AFRICAN AMERICANS AND THE LIVING CONSTITUTION

AFRICAN AMERICANS AND THE
LIVING CONSTITUTION

EDITED BY
JOHN HOPE FRANKLIN AND GENNA RAE McNEIL

SMITHSONIAN INSTITUTION PRESS

WASHINGTON AND LONDON

Earlier versions of Chapter 4 were presented at Howard University, the University of North Carolina in Chapel Hill, and the University of Texas at Arlington. For Chapter 5, the editors acknowledge permission granted by West Publishing Company to reprint excerpts from Mr. Branton's "The History and Future of School Desegregation." *Federal Rules Decisions*, Vol. 109 (1986): 241–52. Parts of Chapter 7, particularly the section on voting, are adapted from the author's book, *Black Votes Count: Political Empowerment in Mississippi After 1965* (Chapel Hill: University of North Carolina Press, 1990). Chapter 8 draws on material previously published in Matthew Holden, Jr., *Racial Stratification as Accident and as Policy* (Charlottesville: University of Virginia, Center for Public Service, 1989); and lectures on the president, Congress, and racial stratification. See also Matthew Holden, Jr., *The Challenge to Racial Stratification*, National Political Science Review Set, vol. 4 (New Brunswick, N.J.: Transcription Publications of Rutgers University, 1993). In addition to the presentation of a version of Chapter 10 at the Smithsonian Institution's symposium, "African Americans and the Evolution of a Living Constitution," the author has published versions of this essay in *Villanova Law Review* 33 (1988), and in the American Bar Association's *Human Rights Journal* 15 (1988). For Chapter 14, the author is grateful for permission to reprint excerpts from "Environmental Justice: New Civil Rights Frontier," *Trial*, July 1993, and "'Environmental Racism': Fact or Fiction?" *Environmental Law*, ABA (quarterly newsletter of the Standing Committee on Environmental Law) 12 (Fall/Winter 1992—93). Remarks by Thurgood Marshall (now incorporated into this volume as Chapter 16) were delivered at the Annual Seminar of the San Francisco Patent and Trademark Law Association, May 6, 1987, and are used by permission of Thurgood Marshall, Jr., and the estate of Mr. Justice Marshall.

Copy Editor: Vicky Macintyre   Designer: Kathleen Sims
Table of Cases Cited: Juliana McCarthy

Library of Congress Cataloging-in-Publication Data
African Americans and the living Constitution / edited by John Hope Franklin and Genna Rae McNeil.
   p.   cm.
   Includes bibliographical references and index.
   ISBN 1-56098-472-4 (casebound). — ISBN 1-56098-471-6 (paperback)
   1. Afro-Americans—Legal status, laws, etc.—History.   2. United States—Constitutional history.   I. Franklin, John Hope, 1915-
II. McNeil, Genna Rae, 1947–
KF4757.A5A44   1995   342.73'0873—dc20   [347.302873]   94-30724

Manufactured in the United States of America 02 01 00 99 98 97 96 95   6 5 4 3 2 1

⊗The paper used in this publication meets the minimum requirements of the American National Standard for Permanence of Paper for Printed Library Materials Z39.48-1984

Cover: Permission to reproduce the photo of Thurgood Marshall and colleagues on the steps of the Supreme Court in 1954 is granted by the NAACP Legal Defense Fund, N.Y.

THURGOOD MARSHALL
IN MEMORIAM

CONTENTS

CONTENTS

FOREWORD

It was more than two centuries ago that a group of thirty-nine men signed their names to work carried out in the punishing heat of a Philadelphia summer. The fruit of their labors was one of the most important documents ever created, the Constitution of the United States. That document is, to be sure, a carefully balanced blend of philosophy and politics that has endured the cataclysm of civil war and the revolutionary social, economic, and technological changes that have transformed the nation in ways that the framers could never have imagined.

A constitution is, as Thomas Paine observed in 1791, "the act of people constituting a government." What the framers created in that summer in Philadelphia was, thus, not the end but the means of the democratic process. The unique genius of the constitution they created can perhaps be best summed up in its three opening words, "We the People." That simple phrase and the powerful idea that underlies it are the key to the staying power of the Constitution. The legitimacy of the government comes only from the people; and the character of the government is rooted in the character of the people.

The history of the Constitution is not just a story of the deliberations of a group of men in a room in Philadelphia. Rather, it is the story of the process they set in motion when they transferred the legacy they had created there, duly signed, to the true heirs identified in the opening phrase. As the heirs, we—the people today—hold the power to preserve and expand that legacy wisely, or to squander it. Thus the work of "we the people" is never done.

During more than two centuries, in the hands of the people, a great democracy continues under construction. At the same time, the "we" has changed considerably, from white men, propertied, educated, and privileged, to today's vastly broader and more diverse multiracial population. The people who are today's custodians of the great legacy of democracy are as varied as the nation is: men and women, rich and poor, from every walk of life and with family trees rooted in every nation on earth—all sharing the responsibilities of citizenship. Changes in the Constitution—won only with great exertion, risk, and sacrifice—have kept faith with the pledge of the Constitution "to form a more perfect union."

In 1988 it was the special honor and privilege of the Joint Center for Political and Economic Studies and the Smithsonian Institution to sponsor a symposium, "Afro-Americans and the Evolution of a Living Constitution." That symposium focused particularly on the contributions of black Americans to the development, vitality, and flexibility of the Constitution. This volume is a testament to black Americans' struggle and achievements. As well, it is a contribution of differing voices to the discourse concerning the continuing capacity of the Constitution to fulfill the noblest ideals of the document.

The struggle of "we the people" to bring black Americans from slavery to the portals of freedom within the framework of the Constitution is, by far, the greatest proof that the Constitution is, indeed, a living document.

EDDIE N. WILLIAMS
President
Joint Center for Political
and Economic Studies

ROBERT McC. ADAMS
Secretary Emeritus
Smithsonian Institution

ACKNOWLEDGMENTS

We are deeply grateful to the many persons who helped in countless ways to bring this volume to completion. Because many of the essays originated in the symposium "Afro-Americans and the Evolution of a Living Constitution" sponsored by the Smithsonian Institution and Joint Center for Political [and Economic] Studies, we must first acknowledge our indebtedness to the staff members of the two institutions. John Whittington Franklin and Neil G. Kotler of the Smithsonian conceived the idea for a symposium and worked to make it a success. We benefited greatly from their creative insights and recommendations. James C. Early, then deputy assistant secretary for public service at the Smithsonian, and Wilton S. Dillon, then director of the Smithsonian's Office of Interdisciplinary Studies, brought essential support to the project. Emma Spriggs contributed her special secretarial skills. Eddie N. Williams, Eleanor Farrar, Milton Morris, Mark Lloyd, Kathleen P. Vander Horst, and Jean Jalloh of the Joint Center helped plan the symposium program and were responsible for raising a substantial portion of the funds that made both the symposium and this volume possible. Carla M. Borden of the Smithsonian served as the publications coordinator and as an editor at the earliest stages of the manuscript.

As we prepared this volume for publication, Joyce Blackwell-Johnson effectively and efficiently served as our research assistant; we are grateful for both the high quality of her work and her zeal. Margaret Fitzsimmons and Mattie

Hackney provided indispensable and exceptional secretarial assistance. Ms. Hackney, Glenda Peace, and Nancy Wilson typed much of the manuscript, and they were ably assisted by Joyce Carpenter and Sandra Chandler-Dillmeyer.

We owe a debt of gratitude to the colleagues and scholars who read portions of this manuscript, the revised essays from the symposium, and newly commissioned essays. We are, as well, appreciative of the work of the staff of the Smithsonian Institution Press who shepherded the volume through its various stages of production, especially Managing Editor Ruth Spiegel and our copy editor Vicky Macintyre. In addition, we wish to thank the librarians and archivists—particularly, those at Duke University, Howard University, and the University of North Carolina in Chapel Hill—who generously gave of their time and expertise and placed their facilities at our disposal. We thank also other skilled professionals, technicians, and members of the support staffs of Duke University and the University of North Carolina at Chapel Hill who assisted and advised us in a variety of ways.

Finally, we further acknowledge the constant, incalculable debt we owe not only to our families—especially, Aurelia Whittington Franklin, "Whit" Franklin, Karen Roberts Franklin, Pearl Walker McNeil, Jesse Jai McNeil, Jr., and Mary Thomas Rogers—but also to our friends for their patience, understanding, advice, and support.

•　　•　　•

The Smithsonian Institution gratefully acknowledges the generous financial support for the symposium and volume from the Ford Foundation, Philip Morris Companies Inc., and the Rockefeller Foundation.

Additional support, also gratefully acknowledged, came from the Gannett Foundation/Gannett Co., Inc./WUSA-TV; the Prudential Foundation; National Constitution Center; West Publishing Company; the Association of Trial Lawyers of America; American Federation of State, County, and Municipal Employees; and Fried, Frank, Harris, Shriver & Jacobson.

JOHN HOPE FRANKLIN
AND
GENNA RAE McNEIL

INTRODUCTION

This volume has its point of departure in several experiences: the bicentennial of the original Constitution of the United States in 1987; a symposium in 1988 on African Americans and the Constitution, which was jointly sponsored by the Smithsonian Institution and the Joint Center for Political (and Economic) Studies; the bicentennial of the Bill of Rights and the retirement of Justice Thurgood Marshall from the Supreme Court of the United States in 1991; and the death of Justice Marshall in 1993. These events prompted serious reflection upon praxis. These events underscored as well the great need for scholarly interpretation of the complex and conflicting meanings of the U.S. Constitution within the light and shadows of Americans' experiences.

Along with the editors of this volume, those who planned the symposium "Afro-Americans and the Evolution of a Living Constitution" identified closely with the bold critique of the Constitution by the sole African American associate justice of the Supreme Court, Thurgood Marshall. Marshall's words sharply punctuated the praise bestowed on the framers of the Constitution in bicentennial observances. The reasons for critical response are worth recounting.

First, of the numerous observances stretching throughout 1987, none had given much attention to the status and condition of African Americans at the time of the writing of the Constitution. Second, African Americans of the

1

eighteenth century were the only group of persons singled out—albeit some-what cryptically—by the framers for special treatment; they deserved more than passing mention during the bicentennial. Third, the Constitution gave African Americans, in stark contrast to others, little about which to cheer. Both remarkable and tragic was the reality that historian James Melvin Washington has so well described:

> The appeal to the doctrine of the "sovereignty of the people" in the Preamble of the Constitution of the United States of America assumed the veracity of the *anthropology of the universality of human equality* pronounced in the American Declaration of Independence. But the Founders could not bypass the problem that African slavery posed for defining American citizenship. The tacit legitimacy of slavery led to the creation of a *herrenvolk* democracy that could not find the national will to abolish slavery without civil war.[1]

It would be at a future date—when the Constitution had evolved through amendments and new interpretation—that African Americans could regard the Constitution as a shield and protector. The 1988 symposium provided an opportunity for scholars, lawyers, and activists to participate in an assessment of the original Constitution, to raise questions about the amended Constitution, and to press for answers regarding America's constitutional crises over power and race. In part, the substance of that dialogue can be found in this volume.

During the early 1990s, many confronted the meaning of the Constitution for African Americans in political-economic and cultural contexts. When the nation commemorated the bicentennial of the Bill of Rights in 1991, it included renewed discussions of civil liberties and race. Some stressed that these amendments collectively represented significant constraints placed upon a new nation by its citizens. Others argued that these first ten amendments made explicit traditionally accepted natural rights, without significantly altering customary notions of black inferiority. An originally excluded race found itself often embroiled in battles over whether veneration of the Bill of Rights justified assaultive, racist speech or the imposition of disproportionate sanctions against African Americans. Clearly, the time had arrived to address the adjudication of interests and the assumption of values inherent in the tradition of constitutionalism inclusive of the Bill of Rights. Aspects of that discourse can be found in this volume.

This volume is also a tribute to the work of Justice Thurgood Marshall, who retired from the U.S. Supreme Court on June 27, 1991, and died on January

24, 1993. A tremendous void has opened up since the passing of this great litigator and jurist, from whom we so often heard not only eloquent defense of the poor and oppressed, but also bold dissents in matters of racial justice, equal protection, and the death penalty. In mourning his death and in celebrating his life, we were compelled to investigate further "the cult of the constitution."[2] The enormous significance of the body of his work—including legal briefs, majority opinions, separate concurring opinions, and dissents—cannot be fully appreciated without reassessing the history of the U.S. Supreme Court in its role as interpreter of the Constitution, reexamining remedies such as affirmative action, and exploring the new frontiers of struggle for civil rights and for racial justice.

The contributors to this volume have expressed a variety of views germane to a serious inquiry into the ideals of this nation, particularly as expressed in its Constitution, and to the struggle of African Americans for justice. Although the authors differ in their disciplines, perspectives, approaches, priorities, and emphases, they share a common concern with the problems of race, constitutionalism, equality, and justice.

The four essays in Part I, "Historical Perspectives," examine the history of the experiences of persons of African descent, our legal status, our aspirations, and our freedom movement. In Chapter 1, Mary Frances Berry looks at the original Constitution and its pro-slavery compromises from an African American perspective. To understand the meaning of the Constitution for persons of African descent in the early national period, Berry insists, it is essential to recognize, as research has shown, that "no matter how one interpreted the language in the Constitution, the slaveholders held the reins of power." Over time, Berry explains, the African American vision of the Constitution evolved from a recognition of "exploitation and exclusion" to "a continuing struggle for inclusion." The status of African Americans in the nineteenth century is the subject of Chapter 2, by John Hope Franklin, who maintains that most free blacks were merely quasi-free. In reality, they were "pariahs" of the nation with "no basis for relief or redress of grievances under the Constitution."

The next two chapters contrast the inclusive quality of the Constitution's expressed ideals with slavery and racial discrimination. In Chapter 3, Darlene Clark Hine documents the struggle for inclusion through the work of African American lawyers in the twentieth century freedom movement—many of them "unheralded local attorneys"—whose competence, creativity, commitment, and courage were manifestations of a whole people's determination to win respect and rights. She notes the close relationship between the National Bar Association's attorneys and the National Association for the Advancement

of Colored People (NAACP) and credits the African American lawyers affili-
ated with the NAACP and the NAACP Legal Defense and Educational Fund,
Inc., with "revolutionizing" constitutional jurisprudence. The case study of
the Baltimore City-Wide Young People's Forum in Chapter 4, by Genna Rae
McNeil, illustrates the endeavors of African American young people to assist
adult supporters of civil rights during the depression era. McNeil also discusses the nexus between racial discrimination and economic disadvantage,
and the initiatives proposed by the Baltimore group in the struggle for racial
justice on the basis of democratic and constitutional ideals.

Part II, "The Post-*Brown* Struggle for Constitutional Change," provides
three lawyers' perspectives on the movement to attack bastions of segregation
and to use the Constitution as an instrument of their destruction. In Chapter
5, Wiley A. Branton, a Southern civil rights litigator, evaluates the assault on
racially segregated public education under the banner of constitutional principles for the twenty-five years after *Brown*. In Chapter 6, George W. Crockett,
Jr., recounts the migration that brought Northern litigators to Mississippi for
limited periods of service to Mississippians as well as to Northern protesters.
His is a personal story of a particular awakening. As Frank R. Parker explains
in Chapter 7, Mississippi is the "ultimate test of whether the promise of the
Fourteenth and Fifteenth Amendments can ever be made a reality," and he
surveys the impact of protest, politics, and litigation on changes in voting,
education, and state employment subsequent to the 1965 Voting Rights Act.
He underscores the necessary intersection of the mass protest movement of
the 1960s and the constitutionally based civil rights litigation that incorporated new legal remedies.

To determine the extent to which effective remedies were implemented or
law and policy sanctioned by the Constitution was changed, it is necessary
to examine the roles of the legislative and executive branches of the federal
government. Part III addresses "Race and Politics of Constitutional Change"
as reflected in executive and congressional leadership. First, in Chapter 8,
Matthew Holden, Jr., discusses the role of the executive branch over several
decades in changing the status of African Americans with respect to what he
calls the "real constitution," "a network of rules that constitute the operative
realities of the political system." Considering the text and interpretation of
the Constitution, Holden examines the policies and practices of presidents
in regard to racial discrimination. In Chapter 9, Gary Orfield discusses the
"relatively progressive" record of Congress in civil rights policy since *Brown*
and compares the activities of Congress with those of the executive branch

and the federal courts. He finds that the major periods of civil rights initiatives were limited to the Reconstruction Era and the period 1964–72. He concludes that Congress played an extremely important role during periods of stalemate or debate on constitutional interpretation and civil rights.

Part IV, "The Legacy of Racial Discrimination: Who Pays the Cost?" broadens the national debate on racial justice and the Constitution by questioning the nation's commitment to ideals of freedom, democracy, and equality in the harsh light of its past and present buttressing of economic inequality and white superiority. Derrick Bell, in Chapter 10, explicates concepts of a "compromise-catalyst role of racism in American policy making" and a "property right" in "'whiteness' . . . recognized and upheld by courts and the society." He argues that African Americans and non–African Americans alike continually pay for the long period of economic exploitation and racial injustice that followed the abolition of slavery. Because the cost extends to the nation as a whole, Bell maintains that it is in the interest of both individual citizens and the nation to recognize the dysfunctional effect of the legacy of racial discrimination.

The First Amendment and the interpretation of the right of free speech are the subject of Chapter 11, by Charles Lawrence III. Inquiring into racist, assaultive speech, or "hate speech," Lawrence observes that "tension . . . sometimes exists between our coexisting constitutional commitments to free speech and equality." Nevertheless, he warns that "it is neither useful nor accurate to frame the debate . . . as one in which the liberty of free speech is in conflict with the elimination of racial oppression." Concurrence in a white supremacist status quo, he argues, is too high a price for an African American to pay for being identified as a proponent of free speech.

"How race permeates America's societal fabric" is the context for the examination of affirmative action in Chapter 12, by W. H. Knight and Adrien Wing. In clarifying the goals of this remedy—namely, "to address the effects of past discrimination" and "to create a community that values racial, ethnic, and gender diversity"—the authors expose the myth of the color-blind constitution and scrutinize Supreme Court decisions concerning affirmative action.

In the broad conception of the struggle for racial justice, Charles Ogletree argues in Chapter 13, the racially disparate treatment of African Americans who come in contact with the criminal justice system cannot be viewed as marginal. "Existing discrimination at every level of the criminal justice system," according to Ogletree, is particularly problematic because it taints data and judgments regarding the correlation between race and crime. Exploring a variety of issues—such as disproportionate arrests and prosecutions, discriminatory stop-and-frisk policies, manipulable drug profiles, police brutality, and the impact of the death penalty on African Americans (a passionate concern of Justice Marshall)—Ogletree investigates grievances and harm identified with violations of the Constitution as well as race-based challenges to arrests and sentencing practices. He concludes that the substitution of the rhetoric of a quest for a color-blind constitution merely "obscures [the] adverse impact of the criminal justice system" on African Americans and other racial-ethnic minorities.

This section closes with Alice L. Brown's essay in Chapter 14 on new civil rights challenges in the environmental arena. Discussing the racial costs connected with the right to a clean, healthy environment, Brown finds that race is the chief predictor of who will "bear a disproportionate share of the burdens attendant to this country's waste and pollution." Brown discusses the constitutional and statutory challenges that minority communities must face in dealing with "environmental degradation, property devaluation, and serious risk to health and safety." With particular attention to case law, Brown explains how "the struggle for environmental protection and social justice has become interwoven with the civil rights movement."

Part V, "Ideals and Costly Compromises," offers two perspectives on the bicentennial of the U.S. Constitution, originally delivered as speeches. In Chapter 15, A. Leon Higginbotham, Jr., explores the theme of the living constitution through a fictional dialogue between Martin Luther King, Jr., and Thomas Jefferson. In conclusion, Higginbotham underscores "the genius of the Constitution and our nation . . . [in] the ability to move beyond the original principles and original vision." Chapter 16 presents Thurgood Marshall's historic address, delivered in May of the bicentennial year, in which he cautioned against celebration that constituted "little more than a blind pilgrimage to the shrine of the original document," which framed a "government . . . defective from the start." Describing the flawed document's limited vision, denial of rights to persons of African descent, and its exclusion of so many of the new nation's population from its pronouncement of "We, the people," Marshall urged his audience to try to understand why some "may more quietly commemorate the suffering, struggle, and sacrifice that has triumphed over much of . . . the original document." Can anything be celebrated? Thurgood Marshall affirms "the Constitution as a living document, including the Bill of Rights and the other amendments protecting individual freedom and human rights."

The "living Constitution" continues to be a work in progress—continually subject to interpretation and amendment. Julius Chambers, a former chief counsel in many cases that marked the struggle for racial justice, brings the volume to a close with some comments on the state of constitutional law as it affected African Americans through 1993. He also makes some insightful observations on the continuing scholarly inquiry and the challenge presented in the struggle for racial justice.

As historians and editors, we have sought to traverse what Michel Foucault has called the "epistemological space specific to a particular period."[3] We brought to this discussion the assumption that in a post-Marshall era, fundamental change to advance the struggle for racial justice in this nation is possible. We brought, as well, confidence in the historical judgment that meaningful changes do occur—even if gradually and incrementally. Ironically, despite the great struggle for freedom and power in recent decades, it is still difficult for African Americans and other advocates of racial justice to hold an open discussion of continuing, pervasive racial oppression and protection of African Americans' constitutional rights without being accused of special pleading. Under the circumstances, this volume has a particularly important contribution to make to the discourse among men and women of different races, cultures, generations, and disciplines.

Our topics were selected to indicate how important it is for the American public to understand not only this nation's history, its political-economic system, constitutionalism, legalism, and racism, but also the experiences of African Americans and our allies as we have challenged injustice. Indeed, the life of the Constitution—particularly during the twentieth century process of resurrecting the Reconstruction amendments' historic purposes—has been changed by feats of the human spirit as well as conquests of power. We hope that this volume can serve as a resource for a people who, in facing a new millennium, must acknowledge a history of accommodating slavery, racism, and hypocrisy, despite a living Constitution.

NOTES

1. James Melvin Washington, "The Crisis in the Sanctity of Conscience in American Jurisprudence," *DePaul Law Review* 42(Fall1992):34.

2. Michael Kammen, *A Machine That Would Go of Itself: The Constitution in American Culture* (New York: Vintage Books, 1987), 22.

8

3. Michel Foucault, *The Order of Things* (New York: Vintage Books, 1973), xi. See, for example, John Hope Franklin and Alfred Moss, Jr., *From Slavery to Freedom: A History of African Americans*, 7th ed. (New York: McGraw-Hill, 1994), *Reconstruction after the Civil War* (Chicago: University of Chicago Press, 1960), and *Race and History: Selected Essays, 1938–1988* (Baton Rogue: Louisiana State University Press, 1989). See also Genna Rae McNeil, "Community Initiative in Desegregation of District of Columbia Schools, 1946–1954," *Howard Law Journal* 22(1979), and *Groundwork: Charles Hamilton Houston and the Struggle for Civil Rights* (Philadelphia: University of Pennsylvania Press, 1983).

PART

I

HISTORICAL PERSPECTIVES ON THE EVOLUTION OF A LIVING CONSTITUTION

MARY FRANCES BERRY

SLAVERY, THE CONSTITUTION, AND THE FOUNDING FATHERS

THE AFRICAN AMERICAN VISION

Neither the U.S. Constitution nor American slavery can be fully understood without examining the proslavery compromises worked out at the Constitutional Convention in 1787. Slavery was expressly sanctioned in three places in Article I, Section 3. Under the three-fifths clause, three-fifths of a state's slaves—euphemistically referred to as "other persons"—were to be counted for purposes of representation in Congress. Another provision required that any direct tax levied in the states be imposed according to population, but only three-fifths of the slaves were to be counted in determining each state's tax levy. Counting slaves helped the South, but taxing slaves partly nullified this benefit. In Article I, Section 8, § 4, any capitation (head tax) or other direct tax had to be consistent with the provision of the three-fifths clause. This meant that slaveholders could pay less. Article I, Section 9, § 1 stipulated that the slave trade was not to end before 1808. States that needed more slaves wanted to continue importing them, whereas the older slave states would have preferred terminating importation immediately. In addition, the Constitution sanctioned slavery through the fugitive slave clause in Article IV, Section 2, and the Article V provision prohibiting any amendment of the paragraph on slave importation before 1808. The cumulative effect of these provisions was the direct ratification of slavery.

Other parts of the original Constitution were also helpful to the institution of slavery. Particularly important were the provisions in Article I that prohibited taxes on exports, because slaveholders depended on the agricultural exports produced by slaves. Furthermore, the electoral college provision on its face gave whites in slave states a disproportionate influence in the election of the president. The three-fifths ratio, which enabled slave states to count nonvoting slaves, increased a slave state's representation and thereby its influence in the electoral college, since the electors were chosen on the basis of congressional representation. The exact purpose of the electoral college is somewhat murky. Some evidence suggests that it was designed to democratize elections by having Congress choose the president. The significant point to recognize in this discussion is its impact on the power of slaveholders.

Another constitutional provision useful to the slave states was that requiring agreement of three-quarters of the states to ratify a constitutional amendment. Slave states could refuse to ratify any constitutional amendment that curtailed or adversely affected the institution of slavery. The U.S. Supreme Court interpreted Article III's accord of diversity jurisdiction to "citizens" of different states as a prohibition on a slave's right to sue in federal court. If the language had said "inhabitants" of different states—assuming that slaves would be inhabitants and not property—there might have been a stronger basis for jurisdiction. But this assumption may be inappropriate on the basis of the evidence.

After Madison's notes became available in 1836, some abolitionists, led by Wendell Phillips, argued that the Constitution was essentially a proslavery document and pointed out still other proslavery provisions.[1] The military clauses in Article IV, Section 4, Phillips said, called on the federal government to protect the states from domestic violence, including slave rebellions; and Article I, Section 8, required the Congress to call forth the militia to suppress insurrections, including slave rebellions.

When I first read Phillips in law school, I was persuaded by his arguments that we had missed a most important proslavery compromise. I researched the debates in the 1787 convention and ratifying conventions and in 1971 published the results in a book focusing on the federal government's role in suppressing black rebellions, *Black Resistance/White Law: A History of Constitutional Racism in America*.[2] (Perhaps the title of the book was too harsh. A senior scholar in the field of constitutional history insisted I had erred, and that everyone already knew there were only three proslavery compromises.)[3] I am still persuaded that Phillips and the other abolitionists who shared these more expansive views were correct. Beyond the three traditionally cited compromises, these other features are correctly considered the framers' handiwork on the subject of slavery.

These slavery provisions have profoundly affected the predominant African American vision of the Constitution over the past two hundred years, African Americans' status, and aspirations. We know a great deal about the thoughts of free Negroes in the period before the Civil War from newspapers, letters, pamphlets, lectures, and speeches. In the first federal census of 1790, taken three years after the Constitution was approved in Philadelphia, most blacks were slaves, but about 59,000 free Negroes were counted, 27,000 in the North and 32,000 in the South. Their numbers grew rapidly between 1790 and 1810, but subsequently the rate of increase dropped sharply because of restraints on manumission and other hardships. By the time the Constitution was written, blacks in the United States were aware that the unequal political, social, and economic opportunities of their group were a consequence of whites' identification of African ancestry with inferiority and subordination. Arguing for greater opportunities for persons of African descent and for the abolition of slavery, numbers of blacks noted that in ratifying slavery the Constitution had betrayed the promises of the Declaration of Independence, which had stated that everyone had a right to life, liberty, and the pursuit of happiness. At the same time, many denounced the hypocrisy of the Declaration for not including blacks as beneficiaries of its promises.

In the years immediately after the Convention, African Americans did not have access to Madison's notes and other materials that have come to light since then, but they were contemporaries of the Constitution makers. In the absence of records of the debates at the Convention, they could, when it suited their purposes, use the very vagueness· of some of the Constitution's wording to support arguments that the Constitution stood for freedom and rights. As petitioners, they noted the potential for antislavery action in the Fifth Amendment of the Bill of Rights and the clauses in the original document pertaining to interstate commerce, general welfare, and the guarantee of a republican form of government. They could—and did—assert that Congress could, therefore, manumit contraband slaves, prohibit the coastal and interstate slave trade, ban slavery from the territories and other property of the United States, enlist slaves in the armed forces, and even take private property for public use by purchasing and emancipating slaves. Although there was no doubt that the Constitution had ratified slavery in the states, it was certainly still open to debate whether some antislavery objectives could be achieved under its provisions.

Most African Americans avoided choosing emigration or attacking the Constitution, preferring instead to advance the antislavery cause by swaddling themselves in arguments emphasizing the Constitution's potential.[4] In short, these African Americans, like some literalists and original-intent adherents today, chose to base their arguments only on the words in the document, insisting that their interpretation of original intent was the only one possible. They asserted that the Constitution could be interpreted in such a way as to support abolition, or at least the containment of slavery.

In those early years of the nation, there was an overriding impression of consensus among African Americans: no matter how one interpreted the language of the Constitution, the slaveholders held the reins of power. To unseat this class would require political action and moral suasion, or, as many others eventually came to agree, it could only be accomplished through the violence of a civil war.[5] African Americans looked to other provisions of the Constitution as they considered their predicament and the means for improvement. They and their white allies were very fond of the First Amendment because it led them to hope that their right to petition the Congress and to assemble in protest would be protected. They were decidedly unimpressed with the Tenth Amendment and the federalism it promoted because states' rights then, as today, permitted discrimination and subordination in the states without interference by the national government. They found, unfortunately, that their protests were not protected automatically from state suppression because in those days the First Amendment applied to federal and not to state action.

Frederick Douglass, a former slave and ardent abolitionist, perhaps best summed up the antebellum view of the Constitution. In 1849 he pointed out that the Constitution's words could be taken to express antislavery sentiment, but that the meaning of the Constitution given to it by the framers and those with the power to interpret it made it a proslavery document. He explained:

> Had the Constitution dropped down from the blue overhanging sky, upon a land uncursed by slavery, and without an interpreter, although some difficulty might have occurred in applying its manifold provisions, yet so cunningly is it framed, that no one would have imagined that it recognized or sanctioned slavery. But having a terrestrial, and not a celestial origin, we find no difficulty in ascertaining its meaning in all the parts which we allege to relate to slavery. . . . [The Constitution] was made in view of the existence of slavery, and in a manner well calculated to aid and strengthen that heaven-daring crime.[6]

When, as a result of the bloodshed and violence of the Civil War and Reconstruction, the Constitution was amended to include the Thirteenth, Fourteenth, and Fifteenth Amendments, the legacy of slavery remained prominent in the African American vision of the new reality. This vision was apparent at the centennial of the Constitution's writing, observed in 1887. Among the approximately seven million African Americans in the country at that time, most of whom lived in the South, the badges of slavery persisted. Frederick Douglass pointed out how much they relied on the Constitution when the promise of freedom seemed abandoned forever:

> I now undertake to say that neither the original Constitution nor the Constitution as amended since the War is the law of the land. That Constitution has been slain in the house of its friends. So far as the colored people of the country are concerned, the Constitution is but a stupendous sham . . . keeping the promise to the eye and breaking it to the heart. . . . They have promised us law and abandoned us to anarchy.[7]

Yet there was more to celebrate in 1887 than there had been in 1787. Slavery was depicted in the centennial exposition floats in Philadelphia, and despite offers of payment, organizers could not find blacks to play the role of plantation slaves. Incongruously, some of the banners in the African American part of the exposition proclaimed enfranchisement and full political rights.[8] Even so, the trend in the South, where most blacks lived, was already well on the way toward almost total disfranchisement.

Slavery was also visible in the African American vision of the Constitution as interpreted by the Supreme Court of the United States. The Court's influence permeated the *Slaughterhouse Cases* that acknowledged the one pervading purpose of the Fourteenth Amendment.[9] The *Civil Rights Cases* further weakened the ability of the Fourteenth Amendment to remove badges and incidents of slavery.[10] Tragically, *Plessy* v. *Ferguson* reduced the badges of slavery to a figment of the black imagination.[11]

Slavery was fundamental in the rationale of white Southerners for the political disfranchisement, economic oppression, and punishment of African Americans. White Southerners argued that African Americans were still not far enough removed from the slave condition to be positive participants in the political process. In the Southern states, where the majority of the black population lived, the recent history of slavery loomed large in the decisions handed down during military reconstruction. Some, for example, prohibited whites from reenslaving black children as "apprentices," and others protected blacks from disproportionately harsh punishment in the criminal justice system. Slavery as context, as definition for all that occurred to African Americans, was prevalent even in the highest state courts.

Throughout the late nineteenth century, when racial fairness appeared impossible, slavery remained an ever-present force both in legal and social affairs. The North Carolina Court, just in time to set the right tone for the centennial celebrations, struck down the statute earmarking taxes paid by Negroes only for the Negro schools and by whites only for the white schools, explaining that because of slavery, "the vast bulk of property yielding the fruits of taxation belongs to the white people of the state and very little is held by the emancipated race." The court hastened to say, however, that it was not questioning the constitutionality of separate schools, or laws forbidding the intermarriage of the races; these were made more necessary by the abolition of slavery.[12]

The centennial period notwithstanding, state courts at the highest levels, the most visible representatives of a justice system in the South, continued to hand down decisions acknowledging the ideals of slavery. The Alabama high court, in refusing to convict, as demanded by "her mistress, a colored girl, 17 or 18 years of age," for burning down the house in which she lived and worked, noted that her confession could be attributed to the fact that "her mistress" routinely disciplined her by whipping. The court did not find whipping, which was a routine punishment administered to slaves, unusual in 1887 but thought since there was no other evidence that the girl set the fire at the house, being locked up and whipped might have meant the confession was false.[13]

Cases declaring the illegitimacy of intimate relations between whites and blacks were common, indicating there were many such relationships and an eagerness to end them. White men were often involved. A case in Yazoo County, Mississippi, decided in the centennial year, involved a white man and "a colored woman" who had been jointly convicted. They had been seen together in bed; he was frequently at her house. She had two mulatto children and he "had been heard to call them his children." The court upheld the conviction. Before slavery became illegal, she could have been his concubine, as was not unusual. After the Thirteenth Amendment was passed, it became important, as the prosecutor told the jury, to maintain appropriate social relations by punishing miscegenation "as a stigma on both races."[14] As in so many things, the North had already shown the importance of strictures concerning interracial sex in a state of so-called freedom, by its laws and policies concerning relationships between blacks and whites.

The courts spoke most directly about slavery in the numerous cases from 1870 to 1900 involving legacies and bequests to freedmen. In a case decided by the Virginia high court in 1887, the descendants of slaves filed a lawsuit after failing repeatedly in their attempts to collect a promised legacy. A plantation owner in Danville had left his fifteen slaves to his heirs in an 1862 will with the understanding that they would be set free seven years after his death and taken to a free state. They were also to be given one half of what they would be worth to his estate and $3,000. He instructed his heirs to pay the money out of a surplus he had in his estate in 1865. He added this provision to this will, and shortly thereafter he died. A few months later, the slaves were freed by the war's results, and they asked for their legacy. The high court decided that the end of the war did not automatically invalidate the former slaves' right to the legacy. As it turned out, however, the heirs did not have to pay them because the legacy, unlike the rest of the estate that the heirs could keep, was to be taken out of the surplus, which was in worthless Confederate money.[15]

Race and the badges of slavery entered into every type of legal matter during the centennial era and thereafter. A court describing the routine issuance of a summons emphasized that it was given to "a white person over the age of sixteen years."[16] All during the proceedings of a tort case in which the value of the life of a black man who was killed accidentally as a result of turning on the light switches for the company where he worked, the court described everyone in racial terms, as did the lawyers and the witnesses: X "a white man" was a witness for the "colored widow," X "(white)" testified that the deceased whose wife was his house servant "was . . . of average intelligence for a colored man."[17] But at least blacks could bring lawsuits and appear as parties—and could sometimes win—which would have been impossible under pre–Civil War restrictions.[18]

The African American vision of the Founding Fathers, of the meaning of slavery, and of the Constitution in 1787 and 1887 was shaped by political, economic, and legal conditions. That vision was consistently suffused with both hope and suspicion of a kind that persists to this day. The Founding Fathers created a framework of government that has served many purposes. In protecting slavery and assuming racial inequality, they made African Americans outsiders from the beginning. They also provided a rationale that could be used by non–African Americans to assume the basic worthlessness, powerlessness, and inhumanity of African Americans as a part of the nation's legacy. Even though by the time of the centennial there had been a great deal of violence and their work had been modified and improved upon, the pall of slavery's influence remained. The pall was still present at the Constitution's bicentennial, although it had diminished somewhat.

An unstated premise of many discussions about intelligence and qualifications is that blackness is associated with inferiority and subordination. In recent years, discussions about African Americans and legal rights under the Constitution have often turned on how far away blacks are from slavery. Many a conversation with a white American has begun, "My grand-daddy did not have any slaves, and anyway slavery was a long time ago and why do we still need to remedy vestiges and discuss redress." But many have also revolved around the economic disparities that continue to plague black communities. In some of these conversations, speakers emphasize the reality of legally enforced slavery, which means blacks should not expect to close the gap and become equal, except for a few extraordinary individuals who ought to be thankful instead of complaining.

The African American vision of the Constitution as it was written in 1787 can be characterized as an affirmation of exploitation and exclusion. By 1887 the Constitution had come to represent inclusion in language but exclusion in reality. Today African Americans see in it a continuing struggle for inclusion. Our lives begin and end taking into account that vision of us crafted by the Founding Fathers in the Constitution. The role we have today they might not have envisioned, but certainly our African American ancestors did.

Because there was slavery, the free Negroes bore the burden of having blackness identified with subordination. Because there was slavery, the Thirteenth, Fourteenth, and Fifteenth Amendments came into being, and because some of the slaves were women, the Nineteenth Amendment was not made fully effective for women of minority groups until the Voting Rights Act of 1965. Because there was slavery, there was Jim Crow and segregation and a race-imbued justice system. Because there was slavery, there were civil rights movements; there was litigation for rights and jail for those who fought for those rights. There were lost jobs and death in the name of improving our lives and the constitutional imperatives under which we live. Because there was slavery, there is debate over remedies and correctives such as affirmative action, school busing, self-help, and black community organization designed to overcome the lingering effects of slavery. Because there was slavery, the most important features of the Constitution are the amending clause in Article V and the power of interpretation by the Supreme Court under Article III. Because there was slavery, the appointment power for Supreme Court justices under Article II, providing for a sharing of power between the president and the Senate has to be kept constantly on our minds.

We need to remember that, interpreting the same Constitution, one group of judges said forced segregation was wrong in 1954 but another said it was perfectly legal in 1896. We must worry about who is appointed to the courts and what they will say in the future. Because there was slavery, we read and hear every day that the United States is not ready for a black man to become president, not just Jesse Jackson. Because there was slavery, we have race and slavery on our minds, and we are likely to keep it on our minds until it is obviously on no one else's minds in ways that constrict the freedom and opportunities of African Americans. Therefore, when we think about everything important to our well-being, including the Constitution and the Founding Fathers, our vision, our African American vision, remains preoccupied and on guard. But perhaps it is not simply because there was slavery, but because the vision of others was shaped by slavery, and because most African Americans still experience unpleasant reminders that we are the descendants of those who were enslaved.

NOTES

1. "The Constitution–a Pro-slavery Compact," in *Selections from the Madison Papers*, ed. Wendell Phillips, 2d ed. rev. (New York: Anti-slavery Society, 1845), 5–9.

2. Mary Frances Berry, *Black Resistance/White Law: A History of Constitutional Racism in America* (Englewood Cliffs, N.J.: Prentice-Hall, 1971).

3. Staughton Lynd advances a similar interpretation in *Slavery, Class Conflict, and the Constitution* (Indianapolis: Bobbs-Merrill, 1967). Lynd also suggests that the Northwest Ordinance, outlawing slavery in the Northwest territory, passed while the convention was in session, was part of the pattern of compromises concerning slavery. See also Staughton Lynd, "The Compromise of 1787," *Political Science Quarterly* 81 (1966): 225–50.

4. David Brion Davis, *The Problem of Slavery in the Age of Revolution* (Ithaca: Cornell University Press, 1975), 130. See also John Hope Franklin and Alfred A. Moss, Jr., *From Slavery to Freedom: A History of Negro Americans*, 6th ed. rev. (New York: Alfred Knopf, 1987), 76–77.

5. Mary Frances Berry and John W. Blassingame, *Long Memory: The Black Experience in America* (New York: Oxford University Press, 1982), 60–66.

6. Frederick Douglass, "The Constitution and Slavery" (*North Star*, March 16, 1849) in *The Life and Writings of Frederick Douglass*, ed. Philip S. Foner, 4 vols. (New York: International Publishers, 1950–), vol. 1, *1817–1849* (1950), 363.

7. Frederick Douglass, "Speech on the Occasion of the Twenty-Fourth Anniversary of Emancipation in the District of Columbia, Washington, D. C., 1886," in *The Life and Writings of Frederick Douglass*, ed. Philip S. Foner, 4 vols. (New York: International Publishers, 1950–), vol. 4, *Reconstruction and After* (1955), 431.

8. Leon Litwack, "Trouble in Mind: The Bicentennial and the Afro-American Experience," *Journal of American History*, 74 (September 1987): 315–37, and notes cited on p. 315. See also Leon Litwack, *Been in the Storm So Long: The Aftermath of Slavery* (New York: Alfred Knopf, 1979), chap. 5.

9. 16 Wallace 36 (1873).

10. 109 U.S. 3 (1883).

11. 163 U.S. 437 (1896).

12. *Puitt v. Gaston County*, 94 North Carolina 709 (1886).

13. *Hoober v. State*, 81 Ala. 51 (1887).

14. *Steward* v. *State,* 64 Miss. 626 (1887).

15. *Allen et al.* v. *Patton Als.,* 83 Va. 255 (1887).

16. *Stolz* v. *Collins,* 83 Va. 824 (1887).

17. *Piedmont Electric Illinois Co.* v. *Patteson's Adm.,* 84 Va. 18 (1887).

18. This material on state courts is drawn from my ongoing research on how white women and black males as well as females fared in cases in the state courts in the South from Reconstruction to 1900.

JOHN HOPE FRANKLIN

RACE AND THE CONSTITUTION IN THE NINETEENTH CENTURY

Much has been written and spoken about the recognition and protection of slavery by the Constitution of the United States. In the year of the Constitution's bicentennial, some critics referred to our basic frame of government as a "flawed" document because of the apparent contradiction between its reference to the blessings of liberty, on the one hand, and its protection of slavery, on the other. (From time to time during the past few years I have made some remarks on the subject myself.)[1] In discussing race and the Constitution in the nineteenth century, I shall resist the temptation to discuss slavery and the Constitution, except where slavery was a clear factor in the manner in which the several branches of the government viewed race under the Constitution.

At the outset, however, we must remind ourselves that race *was* a powerful factor in the establishment of slavery, and for two and a half centuries race was crucial to the maintenance of the institution.[2] In 1640, when three Virginia indentured servants, one black and two white, ran away and were apprehended, the magistrate set the stage for racial discrimination that would persist for more than three centuries. Remember that all three of the fugitive indentured servants were free. The magistrate punished the white indentured servants by adding one year to their indenture. He punished the black indentured servant by sentencing him to a lifetime of service.[3] The remainder of the colonial period would witness a marked distinction between the treatment

21

of whites who were free and blacks who were free, as demonstrated by the Virginia magistrate in 1640. When George Washington was building his revolutionary army, he preferred not to use blacks—slave *or* free. Only the sobering experience of facing more British military power than he had anticipated caused him to reverse his earlier decision and take blacks into the forces fighting for independence. Meanwhile, Massachusetts imposed *taxes* on property-owning free blacks although it barred them from voting. Joseph and John Cuffee, two property-owning, free black businessmen in Massachusetts, refused to pay their taxes because they could not vote. They were promptly slapped into jail.[4] Incidentally, who was it who yelled, "Taxation without representation is tyranny"?

Thus, in the eighteenth century the sense of racial inequality was as pervasive as slavery itself and was often used to justify keeping blacks in bondage. The student at the Harvard commencement in 1773, who argued in his speech that slavery did not violate the law of nature, insisted that blacks were inferior to whites and for the good of all should be kept in subordination.[5] And since the typical African was, in his view, "a child, an ideot [*sic*], madman," his consent was not required before exercising authority over him. "Why," he asked, "should anyone interfere with a stable and beneficent social order, just to pursue some mystical primeval equality?" This question was raised less than two years before the Battle of Bunker Hill.

Fourteen years later, during the fateful year of constitution-making, a group of Philadelphia Negroes, all free, worshipped at the predominantly white St. George's Methodist Church. In November, two months after the close of the Constitutional Convention, the sexton told the black communicants, as they arrived for morning worship, that they were expected to sit in the gallery. They dutifully went to the gallery and took their seats on the front row, kneeling for the prayer service, which, by this time, had already begun. Thereupon one of the trustees seized one of the black worshippers, pulled him from his knees, and informed him that he and his fellow blacks were to sit in the *rear*, not in the *front* row, of the gallery. When the prayer was over, the blacks left the church in a body, and, as Richard Allen later reported, "They were no more plagued with us in the church."[6] Allen went on to found the African Methodist Episcopal Church, the largest black denomination in all Methodism, built not only on Allen's dream of an African American Methodist church, but also, sadly enough, on the arrogance and presumption of superiority of whites over free blacks that characterized the white Christians of St. George's Church in the City of Brotherly Love.

Those who wrote the Constitution brought with them to Philadelphia not only a century and a half of experience with slavery but also a similar period of discrimination against blacks who were *not* slaves. If the framers of the Constitution gave no attention to blacks who were free, it was not because they believed that there should be no distinction among free peoples. Rather, it was because of the framers' preoccupation with slavery at a time when continued discrimination against free blacks was assumed. And they did their work well, extending the slave trade for at least twenty years, counting a slave as three-fifths of a person, and approving the capture and return of fugitive slaves to their masters (Article 1, Sections 2 and 9; Article IV, Section 2). That was the situation when the first Congress under the new Constitution met in 1789. One of the questions to be settled was who was worthy of citizenship in this new nation that aspired to become the model for all future democracies. The question was answered without much debate. Only *white* aliens, the law of 1790 specified, could become naturalized citizens of the United States.[7] The message was clear: any free black person imprudent enough to migrate to the United States could not expect *ever* to become a citizen.

In the First Congress that did so much in setting precedents and patterns for the future and that defined who could become a citizen of the United States, there were no less than twenty who had been members of the Constitutional Convention two years earlier. *Not one* of them raised any objection to barring free blacks from becoming naturalized citizens. Founding Fathers such as Elbridge Gerry of Massachusetts, Roger Sherman of Connecticut, Hugh Williamson of North Carolina, and James Madison of Virginia, the "father" of the Constitution, all acquiesced in this first act of racial discrimination by the first Congress of the United States.

If the First Congress, with such fresh memories of the framing of the Constitution could, with impunity, violate the dignity of persons on the basis of race, it should not be surprising that succeeding congresses enthusiastically followed suit. If such was possible, the Second Congress even went beyond its predecessor in indicating the disesteem in which free blacks were held. In an act establishing a "uniform militia throughout the United States" the Second Congress provided that "each and every free able-bodied *white male citizen* of the respective states . . . who is or shall be of the age of eighteen years and under the age of forty-five . . . shall . . . be enrolled in the militia."[8] In a word, the act told the 5,000 blacks who saw service in the War for Independence and all of whom were freed after the war that their services were not only no longer needed but that once independence was achieved, with their help, they were not worthy to serve in the militia of the United States.

This declaration was not only lacking in grace, but it was also lacking in gratitude. The "white only" militia law repudiated the policy reluctantly accepted by George Washington that black soldiers could serve in the armed forces of the United States, and it embraced the view that the protective arm of the United States must be *white* in order to be effective. Such a policy and such a view launched this country on a policy of racial bigotry that would in the future mar race relations in war as well as in peace.

One other example will suffice to illustrate the view of race expounded by the immediate successors of the framers of the Constitution. In 1801, when the new capital of the United States was established in Washington, the question of governance arose immediately. To make certain that no free blacks in Washington would have a voice in the governance of that city, the Seventh Congress, in its act incorporating the new city, declared that "the city council be elected annually . . . by the *free white* inhabitants of full age, who have resided twelve months in the city and paid taxes therein."[9] The law was enacted when Founding Fathers such as Gouverneur Morris, who had spoken out against slavery in 1787, was in the Senate and Thomas Jefferson was president. And, in the words of the revered Negro spiritual, "They never said a mumblin' word, not a word!" The governance of the new capital city was apparently too important to expose it to the wishes of *all* free men. The wishes and the decisions of white men would be sufficient.

We all take pride in the fact that even as the Constitution was being written, the Congress under the Articles of Confederation enacted its most important piece of legislation, the Ordinance of 1787 or, as it is popularly known, the Northwest Ordinance. It established the process by which territories were to be organized and admitted to the Union as states. A territory could be formally organized when it had a population of 5,000 free male inhabitants, and it could become a state when it had 60,000 free inhabitants. It also forbade slavery in the territory. The ordinance did not specify that the 5,000 male inhabitants should be white for purposes of organizing the territory or that all of the 60,000 inhabitants should be white in order to qualify for statehood.[10]

Since slavery was forbidden in the territory, it is reasonable to assume that free black persons living in the territory would be counted in determining the area's qualification to become a territory and then a state. Yet, when the Tenth Congress enacted legislation in 1808 enabling Indiana to qualify as a territory, that Congress saw fit to limit the suffrage in the territory to *free white males*.[11] In doing so, the Congress of the United States said to all free black inhabitants in the Indiana Territory that *their freedom*, their ownership of property, and even their patriotism did not earn for them the sacred role of participating in the governance of the territory. Since the Constitution had given *states* the authority to determine the qualifications for voters, one would have thought that the Tenth Congress would have given Indiana the opportunity to work through the early stages of this problem and to define the qualifications for voters. Instead, it *told* the Indiana Territory that whatever else it did, it could not permit free blacks to vote. What a remarkable way in which to launch a territory on the road to statehood! Every time I pass through that central Indiana town not far from Bloomington that boasts its strong traditions of Ku Klux Klanism, I wonder how much can be traced to the government's policy toward Indiana in 1808.

The Constitution and the Fugitive Slave Law of 1793 gave ample protection to slaveowners in their effort to recover their runaways. But blacks, even in the free states, who were accused of being fugitive slaves—and who may well have been free—had no protection from false arrests or erroneous accusations. All that the owner or his agent had to do was to bring the alleged fugitive before any federal or state court and, upon proof of identity, that alleged fugitive who could not testify in his own behalf would be turned over to the alleged owner or his or her agent. There was no provision for a trial, no provision for the alleged fugitive to defend himself or herself. Indeed, there was no provision for the alleged fugitive to give testimony in his or her own behalf. An alleged fugitive had no standing before the court anyway. And as we consider the ways in which this law could promote a miscarriage of justice, it is well to remember that there were a quarter of a million free Negroes in the Northern states by 1850 and about as many in the Southern states. With slaveholders and their agents combing the countryside from New Orleans to Boston in search of their runaways, virtually every free person of color was in imminent danger of being taken up and placed in slavery with no opportunity whatever to establish a valid claim to freedom.[12] And the Constitution provided *no protection whatever* to free blacks who could be falsely accused of being slaves.

Small wonder that some states, interested in the rights of human beings regardless of race, discerned a woeful miscarriage of justice in denying to free blacks the elementary rights to which all free persons were entitled. To be sure, a part of the sentiment in the enactment of personal liberty laws in the 1820s and 1830s reflected a virulent opposition to slavery in any and all forms. It was also a vigorous protest by the civil libertarians who saw much that was wrong and morally repugnant in the government's failure to make any distinction between actual runaway slaves and bona fide free blacks who might be wrongfully accused of being runaways.

The 1820 personal liberty law of Pennsylvania was typical of legislation enacted by states that sought to protect the rights of blacks who were not slaves. When the case testing the constitutionality of Pennsylvania's personal liberty law reached the Supreme Court in 1842, Justice Joseph Story, speaking for the Court, declared the Pennsylvania law unconstitutional, since the power over fugitive slaves belonged exclusively to Congress and had been given to Congress by the Constitution. States, therefore, could not legislate in matters relating to fugitive slaves.[13] But what of the rights of free blacks falsely or unjustly accused of being runaways? On this question the Constitution was silent, and the Court offered little comfort to such people except in asserting that perhaps the states did not have a duty to assist the federal government in the rendition of fugitive slaves.

Negro Americans, delivered from slavery in a variety of ways and desperately anxious to enjoy at least a modicum of that freedom, joined with antislavery groups in seeking the civil and legal rights that others enjoyed. It is interesting to observe, however, that in their state and national conventions that met almost annually after 1831, and in numerous addresses to public officials and to their own people, black leaders seldom invoked the Constitution as the source of their anticipated support and protection.[14] From time to time they asked Congress to repeal all laws that made distinctions on the basis of race or color, to no avail, of course. When the Pennsylvania Constitution of 1837 disfranchised blacks, some forty thousand Pennsylvanian free Negroes protested this move. They took their stand, they said, on the basis of the electrifying words in the Declaration of Independence that proclaimed that to protect the inalienable rights of all people "governments are instituted among men, deriving their just powers from the consent of the governed."[15] Not once did they refer to the Constitution of the United States, for their examination of that document revealed nothing to relieve them in that solemn hour of their disfranchisement.

Frederick Douglass was one articulate black man who found no consolation even in the words of the Declaration of Independence. "Are the great principles of political freedom and of natural justice, embodied in that Declaration of Independence, extended to us?" he asked his Fourth of July audience in Rochester in 1852. Answering his own question, he declared, "This Fourth of July is *yours*, not *mine. You* may rejoice, *I* must mourn. To drag a man in fetters into the grand illuminated temple of liberty, and call upon him to join you in joyous anthems, were inhuman mockery and sacrilegious irony."[16]

Even if others did not go as far as Douglass, those blacks who hoped that the Declaration of Independence offered solace and comfort for them were flying in the face of reality. Worse still, as the rights of white Americans were being extended, the rights of black Americans were being diminished. One could see this virtually everywhere. In 1834 and 1835 blacks were disfranchised by Tennessee and North Carolina, respectively, and, as we have seen, by Pennsylvania in 1837. New Jersey and Connecticut followed close behind. From the admission of Maine in 1819 until the end of the Civil War, the constitution written by *every new state* barred blacks from voting. Yet this is precisely the period, 1820 to 1860, in which the franchise was being extended to large numbers of whites who, up to that time, had been voteless.

When Congress enacted a more stringent fugitive slave law in 1850 that had *no provision* for a jury trial or for the alleged fugitive to testify in his own behalf, the 434,000 blacks who were free should have been convinced that they had no reasonable protection under the Constitution and laws of the United States. They condemned the law of 1850 as a natural evil flowing from the Constitution of 1787. Speaking before the State Convention of Ohio Negroes in January, 1851, one Negro delegate said,

> No colored man can consistently vote under the United States Constitution. That instrument also provides for the return of fugitive slaves. And, sir, one of the greatest lights now adorning the galaxy of American literature, declares that the "Fugitive Law" is in accordance with that stipulation;—law unequaled in the worst days of Roman despotism, and unparalleled in the annals of heathen jurisprudence. You might search the pages of history in vain to find a more striking exemplification of the compound of all villainies! It shrouds our country in blackness; every green spot in nature is blighted and blasted by that withering Upas.[17]

Small wonder that the reaction of many free Negroes to the Fugitive Slave Law of 1850 was to flee en masse to Canada, convinced, as Henry McNeal Turner would say a generation later, that there was "no manhood future for Negroes in the United States."

If Congress could disfranchise free Negroes in the territories, as we have seen in the case of Indiana, it should come as no surprise that some branch of the federal government—in this case the Supreme Court—would protect the institution of slavery in the territories. That is precisely what the Court did in the celebrated Dred Scott case. Chief Justice Roger B. Taney not only insisted that slavery was protected by the Constitution in the territories as well as the states, but that blacks, whether slave or free, did not have and had never had any legal standing in the courts of the United States. One is compelled to agree, after this cursory view of the status of blacks in the late eighteenth and early nineteenth centuries, that the chief justice was giving an accurate reading of the nation's history when he referred to the degraded status of blacks in the late eighteenth century. In the most widely quoted passage in the decision, he said:

> It is difficult at this day [1857] to realize the state of public opinion in relation
> to that unfortunate race, which prevailed in the civilized and enlightened por-
> tions of the world at the time of the Declaration of Independence and when
> the Constitution of the United States was framed and adopted. . . . They had
> for more than a century before been regarded as beings of an inferior order,
> and altogether unfit to associate with the white race, either in social or politi-
> cal relations; and so far inferior, that they had no rights which the white man
> was bound to respect.[18]

The chief justice may well have been a better historian than a lawyer, though his judgment about slaveholders as being a part of the civilized and enlightened portions of the world could bear some modification. There is no evidence, however, to contradict his reading of the status of free blacks at the time of the Declaration of Independence and the framing of the Constitution. One looks in vain at that entire miserable period from the writing of the Constitution to the outbreak of the Civil War to find any indication that the Founding Fathers, the fledgling government of the United States, or the great leaders of the nation in the first half of the nineteenth century pursued a policy looking toward any semblance of citizenship or equality for free black Americans. The terrible truth is that by the beginning of the Civil War the status of free black persons had deteriorated to the point that they were pariahs of the land, unwanted, virtually helpless, and with no substantial basis for relief or redress of grievances under the Constitution.[19]

Thus, when the emancipation of the slaves finally came in 1865 with the end of the Civil War and the ratification of the Thirteenth Amendment, there were abundant precedents that could be used to set forth a public policy for the freedmen. They were not the precedents established by more than two centuries of slavery, but precedents established by more than two centuries of discrimination and degradation of free black Americans. What a way to initiate free Negro soldiers in the Civil War, by placing them in a segregated army and giving them less pay for the same rank and service than that given to white soldiers.[20] Small wonder that in 1865 black people—all of them legally free by this time—looked not to the slave experience but to the experience of free blacks to get some notion of what the future held for them.

It was this experience that influenced the conduct of white Americans toward black Americans even after the ratification of the Reconstruction amendments. In *Roberts v. the City of Boston*, which had been decided in 1850, Chief Justice Lemuel Shaw of the Massachusetts Supreme Court declared that Sarah Roberts, a black child, did not have the right to attend the school that she wished to attend, although it was closer to her home than the one she was required to attend. The Boston School Committee had plenary authority, the chief justice said, to determine which primary school a child should attend as long as it was "as well fitted" as other primary schools.[21] Surely over the following century the influence of the decision in the Roberts case, with its incipient doctrine of separate but equal, would exert greater influence over the condition and destiny of black Americans than the Fourteenth Amendment.

Perhaps the one piece of legislation that gave them reason to hope for equality was the Civil Rights Act of 1866. A far-reaching law, it declared that all persons born in the United States, excluding Indians not taxed, were citizens of the United States and such citizens "without regard to any previous condition of slavery or involuntary servitude . . . shall have the same right . . . as is enjoyed by white citizens."[22] When, in the following year, these sweeping provisions became a part of the Fourteenth Amendment, there was even greater cause for optimism.

Thus, it would be reasonable to assume that once the Reconstruction amendments, especially the Fourteenth Amendment, were ratified, race would no longer be a special problem under the amended Constitution. The Thirteenth Amendment had been ratified in 1865, thus eliminating all those cryptic, convoluted references to slavery in the original Constitution. It no longer mattered—or did it?—that in some states the ratification of the Thirteenth Amendment was hotly debated and that a bit of bribery here and there was alleged to be necessary to get the amendment accepted in certain Northern states.[23] At first glance the Fourteenth Amendment seemed so straightforward, so unequivocal. Surely, black Americans would enjoy equal citizenship and equal protection of the laws. And if black Americans were not guaranteed the franchise by the citizenship provision of the Fourteenth Amendment, then it would seem that the Fifteenth Amendment had "wrapped the whole thing up," as President Abraham Lincoln had said in referring to the Thirteenth Amendment when Congress sent it to him for his signature.

It was not nearly so simple as that. The bill that was to give real meaning to the Fourteenth Amendment, the Civil Rights Act of 1875, was in the making for five years, and when it was finally passed it was never effectively enforced. The attorney general did not even provide the U.S. marshals with copies of the bill so that they would be informed about it in order to enforce it. Benjamin Butler, the floor manager of the bill in the House of Representatives, made it clear to a Cincinnati audience that the bill would not permit blacks to enter saloons that served white people. After all, he said, there must be some place where whites could get away from the ubiquitous black race![24]

It was a painful experience for black Americans to learn in 1883 that the Supreme Court declared the Civil Rights Act of 1875 unconstitutional, with the assertion that the Fourteenth Amendment had not authorized Congress to enact laws extending such civil rights to Negroes. It had merely restrained the state, not private persons, from denying equal protection to Negroes. This caused T. Thomas Fortune, the black journalist, to bewail, "The colored people . . . feel today as they have been baptized in ice water."[25] It had already become painfully clear that the Fifteenth Amendment did not provide all the guarantees of enfranchisement for which blacks had hoped; for the Supreme Court said as early as 1876 that the Fifteenth Amendment did not confer the right of suffrage on anyone but merely prohibited the states or the national government from excluding persons from voting on racial grounds.[26]

Meanwhile, it appeared that the Fourteenth Amendment was proving to be of greater benefit to the burgeoning corporate world than to the hapless, powerless blacks. Even before the end of Reconstruction, the Supreme Court had broadened its role of judicial review by passing on the constitutionality of state legislation that sought to regulate businesses ranging from slaughter-houses to railroads to grain elevators.[27] In so doing, the Court greatly enhanced the role of the Constitution in the economic life of the country at a time when the Constitution's role in protecting human rights seemed to be diminishing.

By the time that the case of *Plessy* v. *Ferguson* reached the Supreme Court in 1896, the Court appeared to be in no mood to be distracted from what seemed to have become its major preoccupation, economic growth. Plessy, who thought that the Fourteenth Amendment protected his right to sit anywhere on a Louisiana train, soon discovered that even his fair skin was no protection if his race was known. When he was forced to sit in a rail car set aside for Negroes, he sued and the case eventually reached the Supreme Court. Echoing the assertions made by Chief Justice Shaw a half-century earlier, the U.S. Supreme Court, through Justice Henry Brown, saw no constitutional objection to a Louisiana law requiring separate railway coaches for whites and blacks, as long as the accommodations were equal.[28]

It was not a great distance for the Court to travel three years later in concluding, in *Cumming* v. *Richmond [Georgia] County Board of Education*, that a white high school need not be closed because the county did not have sufficient funds to maintain a high school for blacks also.[29] The logic of *Plessy* and *Cum-*

ming led directly to every conceivable form of discrimination and segregation, most of it unequal, such as the one in 1945 when forty-five blacks, including me, were crammed into a half-coach designed to accommodate twenty passengers, next to the baggage car, on a trip from Greensboro to Durham, while a full coach was occupied by six German prisoners of war, who took much delight in our discomfort.

The nineteenth century closed as it began, just as, indeed, the eighteenth century had closed as it began, as far as race was concerned. The factor of race haunted the relations of whites and blacks in the eighteenth century and dictated not only the relations of master and slave but the relations of whites and blacks who were free. This same factor of race in the nineteenth century dominated the thoughts and actions of proslavery advocates as well as abolitionists, and was a major issue in determining the interpretation of the Constitution and in setting public policy virtually to the end of the twentieth century. Throughout the nineteenth century, white Americans could not bring themselves to subscribe to the view that free black Americans were entitled to the same privileges and rights of citizenship that whites enjoyed. The view that free blacks had no rights prevailed at the time of the framing of the Constitution and was in place when all blacks became free in 1865. This was the basis for the policy and practices that persisted throughout the nineteenth century and for most of the twentieth century.

NOTES

1. See my "Moral Legacy of the Founding Fathers," *University of Chicago Magazine*, vol. 47, no. 4 (Spring 1975), reprinted in John Hope Franklin, *Race and History, Selected Essays, 1938–1988* (Baton Rouge: Louisiana State University Press, 1990).

2. Oscar Handlin, *Race and Nationality in American Life*, (Boston: Little, Brown, 1948), 3–28; and Winthrop D. Jordan, *White over Black: American Attitudes toward the Negro, 1550–1812* (Chapel Hill: University of North Carolina Press, 1968), 44–98.

3. The incident is described in Jordan, *White over Black*, 75.

4. Lamont D. Thomas, *Rise to Be a People: A Biography of Paul Cuffee* (Urbana: University of Illinois Press, 1986), 9–12.

5. The speech, "On the Legality of Enslaving the Africans," is reprinted in Louis Ruchames, ed., *Racial Thought in America from the Puritans to Abraham Lincoln*, vol. 1 (Amherst: University of Massachusetts Press, 1969), 152–56.

6. Charles H. Wesley, *Richard Allen: Apostle of Freedom* (Washington: Associated, 1935), 52–53.

7. *Public Statutes at Large of the United States* (Boston: Little and Brown, 1845), 1: 103.

8. *Public Statutes at Large of the United States* (Boston: Little and Brown, 1845) 1: 271.

9. *Public Statutes at Large of the United States, Seventh Congress* (Boston: Little and Brown, 1846), 2: 195–96.

10. For an illuminating discussion of the problem, see Paul Finkelman, "Slavery and the Northwest Ordinance: A Study in Ambiguity," *Journal of the Early Republic,* 6 (Winter, 1986): 343–70.

11. *Public Statutes at Large of the United States, Tenth Congress,* 2: 469.

12. The manner in which alleged fugitive slaves were treated in the Northern states is discussed in Leon Litwack, *North of Slavery, The Negro in the Free States, 1790–1860* (Chicago: University of Chicago Press 1961), 247–79; and Stanley W. Campbell, *The Slave Catchers: Enforcement of the Fugitive Slave Law, 1850–1860* (Chapel Hill: University of North Carolina Press, 1970), 170–86.

13. *Prigg* v. *Pennsylvania,* 16 Peters 539 (1842).

14. See, for example, Philip S. Foner and George E. Walker, eds., *Proceedings of the Black State Conventions, 1845–1860* (Philadelphia: Temple University Press, 1979).

15. "Appeal of Forty Thousand Citizens, Threatened with Disfranchisement, to the People of Pennsylvania," *The Liberator,* April 13, 1838.

16. Frederick Douglass, "The Meaning of July Fourth for the Negro," in Philip S. Foner, ed., *The Life and Writings of Frederick Douglass,* vol. 2 (New York: International, 1950), 181–204.

17. Quoted in Herbert Aptheker, *A Documentary History of the Negro People in the United States,* vol. 2 (New York: Citadel Press, 1951), 316–17.

18. *Dred Scott* v. *Sandford,* 19 Howard 393 (1857). See, also, Don E. Fehrenbacher, *The Dred Scott Case: Its Significance in American Law and Politics* (New York: Oxford University Press, 1978).

19. Ira Berlin, *Slaves without Masters: The Free Negro in the Antebellum South* (New York: Pantheon Books, 1974); and Litwack, *North of Slavery.*

20. Benjamin Quarles, *The Negro in the Civil War* (Boston: Little, Brown, 1953), 199–213.

21. *Roberts* v. *City of Boston,* 59 Mass. 198; and Leonard W. Levy and Philips Harlan, "The Roberts Case: Source of the Separate but Equal Doctrine," *American Historical Review* 56 (April, 1951): 510–18.

22. Act of April 9, 1866, chap. 31, 14 Stat. 27.

23. LaWanda Cox and John Cox, *Politics, Principle, and Prejudice* (Glencoe, Ill.: Free Press, 1963), 1–30.

24. John Hope Franklin, "The Enforcement of the Civil Rights Act of 1875," *Prologue* 6 (Winter, 1974): 225–35.

25. *New York Globe,* October 20, 1883.

26. *U.S.* v. *Reese,* 92 U.S. 214 (1876), 367.

27. *The Slaughter-House Cases,* 16 Wallace 36 (1873); *Chicago, Burlington, and Quincy Railroad Co.* v. *Iowa,* 94 U.S. 155 (1877); and *Munn* v. *Illinois,* 94 U.S. 113 (1877).

28. *Plessy* v. *Ferguson,* 163 U.S. 537 (1896).

29. 175 U.S. 528 (1899).

DARLENE CLARK HINE

BLACK LAWYERS AND
THE TWENTIETH-CENTURY STRUGGLE
FOR CONSTITUTIONAL CHANGE

The fact that the Constitution of the United States is not only alive after two hundred years but is still evolving as the fundamental law of the land has been attributed to the wisdom and genius of its framers, the majority of whom were lawyers. Most especially, credit is accorded to James Madison, principal architect of the system of checks and balances. Madison ensured, or so he must have imagined, political stability by providing for a bicameral legislature, an executive, and a judiciary. The framers of the Constitution nevertheless left unresolved two discordant issues. At birth, therefore, the new republic was marked by an ambiguous line separating and defining state and national power. In the years to come, this ambiguity would severely test the resiliency of the new government.

Even more propitious than the controversy over state versus federal rights was the struggle to resolve the contradiction inherent in the coexistence of democracy and constitutionally sanctioned slavery, and later, racial inequality. Actually, the two issues became so closely intertwined that it would require two reconstructions—one in the aftermath of the Civil War and another several generations later—to restore the primacy of federal authority over state power and equality of rights over racial subordination. It is the second Reconstruction that commands attention because of its important accomplishments. As political scientist Charles V. Hamilton has pointed out: "Blatant, overt laws requiring segregation of the races were declared unconstitutional, and laws denying and impeding the rights of black Americans to vote were ended. In this sense, the civil rights movement that most people joined (or opposed) was won."[1]

Many individuals, groups, and organizations contributed to the victories of the modern civil rights movement. A wealth of scholarly literature details the changing fortunes of the U.S. Supreme Court and the ideologies of the justices comprising the high tribunal since the 1930s. Scores of autobiographies and biographies examine the lives and contributions of national and of local community black protest leaders in the movement. For the most part, however, historians have neglected to analyze the roles played by the individual local black attorneys who labored behind the scenes, in the shadows of the larger-than-life black protest figures, but without whose labor and expert legal guidance there would have been no second Reconstruction or civil rights revolution.[2]

The business of this essay is not to diminish the brilliance of James Madison's achievement. Rather, I propose that we share the spotlight for the efficacy, longevity, and vitality of the U.S. Constitution with a very special cadre of American citizens, the members of the twentieth-century black bar. It is a daunting task to unravel the tangled tapestry of factors that explain how such a small group of African American lawyers, never at any point exceeding 2 percent of the legal profession, wrought a second emancipation. Between 1910 and 1920 the number of black lawyers increased from about 800 to 950. By 1940, there were 1,350 black lawyers serving a population of thirteen million African Americans. In 1950 the black lawyer population stood at approximately 1,450, and in 1960 it jumped to more than two thousand. The number of black physicians throughout this period was well over four thousand.[3] Unfortunately, little has yet been written about the educational and professional handicaps black lawyers endured and their responses to them.

In their relentless pursuit of equality and freedom for black Americans, black legal soldiers revolutionized constitutional jurisprudence, derailed the strange career of Jim Crow, and made civil rights, as opposed to state rights, the moral imperative of the twentieth century. In other words, black lawyers, working with a number of organizations over long periods of time, transformed constitutional jurisprudence to embrace the primacy of civil rights over state rights, and replaced the doctrine of "separate but equal" with one of equality. This "equalitarian revolution" was the hidden revolution within the modern black rights movement.[4]

This chapter examines the role of the black bar and the institutional infrastructure that sustained it throughout the critical years of 1945 to 1965. During this period black lawyers were involved in more than a dozen favorable cases in the U.S. Supreme Court. Because it is first necessary to identify the black bar, its national leaders, chief strategists, and community-based lawyers, this discussion devotes considerable attention to the development of key black-led legal institutions: the National Bar Association (NBA), Howard University, and the National Legal and Educational Defense Fund, Inc., of the National Association for the Advancement of Colored People (NAACP). These institutions, along with the pivotal civil rights organizations, the Southern Christian Leadership Conference (SCLC) and the Student Nonviolent Coordinating Committee (SNCC), generated the court cases that enabled lawyers to win the substantive judicial decisions. To be sure, the relationship between the black bar and the civil rights protestors was a symbiotic one. The street protests and demonstrations provoked oppressive responses from white police and municipal governmental authorities based upon, as the lawyers put it, a "misapplication of preexisting constitutional laws."[5] This is not an attempt to overemphasize the work of the lawyers and to subordinate the contributions of the leaders of these protest organizations and the demonstrators who bore the brunt of imprisonment and white brutality.

The second part of the discussion highlights a few of the precedent-setting U.S. Supreme Court decisions won by the black bar during the second Reconstruction. A series of brilliantly orchestrated cases secured decisions that desegregated transportation and public schools, reapportioned districts, extended and protected black voting rights, and finally ended restrictive housing covenants. Yet, it is well to recognize that although judicial decisions expanded on the meaning of the Constitution of the United States, they alone would not have effected a revolution in American race relations. Judicial decisions in and of themselves did not contain political or moral authority to force compliance. Judge J. Skelly Wright correctly reminds us that "a compelling moral principle, banned from the political system, was taken up by the Supreme Court and given formal legitimacy, then, when the political system refused the legal principle, as it had the moral one, the idea traveled back into the private sector, back to the people, and created a whole new politics."[6] And much of this new politics was played out in the streets—in demonstrations, marches, sit-ins, and freedom rides.

Still, throughout the period of the modern civil rights movement, the black lawyer was an essential force. As one student maintained, "Black lawyers have been fulcrums on which the see-saw of the civil rights movement was balanced." During this turbulent period, the black lawyer was adviser, mediator, educator, and defendant, depending on the needs of the hour. Black lawyers worked with the civil rights organizations, dealt with opposition attorneys, negotiated with members of white city boards and county officials, joined interracial commissions, posted bonds to liberate thousands from Southern jails, and not infrequently suffered physical attack and had their homes bombed.[7] Burke Marshall has pointed out that "the protestors, demonstrators, and so forth acted at all times with careful legal advice, under a claim of right under the federal constitution to do what they did. . . . To put it another way, the action taken by the members of the protest movement merely asserted legal rights guaranteed by the federal constitution, but denied to them by unconstitutional, and therefore unlawful, local police action."[8] In an exuberant tribute to the black bar, former Atlanta mayor Maynard H. Jackson exclaimed, "When considered in light of the impediments and shackles born of a system of racism and systematic exclusion, the gains of the black lawyer are nothing short of phenomenal."[9] No less effusive, Robert L. Carter declared that the black lawyers "succeeded in transforming the Fourteenth Amendment, and to a lesser extent the Fifteenth Amendment, into a Negro Magna Charta."[10]

Most discussions of the role black lawyers played in the transformation of constitutional jurisprudence, that is, in the elimination of constitutional support for racial segregation and discrimination, begin with Charles H. Houston. The reverence accorded this man and his deeds is not without merit. Houston, born on September 3, 1895, in Washington, D.C., was a graduate of Amherst College. He earned his first law degree in 1922 from Harvard Law School and his doctorate in juridical science the following year. He continued his studies at the University of Madrid, where he studied civil law. From 1924 to 1929 in the firm of Houston and Houston, Charles Houston practiced law with his father in Washington, D.C. Although his legal work was demanding, Houston managed to find time to take an active interest in the fortunes of the Howard Law School and to research the general status of the black lawyer. In 1929 Houston's life changed irrevocably when he accepted the post of vice-dean of the Howard University School of Law, where he served as a full-time administrator until 1935.

No less talented and essential to the black rights struggle than Houston was William Henry Hastie. In 1930 Hastie, a recent graduate of Harvard Law School, joined Houston as a faculty member in the Howard Law School. Hastie was born on November 17, 1904, in Knoxville, Tennessee. He completed his undergraduate study at Amherst College. While engaged in work for the S.J.D. at Harvard, and on leave from the Howard Law School, Hastie participated in his first major black rights case. He assisted (on behalf of the NAACP) Conrad Pearson and Cecil McCoy in defending the right of Thomas

R. Hocutt to enter the school of pharmacy at the University of North Carolina.[11] After Houston resigned from Howard in the mid-1930s, Hastie stepped in to continue the revitalization process.

The Howard Law School had opened on January 6, 1869, with an integrated faculty and student body. Until 1898 students pursued a two-year course of study for the LL.D. degree. In 1898 the course for the LL.D. degree was extended to three years. Before 1904 no tuition fees were charged, only a matriculation fee of $10.00. Up to 1924 the only entrance requirement was a high school education or its equivalent. The administration raised the admission standards in 1924 to two years of standard college work. Clearly, as conditions were in the mid-1920s, Howard Law School was far from becoming what attorney Robert L. Carter later described as "the center of intellectual ferment in black legal circles."[12] Nevertheless, Howard Law School was still deemed to be of higher quality than the only two existing institutions in the entire South that offered legal training to black students, Simmons University in Louisville, Kentucky, and Virginia Union University in Richmond, Virginia. Most white law schools, which with a few exceptions were located in the northeast, excluded blacks.[13]

As early as 1926 Houston had become involved in the affairs of the Howard Law School. Three years before assuming the deanship he had undertaken the challenge of spearheading a special faculty campaign committee charged to raise money to improve the school's law library. Houston believed that the inadequacies of the law library accounted for the refusal of the Association of American Law Schools to recognize the institution. In a widely circulated fund-raising letter, he offered potential contributors a candid assessment of existing conditions. He wrote, "It has no endowment. It has no student loan funds or scholarships. Most of the professors are employed only on part-time; and even in the case of full-time professors their salaries fall below those of the academic professors by hundreds of dollars. The Law Library is not up-to-date."[14] Warming to the task of persuading others to give, Houston provided even more specific details of the law library's needs. "The Howard University Law Library now consists of some 5482 volumes, of which more than 1000 are duplicates and an additional 500 antiquated and out-of-date, leaving a working library of less than 4000 volumes." According to the December 1925 report of the Association of American Law Schools, a recognized law school was expected to own a library of not less than 7,500 volumes.[15]

Thus when Houston accepted the vice-dean's position at Howard Law School, he did so fully cognizant of the needs and challenges. As with so many things in his life, in this, too, he proved successful. With single-minded purpose and unremitting drive, Houston transformed the unarguably marginal enterprise into a school fully accredited and highly respected. Propitiously, Houston's work between 1929 and 1935 at the law school enabled him to train a cadre of young black lawyers imbued with a desire to go South and do legal battle with Jim Crow. At the outset of his tenure as vice-dean, Houston carefully unveiled his vision of what the school would accomplish. "The aims . . . should be to equip its students with the direct professional skills most useful to them, and to give them as deep and as broad a societal background as possible." But Houston articulated an even higher purpose when he declared, "From the standpoint of public function, the Negro lawyer ought to be trained as a social engineer and group interpreter. . . . To qualify such group leaders, the law school must give its students a thorough understanding of the administration of Law with its inherent limitations superimposed with a brief societal background."[16]

Under Houston's leadership, the Howard Law School faculty produced a generation of black lawyers very different from the ones he had criticized in a 1928 report on the status of the black bar financed by the Laura Spelman Rockefeller Memorial Fund, but sponsored by the Howard Law School. Researching the project had been an illuminating and frustrating experience. Perhaps the most significant benefit Houston derived from making the survey and preparing the report was the unique opportunity afforded to travel across the country and to meet and talk to virtually all of the major practicing black lawyers and a few he needed not to have met. While the lack of social conscience of many black lawyers disappointed him, he did manage to identify a handful of key Southern black lawyers who exemplified an admirable spirit of public service. He singled out for special praise N. P. Frederick of Columbia, South Carolina; S. D. Redmond of Jackson, Mississippi; S. D. McGill of Jacksonville, Florida; Scipio A. Jones of Little Rock, Arkansas; and A. T. Walden of Atlanta, Georgia. He acknowledged that "there are some men in the South who are doing real pioneer work for the Negro lawyer . . . trying cases in many instances at the risk of their personal safety."[17] Along more critical lines, Houston railed against the appalling incompetence and absence of social reform work among many black lawyers. He charged, "I think it may be said without much fear of contradiction that the lawyer exerts less influence on the community than any other class of professional man." He elaborated:

> Along strictly professional lines the Negro lawyers have come to the front
> when racial controversies have cropped out in the courts. Scipio A. Jones
> saved the lives of the Elaine rioters by his disinterested work; N. P. Frederick

paved the way for the ultimate acquittal of the Lowmans altho the mob subsequently lynched them. The Chicago lawyers and the Washington lawyers came to the defense of the Negroes arrested during the race riots of 1919 and 1920. W. Ashbie Hawkins is the grand old man who has fought every form of discrimination in Baltimore during the last forty years. But these instances are sporadic. There is no court committee in any town to fight oppression of undefended Negroes; no legal relief organization, and no enthusiasm [a]bout starting one.[18]

The contacts Houston made while working at Howard proved invaluable when in 1935 he left the law school to serve as the first full-time salaried attorney and special counsel for the NAACP. A close colleague and admirer described Houston's work with the NAACP in reverential terms: "He was the architect and dominant force of the legal program of that organization. He guided us through the legal wilderness of second-class citizenship. He was truly the Moses of that journey."[19] Shortly before he relinquished the reigns on this position in 1939, the NAACP separated the litigative functions of the organization in order to receive tax-exempt status and created the NAACP Legal and Educational Defense Fund.

Between 1929 and his death in 1950, Houston devoted his entire professional life and all of his considerable legal talents to laying the groundwork, as historian and biographer Genna Rae McNeil puts it, for the judicial battles that all but dominated the Supreme Court's docket from 1939 through 1965. His colleague, William H. Hastie, in a moving testament to Houston's significance declared, "He lived to see us close to the promised land of full equality under the law, closer than even he dared hope when he set out on the journey and so much closer than would have been possible without his genius and his leadership."[20] Houston possessed many characteristics that won converts to his cause. As described by Dean Erwin N. Griswold of the Harvard Law School, "He was handsome, in a dignified yet forceful way. He was a man who created respect."[21] Griswold announced what the black bar already knew, "It is doubtful that there has been a single important case involving civil rights during the past fifteen years in which Charles Houston has not either participated directly or by consultation and advice. He was a tower of strength in the legal field."[22]

Shortly after Houston assumed the reigns of the NAACP's legal work, he drafted what he called the "Tentative Statement Concerning Policy of NAACP in Its Program of Attack on Educational Discrimination." In it, Houston delineated the three "glaring and typical discriminations" destined to be the targets of concentrated legal action; differentials in teacher's salaries along color lines, inequalities in transportation facilities (which he deemed the basic barrier to the consolidation of rural schools), and inequalities in graduate and professional education offered to whites in universities supported by state funds but denied to black students. Houston was especially concerned with the denial of professional and graduate study to blacks. He believed that the denial of advanced educational opportunity to black students was a white ploy "to perpetuate the inferior status of Negroes," and to prevent the race from developing a viable pool of leaders.[23]

In the 1930s and 1940s, in tandem with his work at the Howard Law School and with the NAACP legal program, Houston oversaw the emergence and maturation of the black bar. Through the force of his personality, the clarity of his vision, the sheer determination of his will, Houston sparked a new social consciousness among black lawyers. He persuaded them to join him in the battle for black rights before the courts. Thus by the eve of World War II Houston had forged critical working relations with dozens of local black lawyers across the country. These linkages became a tightly woven network of the best black legal minds available. On one occasion Houston encouraged a young man contemplating law as a career, "There is an unlimited field in the law for young Negroes who are willing to make the fight." He predicted that "the lawyer is going to be the leader of the next step in racial advancement." If the lawyer was destined to be, as Houston phrased it in 1935, "the trouble shooter," then the site of all the action would, in the coming decades, occur in the South. He declared, "It is obvious that our greatest problems are in the South, where the masses of Negroes suffer the greatest handicaps and discriminations. The Negro lawyer in the South in the next twenty-five years has a chance to reconstruct the entire southern picture."[24]

An abiding conviction that Southern black lawyers would play pivotal roles in the reconstruction of race relations fed Houston's desire to forge close associations between the NAACP Legal Committee and the black bar. He was keenly aware that revolutions of any stripe depended for success upon the depth of the infantry. These local lawyers, or the lieutenants and foot soldiers, often initiated, massaged, and argued in the lower courts the precedent-setting cases. Their involvement in and subsequent cooperation with the NAACP led to the U.S. Supreme Court victories in *Smith* v. *Allwright* in 1944 (ending the white primary), *Shelley* v. *Kraemer* in 1948 (nullifying restrictive housing covenants), and *Brown* v. *Board of Education* in 1954 (desegregating public schools in the South). Then in the years after *Brown*, the local lawyers became the advisers to the leaders of the civil rights movement, playing instrumental roles in linking the courtroom struggles with those battles raging in the streets of Birmingham, Montgomery, Albany, Greensboro, and Selma.

The problems and obstacles impeding the professional development of black attorneys cannot be exaggerated. Some scholars have suggested that in the 1930s the black bar existed in a state of segregated disarray. The problems black attorneys encountered entering the profession and their difficulties in earning a living by practicing law during the 1930s and 1940s have been discussed elsewhere in great detail and need only brief mention here. For the most part, black lawyers possessed inadequate education, substandard training, limited opportunities for professional development and growth, and low professional esteem. Even when highly competent, the American Bar Association refused them membership on the basis of race; potential, even black, clients, regarded black lawyers as inferior; white judges in the South sometimes barred black lawyers from courtrooms; and few law libraries were open to them. The vast majority of the 1,200 black lawyers were relegated to the least desirable and least remunerative areas of practice—criminal offenses, domestic relations, personal injury, and small claims.[25]

Houston's supervision of one of the key agencies for social and legal reform, the NAACP Legal Committee, and his involvement with significant members of the National Bar Association, during the 1930s provided the essential institutional base from which he orchestrated the multifaceted attack on "Jim Crow" and black second-class citizenship. Contemporaries graciously and generously accord Houston a special place of honor and readily acknowledge the debt owed his leadership. Houston, however, would have been the first to admit that the major legal victories of the 1930s and 1940s were accomplished precisely because of the collaboration of an array of talented barristers, including Raymond Pace Alexander, William H. Hastie, Thurgood Marshall, Leon A. Ransom, and James M. Nabrit. These men, virtually all having received their legal training at Howard or Harvard Law School, constituted an elite stratum of the black bar.

Shortly after Houston settled into his new position with the NAACP, he moved to balance the racial composition of the NAACP National Legal Committee, which for most of its existence had been composed of prominent white attorneys. There were exceptions. Black attorneys William Andrews and James Cobb had worked with the legal committee during the 1920s. Among the new black attorneys whom Houston nominated for membership on the committee was Z. Alexander Looby of Nashville, "the best trained and most outstanding lawyer in Tennessee," Houston wrote. He described Alexander P. Tureau of New Orleans as "a leader of the fight against disfranchisement in

Louisiana." Earl Dickerson of Chicago, an assistant attorney general of Illinois, was noted as being "one of the best lawyers in the Middle West." A former president of the National Bar Association, Raymond Pace Alexander of Philadelphia was dubbed "an outstanding trial lawyer of the East." Houston offered special praise for one attorney, Leon A. Ransom of Washington, D.C., describing him as one "of the best legal minds in the Negro race," who had done "more than anyone else upon the Howard University faculty to inspire young law students with social purpose."[26] Scholars August Meier and Elliott Rudwick contend that "with the accession of Houston to the post of special counsel, the transition from white preeminence to black control of the NAACP's legal work was essentially complete."[27]

The black lawyers whom Houston added to the NAACP Legal Committee belonged to a closely knit professional and personal brotherhood. They shared similar educational backgrounds; most of the older ones were trained at Harvard, Yale, and other elite eastern law schools. The majority of the younger men were products of Howard University Law School, where they received instruction from Houston, Hastie, and James Nabrit. These black lawyers maintained a great degree of contact through fraternal, social, business, and professional organizations, especially through the National Bar Association.

Houston, ever on the search for outstanding black legal talent, continuously enlarged the fold. Roy Wilkins, former executive secretary of the NAACP, lauded Houston's special talent for persuading black lawyers to become involved in the civil rights struggle. Wilkins recalled that Houston "was able to get black lawyers interested in civil rights cases because he talked it wherever he went." Similarly, James Nabrit reminisced that "when Houston selected a person to work with him, it was as if the mantle of the Lord had dropped on them, and they would do anything for him."[28]

In September 1936, Houston, while in Reno, Nevada, wrote a revealing memorandum to four black lawyers: Leon Ransom, Z. Alexander Looby, Carl Cowan, and Thurgood Marshall. The memorandum was loaded with praise and instructions concerning the University of Tennessee desegregation case then being sponsored by the NAACP. Ever the cheerleader, Houston first exclaimed, "Congratulations Andy, Looby and Carl. Splendid work; the case seems to be in good shape." What Houston found especially gratifying about the case against the University of Tennessee's School of Pharmacy denial of admission to William B. Redmond II on account of race was the potential it held for mobilizing the black community. He maintained, "That hunch about inspecting the minutes of the board of trustees of the University of Tennessee was one of the best inspirations we have had. When the story is told to

Negroes, I think it will furnish one of the most inspiring episodes in the educational campaign. It shows Negroes that the minutes of so-called white universities are public records, open to inspection of Negroes the same as any other citizen, and that Negroes in proper cases will insist on their rights."[29]

In the case against the University of Tennessee, the university's attorney argued that a Tennessee act of 1901 made it a criminal offense to teach white and Negro students in the same class, school, or college building. Accordingly, the law prohibited the enrollment of any Negro students in the university. The plaintiff, William Redmond, contended that this act of 1901 applied to the physical separation of the races and was entirely consistent with the provisions of the act of 1869, which provided for the admission of Negroes to the University of Tennessee but required that they be instructed in separate classes. The black lawyers argued that William Redmond was not seeking to enter the same classes with the white students in the School of Pharmacy, but rather that he was entitled to admission to the school and that it was incumbent on the trustees of the university to provide him separate instruction in accordance with the acts of 1869 and 1901. The black lawyers further insisted that the University of Tennessee's denial of admission to him on account of color violated the Fourteenth Amendment to the Constitution. The Chancery Court of Shelby County, Tennessee, in Memphis, dismissed the petition for mandamus holding that "there was no pharmaceutical school in Tennessee in which a Negro student was eligible to enroll but ruled that the State of Tennessee did not violate the Fourteenth Amendment by limiting the School of Pharmacy of the University of Tennessee to white students only."[30]

During the local court arguments, Ransom and Houston introduced two strategies that would become standard features of desegregation litigation over the next twenty years. Ransom identified and called for testimony from black professionals, in this instance two practicing pharmacists. He used their testimony to establish "conclusively that there is a real need for Negro pharmacists in the State of Tennessee as well as the entire South, and that Negroes are not confined, in this profession, to practice solely within their own race." The second point hammered home by Houston focused on the state's failure to provide adequate pharmaceutical training for blacks and that this created a "great menace to the health of the good white people of the South." Eventually, after a couple of adverse decisions, the NAACP abandoned the case. Its significance lies in being the mirror reflecting Houston's leadership style and thoughts on the roles of the black lawyer.[31]

The memorandum, however, goes far beyond commenting on the specifics of the Tennessee desegregation case. In it Houston explained why he removed himself from direct formal involvement in the case and elaborated upon the philosophical rationale for including as many top-notch, well-trained, care-fully selected local black attorneys as possible in the civil rights cases. Further, he discussed relations between the antisegregation court cases of the black bar and the activism of community leaders.

After the first round of arguments in the *Redmond* v. *University of Tennessee School of Pharmacy* case, Houston withdrew, declaring, "This is no star perfor-mance." Houston believed that no one person or lawyer should ever be indis-pensable to a given case. He insisted, "My ideal of administration is to make the movement self-perpetuating so that the loss of the head or any set of members will not hamper progress." The achievement of a "self-executing" administration, Houston asserted, is possible only "where all subordinates have been so well trained and posted about the program that any one of them is able to step into the chief's shoes any minute and carry on with no loss of stride." He concluded with characteristic modesty, "My greatest satisfaction in these cases is to find I can let go and the colleagues carry on as well, if not better than I can."[32]

In positing this philosophy of "self-executing" leadership, Houston was in no way attempting to drop out of the legal battle against segregated educa-tion. Rather, it was critical to his overall program to take a back seat in the early years of this desegregation of education campaign. Houston's decision was based on a desire for self-protection and the protection of other black lawyers, and on a realization of the importance of maintaining local black confidence and support: "There is safety in sudden switching and changing, and rotation of counsel. If the opposition gets the belief that I am the only person to worry about and that if I am removed all trouble will be over, it will concentrate on removing me by disbarment proceedings, public embar-rassment, criminal charges, or otherwise." Houston desired to spare local black lawyers from the threat of white reprisals and retaliations. He reasoned that if the white opposition understood that "it will not accomplish anything by my removal or by removal of any set of lawyers, it will not waste time on personal reprisals but will accept the fact that it has to fight a movement and concentrate on technical defenses and defenses to the merits."[33]

Wisely, Houston urged his colleagues to continue to emphasize, when speaking to the press or local audiences, that "these cases are not my cases, but the manifestation of a spontaneous local demand on the part of the citi-zens, and that for every one of us who for any reason drops out, there remains a dozen to take his place." Houston resolved that white opposition and harass-ment of the black attorney along with the "cry of outside interference and agitation" would be muted if "we can show a bushel of lawyers than if we have to have one or two men running all over the country on emergency calls just like a fire engine or wrecking crew."[34]

Houston's decision to move into the background in order to maneuver behind the scenes did not reflect either a diminution of personal interest or decreased professional involvement in the local school desegregation cases. To his "boys," as he referred to them, Houston demanded, "just keep me fully advised of everything." He warned them, "and for God's sake don't let them catch us asleep on technicalities and don't let anything go by default." Houston remained ever mindful of the powerful white personal and institutional resistance they confronted. At one juncture, he lamented that, "against us we have all the forces of state governments." He knew that any losses or mistakes would be blamed on him, "as the responsible authority." After all, he recalled having once advised "Andy and the boys the line between a bitch and a son-of-a-bitch was mighty fine." More seriously, he reiterated, "The only thing I can do is pick our associates with all possible care and insist on being kept advised of all developments so as to be able to counsel with the fellows if I think things are not developing as they should." He added, in wry humor, "If success comes the boys can have it, and I won't have such a long distance to fall when the reaction comes and the second-guessers get busy."[35]

The caring and cooperative working pattern Houston evidenced with the trio of black attorneys handling the *Redmond* v. *University of Tennessee* case became his trademark. He offered advice, encouragement, and attention to detail. To Sidney Redmond, black attorney in St. Louis, Missouri, whom Houston retained to handle the local legal work in the more successful *Missouri ex rel. Gaines* v. *Canada* case, he cautioned, "Remember that it is not your job to find a client. I don't want you to be put in the position of fomenting litigation. I want the newspapers or interested laymen to find you your client. All I want you to do is make the investigation and disclose the rotten conditions."[36]

When Redmond expressed anxiety about not moving quickly enough, Houston cautioned him, "I am not anxious for you to rush the case simply to get action. . . . The issues involved are so big that we cannot afford to omit any detail of preparation in a hasty attempt at grandstand play. So as long as you are working, be assured that I will not become impatient because suit is not filed within the next few days."[37] Moreover, when the beleaguered Redmond encountered difficulties working with the local leaders of fraternity and sorority groups, Houston wrote with empathy, "I appreciate the difficulty you face in working with your group. The same thing has happened in every state we have entered. Frankly, the university program has slowed down to a walk for lack of suitable candidates both in the front line and in reserve." He emphasized that the work with the fraternities and sororities, albeit often frustrating, was necessary in order "to undergird the educational program with more popular support." He reminded his colleague, "What we must realize is that we are marking out new ground and that very few persons have the pioneer spirit. Consequently, do not be dismayed by the timidity and general unreliability of many of those with whom you come in contact."[38]

The same determination, patience, guidance, and commitment Houston demonstrated while working with the local black lawyers in the aborted *Tennessee* case can be seen in his interactions with the members and leaders of the National Bar Association. As mentioned earlier, many have stated that the black bar was in a state of segregated disarray during the 1930s, some would add the 1940s, as well. Certainly the legal profession was segregated, but the notion that the black bar was in disarray depends on the perspective of the observer. Actually, the allegation of disarray is more a testament to the vast differences in status and resources between the black and white bars than a comment on individual black lawyers. Fully a generation before the black lawyers organized the National Bar Association, white lawyers of the American Bar Association (ABA) had already engaged in and completed the whole process of professionalization. Of course, the issue of admitting blacks to membership was not resolved until much later.

That blacks found it virtually impossible to win admission into the majority of law schools in the country is well documented. It is also important to recognize the treatment meted out by the American Bar Association. In 1912 the ABA expelled black member William H. Lewis, a graduate of Amherst College and Harvard Law School, who in 1910 had been an assistant attorney general for the United States. Apparently he had gained membership in the ABA before his racial identity was known. The leaders defended their purge arguing that the ABA was intended to be a social organization. It was only the concern and adamant protests of former ABA president and NAACP official Moorfield Story that persuaded the organization to ameliorate the racial policy.

In response to Story's objection, the ABA amended a resolution so as to permit all existing black members to remain, but it barred all future African Americans. Refusing to give in, Story argued, "in my judgment the American Bar Association is not a social organization. It claims to represent the whole American Bar, and its recommendations are made on that basis. I think, therefore, it cannot exclude from membership persons who are in other respects entirely fit, merely because their complexion is dark, or their race different from that of other members."[39] Although the ABA convention in 1914 lifted the color bar, a new resolution was adopted calling for full disclosure of race on all applications. Needless to say, this tactic allowed local and state bar associations to weed out all black applicants and thus effectively preserved the ABA's racial purity. Not until 1943 would black lawyers shatter the color bar of the ABA.

By any measure, the difficult terrain separating black and white legal professionals posed major challenges to the few black lawyers practicing in the 1920s. None of these men and women possessed the resources, time, and institutional support they needed to surmount the obstacles in the path of their professional development. By the end of World War I, all of the dozen or so black law schools lacked endowments, adequate operating expenses, libraries, enough full-time teachers, or scholarships for their impoverished students. The majority of the black lawyers engaged in the least remunerative practices. To add to these difficulties, there was a deeply entrenched public stereotype of the black lawyer as an incompetent, shady character whose race prevented him from winning respect from either judges or juries. According to one student of the profession, "the legal insecurity of the Negro is such that the Negro lawyer has but little chance before a Southern court. Protection by a 'respectable' white person usually counts more in the South for a Negro client than would even the best representation on the part of a Negro lawyer."[40]

As the experiences of early black attorneys in Tennessee illustrate, white colleagues and white citizens proved intractable in their resolve to drive black lawyers out of the profession. Historian Lester Lamon observed, "Black lawyers who fought legal discrimination too vigorously often found themselves in professional or physical danger from irate white citizens." In 1920 the Tennessee Bar Association barred the combative Robert L. Mayfield, a graduate of Howard Law School, who had fought for eight years to keep his license. When Chattanooga attorneys Noah W. Parden and Styles L. Hutchins saved Ed Johnson, convicted of rape, by appealing to the U.S. Supreme Court in 1906, they suddenly found it safer to move to Oklahoma. After Justice John Marshall Harlan granted Johnson a stay of execution, the white citizens took him from the Hamilton County jail and lynched him.[41]

What is remarkable about the black bar during the 1930s is not its disarray, but the professionalization of the approximately 1,300 black lawyers then practicing in the country. The 1930s saw the rise of a more militant definition of the proper role the black lawyer should play in black and American society. This coming together of the black bar occurred during the first phase of the modern civil rights movement.

In the first decade of its existence, the National Bar Association accomplished more in the realm of elevating the black lawyer's self-esteem than in contributing to the science of law, or removing the shackles of legal oppression from the black community. But self-esteem, pride, and respect were urgently needed if black lawyers were to assault Jim Crow and repair the derogatory stereotypes of their profession prevalent across the country.

Charles Houston was preeminent among the small cadre of well-trained, visible, and respected black lawyers who shaped the militant activistic twentieth-century role of the black lawyer. Houston preached the gospel holding that the Constitution was the chief weapon to demolish the edifice of legal inequality. Going one step further, Houston asserted that the judges serving on the U.S. Supreme Court more often than not decided cases on the basis of previous principles established in earlier cases. He continued that these judges showed a marked reluctance to decide cases on constitutional grounds. The strategy was clear. In order to effect fundamental constitutional change and to remove the legal barriers thwarting black advance, black lawyers had to take up to the U.S. Supreme Court a series of cases that would establish important precedents. All engaged in the struggle knew that this course would take decades to execute fully.[42]

Jesse Heslip of Toledo, Ohio, a graduate of Harvard Law School and student of Felix Frankfurter, counseled his colleagues in his 1932 NBA presidential address, "We must become thoroughly grounded in constitutional law; we must be ready to face the nation's highest tribunal in search of justice for ourselves."[43] Houston similarly declared that blacks needed their "own constitutional lawyers" because, as he contended, "no one can prepare or present Negroes' cases as well as a trained Negro."[44]

Each president of the NBA echoed identical sentiments emphasizing the black lawyer's obligation to honor the social contract that had gradually emerged with the black community. No one questioned the necessity of the black lawyer to recognize that his fate and that of the black community were inextricably interwoven. Indeed, succeeding NBA presidents consistently preached the centrality of court litigation in the whole quest for black rights. Eugene Washington Rhodes, president in 1933, declared, "The cause of the race will be advanced in exact proportion to the strength and militancy of the bar. . . . The sole bulwark of protection for Negroes are courts of the law. There is no other way out."[45]

Throughout the 1930s and early 1940s, leading black barristers accepted and exhorted that the Constitution of the United States was not only an important expression of values and principles but was also the source of authority for legal and political rules and the institutions that could affect the course of social change. Houston and his colleagues advocated that blacks and other minorities, since they were unable to influence significantly the executive and legislative branches of the government by means of the ballot, should try to achieve their social, educational, and political rights through the courts. For the dispossessed, disfranchised, and disinherited, the law was, in Houston's opinion, the most accessible instrument with which to win civil rights.[46]

Houston's definition of the black lawyer's role grew out of his belief that the lawyer, while at heart a trouble shooter, was also a social critic and activist. Houston, in short, believed that the lawyer should devote his skills and talents to winning black rights through litigation. Yet, while this litigation was under way, the lawyer should also be engaged in activities to mobilize black community residents to protest and agitate for their rights in other arenas.[47] Houston himself attempted to stir up the black communities. In numerous articles published in the NAACP's *Crisis*, he provided instruction on "How to Fight for Better Schools," how to find suitable plaintiffs, raise funds, and organize suits, and the importance of educating white Americans to the true nature and extent of black oppression.[48]

Actually, Houston's views were entirely consistent with those of the early leaders of the National Bar Association, which was founded in 1925. The moving force behind the formation of the NBA was George H. Woodson of Des Moines, Iowa. Woodson was born in Wytheville, Virginia, in 1865 and graduated from Howard Law School in 1895. He practiced law in Iowa until his death in 1933.[49] The men and women who planned and organized the black bar agreed that its objectives would be

> the advancement of the science of jurisprudence, and in addition to form a nationwide organization of practicing attorneys of the Negro race in an endeavor to strengthen and elevate the Negro lawyer in his profession and in his relationship to his people; to improve his standing at the bar of the country, and to stress those values that would serve to enhance the ethics of his practice and conduct, to condemn actions that have a tendency to lessen respect for the lawyer and to create a bond of true fellowship among the colored members of the Bar of America for their general uplift and advancement and for the encouragement of the Negro youth of America who will follow their choice of this profession.[50]

Indeed, little philosophical difference distinguished Houston from NBA stalwart Raymond Pace Alexander. A native of Philadelphia, Alexander was educated at the University of Pennsylvania, Columbia University, and Harvard Law School, from which he was graduated in 1923. He then returned to Philadelphia to practice law. At the first NBA convention, Alexander declared, "We owe the law more than merely using it as a means of making a livelihood. . . . We owe to our people, who, more than any other people are in need of our services, a duty to see that there shall be a quick end to the discrimination and segregation they suffer in their everyday activity."[51] Subsequent NBA presidents adhered to the social contract of race service. For years, Leon Ransom served, without pay, as the chief counsel of the *University of Tennessee* cases.[52] In exchange for the support, respect, and loyalty of the masses of blacks, the race lawyers prepared the legal cases designed to overthrow the constitutional foundation for white supremacy and to remove the shackles of black subordination.

Writing in the first issue of the NBA's *National Bar Journal* in 1941, Raymond Pace Alexander asserted, "The National Bar Association is really the development of the American Negro's belief in himself." He concluded, "As the American Negro lawyer began through this Association to develop a belief in himself, his efforts in crusading for equal justice for the Negro citizens in their fight to improve their civic status took on a new and vastly important aspect." To substantiate his conclusions, Alexander enumerated the twenty cases heard by the U.S. Supreme Court between 1923 and 1940 that dealt with black rights. Each case had a black lawyer on the defense team and every black lawyer so involved, according to Alexander, was a member of the National Bar Association.[53]

It was during the 1940s that the NBA came of age. The annual conventions were well attended, membership soared, and black lawyers launched their own official organ, the *National Bar Journal*. The topic of most of the articles published in the journal concerned the various civil rights activities of the members. Charles Houston, William Hastie, Thurgood Marshall, and other members of the NAACP Legal Defense Fund, Inc., delivered papers and reported on the various litigations sponsored throughout the country. Virtually all of the key NBA performers had some connection with the Defense Fund, Inc. Clearly, so much cross-fertilization of ideas and strategies occurred that it is difficult to determine where the NBA ended and the Legal Defense Fund began.

It is significant that between 1938 and 1954 the NAACP and NAACP Legal Defense and Educational Fund, Inc., under the leadership of Houston and his successor, Thurgood Marshall, argued six antisegregation education cases before the U.S. Supreme Court.[54] These educational cases fell into three broad categories: "suits seeking to equalize the desegregation of public graduate and professional schools, suits seeking to equalize the salaries of black and white teachers, and suits occasioned by the inequalities in the physical facilities at black and white elementary and secondary schools.[55]

Inexorably, black lawyers—beginning with Houston, Hastie, and Marshall, aided by Ransom, Nabrit, Lovett, and scores of unheralded local attorneys—persuaded the U.S. Supreme Court in litigation from *Gaines* to *Brown v. Topeka Board of Education* to reject the doctrine of "separate but equal." Through their compelling arguments they persuaded the Court to reinterpret constitutional equal protection of the law and establish a new standard of equality. In so doing they revolutionized constitutional jurisprudence and made civil rights, as opposed to states rights, the moral imperative of the twentieth century. Black lawyers have made a most significant contribution to the evolution of a living Constitution. Their efforts have benefited all Americans. Thus no celebration of the U.S. Constitution can justifiably ignore the feats of Charles Houston and the black bar.

NOTES

1. Charles V. Hamilton, quoted in Charles W. Eagles, *The Civil Rights Movement in America* (Jackson: University Press of Mississippi, 1986), 97. For a general treatment of the ambivalent relationship of African Americans with the Constitution, see Donald G. Nieman, *Promises to Keep: African-Americans and the Constitutional Order, 1776 to the Present* (New York: Oxford University Press, 1991).

2. There are noteworthy exceptions. The most recent study is J. Clay Smith, Jr., *Emancipation: The Making of the Black Lawyer, 1844–1944* (Philadelphia: University of Pennsylvania Press, 1993). For excellent studies of two black lawyers, see Gilbert Ware, *William Hastie: Grace under Pressure* (New York: Oxford University Press, 1984); Genna Rae McNeil, *Groundwork: Charles Hamilton Houston and the Struggle for Civil Rights* (Philadelphia: University of Pennsylvania Press, 1983). For discussion of local black lawyers, see Robert L. Gill, "The Role of Five Negro Lawyers in the Civil Rights Struggle," *Quarterly Review of Higher Education among Negroes* 31 (July 1963): 31–58; Irvin C. Mollison, "Negro Lawyers in Mississippi," *Journal of Negro History* 25 (January 30): 38–71; "Commentary: Negro Lawyers, Negro Members of the Alabama Bar," *Alabama Law Review* 21 (1969): 306–31; "Virginia Section: The Negro Lawyer in Virginia: A Survey," *Virginia Law Review* 51 (1965): 521–45.

3. Kenneth S. Tollett, "Black Lawyers, Their Education and the Black Community," *Howard Law Review* 17 (1972): 332–33, 336, 347; Smith, *Emancipation*, 52.

4. Philip B. Kurland, "Foreword: Equal in Origin and Equal in Title to the Legislative and Executive Branches of the Government," *Harvard Law Review* 78 (1964): 143.

5. Walter J. Leonard, "The Development of the Black Bar," *American Academy of Political and Social Science* (1973): 141.

6. J. Skelly Wright, *Amistad Symposium on Southern Civil Rights Litigation Records for the 1960s* (New Orleans: Dillard University, Amistad Research Center, 1978): 9; Derrick A. Bell, Jr., *Race, Racism and American Law* (Boston, Little, Brown, 1980), 302. Bell reminds us that many of the black protest cases were actually lost in the courts.

7. Donald L. Hallowell, "The Black Lawyer and the Human and Civil Rights Struggle," *Harvard Law School Bulletin* 22 (February 1971): 18–21. Members of the earlier generation of black lawyers were not infrequently assaulted. On February 27, 1942, Leon A. Ransom was attacked by a former deputy sheriff in the hall of the Davidson County Courthouse in Nashville, Tennessee. The *Crisis* reported, "The attack came when Ransom walked out into the hall from the courtroom where he was sitting with Z. Alexander Looby, local NAACP attorney, on a case involving the exclusion of Negroes from a jury. . . . When the scuffle began, Negroes who would have aided Ransom were held back by a former constable (white) named Hill, who drew his gun and shouted: 'We are going to teach these northern Negroes not to come down here raising fancy court questions'" (April 1942, 137).

8. Burke Marshall, "The Protest Movement and the Law," *Virginia Law Review* 51 (1965): 795; Constance Baker Motley, "The Role of Law in Effecting Social Change," *Crisis* 85 (January 1978): 24–28.

9. Maynard H. Jackson, "The Black American and the Legal Profession: A Study in Commitment," *Journal of Public Law* 20 (1971): 379.

10. Robert L. Carter, "The Black Lawyer," *Humanist* (September/October 1969): 12.

11. Robert C. Weaver, "William Henry Hastie, 1904–1976," *Crisis* 83 (October 1976): 267–70; Ware, *Hastie*, 142–43.

12. Carter, "The Black Lawyer," 12; Smith, *Emancipation*, 41–46.

13. Leonard, "Development of the Black Bar," 140; Tollett, "Black Lawyers, Their Education, and the Black Community," 326–57; Marcia Graham Synnott, *The Half-Opened Door: Discrimination and Admissions at Harvard, Yale, and Princeton, 1900–1970* (Westport, Conn.: Greenwood Press, 1979), 47–52, 134, 174–76, 218–20; Ernest Gellhorn, "The Law Schools and the Negro," *Duke University Law Review* (1968): 1069–97.

14. Chicago philanthropist Julius Rosenwald contributed $2,500 to the campaign on the stipulation that the school raise an additional $500 from among its alumni or friends. Charles Houston, A Personal Message to Friends, April 12, 1926. Julius Rosenwald Papers, Box 19, Folder 6, University of Chicago Library, Chicago. Houston to Rosenwald, April 28, 1926; see also Houston to Judge Julian W. Mack, January 8, 1926, Rosenwald Papers, Box 19, Folder 6. Houston outlined the campaign and described what he hoped to obtain from various groups. "We are also working on a regional organization of Negro lawyers into Bar Associations, and hope to draw support for the library from that. Through such an organization or organizations we would tap most of the alumni of the law school. I want the students and alumni in particular, and the Negro business in general, to feel an ever increasing responsibility for our legal education, and to develop the habit of systematic contributions upon which we can rely for its support."

15. Houston to Judge Julian W. Mack, January 8, 1826.

16. Genna Rae McNeil, "To Meet the Group Needs: The Transformation of Howard University School of Law, 1920–1935," in *New perspectives in Black Educational History*, ed. Vincent P. Franklin and James D. Anderson (Boston: G. K. Hall, 1979), 156–57.

17. Charles H. Houston, Report, Status of Negro Lawyers, May 3, 1928, 10. Laura Spelman Rockefeller Memorial Fund (Hereafter LSRMF), Box 101, Folder 1018. Rockefeller Archive and Research Center, North Tarrytown, New York.

18. LSRMF, Box 101, Folder 1018, 11–12.

19. William H. Hastie, "Charles Hamilton Houston, 1895– 1950," *Negro History Bulletin* 13 (June 1950): 207–8; Leonard, "The Development of the Black Bar," 134–43.

20. Hastie, "Charles Hamilton Houston, 1895–1950," 208.

21. Hastie, "Charles Hamilton Houston, 1895–1950," 210.

22. Hastie, "Charles Hamilton Houston, 1895–1950," 213.

23. Charles H. Houston, "Tentative Statement Concerning Policy of NAACP in Its Program of Attack on Educational Discrimination." July 12, 1935. NAACP Administration Files, C-197, Library of Congress, Washington, D.C.

24. Houston to J. Reuben Sheeler, October 18, 1935, NAACP Legal Files, D-96.

25. Jerold Auerbach, *Unequal Justice: Lawyers and Social Change in Modern America* (New York: Oxford University Press, 1976), 212–16; Smith, *Emancipation,* 543–46, 577–78.

26. Darlene Clark Hine, *Black Victory: The Rise and Fall of the White Primary in Texas* (Millwood, N.Y.: Kraus Thomson, 1979), 188. When Leon Ransom died in 1954, Arthur E. Spingarn observed, "While many talented lawyers became too busy with their private affairs to devote much time to public service, Dr. Ransom over the years gave brilliant and devoted attention to legal cases in the civil rights field, often with no more reward than his bare expenses and the satisfaction of having established a new frontier in civil rights law for the benefit of his people." Thurgood Marshall likewise declared, "Negro Americans, whether they know it or not, owe a great debt of gratitude to Andy Ransom and men like him who battled in the courts down a span of years to bring us to the place we now occupy in the enjoyment of our constitutional rights as citizens. In helping to build up the NAACP legal program step by step, in the skill which he gave to individual cases and to the planning of strategy, Dr. Ransom left a legacy to the whole population." *Crisis* 59 (October 1954): 494.

27. August Meier and Elliot Rudwick, "Attorneys Black and White: A Case Study of Race Relations within the NAACP," in *Along the Color Line: Explorations in the Black Experience,* ed. August Meier and Elliott Rudwick (Urbana: University of Illinois Press, 1976): 154; Smith, *Emancipation,* 16–17.

28. Hine, *Black Victory,* 189–92.

29. Houston to Leon Ransom, Z. Alexander Looby, and Carl Cowan; to Sidney Redmond and to Thurgood Marshall, September 17, 1936; NAACP Papers Box D-96, Library of Congress, Washington, D.C.

30. News release concerning University of Tennessee case, 1937. Tennessee had no scholarship provisions for Negro students, so that it made no provisions for pharmaceutical instruction for Negroes either at an institution within the state or by scholarship outside the state. Memorandum from Charles Houston to Roy Wilkins, April 22, 1937, NAACP Papers, Legal Files, Box D-97. Also see *State of Tennessee ex. rel. William B. Redmond II v. O. W. Hyman* and A Statement Regarding the Mandamus Suit by a Negro Citizen for Admission to the School of Pharmacy, March 21, 1937, by Z. Alexander Looby, Leon Ransom, and Charles Houston. NAACP Legal Files, D-97.

31. Office Memorandum on (William) Redmond Case by Leon A. Ransom, December 16, 1936, NAACP Legal Files, D-96; Mark V. Tushnet, *The NAACP's Legal Strategy against Segregated Education, 1925–1950* (Chapel Hill: University of North Carolina Press, 1987), 55.

32. Memorandum of Leon Ransom on the Redmond Case, December 16, 1936, NAACP Legal Files, D-97.

33. Memorandum of Leon Ransom on the Redmond Case.

34. Memorandum of Leon Ransom on the Redmond Case.

35. Memorandum of Leon Ransom on the Redmond Case.

36. Houston to Sidney R. Redmond, July 15, 1935, NAACP Legal Files, D-94. See also 305 U.S. 337 (1938), *Missouri ex rel. Gaines* v. *Canada.*

37. Houston to Redmond, October 4, 1935, NAACP Legal Files, D-94.

38. Houston to Redmond, December 26, 1935, NAACP Legal Files, D-94.

39. William B. Hixson, Jr., *Moorfield Story and the Abolitionist Tradition* (New York: Oxford University Press, 1972), 118–19; Smith, *Emancipation,* 543–46.

40. Arnold Rose, *The Negro in America* (New York: Harper and Row, 1944), 112.

41. Lester C. Lamon, *Black Tennesseans, 1900–1930* (Knoxville: University of Tennessee Press, 1977): 9–10.

42. Genna Rae McNeil, *Groundwork,* 6–7.

43. Meier and Rudwick, "Attorneys Black and White," 145.

44. Meier and Rudwick, "Attorneys Black and White," 171; *Houston Informer and Texas Freeman,* July 16, 1932.

45. Fitzhugh L. Styles, *Negroes and the Law* (Boston: Christopher, 1937), ix; Smith, "The Black Bar Association," 660.

46. McNeil, "To Meet the Group Needs," 157.

47. McNeil, "To Meet the Group Needs," 33; Veteran Alabama black attorney Arthur D. Shores boasted in "The Negro at the Bar, The South," *National Bar Journal* 4 (1944), 271, that "No greater opportunity is offered anywhere in the country to raise the level of the Negro through the efforts of the Negro lawyer and be amply compensated, than here in the Deep South."

48. Tushnet, *The NAACP's Legal Strategy,* 43–44; Charles H. Houston, "Don't Shout Too Soon," *Crisis* 43 (March 1936): 79, 91. See also Richard Kluger, *Simple Justice the History of Brown v. Board of Education and Black America's Struggle for Equality* (New York: Alfred A. Knopf, 1976), 346–66.

49. J. Clay Smith, "The Black Bar Association and Civil Rights," *Creighton Law Review* 15 (1962): 651–75.

50. Raymond Pace Alexander, "Foreword-Editorial: The National Bar Association— Its Aims and Purposes," *National Bar Journal* 1 (July 1941): 1–2.

51. Auerbach, *Unequal Justice: Lawyers and Social Change in Modern America,* 212; Smith, *Emancipation,* 560.

52. Mark V. Tushnet, *The NAACP's Legal Strategy against Segregated Education 1925–1950,* 102.

53. The cases included the Elaine, Arkansas, riot case, *Moore* v. *Dempsey,* 261 U.S. 86 (Feb. 19, 1923); the New Orleans residential segregation case, *Harmon* v. *Tyler,* 273 U.S. 668 (1926); the two white primary cases, *Nixon* v. *Herndon,* 273 U.S. 536 (March 7, 1927), and *Nixon* v. *Condon,* 286 U.S. 73 (May 2, 1932); the residential segregation case, 10 *City of Richmond* v. *Dean,* 281 U.S. 704 (1930); right to a fair trial free from torture to extract confessions, *Brown, Ellington and Shields* v. *State of Mississippi,* 297 U.S. 278 (February 17, 1936); right of blacks to serve on juries, *Joe Hale* v. *Commonwealth of Kentucky,* 303 U.S. 613 (April 11, 1938); and right of blacks to picket a store in their neighborhood to force employment of blacks, *New Negro Alliance* v. *Sanitary Grocery Company,* vol. 82, no. 13 L.Ed. Adv. Opinion Supreme Ct. (the picketing was done by black men and women members of the New Negro Alliance, a civic association). See also *Missouri ex rel. Gaines* v. *Canada [Registrar, University of Missouri]* (December 18, 1938). In this momentous decision the Court ruled, "By the operation of the laws of Missouri a privilege has been created

for white law students which is denied to Negroes by reason of their race. The white resident is afforded legal education within the State; the Negro resident having the same qualifications is refused it there and must go outside the State to obtain it. That is a denial of the equality of legal right to the enjoyment of the privilege which the State has set up and the provision for the payment of tuition fees in another State does not remove the discrimination" (*Missouri ex rel. Gaines* v. *Canada*, 305 U.S. 337 [1938]). Missouri accordingly was found guilty of having violated the equal protection of the laws clause of the Fourteenth Amendment. This case was argued by Sidney Redmond, who in 1941 was the president of the NBA, and Charles Houston (Tushnet, *the NAACP's Legal Strategy against Segregated Education, 1925–1950,* 70–77). In *Chambers* v. *Florida*, 309 U.S. 227 (Feb. 12, 1940), black lawyers argued a case involving torture used to extract confessions. Two identical ones were also argued, *Canty* v. *Alabama*, 309 U.S. 629 (March 11, 1940), and *White* v. *Texas*, 309 U.S. 631 (March 25, 1940). A series of cases involving the equalization of teachers' salaries included *School Board of the City of Norfolk, Va.* v. *Alston*, 85 L.Ed. 81, (Oct. 28, 1940). In *Hansberry* v. *Lee*, 85 L.Ed. 11 (November 12, 1940), the argument revolved around the use of a restrictive covenant. In a case concerning the refusal on the part of interstate carriers to give first-class accommodations to blacks traveling between states, *Congressman Arthur W. Mitchell* v. *The Illinois Central Railway*, the Court ruled that blacks who purchased first-class tickets may not be denied pullman berths or any of the accommodations that went with first-class tickets for interstate rides. All of these cases are discussed in Raymond Pace Alexander, "The National Bar Association—Its Aims and Purposes," *National Bar Journal* 1 (1941): 5–14. For a discussion of major civil rights cases between 1954 and 1964, see Robert L. Gill, "The Negro in the Supreme Court, 1954–64," Part I, *Negro History Bulletin* 28 (December 1964): 51–52, 65; Part II, *Negro History Bulletin* 28 (January 1965): 86–88; Part III, *Negro History Bulletin* 28 (February 1965): 117–19.

54. *Missouri ex rel. Gaines* v. *Canada*, 305 U.S. 337 (1938); *Sipuel* v. *University of Oklahoma*, 332 U.S. 631 (1948); *Fisher* v. *Hurst*, 333 U.S. 147 (1948); *Sweatt* v. *Painter*, 339 U.S. 629 (1950); *McLaurin* v. *Oklahoma State Regents*, 339 U.S. 637 (1950); *Gray* v. *University of Tennessee*, 342 U.S. 517 (1952). The "infamous" *Brown* was actually four state cases: *Brown* v. *Board of Education of Topeka*, 98 F. Supp. 797 (D. Kans. 1951); *Briggs* v. *Elliot*, 103 F. Supp. 920 E.D.S.C. (1952) from South Carolina; *Davis* v. *School Board of Prince Edward County*, 103 F. Supp. 337 (E.D. Va. 1952), Virginia; and *Gebhart* v. *Belton*, 33 Del. Ch. 144, 91 A. 2d 137 (1952) from Delaware. A fifth companion case, *Bolling* v. *Sharpe*, 347 U.S. 497 (1954), was argued the same day for the District of Columbia. See "The Fight for Equal Justice under Law: Report of the Legal Department," *NAACP Annual Report, 1947,* 20–33; "It Is So Ordered: Report of the Legal Department," *NAACP Annual Report, 1954,* 23–40.

55. Tushnet, *The NAACP's Legal Strategy,* 34.

GENNA RAE McNEIL

YOUTH INITIATIVE IN THE AFRICAN AMERICAN STRUGGLE FOR RACIAL JUSTICE AND CONSTITUTIONAL RIGHTS

THE CITY-WIDE YOUNG PEOPLE'S FORUM OF BALTIMORE, 1931–1941

An "is/ought" dichotomy has underscored the existential challenge of being an African American since the first Africans set foot in the British colonies. Definition of African people as Other, because of race, and political exclusion from the citizenry have made struggle the daily lot of African Americans. A sense of self beyond such a struggle and affirmation of human equality have made blacks' quest for self-development perennial. African Americans have petitioned, protested, prayed, demonstrated, litigated, initiated dialogue with governing authorities, fought, and sometimes died seeking to express in this society the whole measure of our humanity.[1]

Even before the nation's founding, persons of African descent appealed to colonial legislatures for freedom and natural rights.[2] Following the ratification of the Constitution of the United States, eighteenth-century African Americans continued their struggle, encouraged by the Declaration of Independence and the lofty language of much of the Constitution. As early as 1797, persons of African descent petitioned the U.S. Congress for release from oppression, which they argued was not only morally wrong and inconsistent with beliefs regarding natural rights, but also a "direct violation of the declared fundamental principles of the Constitution."[3]

Some scholars attribute to the text of the Constitution the longevity of the United States of America, despite its multiethnic character and internal conflicts over rights and power. Alfred Kelly and Winfred Harbison argue that "while its provisions are sufficiently specific and detailed to provide a necessary element of stability to government, [the Constitution] has nonetheless proved to be broad and general enough in its institutional arrangements and grants of power to allow for steady growth of the 'living constitution' to meet the altered requirements of a changing social order."[4] Other scholars, such as Vincent Harding, emphasize that racial conflict has been avoided not only because of the fundamental belief of African Americans in human equality, freedom, and justice, but also because of our majority's centuries-old patient, tenacious, and consistent "offering [of] an opportunity for America to be true to its most democratic pronouncements."[5] Most African Americans have chosen "persistent, costly questioning" of the meaning of "all men are created equal," or the identity of "we, the people," over widespread violent revolution.[6] Although African American history includes rebellion, most black Americans, Mary Frances Berry and John Blassingame have observed, "have protested discrimination and segregation *in the name of the Constitution and the Declaration of Independence.*"[7]

The expansive quality of the Constitution's language and its amendment provision prevented the framers from having the last word, despite their failure to reconcile racial oppression with "we the people's" entitlement to liberty. During the first three-quarters of the twentieth century, protagonists and antagonists in the struggle over white supremacy, racial discrimination, and equality demonstrated the capacity of an evolving federal constitution both to encompass varied understandings of human rights and to inspire movements for freedom and justice.[8] Believing ourselves fully justified on constitutional and moral grounds, unprecedented numbers of African Americans, regardless of socioeconomic status, participated in the civil rights and black liberation movement of the 1950s and 1960s.

In the 1960s this movement was often led by African American youth and young adults, who contributed energy, militance, impatience, innovation, and a sense of urgency to the fight for rights, freedom, and justice. Our activities came on the heels of the earlier experiences in the century of African American youth seeking to define as well as secure full freedom in the land of their birth, the United States of America.

The activities of one particular youth organization, the City-Wide Young People's Forum of Baltimore, between 1931 and 1941, illustrate the effectiveness and significance of youth leadership supported by intergenerational cooperation in the struggle *against* racial oppression and *for* recognition of African Americans' constitutional rights. The Baltimore City-Wide Young People's Forum also demonstrates that the Constitution lives not only through the capacity of its language and its symbolic significance, but also through the praxis of young African Americans. They courageously asserted their right to self-definition, self-determination, and a positive vision of a racially just, democratic society as they challenged those holding the reigns of power.

THE SETTING

The Great Depression was an era of "utter distress and pessimism" for African Americans in general. Before the crash of 1929, African Americans were already familiar with hardship, as a result of racial oppression and poverty or race-based economic discrimination. Within a few years, millions of Americans—of all races—were unable to support either their families or themselves in any occupation. When businesses and banks began failing, more African Americans than ever joined the ranks of the unemployed and poor. Increasing numbers found "added to the denials of freedom and democracy . . . the specter of starvation."[9]

Baltimore, Maryland, differed little from the rest of the United States during the Great Depression, and its African American population suffered similarly. In 1930 the African Americans in Maryland numbered 276,379, or 16.9 percent of the state's population of 1,631,526. Baltimore had a total population of 804,874, of which 662,168 were Caucasian and 142,106 (17.6 percent) were African American. Before the depression, 47,900 African Americans of Maryland worked in domestic and personal service, 36,612 in unskilled and semiskilled jobs with various industries, and 21,793 in agriculture. Few were landowners or self-employed. Fewer still were employed in transportation (12,601), trades (7,828), the professions (5,302) or public service (1,914).[10]

As the depression deepened, policies and practices of racial discrimination intensified and further reduced not only the living conditions of all African Americans but also the expectations and aspirations of school-age children and college youth. Nevertheless, parents and grandparents continued to encourage African American youth to acquire a formal education through college and university levels. Education was valued beyond its function in the marketplace. Thus, in the academic year 1929–30, more than 20,800 African American children in Baltimore were attending elementary school and 2,149 high school. In 1929, 295 of Baltimore's African American youth graduated from high school. During the late 1920s and the early 1930s, the increase in African Americans attending school was so great that the Frederick Douglass

High School, Baltimore's only African American high school offering a college preparatory curriculum, was crowded with students. The budgetary shortfalls of the depression notwithstanding, parents pressured the administrators of the schools to provide better opportunities and facilities within the segregated school system.[11]

The top priority of most of Baltimore's African Americans at this time was to secure an education for their children and ensure the survival of their families, rather than to protest discrimination or segregation in transportation, public facilities, workplaces, private restaurants, and clubs. It is also important to note that the Baltimore branch of the National Association for the Advancement of Colored People (NAACP) was moribund by 1931. Tragically, for Maryland's African Americans, lynchings in the United States, and specifically on the Eastern shore of Maryland, were a painful reminder of how little value Caucasians placed on the life of an African American. As Lillie Carroll Jackson and Thurgood Marshall, two African American proponents of civil rights from Baltimore, described it, Maryland was "a mean state," "way up South."[12]

FOUNDING AND ORGANIZATION OF THE FORUM

The situation endured by African Americans in Baltimore troubled many, especially the young people studying hard in schools and colleges or just returning from college with their degrees and their dreams for the future. In the summer of 1931, explained William Dorsey, a young African American Baltimorean, "these young people had nothing to do." Upon graduating from the University of Pennsylvania, eighteen-year-old Juanita E. Jackson, another young African American Baltimorean—whose mother, Lillie Carroll Jackson, was a school teacher as well as property owner, and whose father, Keiffer Jackson, was a promoter and exhibitor of religious films—returned home to face unemployment. Both she and her sister Virginia, who was an artist and graduate of the Pennsylvania Museum's School of Art in Philadelphia, felt obligated to return to segregated Baltimore. Throughout the years of their higher education, their mother had challenged them "to help [their] people" and admonished: "You're not to come back and separate yourselves into an intelligent few, but to give back so our people can be free."[13]

Having experienced Philadelphia, both Jackson sisters found it impossible to tolerate either joblessness or racial segregation without some resistance. Juanita, however, was anxious to initiate some action that would incite group protest and bring other youth to her side. Late in the summer of 1931, she received an invitation from Clarence Mitchell (a Lincoln University graduate who would later become the NAACP's chief lobbyist) to attend a "town hall" meeting at the home of Elisabeth Coit Gilman, a prominent Socialist and the daughter of the first president of Johns Hopkins University. Jackson's attendance had unforeseen results. For Jackson, the meeting provided an opportunity to discuss ideas about change in the city and the nation. She shared with her family and with Clarence Mitchell her idea that African American youth and the young adults of Baltimore should host a forum regularly, at which invited speakers could address specific topics and answer young people's questions about Baltimore's problems and the changes needed there.[14]

Juanita Jackson had gained some experience in developing, planning, and promoting programs (including a recital by Paul Robeson) when she was a member of the Alpha Kappa Alpha (AKA) sorority while in college with her sisters. That experience and her involvement with the Methodist church gave her the skills she needed to spread the word about the proposed youth forum among other young African Americans of Baltimore. With the support of Clarence Mitchell, her parents, and both of her sisters—Marian, a singer, and Virginia— Juanita Jackson held a September planning session. In less than a month, she called to order the first meeting of a Baltimore African American youth forum. On Friday evening, October 2, 1931, Jackson, Mitchell, and a steering committee of young people presented their first public program at the Sharpe Street Memorial Methodist Episcopal Church. So great was the interest following the first meeting that on October 24 young African Americans "from all over the city of Baltimore formally organized themselves into the City-Wide Young People's Forum."[15]

The City-Wide Young People's Forum gave new meaning to a Friday night out for one hundred African American young people between the ages of sixteen and twenty-four. As one young man explained, after days of unsuccessful job-hunting, the forum offered something challenging to "occupy their minds." The forum's meetings attracted larger audiences every Friday. In the first year, 1931–32, they averaged 500. The organizers minimized differences and emphasized common concerns among the youth. Young people from working-class, middle-class, and upper-class backgrounds of Baltimore's African American neighborhoods, who represented twenty black churches and as many as six protestant denominations—including Methodist, Episcopal, Baptist, African Methodist Episcopal (A.M.E.), African Methodist Episcopal Zion (A.M.E.Z.), and Presbyterian—eagerly participated in the City-Wide Forum.[16]

Forum members elected many of the organizers and steering committee members to positions of leadership, naming founder, Juanita Jackson, president. Other college students or graduates, Howard Cornish, Maceo Howard, Elmer Henderson, and Clarence Mitchell became vice-presidents of the forum. Through elections and appointments, members and presiding officers broadened the forum's base. Community young people of different ages, socioeconomic statuses, and educational levels filled the positions of recording secretary, financial secretary, treasurer, and chairpersons of the standing committees. They headed the ways and means, publicity, courtesy, membership, program, constitution and research, student aid and scholarship, auditing, and sick committees. The forum also boasted an usher board, dramatic unit, chorus, trio, and orchestra of African American youth. Because they wanted to maintain good relations with adults of their parents' and grandparents' generations, the youth selected one older adult as an officer and two older adults as advisers. They elected as corresponding secretary the wife of a physician, Mrs. Katherine White, a former secretary who had considerable skills as well as financial resources at her disposal. W. A. C. Hughes, Jr., the son of a prominent African American clergyman, advised the forum on legal matters. The president's mother, Lillie Carroll Jackson, enjoyed the permanent but unofficial status of general adviser. She assisted the young people with a variety of tasks from arranging for meeting space, to counseling the forum officers on how to maintain a progressive, "palatable," community-supported group.[17]

The original purposes of the City-Wide Young People's Forum were fivefold:

1. To afford the people of Baltimore the opportunity to be informed by experts . . . on the variety of problems which confront them and to discuss freely their ideas . . . ;

2. To establish an intelligent, trained young people's leadership engaged in a constructive program with city-wide influence;

3. To convert many of the older people to an interest in and love for young people through the knowledge of and contact with a steady, sane and intelligent group of young leaders;

4. To afford an opportunity for young people to make fruitful inter-racial contacts on a ground of common interest;

5. To stimulate the consciousness of values in life which are not found in material things alone . . . ; to establish a contact with the Divine which will give courage, renew hope, inspire thankfulness and release the physical, mental, and spiritual energies that men may better understand God's laws and thus intelligently cooperate with Him to accomplish His plan.[18]

62

In subsequent years, these purposes changed to reflect new priorities and attitudes of the forum's members. In its second year, 1932–33, two additional purposes were added and ranked third and fourth: "to open up avenues and create opportunities of employment for efficient qualified young people" and "to discover and develop the talent and rare ability of young people who have not the means of helping themselves."[19] By 1937, members focused on "developing an intelligent, militant youth leadership engaged in a constructive program with city-wide influence." This priority was second only to the forum's commitment to disseminating information and to taking action "to inform the people of Baltimore about the political, social, and economic problems which confront them and upon the resultant understanding to afford an opportunity for organized united action on some of the important issues."[20]

PROGRAMS AND PROJECTS

The programs and projects of the City-Wide Youth Forum put the group's purposes into action. They included a weekly lecture series, advocacy of equal employment opportunities, promotion of equal rights at state and national levels, participation in partisan politics, and special programs to develop leadership among African American youths.

The Weekly Lecture Series

The forum's weekly lecture series became one of its most important activities. With the zeal of crusaders, forum leaders sought keynote speakers from among experts in various fields who could inform, inspire, and motivate audiences during the Friday night programs held every week between October and May. Motivation, the forum officers believed, was the key to sparking interest in activism. The list of the forum's speakers and topics emerged from both the executive committee's deliberations and audiences' choices during the weekly meetings. Topics most frequently reflected the expressed interests and needs of the African American community; forum members reported that "many times there c[a]me requests from the audience for certain subjects to be discussed."[21]

Forum programs between 1931 and 1941 boasted a great variety of speakers and subjects. In its first year, historian Charles H. Wesley gave a talk entitled "The Negro and American Industrialism," and Congressman Oscar DePriest spoke on "Our Rights as Citizens." Because subjects and speakers were selected to "meet vital needs" of African Americans, subsequent seasons revealed considerable diversity as well. Distinguished African Americans and Caucasian Americans appeared before forum audiences. Speakers included W. E. B. Du Bois (nationally known scholar, author, activist, and pan-Africanist); Mary McLeod Bethune (president of Bethune Cookman College); William Patterson (the African American Communist attorney and executive secretary of the International Labor Defense [ILD]); Nannie Helen Burroughs (founder of the National Training School for Girls in Washington, D.C., and a national Baptist leader); Elisabeth Gilman (Socialist-reformer); reform-minded attorneys such as Charles Hamilton Houston and Thurgood Marshall; civil rights executives of the NAACP such as Walter F. White, William Pickens, and Roy Wilkins; gifted poet-professors such as James Weldon Johnson and Sterling Brown; social scientist E. Franklin Frazier; Africanist Leo Hansberry; and the internationally celebrated African American Communist and labor activist, Angelo Herndon. Topics ranged from emergency relief, a comparison of the abilities of African American and Caucasian children, the African origins of the Negro, the criminal justice system, political radicalism, and the NAACP's campaign against segregation to world peace. After 1933, the forum's audiences, which were usually African American but occasionally bi-racial, rarely numbered less than six hundred persons and at times reached two thousand or more. During the ten years of its activities, the forum had an estimated total attendance of 333,000.[22]

Forum members found unforgettable several speeches and speakers. Nannie Helen Burroughs of Washington, D. C., who spoke often, delivered an address on December 8, 1933, entitled, "What Must the Negro Do to Be Saved?" Burroughs told the two thousand people assembled at Baltimore's Bethel A.M.E. Church that African Americans should "chloroform . . . 'Uncle Toms.'"[23]

Negroes like that went out of style seventy years ago. They are relics and good for museums. I don't care whether they are in the church as the preacher; in the school as the teacher; in the ward as a politician. . . .

The Negro is oppressed, not because he is a Negro—but because he'll take it. Negroes, . . . organize yourselves. . . . We need mental and spiritual giants who are aflame with purpose.

The Negro must serve notice on the world that he is ready to die for justice. To struggle and overcome and absolutely defeat every force designed against us is the only way to achieve.[24]

In March 1935 James Weldon Johnson, a former national NAACP executive and a professor of creative literature from Fisk University, gave a speech that rivaled Burroughs's in popularity, "The Creative Genius of the Negro." This extraordinary poet, novelist, professor, and activist attracted more than 2,000 persons, 400 of whom were Caucasians from Goucher College, Enoch Pratt Library, and Johns Hopkins University. "We should be proud!" Johnson declared, and each "forumite" felt a surge of pride, Rebecca Evans recalled. The message and the man had a tremendous impact on the assembled African American young people. Printed on the forum song cards under the title "National Negro Anthem" were James Weldon Johnson's words, "Lift Every Voice and Sing" (his brother Rosamond had written the music). That evening, few were not moved as the eloquent lecture ended and majestic music filled the sanctuary of Bethel A.M.E. Church.[25]

Advocacy of Equal Employment Opportunities

With a regular following, the youth of the forum used Friday night programs to seek support for their civil rights endeavors and their campaigns for jobs in Baltimore. In accordance with its purpose of "open[ing] up avenues of employment for efficient qualified young people," the forum initiated employment projects in 1933.[26] As a matter of policy, forum members set objectives for their collective activism after consultation with adult advisers, input from older adult community leaders, some polling of the interest of the larger African American community during weekly meetings, and final deliberations by the forum's executive committee.[27] Forum members sought tangible results in four areas of employment. Their objectives were to (1) enable African Americans to apply for positions on the staff of the Enoch Pratt Free Library, a tax-supported institution, and obtain training to qualify for positions; (2) see an "increase in the number of [African American] welfare workers employed by the Family Welfare Association"; (3) gain positions for African Americans in retail stores located in black neighborhoods or having large numbers of African American customers; and (4) achieve equitable distribution of positions in the public school system.[28]

Fighting segregation and addressing the unemployment problem in connection with education, libraries, and schools, members initiated their own campaigns in the forum's second year (the first and fourth objectives). Organizing, petitioning, negotiating, and litigating, forum members enjoyed some success between 1933 and 1941, as well as after the organization formally disbanded. Salary equalization for teachers and Pratt Library admissions, in particular, interested forum members, even after they ceased to meet. Former forum members often worked closely with the NAACP. For example, by April 1933 forum members had collected six thousand signatures on a petition protesting the Enoch Pratt Free Public Library's unconstitutional racial discrimination. In April 1937 six young African American women had qualified for library positions and three for academic training. Louise Kerr, a secretary of the forum, later demanded training for librarianship at the library, and in 1945 federal judges ruled in her favor, arguing that barring Kerr from the training school of Pratt was a violation of her constitutional rights. The forum's legal adviser, W. A. C. Hughes, Jr., guided the young people through conflicts with institutions and governmental authorities.[29]

Success with the second objective came more quickly. Following a forum campaign in coalition with the Urban League of Baltimore, sixteen social workers (two of whom were forum members) were appointed by the Baltimore Emergency Relief Commission during 1933 and 1934. Inspired by Charles Houston's broad claims for use of the U.S. Constitution's Fourteenth Amendment to "Sue Jim Crow out of Maryland," forum members petitioned and were prepared to enter into litigation against the city to secure employment of African Americans as policemen, firemen, and civil servants for municipal agencies.[30]

Successful mobilization of African Americans in Baltimore for a "Buy Where You Can Work" campaign (the third objective) was a tribute to the energy, enthusiasm, and constant effort of forum members and the trust they had earned through community involvement. Following the presentation of the idea to the executive committee by a nondenominational evangelist, the Reverend Kiowa Costonie, the officers brought the proposed project to the attention of the forum's audience. As with other activities, the forum launched this project with strong support in the African American community, once consensus was reached. The target of the forum's campaign was the grocery store chain, the Great Atlantic and Pacific Stores, better known as "A & P." A & P had never hired any African Americans to work in the stores located in black neighborhoods; no amount of verbal persuasion had convinced managers of the need to begin such hiring. The forum organized the boycott and picketing not only by disseminating information at weekly meetings of the forum and at the worship services of local churches, but also by publicizing the campaign against A & P in the *Baltimore Afro-American*. In November 1933 a mobilized African American community demanded that the executives of A & P hire African Americans to work in the A & P stores located in African American neighborhoods or suffer an African American boycott. The forum's boycott began on November 18 with scores of clergypersons and about forty churches supporting the effort. Approximately five hundred young people and their parents picketed at every A & P store in the African American neighborhoods of Baltimore. The boycott continued until November 21, leaving the targeted A & P stores with "*no* African-American customers," according to reports. The A & P regional management yielded to the demands. By December 1933, thirty-eight young men were employed as full- or part-time clerks through A & P's inauguration of a new hiring policy.[31]

Forum protesters were not satisfied with the A & P victory alone. On its momentum they targeted stores in the 1700 block of Pennsylvania Avenue. There Caucasian merchants depended on African Americans for a large volume of their retail business, yet hired no African Americans. Aware of the forum's successful picketing of A & P stoies, the merchants of 1700 Pennsylvania Avenue acted collectively, immediately after the forum began its picketing of the Pennsylvania Avenue stores with approximately two hundred persons. Litigating to enjoin the actions of the picketers whose presence discouraged customers, proprietors of the shops secured a temporary injunction from the court and i ; March 1934 a permanent injunction. The Honorable Albert S. J. Owens ruled the complaint of the owners valid with respect to the disruption of business. Clarence Mitchell voiced the sentiments of other forum members and their lawyer, W. A. C. Hughes, Jr., when he wrote that Judge Owens "did not administer justice in the case, but . . . the law. His knowledge of the law, however, is apparently not such as teaches him to weigh the forces of hunger, moral decay, idealism, and lack of employment opportunity when making a decision."[32]

Promotion of Equal Rights
at State and National Levels

The young people of the forum boldly involved themselves in the affairs of the state and the nation. Representing the forum and in cooperation with other civic or national groups, members protested racial injustice and denials of equal rights, which they believed to be a violation of the Constitution. Finding segregation constitutionally objectionable, insulting, and offensive, members of the forum joined the Committee for the Repeal of the Maryland Jim Crow Laws in 1932. In March of 1934, members and friends sent one thousand letters to Maryland congressmen urging them to support Representative Oscar DePriest in his effort to eliminate segregation from the restaurants of the House of Representatives and the Senate. Concerned about the rights of African Americans in the criminal justice system, the forum raised money in 1932 to aid the defense of Euel Lee, who was accused of murder. In that case, Lee's radical attorney, Bernard Ades, successfully argued against the exclusion of African Americans from Maryland's juries. For themselves and others, the forum's young people supported the efforts of the national NAACP to eliminate discrimination in public education. Initially at Lillie Jackson's urging, and later allied with a revitalized local NAACP, the forum gathered spectators for Charles Houston's and Thurgood Marshall's arguments on behalf of Baltimore's Donald G. Murray, a college graduate seeking admission to the University of Maryland's Law School.[33]

The forum's members demonstrated against lynching and supported antilynching legislation. In the wake of the George Armwood lynching, a forum representative participated with the local Citizens' Committee in meetings with Governor Albert Ritchie regarding conviction of the lynchers victimizing African Americans during the early 1930s. In 1934 the forum secured one thousand signatures to letters of support for the Costigan-Wagner federal antilynching bill and the forum's president, Juanita Jackson, testified at the U.S. Senate's hearings on that bill. In 1935 the forum was a leading participant in the national Cooperative Committee against Lynching.[34]

Partisan Political Involvements

Almost immediately upon its organization, the forum joined Carl Murphy, the *Baltimore Afro-American*'s publisher, and other concerned citizens in demands for political candidates' and incumbents' accountability to African American constituents in Baltimore. Forum members regularly invited a politician from the Democratic, Republican, Socialist, or Communist parties to make the case for that party's leadership at preelection symposia. The forum's youth leadership challenged politicians on issues of racial discrimination, as well as their positions regarding conditions in Baltimore, the state, and the nation.

Yet the forum members' contacts with the political left were not limited to symposium presentations. In 1934 Clarence Mitchell, a forum vice-president, ran for a seat in Maryland's House of Delegates, as representative of Baltimore's fifth district. He wanted to be more directly involved in offering political solutions to the problems faced by African Americans and was dissatisfied with Democrats and Republicans. Mitchell's campaign marked the first time that an African American's name had ever appeared on the ballot for the racially mixed fifth district.

Although Clarence Mitchell was not ideologically a proponent of socialism, he appreciated Elisabeth Gilman's and Norman Thomas's civil rights advocacy and opposition to the traditional parties. Mitchell chose to use "the

Socialist party label, [but] . . . was running independent."[35] Mitchell gave only partial support to the Socialist ticket on which Gilman was running as a candidate for the U.S. Senate and Johns Hopkins University professor Broadus Mitchell as a candidate for Maryland's governorship. With the public support of the forum and the *Afro-American* for the Socialist candidates, Mitchell campaigned as an alternative to the status quo for all citizens. Despite the traditional Republican voting patterns of African Americans in Baltimore, he waged a vigorous fight. Nevertheless, Mitchell lost, as did his running mates. According to a forum canvas of November 1934, however, Clarence Mitchell "polled over 1700 votes." The forum, Murphy, Lillie Jackson, and Gilman considered this a respectable showing in the fifth district. Unfortunately, the loss represented a failure to persuade African Americans to assert their political independence from the Republican party. Significant defection from the party of Abraham Lincoln to the Democratic party came just two years later when African Americans favoring Franklin Roosevelt's New Deal policies participated in the 1936 campaign and election. As the *Afro-American* editorialized, African Americans of Baltimore missed "the best opportunity in the history of the city to send a representative to the House of Delegates."[36]

Special Programs for African American Youth Leadership Development

The forum's leaders perceived the development of youth consciousness and leadership among African Americans to be dependent, in part, on fostering more positive human relations and facilitating higher education. They considered these essential for the civil rights struggle and a desegregated society. As a consequence, the forum's activities included efforts to promote better interracial relations such as a biracial "Good-Will Tour" of African American businesses, institutions, and homes followed by speakers and discussion. It also included specific activities to address the chasm between youth and older adults, such as open discussions after lectures and frank dialogue in the context of committee work. In 1933 the forum reported that the "gap of conflicting ideas and misunderstanding separating the young people and the adults is beginning to be bridged. Both discuss their views in the open forum so that each has been enlightened. . . . [Moreover] the respect and admiration of the older people has increased as [young people] have put over a program that was said could not be successfully done."[37] Among youth of differing backgrounds and socioeconomic status, "Forum Frolics" became recreational opportunities for meeting "together on grounds of mutual interest." These gatherings every second Saturday evening in the month "enriched the recreational experiences of [the] young people" and facilitated the "form[ation of] friend-ships."[38]

The forum awarded scholarships and sponsored events to raise funds for leadership development among African American youth. Support of African American educational institutions received the special attention of the forum's officers and particularly its program committee. The forum created in its first year "a scholarship fund in order that worthy young [Frederick] Douglass High School graduates with potentialities' for leadership might be trained in Morgan College and the National Training School for Girls."[39] In the follow-ing year, the forum added to its recipients of aid, Bethune-Cookman of Florida and Palmer Memorial Institute of North Carolina, founded by African Ameri-can female educators, Mary McLeod Bethune and Charlotte Hawkins Brown, respectively.[40] When the forum sponsored inspiring and effective programs for youth development, it prompted organizations and churches supportive of higher education and civil rights to provide additional support for other programs. In 1932 the Allen Christian Endeavor League of Trinity A.M.E. Church pledged "prayers and hearty cooperation" as it formally advised forum president Juanita Jackson that "this forum is getting far-reaching results in our churches."[41]

Results in youth leadership development could be seen in several public programs of the forum. Although the forum occasionally sponsored debates such as the international debate between Lincoln University of Pennsylvania and the British Union of England, it *annually* hosted an "Inter-Collegiate Ora-torical, Vocal and Instrumental" contest.[42] The Inter-Collegiate Contests— which usually included students from Morgan, Hampton, Howard and Lincoln University (Pennsylvania)—offered African American young people opportunities to hone their skills, present their talents, and develop self-confidence while entertaining a generous audience. The forum's extensive programming and practical purposes in conjunction with its youth leadership development and civil rights advocacy prompted the *Atlanta Daily World* to declare of Jackson and the forum in 1936: "The gifted young woman orga-nized the now *nationally known* City-Wide . . . Forum in Baltimore, the largest similar forum in the country."[43]

CONTEMPORARY LEADERS' ASSESSMENTS OF THE FORUM

The positive influence of the City-Wide Young People's Forum was the subject of comments by local and national leaders. To garner support, the youth solicited comments from famous speakers. As early as the 1932–33 season, Elmer Carter, editor of *Opportunity* Magazine, wrote to compliment forum members on their "fine organization," adding, "I have traveled a good deal and I have never seen a forum which approaches yours in the efficiency of its administration." Others who praised the forum included Mary McLeod Bethune, W. E. B. Du Bois, Walter White, P. B. Young, Howard Murphy of the *Afro-American*, and Nannie Helen Burroughs. The editor of the *Norfolk Journal and Guide*, P. B. Young extolled the forum's virtues, after he appeared on one of its programs. "I believe that I can say in all sincerity that for adopting a program and following it with determination and courage the Young People's Forum has no close rival." Focusing on Baltimore, Howard Murphy celebrated the forum's service in the community: "It keeps the community in close relationship with the present-day trends, both political and social." After several appearances before forum audiences, Nannie Helen Burroughs announced without equivocation, "The City-Wide Young People's Forum . . . is the best, most progressive and analytical organization of Negro young people in America. It feels, thinks, believes, acts. It gives good account of its self-imposed responsibilities. It is socially sound in its attitude and spiritually dynamic in its deeper, inner life."[44]

FUNDING THE WORK OF THE FORUM

The forum was able to maintain its program as well as its members' independence, militancy, and risk-taking, for a decade in large measure because it received support from individual African Americans, African American institutions, liberal and radical Caucasians, black businesses, and Caucasian entrepreneurs with African American clientele. The expenses of the forum's activities were covered by financial contributions, but the implementation of programs often depended on donations of time, resources, talent, or skills. The free-will offerings collected by the forum's ushers from those attending the weekly lectures were necessary but not sufficient to sustain the organization. The leadership turned to sympathetic older adults, and foremost among individual sponsors was Carl Murphy, the owner-publisher of the *Baltimore Afro-American*, which forum members called the "liberation newspaper." Murphy not only gave the forum free publicity for its weekly meetings and reported on its lectures, but also assigned reporters to cover its programs, protests, and political activities. When forum members attacked racial discrimination or proposed progressive civil rights stances, Murphy's paper could be relied upon to offer a supportive editorial. In addition, Murphy regularly donated substantial sums of money to the forum. Annually, as owner of the *Afro-American*, he joined other entrepreneurs in buying advertisements (at a cost of $2.50 per quarter page) for the souvenir program of the forum's Inter-Collegiate Contest.[45]

Between 1932 and 1941 quarter-page advertisements increased from forty to seventy; the number of half- and full-page advertisements increased at a similar rate. Among institutional and corporate advertisers were Sharpe Street Memorial Community House, Holland Funeral Service, Liepman's Clothing Store, Lowenthal's Shoes, Mt. Auburn Marble & Granite, Hamlette Home Bakery, Herald Commonwealth Printing, Majestic Hotel, Gordon's Dining Room, Central Fire Insurance, and Regal Theatre, as well as the *Afro-American*. For the Inter-Collegiate Contest and other programs, the forum solicited patrons and sponsors who gave liberally. Between 1932 and 1941, forum programs listed from 150 to 500 sponsors or patrons who enjoyed disparate levels of economic security and came from different backgrounds. In response to the weekly solicitations of the forum following its lectures, some had only coins to contribute while others gave a few dollars. Each, Juanita Jackson believed, responded according to his or her ability. Still others, in addition to Carl Murphy, were major contributors. These, recalled Jackson, included Howard W. Jackson (mayor of Baltimore); David Weiglein (superintendent of schools); Francis Wood (director of colored schools); John Spencer (the president of Morgan, a Caucasian); Elisabeth Gilman (one of the original supporters of the forum); William Jones (the city editor of the *Baltimore Afro-American* and "big brother" of the forum's youth); Thomas Kerr (a prominent African American pharmacist and father of Louise Kerr, a forum secretary); Mason Hawkins (principal of Douglass High School); and David Ellison (councilperson of the fourth district).

Many older adults were praised by the forum's leadership for "not only their presence and verbal expressions, but [also] . . . their liberal contributions when financial assistance was imperative."[46] African American and Caucasian organizations, businesses, and institutions that placed advertisements in souvenir programs also often contributed prizes to the forum. Individual contributors and volunteers who provided office or meeting space, prepared luncheons or donated labor represented more than dollars to the young people of the forum. They recognized clearly that the forum could offer its programs free of any admission charge because of this "splendid support and cooperation of adults."[47]

The ecumenical character of the forum and its broadly based community membership led churches to provide invaluable support. Although the forum's perceived "radicalism" was the reason that the pastor of Sharpe Street Methodist Church refused to provide space for its weekly meetings in 1932, his behavior was atypical. In that same year the Reverend A. C. Clark and the congregation of Bethel A.M.E. Church welcomed the forum's youth for meetings in that church's sanctuary. The congregation, as well, collected special offerings for the forum. Methodist youth leaders urged the young people of the Epworth League to be an integral part of the forum. Methodist women prepared meals for luncheon meetings to that end. Churches of the Methodist denomination and other Protestant denominations annually sponsored the City-Wide Forum's Christmas Banquet. Announcements of forum programs from pastors or interested members of the more than twenty churches of the six participating denominations generated greater interest and larger audiences. Most important, so many well-known pastors and popular black churches supported and cooperated with the forum that most of the churches' members believed it a credible, positive vehicle for the pursuit of worthy causes. Assessing the efforts of sympathetic, participating older adults in churches and elsewhere throughout the city, state, and region, the forum's leadership explained: "Their [Older adults'] support and cooperation . . . facilitated the tremendous spiritual task attempted—the lifting of the spirits of the people during the depression; the feeding of intellectual, aesthetic, and spiritual food that they might not come out of these crushing times with distorted visions. For 'where there is no vision the people perish.'"[48]

CONCLUSIONS

For a decade, from 1931 to 1941, the City-Wide Young People's Forum of Baltimore focused attention on the need for change in the conditions and social status of African Americans suffering because of racial and race-based economic discrimination. African American young people in Baltimore—with the advice, assistance, and cooperation of older adults in the African American neighborhoods of Baltimore—provided leadership in a variety of educational, political, and advocacy endeavors. The forum effected change for African Americans in Baltimore while serving as a catalyst for political action, employment, and civil rights activism. Although the early years of the Great Depression spread distress and pessimism among all blacks, the African American youth and young adults of Baltimore's City-Wide Young People's Forum were able to rise above the general despair to demonstrate that they could sustain an organization, advocate genuine equality of rights under the Constitution and human rights, change the conditions of life for African Americans in their city, and improve intergenerational relations in the African American community.[49] There are a number of reasons for their success.

First, in the midst of an oppressive society, their peers and older adults created a nurturing environment for the African American young people of the forum and encouraged their hopes and aspirations. Within the African American community of Baltimore, forum members could receive financial support, find allies, and talk with and be heard by some parents, siblings, teachers, clergypersons, and other African American professionals. At various times, the forum's supporters did one or more of the following: stressed the importance of education; discouraged idleness; refuted or disregarded Negro inferiority theories; encouraged the use of talents; emphasized the importance of faith; encouraged the maintenance of a relationship between the forum and black institutions such as colleges, churches, and the press; challenged young people to advocate their rights nonviolently; urged them to explore alternatives for social change; and supported the forum's programs, projects, and protests.

Second, African American leaders of local, regional, and national reputation—some of whom were heroes of the young people—responded affirmatively to invitations of the forum early in its life and gave to the lecture series prestige, substance, and public appeal. Publicized in the African American press, the forum's activities with widely recognized speakers attracted larger African American—occasionally biracial—audiences and significant financial contributions to the organization.

Third, the relationship between the national office of the NAACP and the forum was symbiotic. The lecture appearances of national NAACP leaders within the forum's first six years gained the attention and financial support of both youth and adults. In the early absence of a strong, active local NAACP, the national NAACP staff devoted more rather than less time and energy to presenting the association's programs at the forum's meetings. The forum served as a training ground for civil rights advocacy and the conduit for information regarding recommendations or programs of the national NAACP. The emphasis of the national NAACP on using the Constitution to obtain legal recognition of civil rights both inspired the forum members and affirmed the propriety of the forum's activism.

Fourth, when making decisions, the forum functioned democratically, particularly to identify topics or speakers for the lectures and to initiate civil rights protests. The forum's officers clearly understood that its success required broadly based community support and that needs of African Americans could not be met if the voices of the African Americans of differing socioeconomic statuses were never heard. Consistent use of democratic procedures for decision-making and the implementation of democratically reached decisions not only assumed but also generated support by and confidence among black Baltimoreans of different social backgrounds, religious affiliations, and ages.

Fifth, the forum's overarching commitment to racial equality and justice in conjunction with its stated intention of improving the conditions of life for African Americans forged and sustained a goal-oriented rather than personality-based relationship between Baltimore's wider African American community and the forum's youth. The forum's structure incorporated the advice and support of older reform-minded African American adults and, while retaining its youth and young adult leadership, avoided depending on a single charismatic leader. This relationship, specifically as demonstrated among regularly participating older adults, those African Americans of the community attending the forum's programs or affected by projects, and the forum's youth, was characterized by sincere efforts to incorporate and maintain several noteworthy features: authentic, common commitment to desegregation, human and constitutional rights, racial equality, and justice; a fundamental assumption that individuals in each age group, regardless of socioeconomic status, could make a valuable contribution to the life of the forum, as well as to the struggle for rights and racial justice; mutual respect, regardless of age, class, or gender; multidirectional sharing of knowledge and information; agreement regarding the use of democratic social-decision procedures incorporating negotiation and consensus; shared responsibilities and mutual accountability in the implementation of programs and projects; encouragement of sacrifice and of the assumption of risks perceived to be reasonably related to either the accomplishment of the forum's purposes, specifically, or the pursuit of racial equality and justice; and an affirmative duty to engage in principled practices and ethical conduct within the contexts of both the forum and the larger struggle.

Sixth, the forum cultivated a relationship with and effectively interpreted its importance to the independent African American press, specifically the *Baltimore Afro-American*, which was known for informing the African American community and was purchased widely. This resulted in the publisher's personal support, publicity in the newspaper, and the paper's endorsement of the forum's projects. This support gave the forum additional credibility.

Seventh, the interdenominational character of the forum and the cooperation of African American churches contributed significantly to its success. Large numbers of youth were members of churches. An African American

Protestant church provided space for meetings. Several pastors and members of congregations were sufficiently concerned about keeping young people in their churches that they made a point of listening to the youths' concerns, making the forum's announcements, attending forum meetings, and providing funding or other support. Some clergypersons helped lead the forum's public campaigns and protests in pursuit of employment and rights. As clergy and congregations endorsed the forum's activities, the credibility of the forum and its viability increased.

Eighth, the forum fostered interracial cooperation based upon principled support of its purposes and counseled against forming permanent alliances with any political party that African Americans could not hold accountable. Forum members invited non–African Americans who opposed segregation, racial discrimination, and the denial of equal rights to attend the forum's meetings, ally themselves with the forum in its advocacy campaigns, address the forum in its lecture series (regardless of political affiliation), and financially support the forum's activities. The forum also provided opportunities for its constituency to hear the political positions of candidates across the political spectrum in preelection symposia, and occasionally forum members allied themselves with non–African American radicals. The forum mobilized its membership to campaign on behalf of and garner the support of registered voters for candidates who advocated African Americans' equal rights and would be accountable to them.

The City-Wide Young People's Forum has historical significance beyond these findings. To begin with, it offered evidence of African American adults' willingness to recognize and respond to youth leadership in pursuing common goals and objectives. Second, the commitment of youth and older adults to racial equality and justice—as expressed in concrete objectives—forged intergenerational cooperation in a situation that might otherwise have sparked dysfunctional intergenerational conflict. Third, the forum achieved national stature through its advocacy of civil rights. Because of this, Walter White of the NAACP could better observe the efficacy of the leadership of youth and young adults who demonstrated principled conduct, militancy, and activism in local settings. He could, then, draw from the forum's elected leadership, specifically its highly skilled organizer and first president, Juanita Jackson, to launch a nationwide NAACP youth movement.

Finally, Baltimore's City-Wide Young People's Forum was not only a training ground for youth leadership, but also a catalyst for a national NAACP campaign to organize youth in the struggle for racial equality and justice. While involvement with the AKA sorority and the Methodist Youth Council provided valuable experiences, Juanita Jackson's success as the NAACP's youth organizer was largely the result of her practical experience in building, organizing, and sustaining the Baltimore movement of African American youth with vastly different socioeconomic backgrounds. Although after 1934 the national NAACP emphasized a legal assault on segregation through planned litigation in class actions to overturn racially discriminatory legal precedents, organization of African Americans at local levels remained a recurrent and important theme. Launching a national NAACP youth movement in 1935 was an indispensable element of grass-roots organizing. (Sustaining youth interest in the South had, as well, consequences for Ella Baker's fieldwork during the early 1940s.) In 1935 Juanita Jackson became special assistant to the NAACP's national secretary, Walter White, with a specific mandate. Jackson wrote a constitution for NAACP youth, organized youth councils, held conferences with youth, and urged councils to diversify their methods of pursuing racial justice. This had a profound impact on the later civil rights movement.[50]

When called upon to develop a youth movement for the NAACP, Jackson inspired young people with a sense of their potential power to effect change. As she traveled throughout the United States on behalf of the NAACP, she embodied the experience of a youth organization's activism and empowerment. As African American youth and young adults expressed dissatisfaction with the status quo, Juanita Jackson challenged them to petition, protest, boycott, demonstrate, and also to use African American attorneys armed with a racially just interpretation of the Constitution to secure freedom and equal rights. These methods of civil rights advocacy as well as local initiative, participatory democracy, and youth leadership caught the imagination of young people throughout the United States.[51] The full flowering of seeds planted in the 1930s would occur in the 1960s, but youth councils would remain active leaders in the struggle of African Americans for justice and rights under new interpretations of the Constitution, even in the intervening decades.[52]

NOTES

Earlier versions of this essay were presented at Howard University, the University of North Carolina in Chapel Hill, and the University of Texas at Arlington. I am grateful to colleagues at these institutions for their helpful comments. I particularly wish to acknowledge, with appreciation, the advice and assistance of Mary Frances Berry, Clayborne Carson, Marvin Dulaney, John Hope Franklin, Kathleen Underwood, and James Melvin Washington who perceptively read versions of this essay. Analysis presented here is based upon research the author is doing on social movements and youth organizations. Contributions of Carla Jean McNeil Jackson and Wekesa Madzimoyo, however, are also gratefully acknowledged.

1. See V. P. Franklin, *Black Self-Determination*, rev. ed. (Westport, Conn.: Lawrence Hill, 1992); Mary Frances Berry, *Black Resistance/White Law* (Englewood Cliffs, N.J.: Prentice-Hall, 1971); and Thomas C. Holt, "African-American History," in *The New American History*, ed. Eric Foner (Philadelphia: Temple University Press, 1990), 211–29. See also Darlene Clark Hine, ed., *The State of Afro-American History* (Baton Rouge: Louisiana State University Press, 1986).

2. See, for example, Herbert Aptheker, ed., *A Documentary History of the Negro People in the United States* (New York: Citadel Press, 1951), and such documents as "Slave Petitions for Freedom during the Revolution" 1:970, et seq.

3. "The Earliest Extant Negro Petition to Congress, 1797," in *A Documentary History*, ed. Aptheker, 1:43.

4. Alfred Kelly and Winfred Harbison, *The American Constitution* (New York: W. W. Norton, 1976), 12.

5. Vincent Harding, *Hope and History* (Maryknoll, N.Y.: Orbis, 1990), 108.

6. Harding, *Hope and History*, 108. See also the Declaration of Independence and the preamble to the U.S. Constitution.

7. Mary Frances Berry and John W. Blassingame, *Long Memory* (New York: Oxford University Press, 1982), 386 (emphasis added). See also Berry, *Black Resistance/White Law*.

8. See Derrick Bell, *Race, Racism and American Law*, 3d ed., rev. (Boston: Little, Brown, 1992); Mary Frances Berry, *Why ERA Failed: Politics, Women's Rights and the Amending Process* (Bloomington: Indiana University Press, 1986), 1–2, 4–10; and Nathan I. Huggins, *Black Odyssey*, 2d ed., rev. (New York: Vintage Books), xi, xii. For general documentary evidence, see Richard Bardolph, ed., *The Civil Rights Record: Black Americans and the Law, 1849–1970* (New York: Crowell, 1970); Albert P. Blaustein and Robert L. Zangrando, eds., *Civil Rights and the American Negro: A Documentary History* (New York: Trident Press, 1968); Joanne Grant, ed., *Black Protest: History, Documents and Analysis, 1619 to the Present*, 2d ed. (New York: Fawcett Premier, 1968); and Donald Nieman, *Promises to Keep: African Americans and the Constitutional Order, 1776 to the Present* (New York: Oxford University Press, 1991). For general studies or overviews of the civil rights movement/black revolution, see, for example, Robert Brisbane, *Black Activism: Black Revolution in the U.S., 1954–1970* (Valley Forge, Pa.: 1984); Vincent Harding, *The Other American Revolution* (Los Angeles, Calif.: Center for Afro-American Studies at UCLA, 1980); Manning Marable, *Race, Reform and Rebellion: The Second Reconstruction in Black America, 1945–1982* (Jackson: University of Mississippi Press, 1984); Edward Peeks, *The Long Struggle for Black Power* (New York: Scribner, 1971); and Harvard Sitkoff, *The Struggle for Black Equality* (New York: Hill and Wang, 1981). For a study of the period of the 1950s through the mid-1960s, see, for example, Lerone Bennett, *Confrontation: Black and White* (Chicago: Johnson Publications, 1965).

9. John Hope Franklin and Alfred A. Moss, *From Slavery to Freedom*, 6th ed., rev. (New York: Alfred Knopf, 1987), 342.

10. See Department of Commerce, Bureau of the Census, *Census of Population AL-MO*, 15th Census of the U.S., vol. 3; and *Fifth Decennial Census, 1930*. See also Ann E.

Argersinger, *Toward a New Deal in Baltimore* (Chapel Hill: University of North Carolina Press, 1988), which discusses the renaissance of voluntarism and rise of new constituencies during the New Deal as well as the depression in Baltimore.

11. See Department of Commerce, Bureau of the Census, *Census of Population AL-MO.*, 15th Census of the U.S., vol. 3. See also Maryland Commission on Higher Education, Report to the Governor and the General Assembly [1931], 25; Clarence Gregory, "The Education of Blacks in Maryland: An Historical Survey" (Ed. diss., Teachers' College of Columbia University, 1976).

12. Lillie Jackson and Thurgood Marshall quoted in Juanita Jackson Mitchell, Untitled address to the 46th Annual Convention of the National Association of Negro Business and Professional Women (typescript) (Baltimore, 1982), 3, 5, Personal Papers of Juanita Jackson Mitchell (hereinafter JJM Papers), Baltimore, Md. (Hereinafter "Address to NBPW"). Interviews with Juanita Jackson Mitchell, January 3, 21, and 22, 1987; see, for example, Arthur Raper, *The Tragedy of Lynching* (Chapel Hill: University of North Carolina Press, 1933).

13. William Dorsey in untitled audiovisual taped recording of reunion of members of the City-Wide Young Peoples Forum (hereinafter "Reunion") (Baltimore, December 27, 1985); Juanita Jackson Mitchell, Address to NBPW, 1982, JJM Papers. See also interview with Juanita Jackson Mitchell, Baltimore, Md., January 3, 1987.

14. Interviews with Juanita Jackson Mitchell, Baltimore, Md., January 3, 21, and 22, 1987.

15. City-Wide Young People's Forum (CWYPF), "Inter-Collegiate Oratorical, Vocal and Instrumental Contest" (hereinafter, Inter-Collegiate Program), Baltimore, 1932, JJM Papers.

16. Inter-Collegiate Program, 1932, JJM Papers; William Dorsey and Elmer Henderson in "Reunion" (Baltimore, December 27, 1985).

17. Inter-Collegiate Programs, 1932 and 1933, JJM Papers; interview with Juanita Jackson Mitchell (JJM), January 3, 1987; and Reunion (Baltimore, December 27, 1985). Like Clarence Mitchell, Elmer Henderson maintained a life-long interest in challenging racist denials of equal rights and would become a litigant in an interstate travel case opposing segregation on the Southern Railway (*Henderson* v. *United States* [339 US 816 (1950)]). Henderson also served as a field director for the Fair Employment Practice Committee (FEPC) and in 1943 as Baltimore's second African American "director of colored schools," succeeding Francis Wood.

18. Inter-Collegiate Program, 1932, JJM Papers.

19. Inter-Collegiate Program, 1933, JJM Papers.

20. Inter-Collegiate Program, 1937, JJM Papers.

21. Inter-Collegiate Program, 1933, JJM Papers; and interview with Juanita Jackson Mitchell, January 3, 1987.

22. Inter-Collegiate Programs, 1932–1937, 1940, 1941; interview with Juanita Jackson Mitchell, January 3, 1987. According to the census, the population in Baltimore was 859,100 in 1940. The African American populace numbered 165,843 in 1940. See *The Sixth Decennial Census, 1940; A Final Report*, vol. 1: *Number of Inhabitants* (Washington, D.C.: Government Printing Office, 1942), 464, and vol. 2: *Characteristics of the Population* (Washington, D.C.: Government Printing Office, 1943), 571.

23. "Reunion" (December 27, 1985); Inter-Collegiate Program, 1934; and clippings of *Baltimore Afro American*, week of December 9, 1933, and *California News*, December 21, 1933, from album of clippings, JJM Papers.

24. Clippings of *Baltimore Afro-American*, week of December 9, 1933, and *California News*, December 21, 1933, from album of clippings, JJM Papers.

25. Inter-Collegiate Program, 1935; Rebecca Evans in "Reunion" (27 December 1985); song card of CWYPF, JJM Papers; interviews with Juanita Jackson Mitchell, January 8 and 22, 1987.

26. Inter-Collegiate Program, 1933 and 1934, JJM Papers.

27. Interview with Juanita Jackson Mitchell, January 21 and 22, 1987.

28. Inter-Collegiate Program, 1933, JJM Papers.

29. Interview with Juanita Jackson Mitchell, January 3, 1987; *Kerr v. Pratt*, 149 F 2d 212 (1945); Inter-Collegiate Programs, 1933, 1934, and 1935, JJM Papers. See also Genna Rae McNeil, *Groundwork* (Philadelphia: University of Pennsylvania Press, 1983), chap. 10.

30. Interview with Juanita Jackson Mitchell, January 3, 1987; and Inter-Collegiate Programs, 1933–35, JJM Papers.

31. Clippings of *Baltimore Afro-American* regarding Costonie and boycott (n.d., ca. November 1933), album, JJM Papers; Maceo Howard in "Reunion" (December 27, 1985); Inter-Collegiate Programs, 1934 and 1937, JJM Papers; interview with Juanita Jackson Mitchell, January 3, 1987; *Minutes of the Executive Board of CWYPF,* 1933–34, 18–20, JJM Papers. In less than a year, two of the new clerks had been promoted to assistant managers.

32. Clarence Mitchell, "Observations and Reflections: Law vs. Rights," *Baltimore Afro-American*, June 2, 1934, clipping, JJM Papers; interview with Juanita Jackson Mitchell, January 3, 1987; Minutes of Executive Board, 1933–34, JJM Papers.

33. Interviews with Juanita Jackson Mitchell, January 3 and 22, 1987; Inter-Collegiate Programs, 1933–35, JJM Papers; "In re Bernard Ades" (March 1934), Houston from files (Washington, DC); *Pearson v. Murray*, 182 A. 590 (1936).

34. Interviews with Juanita Jackson Mitchell, January 3 and 22, 1987; Inter-Collegiate Programs, 1933, 1935, and 1937, JJM Papers. See *Minutes of Executive Board of CWYPF,* 1933–34, JJM Papers; List of witnesses to appear for Hearings on Costigan-Wagner Bill, 3–4, JJM Papers; and program of Cooperative Committee against Lynching, February 1935, JJM Papers. See also G. R. McNeil *Groundwork* (Philadelphia: University of Pennsylvania Press, 1933), 137–39.

35. Denton Watson, *Lion in the Lobby* (New York: William Morrow, 1990), 98.

36. "Reunion" (27 December 1985); Inter-Collegiate Program, 1935, JJM Papers. (Of the 16,000 registered African-American voters in the fifth district, approximately 10,900 voted.) See also *Afro-American* editorial quoted in D. Watson, *Lion in the Lobby,* 97–100.

37. Inter-Collegiate Program, 1933, 1 and 3, JJM Papers.

38. Inter-Collegiate Program, JJM Papers 4.

39. Inter-Collegiate Program, 1932, JJM Papers.

40. Inter-Collegiate Program, 1933, JJM Papers.

41. Robert L. Henson, pres., Allen Christian Endeavor League Trinity A.M.E. Church to Juanita Jackson Mitchell, January 20, 1932, JJM Papers.

42. See "Programme," International Debate, British Union of England vs. Lincoln University, Pennsylvania, held at Grace Presbyterian Church, November 24, 1931. See also, for example, Inter-Collegiate Programs, 1932–1934, 1941, JJM Papers.

43. Lucius Jones, "Juanita Jackson Proved Heroine of Movement," *Atlanta Daily World*, November 20, 1936, 1 and 6; album, JJM Papers. Youth of other cities, such as Atlanta, attempted to organize and duplicate the success of Baltimore's forum.

44. Inter-Collegiate Programs, 1935, 1936, and 1939, JJM Papers.

45. Inter-Collegiate Programs, 1932–39 and 1941; Interviews with Juanita Jackson Mitchell, January 3 and 21, 1987; Frazier Armstead in "Reunion" (December 27, 1985).

46. Inter-Collegiate Program, 1933; Inter-Collegiate Program, 1932, and interview with Juanita Jackson Mitchell, January 21, 1987.

47. Inter-Collegiate Program, 1933, 4.

48. Inter-Collegiate Program, Interviews with Juanita Jackson Mitchell, January 3 and 22, January; Inter-Collegiate Programs, 1932–37. Major denominations participating were A.M.E., A.M.E.Z., Baptist, Episcopal, Methodist, and Presbyterian.

49. Franklin and Moss, *From Slavery to Freedom*, 342.

50. Interviews with Juanita Jackson Mitchell, January 3 and 22, 1987; clipping, *Atlanta Daily World*, November 22, 1936, album, JJM Papers. See Administrative Files, 1935 et seq., particularly correspondence of Juanita Jackson, *Constitution of the NAACP Youth Council*, and Youth Files, NAACP Records, Library of Congress, Washington, D.C. Cf. Carol Mueller, "Ella Baker and the Origins of 'Participatory Democracy,'" in *Women in the Civil Rights Movement*, ed. Vicki L. Crawford, Jacqueline Rouse, and Barbara Woods (Brooklyn: Carlson, 1990). See also G. R. McNeil, *Groundwork*, 140–45, 220–22.

51. Interview with Juanita Jackson Mitchell, January 3, 1987. See Youth Files, NAACP Records, Library of Congress. See also, for example, letter of Jackson to Youth Officers, May 29, 1936, in re. youth conference, NAACP Correspondence, JJM Papers; Juanita Jackson Mitchell, Address to NBPW, 1982, JJM Papers; Richard Kluger, *Simple Justice* (New York: A. Knopf, 1975); and Carol Mueller, "Ella Baker," 51–70. See also clipping, *Atlanta Daily World*, November 20, 1936, album, JJM Papers.

52. Aldon Morris, *Origins of the Civil Rights Movement* (New York: Free Press, 1984), 188–89, 198–99. See also Manning Marable, *Race, Reform and Rebellion* (Jackson: University of Mississippi Press, 1985); and Clayborne Carson, *In Struggle* (Cambridge: Harvard University Press, 1980).

PART

II

THE POST-*BROWN* STRUGGLE FOR CONSTITUTIONAL CHANGE

WILEY A. BRANTON

RACE, THE COURTS, AND CONSTITUTIONAL CHANGE IN TWENTIETH-CENTURY SCHOOL DESEGREGATION CASES AFTER *BROWN*

A PARTICIPANT'S PERSPECTIVE

Through the courts, members of racial minority groups have in many instances been able to gain equal rights before the law well in advance of the enactment of any legislation on the particular point. The Supreme Court of the United States did not enact legislation but made those historic decisions on the basis of its interpretation of a "living Constitution." These cases had to do with protecting or upholding the rights of African Americans in such matters as voting (not only in general elections, but also in party primaries and with respect to political districts, which were gerrymandered in a manner that diluted black voting strength), housing (where the particular concern was to prohibit the enforcement of racially restrictive covenants), interstate travel (where the emphasis was on enjoining segregation of interstate passengers on trains and buses), and jury service (where the objective was to quash jury panels and grand juries practicing systematic exclusion of black people). As well, the Court has struck down a number of racially neutral laws applied for the purpose of racial discrimination.[1]

Predictably, after the Court ruled in *Brown (I)* that racially segregated education violated the constitutional right of equal protection and in *Brown (II)* that compliance with *Brown (I)*'s holding was to be accomplished by the states with "all deliberate speed," the decisions were met with massive resistance in the South.[2] In Little Rock, Arkansas, however, black people seemed to be making some progress toward desegregation. During the years immediately following

Brown (II), I filed suit on behalf of black students and parents in Little Rock to accelerate the desegregation process and to broaden its scope in regard to school grades.[3]

As I recounted for the producers of the documentary, *Eyes on the Prize*:

> Under the so-called Blossom Plan of gradual desegregation, nearly three to four hundred black children were supposed to enroll at the high school level in Little Rock beginning in 1957, because of where they lived. But as the summer went by, and Little Rock decided, 'oh my God, this thing that we've been pushing is on us,' they started putting up all kinds of barriers. They required black children who wanted to go to white schools to register. Approximately seventy-five black kids signed up to go to Central High School. Then as the opening of school approached, the number went down. . . . And they made . . . sure that they did not include a single one of the plaintiffs [thirty-three black children and their parents] who had been selected by the NAACP. Those whom we recognize in history today as the Little Rock Nine were the nine children whose parents, and themselves, decided they were going to go. But you could not have selected . . . nine finer youngsters.
>
> We became concerned about the board's dilution of [its] own court-approved plan, and we were going into federal court to compel the Little Rock School Board to do what it had represented that it was going to do, when [Governor] Faubus pulled the rug out from under everybody.[4]

A few days before the Little Rock public schools were to open, an order came from the state court enjoining the implementation of the desegregation plan. Although a federal court had overruled the state court, Governor Orval Faubus ordered the Arkansas national guard to block the entry of the nine black children to Central High School. Little Rock became the scene of a major confrontation between state and federal authorities when President Dwight D. Eisenhower nationalized the Arkansas guardsmen and sent U.S. Army troops, as well, to disperse white mobs. Little Rock's defiance of federal authority, which had been viewed on national television by millions, compelled Eisenhower reluctantly to become the first president since Reconstruction to use federal troops in the protection of African Americans' constitutional rights.[5]

For *Cooper v. Aaron*, the first school decision of the U.S. Supreme Court after *Brown (II)*, the Court convened to review the petition of the Little Rock School Board, in which the board requested a stay of the 1958 integration plan because of public hostility. The plaintiffs' attorneys argued that normal educational activities could not be conducted if the black students were permitted to attend Central High School. Thurgood Marshall and I, for the respondents, stressed the constitutional rights of the black children. During 1958, in an opinion that was unanimous, the U.S. Supreme Court chronicled the state of Arkansas's defiance of the *Brown* mandate and held that despite whites' violence and hostility, the plaintiffs' request for a delay could not be honored. The Supreme Court's decision in *Brown (I)* was to be recognized as the appropriate interpretation of the Constitution, "the supreme law of the land," and the state was obligated to use its authority to control the violent behavior of citizens in Little Rock, which the Court found traceable to the conduct of state officials opposed to desegregation.[6] The nine justices declared:

> The constitutional rights of children not to be discriminated against in school admission on grounds of race or color declared by this Court in the *Brown* case can neither be nullified openly and directly by state legislation or state executive or judicial order, nor nullified indirectly by them through evasive schemes for segregation whether attempted 'ingeniously or ingenuously.'[7]

Nonetheless, school boards, state legislators, state executives, and state judges continued in their attempts to evade the constitutionally imposed duty to dismantle de jure segregation in public schools of various states. In *Griffin* v. *School Board of Prince Edward County*, a county school system in Virginia had remained closed for four years to avoid desegregation, and public funds were used to support white private schools. The U.S. Supreme Court in *Griffin* declared ten years after *Brown (I)* that the time for "deliberate speed" had run out and that this phrase could no longer justify the denial of constitutional rights to black children seeking a desegregated education. Yet, deprivation of constitutional rights continued to be the order of the day.[8]

Not until the Supreme Court decided *Green* v. *School Board of New Kent County* of eastern Virginia in 1968 did these evasive schemes begin to come to a halt. Justice William J. Brennan, Jr., for the Court asserted that *Brown II* was a command to dismantle racially segregated dual systems: "School boards . . . operating state-compelled dual systems were . . . clearly charged with the affirmative duty to take whatever steps might be necessary to convert to a unitary system in which racial discrimination would be eliminated root and branch." He cited *Cooper* v. *Aaron*, among other cases, to clarify the position of the Court. Before concluding, once again the Court declared that the "all deliberate speed doctrine" was no longer operable; "the time for mere 'deliberate speed' has run out." The Court added that "[the] burden on a school board today is to come forward with a plan that promises realistically to work and promises realistically to work *now*."[9]

Nonetheless, during the very next term Justice Hugo L. Black found it necessary to reiterate that "the phrase 'with all deliberate speed' should no longer have any relevancy whatsoever in enforcing the constitutional rights of Negro students" in the Mississippi case of *Alexander* v. *Holmes County Board of Education*.[10]

> The question presented is one of paramount importance, involving as it does the denial of fundamental rights to many thousands of school children, who are presently attending Mississippi Schools. . . . [C]ontinued operation of segregated schools under a standard of allowing "all deliberate speed" for desegregation is no longer constitutionally permissible.[11]

These cases and the tortuous history they represent provide the context for any discussion about the course of school desegregation. This context is important because when one thinks of it, the truth of the matter is that school desegregation did not begin in earnest until 1971, with *Swann* v. *Charlotte-Mecklenburg Board of Education* when, for the first time, the Supreme Court actually directed the district court to provide specific types of remedies, including student transportation, to school desegregation plaintiffs in North Carolina.[12]

In rapid succession after *Swann*, school districts across the South began the process of dismantling their dual educational systems. The 1973 decision in *Keyes* v. *School District No. 1* of Denver, Colorado, extended the school desegregation process to northern non–de jure school districts and in the next year the Detroit, Michigan, case of *Milliken* v. *Bradley* set forth the standard for interdistrict, metropolitan-wide, school litigation. *Milliken (II)*, which was decided in 1976, defined the circumstances in which compensatory programs and other educational enhancements were appropriate. Further development of the legal standards for determining continuing liability and the consequent affirmative duty of school districts with a history of prior segregation was set forth in *Dayton [Ohio] Board of Education* v. *Brinkman (I)* of 1977, *Dayton (II)* of 1979, and *Columbus [Ohio] Board of Education* v. *Penick*, also decided in 1979.[13]

School desegregation cases are not as simple as they once were. Once, they presented the issue of the admission of one or a number of students to schools that practiced blatant racial discrimination. The cases now present complex issues brought as class actions, often against numerous defendants, including local, state, and federal governmental officials. Moreover, the modern-day school desegregation suit may include claims that involve the actions of not only school officials, but also of the actions of governmental officials and private individuals in the areas of housing, transportation, and urban planning. And instead of focusing on present efforts to bar black children from the schoolhouse door, the desegregation suits with which the courts are grappling may involve the scrutiny of segregative actions and effects spanning decades.

School boards that have finally implemented successful desegregation plans are seeking court permission to dismantle them and thus return to segregated schools, citing.*Pasadena City Board of Education* v. *Spangler.*[14] Courts are being called upon to determine what "unitary status" really means, and what the obligations of school districts are once they have been released from court jurisdiction. It is one thing to hold, as *Spangler* did, that a unitary school district is not obligated to make yearly adjustments to maintain any particular level of desegregation or strict racial percentages in each school. It is quite another thing for a school district with a de jure history that has finally implemented an effective plan rendering it unitary to undo the plan and revert to segregated status.

On the other hand, courts understandably do not want to be in the position of permanently supplanting local officials by overseeing the day-to-day operation of local school districts. Undoubtedly, the resolution of these cases, while not easy, will be aided by the jurisprudential principle under which the equitable power of a district court cannot be invoked absent a constitutional or statutory violation. Only upon the default of a school district of its constitutional obligation can a court exercise its authority.[15] In other words, the condition that offends the Constitution is governmentally caused segregation.

In addition to the unitary status issue cases, federal appellate courts will continue to witness an increase in a number of cases that raise "second-generation" issues—disproportionate assignment of minority students to special education classes, especially those for the emotionally mentally retarded (EMR). In many instances the assignments may not always appear on their face to be racially discriminatory. Often the standards for referral are lacking in clarity or objectivity, leaving room for a teacher or counselor to classify a student in a manner that will forever stigmatize him or her, and that may in fact become a self-fulfilling prophecy insofar as it may retard a child's intellectual development.

These cases present difficult factual inquiries. On the one hand, if a child is, in fact, emotionally handicapped or learning disabled, special attention may not only be desirable; it may be critical. On the other hand, where a substantial number of black or minority children are being relegated to special education classes, the question arises as to whether these programs are being used to effectuate another form of school segregation.

A related second-generation issue is the discriminatory tracking of black students into lower-rung academic courses and the concentration of white students in classes for the gifted and talented. Like assignments to special education classes, tracking assignments may be made with considerable discretion on the part of teachers and counselors. Although the stigma may not be as damaging as an EMR label, a discriminatory tracking system may have lifelong effects on the educational and employment opportunities of its victims. These claims are becoming more common in school desegregation cases and will undoubtedly be brought to federal appellate courts for further review.

The most complex issues are presented in the multidistrict, metropolitan-wide cases. Whether operating solely in their self-interest or as a fiduciary for their students, these districts recognize that their continued viability as healthy educational institutions is partly dependent upon their ability to maintain racial diversity. While their interests may not completely coincide with those of black plaintiffs in these interdistrict cases, there is a substantial identity of interests.

In the interdistrict case, a majority black or other minority school district is facing severe fiscal crises precipitated in part by the inability to prevail in tax elections or to win voter approval for bond issues, and in part by an eroding tax base that may be linked to the exodus of white families from urban dwellings. Such cases are further characterized by inferior physical facilities as a result of deferred maintenance and capital improvements, by overcrowded classrooms, and by inadequate academic programs. These school districts are virtually bankrupt—fiscally and educationally.

The resultant deprivation of educational opportunity is no less damaging than that identified by the Court in *Brown*. As deplorable as these conditions may be, the relevant question for a federal court is whether they are attributable to a constitutionally cognizable violation, which has contributed to the current condition. Whether they are, of course, depends on the facts of the particular case.

With hindsight, it is now possible to see that de jure statutes were not the only forces to have an impact on school segregation; they were merely the most obvious. Segregative actions and policies spanning decades, taken by federal, state, and local officials in the school and housing arenas, have conspired to create systems of segregation that have had intergenerational effects on entire metropolitan areas. In short, we now know that, in some instances, in order to identify the root causes of school segregation we must determine the manner in which entire metropolitan areas have come to be racially segregated. Whether in cases involving the issue of unitary status or in interdistrict cases school desegregation, litigation is unlikely to proceed without housing-related claims. It is abundantly clear that school and housing segregation are inextricably linked. Whether the issue is the federal government's role through the location of public or subsidized housing, or a local community's role through zoning practices aimed at excluding minorities, the housing issue is likely to be presented in the vast majority of future school desegregation cases before federal appellate courts.

This undertaking involves complex factual inquiries in which thousands of documents may be relevant and hundreds of witnesses may have knowledge, and they may require the elucidation of expert witnesses from a variety of disciplines. The litigation costs and judicial expenditure of time have increased exponentially. The records have become unwieldy. Given the already overburdened workload of the appellate court and concern about the limits of justiciability, undoubtedly there must be frustration about the ability of the courts to properly decide these controversies. Yet, despite these difficulties, the Supreme Court must recognize the monumental importance of these cases to the individuals involved and the communities in which they live. The claims are not frivolous; the disputes are real and the stakes are high. The status of a racial minority often translates into political powerlessness, and where majoritarian prejudices foreclose any possibility of relief through political processes, the power of a federal court is often the last avenue of recourse: "[P]rejudice against discrete and insular minorities may . . . [tend] seriously to curtail the operation of those political processes ordinarily to be relied upon to protect minorities, and . . . may call for a correspondingly more searching judicial inquiry."[16]

Black children in public schools are still experiencing, in the words of Jonathan Kozol, intellectual "death at an early age."[17] While many factors contribute to this fatal malady, the cancerous actions of governmental officials remain paramount. There are those who argue that it is time to close the books on this chapter of our nation's history. To do so would not close the books but would turn back the pages to a chapter in which racial discrimination was not legally redressable and the Constitution was lifeless and fatally flawed.

Racial and other forms of discrimination still exist in many areas of American life. The statement of the late Chief Justice Earl Warren, speaking on May 15, 1970, at a session of the NAACP Legal Defense and Educational Fund, Inc.'s Institute on the crisis in American justice, is no less valid today.

Our Nation stands at a crossroads. As we face the future, we must make a choice on which we will travel. One leads to that plural society to which we rededicate ourselves whenever we repeat the Pledge of Allegiance—

> "I pledge allegiance to the flag of the United States of America and to the republic for which it stands, one nation under God, indivisible, with liberty and justice for all."

That road leads to the unity of purpose and action which will make life meaningful for all. The other road would divide us into segments of discontented people with a divisiveness that leaves no room for the happiness and contentment of the children of any of us in the foreseeable future.[18]

Racial discrimination cannot be eradicated without the support of all people who believe in the Constitution of the United States.

NOTES

Wiley A. Branton (1923–1988), with George Crockett, was one of the few participants in the Smithsonian conference of 1988 on African Americans and the Constitution who was an active advocate and litigator of civil rights and liberties before and after the sit-ins of 1960. As chief counsel for the African American children and parents in 1957–58, Branton played an indispensable role with Daisy Bates in the NAACP's struggle at the local level to actualize the personal and present rights of African Americans of Little Rock, Arkansas. His later activism in the South while serving as the director of the Southern Regional Council's Voter Education Project in Atlanta, Georgia, at the same time as the James Meredith case in Mississippi persuaded him of the need for bold and direct federal protection of constitutionally guaranteed rights. His remarks at the conference clearly focused on federal conduct and responsibilities with respect to equal protection and school desegregation. Branton became ill and passed away in 1988 before having the opportunity to note all authorities, and to expand upon his remarks. The editors have taken the liberty of adding citations and including recollections that Branton made on other occasions, which either supplement or support his remarks prepared in 1988. The editors acknowledge permission granted by West Publishing Company to reprint excerpts from Mr. Branton's "The History and Future of School Desegregation." *Federal Rules Decisions*, Vol. 109 (1986): 241–52.

1. See, for example, *Guinn* v. *United States*, 238 U.S. 347 (1915), invalidating grandfather clauses; *Smith* v. *Allwright*, 321 U.S. 649 (1944), outlawing white primaries; *Gomillion* v. *Lightfoot*, 364 U.S. 339 (1960), forbidding racial gerrymandering; *South Carolina* v. *Katzenbach*, 383 U.S. 301 (1966), upholding the constitutionality of the 1965 Voting Rights Act; *Shelley* v. *Kraemer*, 334 U.S. 1 (1948) and *Hurd* v. *Hodge*, 334 U.S. 24 (1948),

invalidating judicial enforcement of racially restrictive covenants; *Morgan* v. *Virginia*, 328 U.S. 373 (1946), declaring unconstitutional a state statute requiring segregation in interstate buses; *Henderson* v. *United States*, 339 U.S. 816 (1950), invalidating segregation on trains during interstate travel; *Powell* v. *Alabama*, 287 U.S. 45 (1932), *Norris* v. *Alabama*, 294 U.S. 587 (1935), *Patton* v. *State of Mississippi*, 332 U.S. 463 (1947), and *Swain* v. *Alabama*, 380 U.S. 202 (1965), regarding unconstitutional jury discrimination; and *Reitman* v. *Mulkey*, 387 U.S. 369 (1967) and *Hunter* v. *Erickson*, 393 U.S. 385 (1969) outlawing facially neutral laws masking invidious discrimination.

2. *Brown* v. *Board of Education* (I), 347 U.S. 483 (1954) and *Brown* v. *Board of Education* (II), 349 U.S. 294 (1955).

3. See Derrick A. Bell, *Race, Racism and American Law* (Boston: Little, Brown, 1973), 454–61, *passim*; Manning Marable, *Race, Reform and Rebellion* (Jackson: University Press of Mississippi, 1984), 42–48 *passim*; John Hope Franklin and Alfred Moss, *From Slavery to Freedom*, 6th ed. rev. (New York: Alfred A. Knopf, 1987), 366–69, 436–39; and Henry Hampton and Steve Fayer, with Sarah Flynn, compilers, *Voices of Freedom* (New York: Bantam Books, 1990), 36–52 *passim*.

4. In Hampton et al., *Voices of Freedom*, 40–41. The producer of the documentary *Eyes on the Prize* has published with others an excerpt from an interview with Wiley Branton, a portion of which has been added by the editors to Branton's Smithsonian remarks on the Little Rock case.

5. See Marable, *Race, Reform and Rebellion*, 45; Franklin and Moss, *From Slavery to Freedom*, 436; and Lerone Bennett, *Before the Mayflower* (Baltimore: Penguin Books, 1966), 318–19, 403.

6. See *Cooper* v. *Aaron*, 358 U.S. 1 (1958), in which the Court cited both *Marbury* v. *Madison*, 1 Cranch 137 (1803), on the Court's power of judicial review, and *Buchanan* v. *Warley*, 245 U.S. 60 (1917), on the issue of disorder and state action. See also Derrick Bell, *Race, Racism and American Law* (Boston: Little, Brown 1973), 457, n. 45.

7. *Cooper* v. *Aaron*, 358 U.S. 1 (1958). Citations have been omitted in quotation.

8. See *Griffin* v. *School Board of Prince Edward County*, 377 U.S. 218 (1964). Litigation in Prince Edward County, Virginia, began in 1951 and was heard on the consolidated *Brown I* case. The county permitted African American children to do without public schooling while the county contributed to the support of private, segregated schools for Anglo and European Americans.

9. *Green* v. *School Board of New Kent County*, 391 U.S. 430 (1968), at 437–38 and 439.

10. *Alexander* v. *Holmes County Board of Education*, 396 U.S. 1218 at 1220 (1969). See also 396 U.S. 19 and 24 L.Ed. 2d. 19 (1969).

11. *Alexander* v. *Holmes County Board of Education*, 396 U.S. at 20.

12. *Swann* v. *Charlotte-Mecklenburg Board of Education*, 402 U.S. (1971).

13. See *Keyes* v. *School District No. 1, Denver, Colorado*, 404 U.S. 1036 (1972) and 413 U.S. 189 (1973); *Milliken* v. *Bradley* (I), 418 U.S. 717 (1974), and *Milliken* v. *Bradley* (II), 433 U.S. 267 (1977); *Dayton Board of Education* v. *Brinkman* (I), 433 U.S. 406 (1977), and *Dayton Board of Education* v. *Brinkman* (II), 443 U.S. 526 (1979); and *Columbus Board of Education* v. *Penick*, 433 U.S. 449 (1979) and 99 S.Ct. 29. Compare discussion of Derrick Bell, "The Quest for Effective Public Schools," in Derrick Bell, *Race, Racism and American Law* (Boston: Little, Brown, 1980), 364–444.

14. *Pasadena City Board of Education* v. *Spangler*, 427 U.S. 424, 96 S.Ct. 2697, 49 L.Ed. 2d. 599 (1976).

15. *Swann* v. *Charlotte-Mecklenburg Board of Education*, 402 U.S. 1 at 16, 91 S.Ct. 11267, 1276, 28 L.Ed. 2d. 554 (1971).

16. *United States* v. *Carolene Products Co.*, 304 U.S. 144 at 152–53, n. 4, 58 S.Ct. 778 at 783 n. 4, 82 L.Ed. 1234 (1938).

17. Jonathan Kozol, *Death at an Early Age* (Boston: Houghton Mifflin, 1967).

18. Annual Report of the NAACP Legal Defense and Educational Fund, Inc., 1970.

GEORGE W. CROCKETT, JR.

REMEMBERING LITIGATION, PROTEST, AND POLITICS IN MISSISSIPPI DURING THE CIVIL RIGHTS MOVEMENT

The twentieth century has seen great changes in the status of black Americans in our society, not because of changes in the Constitution of our land, but because of fundamental changes in the *interpretation* and implementation of that Constitution.

The twentieth century has brought us to new battlegrounds. Although the Constitution was written more than two hundred years ago, it has no life or meaning for black Americans unless people breathe life into it by living it. *That* has been the struggle of the twentieth century. It has meant the most wrenching, bitter battles of all, not only to change the habits, the thinking, and the practices of those who are charged with implementing existing constitutional law, but also to eliminate the racism still enmeshed in the consciousness of far too many Americans.

Through a multidimensional approach to the problem, African Americans have enlisted the support of other oppressed groups in our society—the poor, women, youth, and other minority groups such as Hispanics and Native Americans—in the struggle for equality. The tactics have been as varied as the people of this nation. They range from nonviolent refusals to give up a seat on a bus to violent confrontations; from legal challenges of local segregation laws to national legislative initiatives such as the Voting Rights Act; from a busload of youth registering voters in Alabama to the election of twenty-three black members of Congress and the candidacy of Jesse Jackson for president of the United States.

The peak of this movement occurred in the 1960s, when the forces of change made their most profound impact on our nation and its commitment to equality. My own involvement in this movement grew out of my legal training and especially my membership in the National Lawyers Guild. As vice-president of the guild during the summer of 1964, I went to Jackson, Mississippi, to organize the field office of the Committee for Legal Assistance in the South. My specific objective was to set up a structure that would allow lawyers from all over the country to come to Mississippi for a week (or more, if they were so inclined) to offer legal assistance to the civil rights demonstrators there.

Such a project was necessary because there were at that time only five African American lawyers in the whole of Mississippi—and only four of them were willing to take civil rights cases. They were all located in Jackson. There were *no* black lawyers in any other area of the state. Few, if any, nonblack lawyers from Mississippi would take a civil rights case. Nor would they move the admission of out-of-state lawyers to take these cases. In fact, virtually the entire bar in the South had refused to provide effective legal representation to African Americans and their white supporters in the effort to achieve the constitutional rights of the former. Local judges, who would have been forced to *assign* the cases to local lawyers unwilling to volunteer, were happy to see the out-of-state lawyers appear.

It was not easy for either the lawyers or the local residents to participate in our project. The lawyers had to pay their own way to and from Mississippi, some from as far away as California and Washington state. While in Mississippi, most of them stayed with local African American families, even though most of the lawyers who were not black had had little or no contact with blacks before this. The lawyers paid for all of their own expenses. Because they were not getting paid for their services, it was difficult for most to stay more than one week. Some did stay for two weeks, however. Most of the lawyers who came were white and faced the personal dangers inherent in the situation. They never knew if someone walking down the street or driving by might suddenly feel compelled to take out his or her resentment against what was being done for African Americans. For this reason, we instituted a rule that whenever our volunteer lawyers left the Jackson area, they were to call the home office on a regular basis to let us know they were still among the living. Some of the African American families and individuals were reluctant to have these lawyers stay in their homes. The danger from the white community was very real. That, added to the natural reluctance to open one's home to strangers, made participation a difficult decision.

The National Lawyers Guild's committee and its volunteers worked out of four rooms above a store at 507½ North Farish Street in Jackson—not exactly an address in the history books! It was not near the downtown area or the courthouse; no one was willing to give us that kind of help. It was more like a loft; the makeshift office was above the store with a funeral parlor next door. We had a full-time staff of four who helped coordinate our efforts, only one of whom was paid. We had some supplies, a mimeograph machine, and we had enthusiasm! Sixty attorneys from all over the country took part in this project.

We would receive calls from the area, advising us that an individual or group had been arrested while protesting in Greenwood, for example. We would contact the people we had stationed closest to Greenwood, and they would begin the task of representing those individuals. Whether it required writing briefs, ascertaining the details of the arrest, or renting a plane and flying to wherever the judge was holding court that day, our lawyers would do what was necessary to protect the rights of our clients.

In a way, what we did in Mississippi in 1964 was a microcosm of the twentieth-century struggle for civil rights. Of course, we were concentrating on the legal representation of our clients. Our lawyers were counseled *not* to consider themselves protestors or participants in the demonstrations that were taking place in Mississippi. From the passionate involvement of those who participated, it was clear that their hearts and minds were committed both to the protests and to active resistance against the segregation so vividly exhibited there. We received the backing of several powerful political figures, including Senators Hubert Humphrey, Jacob Javits, Phillip Hart, and Pat McNamara. In hindsight, it is clear that the political power of Southern blacks, which has become so evident in the 1990s, grew out of the seeds sown in the 1960s by all the people who worked in the South for civil rights and minority political empowerment.

I remember one instance in which all the elements of the struggle came very close to home for me. I got a call late one night in our office in Jackson from a young man by the name of Michael Schwerner. He was working out of the office of the Congress of Racial Equality (CORE) in Meridian, Mississippi. He said the church in Philadelphia, Mississippi, in which they had been holding "freedom classes," had been burned. He wanted to know what could be done legally to challenge this harassment. I told him to gather the facts and witnesses, and I would be there Monday morning. On the way to Meridian that Monday with several of my colleagues, we heard over the radio that Michael Schwerner and two other young people working in the movement had disappeared. When we got to Meridian, we were met by a crew from CBS News, who warned us that Philadelphia was extremely tense. We decided to go anyway. We did not know where the sheriff's office was and our attempts to get information at a gasoline station outside town only alerted persons in Philadelphia to the fact that we were coming. They lined the streets and crowded the hallway, trying to stop us from seeing the sheriff and finding out the location of the church. When we finally did see the sheriff (a big, tobacco-chewing man), he made certain everyone in the hallway heard his directions to the church. By the time we got back to our car, we had decided that finding the young man who had called me, Michael Schwerner, was probably impossible and that the situation was too tense to continue. We went back to Jackson. Three weeks later, they found the bodies of Michael Schwerner, Andrew Goodman, and James Chaney.

The decade of the 1960s was neither the beginning of the twentieth-century civil rights movement nor the end. It was, nevertheless, a time of remarkable change. A convergence of *all* the elements of the African American civil rights struggle in the 1960s—the protests, the politics, and the pursuit of the equal justice under the law—made a profound change in the racial landscape of America. America's conscience was awakened by writers, religious leaders, and philosophers. This, along with the courage of individuals who demanded their rights to housing, transportation, public accommodations, political empowerment, and education, not to mention the persistence of those who believed in racial justice and the rule of law, enabled us to achieve much in a short time.

I am proud to have been a part of such a time. I continue to hope that the changes wrought then will have a profound and lasting impact on future generations as they strive to meet the challenge of our living and evolving Constitution.

FRANK R. PARKER

POLITICAL AND SOCIAL CHANGE
IN MISSISSIPPI SINCE 1965

T he ultimate test of whether the promise of the Fourteenth and Fifteenth amendments can ever be made a reality has always been Mississippi. Historically, Mississippi has had the highest percentage of black
people of any state (1960–42 percent; 1970–38 percent; 1980–35 percent)
and has been the scene of the most intransigent resistance to the constitutional rights of black people. It was Mississippi that led the South in black
disfranchisement with the Mississippi Plan of 1890, led the country in recorded lynchings (534 from 1882 to 1952), and developed the most oppressive "Jim Crow" political, social, and economic system.

For black people in Mississippi in 1965, there was no "living constitution."
In fact, it was a dead constitution. Constitutional protections against state-
imposed racial discrimination in every area of public life, voting, education,
public employment, and jury selection were all but completely ignored.

Although most Southern states had begun to dismantle their Jim Crow systems during the period 1954 to 1965, as late as 1965 Mississippi was still a
rigidly segregated state. As Anthony Lewis of the *New York Times* commented,
"The revolution that so profoundly changed American race relations between
1954 and 1964 stopped at the borders of Mississippi."[1] After five years of civil
rights protest, voter registration drives, and community organizing by Student
Nonviolent Coordinating Committee, Southern Christian Leadership Conference, Congress of Racial Equality, and the National Association for the

Advancement of Colored People (NAACP)—efforts that were more intense than anywhere in the South—only 6.7 percent of the eligible adult black population was registered to vote (28,500 out of a black voting age population of 422,273), there were no black elected officials outside the all-black town of Mound Bayou, not a single school district had dismantled its racially segregated schools, and most of the black people who had jobs were employed as field hands or household servants. Civil rights protests aimed at eliminating this rigid segregation were ruthlessly suppressed by police harassment, economic reprisals, and Ku Klux Klan terrorism.

This chapter provides a brief overview of the impact of civil rights protest, politics, and litigation on political and social change in Mississippi in the post-1965 period. Special attention is given to the role of constitutional litigation as an instrument of social change in the areas of voting, education, and state employment.

VOTING

During the early 1960s, case-by-case litigation proved inadequate to remedy the massive exclusion of blacks from the political process. From 1961 to 1965 half of the Justice Department's voting discrimination and harassment lawsuits in the South were filed in Mississippi, but these cases failed to make more than a slight dent in the political exclusion of black citizens. More was needed. In 1965 Congress passed the Voting Rights Act to enforce the constitutional guarantees of the Fourteenth and Fifteenth amendments.[2]

The Voting Rights Act of 1965 was primarily the product of the black-led civil rights protest movement. Martin Luther King's philosophy and strategy of massive nonviolent civil disobedience had predictable consequences. After black people were subjected to police dogs, fire hoses, and the police charge at the Edmund Pettus bridge in Selma, Alabama, Congress was spurred to decisive action. After the Selma bridge incident, Senator Walter Mondale (Minnesota) is reported to have said: "Sunday's outrage in Selma, Alabama, makes passage of legislation to guarantee Southern Negroes the right to vote an absolute imperative for Congress this year."[3]

The Voting Rights Act did primarily three things. First, it struck down the literacy tests, the other discriminatory voter registration tests, and the poll tax that had been used since 1890 to deny black people in the South the right to vote. Second, it authorized the Justice Department to send federal registrars and poll watchers into Southern states to register voters and to ensure that elections were conducted fairly. Third, and most important for the post-1965 era, in Section 5 it required all states and localities in which voter-registration tests were suspended to submit any changes in their voting laws either to the Justice Department or to the federal district court in Washington for approval before they could be implemented.

As a result of the passage of the Voting Rights Act, within two years black voter registration rates in every Southern state jumped to more than 50 percent of the black voting age population.[4] Mississippi's black voter registration rate ballooned from 6.7 percent in 1965—the lowest in the South—to 59.9 percent in 1967—the highest of any state covered by the Voting Rights Act. In this brief two-year period, black voters in Mississippi went from 5 percent of the statewide electorate to 28 percent.

Contrary to popular expectations, however, the Voting Rights Act did not eliminate all the barriers to equal black political participation. In fact, the dramatic increases in black voter registration produced by the act triggered a "massive resistance" by the state's white supremacist establishment that ushered in a whole new "second generation" of discriminatory devices aimed at nullifying the newly gained black vote.

Once again, Mississippi led the way. Deprived of the legal authority to deny blacks the right to register and vote, the Mississippi legislature in its political massive resistance session of 1966—within ten months after the Voting Rights Act became law—enacted a host of measures aimed at diluting black voting strength. Among other measures, the state legislature gerrymandered the congressional district lines to eliminate the black majority Delta congressional district and to divide it among three of the five districts; increased the number of multimember districts in which state legislators ran countywide (or in combinations of counties) for the state legislature; authorized counties to switch from district to at-large, countywide elections for members of both the county boards of supervisors and county school boards; increased greatly the qualifying requirements for independent candidates for office, most of whom were black; and abolished elections for county school superintendents in a number of majority black counties.

The primary purpose of these measures was to eliminate or minimize the number of black-majority election districts in which black voters would be able to elect candidates of their choice. Mississippi's political massive resistance tactics had an immediate impact. In 1967, in the first statewide elections after the Voting Rights Act became law, only 22 out of 127 black candidates who ran or attempted to run for office were elected to only a handful of the more than 2,000 state, county, and district offices that were to be filled. The changes in election rules enacted by the state legislature in 1966 were a primary factor in the massive defeat of black candidates in the 1967 elections. This strategy of massive political resistance was not limited to Mississippi. Similar tactics were employed throughout the South to dilute the black vote and to prevent black candidates from being elected.[5]

Success in overcoming these vote-dilution devices was critical to the goal of equal political participation for black voters. Without victory over these devices, all prior successes—the striking down of the white primary, the literacy tests, and the poll tax—would be negated. Black voters would be able to register and vote, but they would be unable to elect candidates of their choice who would be accountable to them on election day.

Initially, the Supreme Court was unprepared to cope with these new pressures on the right to vote and in 1967 rejected a constitutional challenge to the racial gerrymandering of Mississippi's five congressional districts.[6] As a result, black voters were denied the opportunity to elect a black member of Congress for another twenty years. Finally, after additional litigation under the Voting Rights Act, Mike Espy, a black lawyer from Yazoo City, was elected to the U.S. House of Representatives in 1986 from a reconstituted Delta congressional district.[7]

Similarly, the federal courts resisted black voters' claims that at-large legislative elections diluted black voting strength. Black voters were denied all but token representation in the Mississippi legislature: from 1967 to 1975, only one black was elected out of a total of 174 legislators; from 1975 to 1979, there were four black legislators out of 174. Legislative reapportionment litigation, including nine trips to the Supreme Court, went on for fourteen years until seventeen black state legislators were elected from single-member districts in the 1979 state legislative elections.[8]

Two Supreme Court decisions have been critical to overcoming this second generation of disfranchising devices. In 1969 in the case of *Allen* v. *State Board of Elections*,[9] which involved three Mississippi cases litigated by the Lawyers' Constitutional Defense Committee and the Lawyers' Committee for Civil Rights under Law, the U.S. Supreme Court ruled that all voting law changes that diluted the effectiveness of black votes must be submitted for federal preclearance pursuant to Section 5 of the Voting Rights Act. The Court ruled that preclearance is required even if the voting law changes did not directly interfere with the right to register or cast a ballot. In the case challenging the Mississippi legislature's statute authorizing changes to at-large county supervisor elections, the Court ruled: "This type of change could . . . nullify [black voters'] ability to elect the candidate of their choice just as would prohibiting some of them from voting."[10] The Supreme Court, for the first time in a case raising actual racial discrimination claims, recognized that the right of black citizens to vote can be affected as much by vote dilution as by vote denial. This recognition makes the Supreme Court's decision in *Allen* v. *State Board of Elections* the *Brown* v. *Board of Education* of voting rights.

The *Allen* decision was of critical importance to black political advancement in the South both because it found that vote dilution could violate the Voting Rights Act and because it expanded the protections of the preclearance requirement of Section 5. States and localities covered by Section 5 of the Voting Rights Act were compelled to submit any and all voting law changes, no matter how minor, either to the Justice Department or to the federal district court in Washington, D.C., before implementation. Since 1969 the Justice Department has lodged Section 5 objections to more than 2,000 voting law changes in the South, including congressional redistricting and legislative reapportionment plans in every covered state.[11]

The second landmark U.S. Supreme Court decision in the voting rights area was the *White* v. *Regester* decision of 1973, in which the Supreme Court ruled that at-large legislative districts in Texas were unconstitutional.[12] In *White* v. *Regester*, the Supreme Court established the principle of minority vote dilution, recognized in the *Allen* decision, as a constitutional prohibition. The Court held that the Fourteenth Amendment prohibits methods of election that deny minority voters an equal opportunity "to participate in the political processes and to elect legislators of their choice."[13] The Supreme Court's decision in *White* v. *Regester* was critical because some structural devices that dilute minority voting strength are not subject to federal preclearance under Section 5 of the Voting Rights Act, either because they were adopted before the Voting Rights Act became law or because they are used in states not covered by Section 5. For example, Jackson, Mississippi, adopted at-large city council elections in 1912. After 1965, citywide voting prevented black voters in Jackson from electing candidates of their choice to the city council, but Jackson's at-large voting system was not subject to Section 5 preclearance because it was adopted before 1965. Black voters seeking relief therefore were required to file a constitutional challenge to Jackson's at-large city council election system and to litigate their case under the *White* v. *Regester* standard.[14]

From 1973 to 1980 the *White* v. *Regester* decision was the chief vehicle for constitutional challenges to discriminatory at-large elections and racial gerrymandering of district lines not covered by Section 5. Scores of cases were filed and won. The usefulness of *White* v. *Regester* was severely undermined in 1980, however, when the Supreme Court in *City of Mobile* v. *Bolden* reinterpreted the

Fourteenth Amendment standard to require proof of discriminatory intent.[15] As a result, court rulings that had invalidated discriminatory methods of election under *White* v. *Regester* were reversed because of the failure to prove discriminatory intent. Discriminatory intent is very difficult to prove. Public officials do not often make public statements exhibiting a discriminatory intent, and actions taken for a discriminatory intent frequently can be disguised by a nondiscriminatory justification. Moreover, white federal judges usually are unwilling to brand local public officials as racists to grant relief to black litigants. These factors, among others, prompted Congress in 1982 to amend Section 2 of the Voting Rights Act to restore the *White* v. *Regester* standard as the statutory standard for determining violations of the Voting Rights Act. Under this 1982 amendment, Section 2 now prohibits any voting law or practice that results in discrimination, regardless of its intent.[16]

Section 2 of the Voting Rights Act, as amended, has been phenomenally successful. The Justice Department estimates that since 1982 more than 1,300 jurisdictions have changed their methods of electing officials in response to litigation or the threat of litigation under Section 2.[17] Section 2 has been applied in the South and throughout the nation to strike down discriminatory congressional redistricting, at-large elections for state legislators, at-large city council elections in northern cities, at-large state judicial elections, and discriminatory voter registration procedures that limit black citizens' opportunities to register to vote.[18]

What impact have these developments had on Mississippi, the test case of progress in equal rights? The voting rights litigation of the 1970s and 1980s has removed many of the barriers to black political participation and has spurred black political mobilization. As a result, Ray Mabus, a progressive young governor, was elected in 1987 with less than half of the white vote but with 90 percent of the black vote.[19] By January 1990 Mississippi had 669 black elected officials, including a member of Congress, a state supreme court justice, 22 state legislators, 68 county supervisors, and almost 300 city council members.[20] Mary King, a former civil rights worker in Mississippi and author of *Freedom Song, A Personal Story of the 1960's Civil Rights Movement*, noted in a 1987 *New York Times* interview:

> People often ask me if I believe any progress has really been made in civil rights. . . . I tell them that it may have taken 23 years, but a black lawyer, Mike Espy, was elected last fall to Congress from a majority black district in the Mississippi delta. Back in 1964 those black counties didn't have a single black registered voter.[21]

TABLE 7.1
Local Expenditures per Pupil in Mississippi, 1961–62 (dollars)

County District	White	Negro
Humphreys	116.62	15.35
Coaboms	139.33	12.74
Sunflower	127.36	11.49
North Panola Consolidated	104.28	1.76
Leflore	175.38	9.52
Yazoo	245.55	2.92
West Tallahatchie	141.95	13.47

Source: U.S. Commission on Civil Rights, Voting in Mississippi (Washington, D.C.: Government Printing Office, 1965), 45.

This is not to say that all barriers to equal black participation in the electoral process have been removed; they have not. The percentage of black elected officials nationwide remains small as compared with the total of all elected officials.[22] Throughout the South and in other parts of the country, the equal voting rights of black citizens continue to be denied by discriminatory redistricting, at-large elections, barriers to black voter registration, and other discriminatory devices that limit black voting influence.

EDUCATION

There can be no doubt that racial segregation in education was extremely damaging to both black and white schoolchildren in Mississippi. Black schoolchildren frequently attended inadequate school facilities in which they were educated by poorly trained teachers. Years after the Brown decision, the per pupil expenditures of heavily black counties show shocking disparities between white and black children (see Table 7.1).[23] Racially segregated schools produced attitudes of racial inferiority in some black students and attitudes of racial superiority in white students.

Census statistics for 1960 show the damaging impact this system had on black citizens in Mississippi. Half of the black population had completed only six years of school or less, and more than 32,000 black adults had no formal education at all. By comparison, more than half of all white adults had completed eleven or more years of education. Only 7.6 percent of the black population were high school graduates, as compared with almost 42 percent of adult white Mississippians.

Of all the Southern states, Mississippi was the last to begin complying with the *Brown* decision, and this was under the force of Fourteenth Amendment litigation. Petitions circulated throughout the state by the NAACP and other groups after 1954 failed to produce any results. The first school desegregation lawsuits were not filed until 1963 and these were entered against only five school districts. By the 1964–65 school year, only 57 of Mississippi's 280,000 black schoolchildren attended formerly all-white schools. One year later, the overall desegregation rate for Mississippi stood at 0.02 percent—the lowest in the South.[24]

Most of Mississippi's school districts were desegregated by federal court litigation—sixty-two school desegregation lawsuits were litigated in Mississippi by the Department of Justice and the NAACP Legal Defense and Educational Fund, Inc. (LDF), and forty-two districts were desegregated by the Department of Health, Education, and Welfare (HEW) under the threat of loss of federal funds.[25]

As in other Southern states, the school desegregation process in Mississippi developed in two stages, the "freedom-of-choice" stage and the "school-integration" stage. Under court orders to desegregate or under HEW mandates, all Mississippi school districts initially adopted freedom-of-choice school desegregation plans under which students theoretically were given the opportunity to choose which school to attend. In practice, this meant that black students could obtain a desegregated education only by transferring to the white schools. Frequently, these freedom-of-choice plans began with the first grade and proceeded one grade a year for each succeeding school year.

Little school desegregation actually was accomplished under this system. Freedom of choice placed the burden of desegregation on black parents and schoolchildren. School officials erected numerous administrative barriers to black students transferring to white schools. Moreover, black families choosing to send their children to the white schools suffered from Ku Klux Klan terrorism and violence, harassment of black children in school by white students and teachers, and economic reprisals, including eviction from their homes and loss of credit and jobs. Freedom-of-choice plans generally left the black schools all black, and resulted in very little integration of the white schools.[26]

In *Green v. School Board of New Kent County*, a Virginia case decided in 1968, the U.S. Supreme Court held that freedom of choice plans were constitutionally inadequate when they failed to achieve full school desegregation.[27] Justice Department and LDF attorneys responded by filing motions in twenty-three pending cases involving a total of thirty-three school districts in the U.S. District Court for the Southern District of Mississippi seeking new, more effective desegregation plans. When the district court denied any relief, the U.S. Court of Appeals for the Fifth Circuit reversed and ordered that new plans should be implemented by September 1969 for the 1969–70 school year. The Fifth Circuit found that under freedom of choice not a single white child attended a Negro school in any of the districts, the percentage of Negro children attending white schools ranged from zero to sixteen percent, there was only token faculty integration, and school activities continued substantially segregated.[28]

Under political pressure from Mississippi Senator John Stennis, the Nixon administration then switched sides, and in August 1969, the Justice Department asked the Fifth Circuit for a one-year delay in implementing school desegregation plans that already had been approved by HEW's technical assistance staff. The Fifth Circuit granted the Justice Department's request for further delay. The LDF attorneys then sought relief from the Supreme Court, and the Court in October reversed the Fifth Circuit's decision. In *Alexander* v. *Holmes County Board of Education* the justices ruled that "continued operation of segregated schools under a standard of allowing 'all deliberate speed' for desegregation is no longer constitutionally permissible. . . . [T]he obligation of every school district is to terminate dual school systems at once and to operate now and hereafter only unitary schools."[29] The *Alexander* decision marks an important turning point in the school desegregation effort. As scholar Gary Orfield noted, "the Court declared that the time for gradualism was over, and that southern districts must correct violations immediately."[30]

Nine days later, the Fifth Circuit ordered all thirty school districts to begin implementing the HEW plans in December 1969, in the middle of the 1969–70 school year.[31] The Fifth Circuit's decision was unprecedented. Never before had an appeals court ordered simultaneous desegregation of thirty school districts in the middle of a school year, particularly over the opposition of the executive branch.[32] Within ten months, 146 of Mississippi's 148 school districts had been forced to abandon ineffective freedom-of-choice plans and to adopt new desegregation plans that revised attendance boundaries and employed a variety of remedies, including zoning, pairing, and busing, to achieve fully integrated school systems.

The school desegregation litigation of the 1960s and early 1970s dismantled the de jure dual, racially segregated school systems in Mississippi and generally eliminated the one-race schools and the one-race faculties. This litigation, however, did not completely eliminate racial segregation in the schools. By 1980 only 23.6 percent of the black students were in schools that were 90 to 100 percent black.[33] By 1987, the percentage of black students attending 90 to 100 percent black schools increased to 38.7 percent.[34] The level of actual integration experienced by black schoolchildren has been mitigated by "white flight" to all-white private academies, ability grouping, tracking, and other systems that generally separate white and black students.

Data from Mississippi confirm national studies that school desegregation has had positive benefits. School desegregation has increased the educational achievement of black students and has promoted attitudes of racial tolerance among Mississippi whites.[35] By 1981, 69 percent of white Mississippians surveyed expressed support for public school integration.[36]

In the two decades of school desegregation from 1960 to 1980, federal and state funding for education increased, education and teaching methods were reformed, and teacher qualifications were increased. Mississippi also became more urbanized and industrialized. The changes that occurred during this period, a major one being school desegregation, have produced substantial improvements in educational attainment among black people in Mississippi. According to census statistics, the median educational attainment for blacks in 1980 was 9.4 years of schooling, compared with six years in 1960. By 1980, 33 percent of all black adults were high school graduates, compared with only 7.6 percent in 1960, and 60 percent of all young black adults eighteen to twenty-four years of age had completed high school.[37]

EMPLOYMENT

The enactment of Title VII of the Civil Rights Act of 1964, which outlawed racial discrimination in employment by private companies, marks the beginning of the desegregation of the Mississippi work force. Enforcement efforts by the Equal Employment Opportunity Commission, which opened an office in Jackson in the early 1970s, and Title VII lawsuits have gone far to open up employment opportunities for black people across the state. However, the Civil Rights Act of 1964 did not prohibit racial discrimination in employment by state and local governmental agencies until 1972. Before 1972, employment discrimination cases against governmental agencies had to be filed under the Fourteenth Amendment and general federal civil rights law (42 U.S.C.). Constitutional litigation in Mississippi contributed significantly to the development of national legal standards for job discrimination cases.

In May 1970, in an incident widely known as the "Jackson State massacre," two young black men were shot and killed and twelve young black people were seriously wounded when officers of the all-white Mississippi Highway

Patrol without provocation fired a twenty-nine-second barrage of gunfire into a crowd of black students and neighborhood residents at Jackson State University.[38] One of the outcomes of the "Jackson State massacre" was the filing of an employment discrimination lawsuit against the Highway Patrol on behalf of two black men who had been denied application forms for patrol officer positions. This case, *Morros v. Crisler,* and another case, *Wade v. Mississippi Cooperative Extension Service,* were the first two state government employment discrimination cases filed in Mississippi's recent history.

Since 1938, when the Highway Patrol was formed, it had never employed a black person as a sworn officer, and the only blacks it had ever hired were janitors and cooks at its training academy. After a trial, the district court found that this constituted a pattern and practice of racial discrimination in employment that violated the Fourteenth Amendment, although "unintentional," and entered a court order prohibiting racial discrimination in hiring and terms and conditions of employment. The district judge refused, however, to order any hiring quotas or any other form of affirmative hiring relief.[39]

In the next two years, the Highway Patrol hired ninety-one whites as patrol officers but only five blacks (and a sixth black recruit in training school). One of the reasons for this low black hiring rate was that after the district court's injunction was entered, the patrol for the first time adopted a hiring examination, the Army General Classification Test, a test that had been developed by the army during World War II for making job assignments, not for screening out applicants. During the two years in which it was administered by the patrol, 299 of the 449 whites who took the test received passing scores (a pass rate of 66.6 percent), while only 25 of the 194 black applicants passed (a pass rate of 12.9 percent).

Plaintiffs appealed the district court's refusal to grant more relief. The Fifth Circuit Court of Appeals sitting en banc ruled that the patrol's hiring and testing statistics since 1971 showed that the district court's order was insufficient to eliminate the effects of past racial discrimination. The Fifth Circuit ordered additional recruitment measures, reexamination of the patrol's hiring criteria, and "some affirmative hiring relief," which could take the form of *"temporary* one-to-one or one-to-two (white-black) hiring, the creation of hiring pools, or a freeze on white hiring, or any other form of affirmative hiring relief until the Patrol is effectively integrated."[40] Circuit Judge J. P. Coleman, in his dissent, suggested that the patrol should be ordered to hire all minimally qualified black applicants.[41]

The Fifth Circuit's opinion in *Morrow v. Crisler* had a significant impact on employment discrimination litigation in the South. The *Morrow* case was one of the first cases—and certainly the first against a governmental agency—in which the Fifth Circuit had ordered quotas or other affirmative hiring relief to eliminate the effects of past discrimination.

Subsequent developments have proven the effectiveness of race-conscious remedies in employment discrimination cases. After further hearings, the district court ordered the patrol to revise its recruitment and testing procedures and to hire all black applicants who met the minimum nondiscriminatory qualifications.[42] The first recruit training class held after the district court's new order was three-quarter's black, and since then training classes have been one-third to one-half black or more. As of 1988, 20 percent of the patrol's 305 troopers were black and have included a black troop commander (captain), a black personnel officer (captain), and two blacks serving as assistant inspectors in charge of two of the patrol's nine districts.[43]

The second constitutional employment discrimination case filed, *Wade* v. *Mississippi Cooperative Extension Service*, had a similar history. The district court found unlawful racial discrimination in hiring, promotions, job assignments, and other terms and conditions of employment, and prohibited further discrimination. Like the district court in the highway patrol case, however, the court refused to order any affirmative hiring relief.[44] Four years later, in 1978, when it was presented with evidence that its "don't-discriminate" decree had proven to be ineffective, the district court ordered, subject to the availability of qualified applicants, one black hired for each white hired and one black promoted for each white promoted until the extension service was 20 percent black at all levels.[45]

Although court decrees requiring quota hiring and promotions and other forms of affirmative hiring relief have come under criticism, including attacks by the Reagan and Bush administrations, they were consistently affirmed by the Supreme Court when necessary to overcome the effects of past discrimination and to provide equal employment opportunities for minority citizens and women.[46] The history of constitutional employment discrimination litigation in Mississippi in the 1970s shows that this relief in many cases was necessary to overcome the numerous barriers employers can erect to prevent the hiring or promotion of qualified black employees even after the employers have been ordered to stop discriminating.

Employment discrimination litigation under the Fourteenth Amendment was severely curtailed when, in a 1976 District of Columbia job discrimination decision, *Washington* v. *Davis*, the Supreme Court held that the Fourteenth Amendment required proof of discriminatory intent.[47]

CONCLUSION

Once the mass protest movement of the 1960s succeeded in persuading Congress to pass the Civil Rights Act of 1964 and the Voting Rights Act of 1965, the civil rights movement was required once again to litigate in the federal courts to enforce the requirements of this legislation and to establish constitutional and statutory civil rights protections for black Americans. Protest demonstrations and grass-roots electoral activism in Mississippi simply were insufficient to overcome racial gerrymandering and at-large elections, rigidly segregated public schools, and an all-white Highway Patrol.

The constitutional-based civil rights litigation of the late 1960s and early 1970s responded to real human needs in Mississippi. Seth Ballard, a black community leader in Jefferson County, was prevented from running for county school superintendent when the Mississippi legislature abolished elections for the position; black parents in Jackson wanted a better education for their children; and Charlie Wade in Holmes County was fully qualified to be county agent but his county board of supervisors would not accept a black person in the position.

During this period, civil rights litigation dramatically altered the governmental, educational, and employment structures of Mississippi, and the impact of those changes is still being felt. What were the critical elements that gave rise to this litigation and led to those changes?

First, the changes could not have taken place if the black community leadership had not been alert to the discrimination to which black citizens were being subjected and persevering enough to carry through years of litigation and appeals to higher courts until success finally was achieved.

Second, lawyers needed the skills and legal talent to devise new legal strategies and to overcome scores of adverse decisions at the district court level in Mississippi from District Judge Harold Cox and his associates to win on appeal either to the Fifth Circuit or to the U.S. Supreme Court. That many of the landmark decisions came in Mississippi cases is no accident. Largely as a result of the Mississippi Freedom Summer of 1964 and the high level of civil rights work in the state, three national civil rights legal organizations—the NAACP Legal Defense Fund, the Lawyers Constitutional Defense Committee, and the Lawyers' Committee for Civil Rights under Law—established full-time, staffed offices in Jackson in 1964 and 1965. (In 1964 the National Lawyers Guild, a progressive legal organization, opened an office for a short period in Jackson, as well.) No other state in the South during this period had such a critical mass of outside legal talent based in the state to litigate such complex and expensive federal court lawsuits.

Third, federal judges had to be sensitive and responsive to the legal claims of black citizens. There is nothing in the language of the Fourteenth or Fifteenth Amendments that says black voters have a right to elect candidates of their choice to the Mississippi legislature in single-member legislative districts, that black schoolchildren have a right to be bused to desegregated schools in the middle of the school year, or that black men and women have a right to be state troopers. Each of these cases required the application of the general principles of the post–Civil War amendments to the specific facts of each case. In each case, there were court precedents that could be construed as pointing the other way. Success depended upon federal judges recognizing the validity of the arguments made on behalf of black litigants and responding to the fundamental injustice of racial discrimination.

Fourth, the success of much of this litigation depended upon the formulation of new legal remedies, such as the creation of 65 percent black supermajority election districts, cross-town busing, and racial hiring and promotion quotas. These remedies produced some hostility on the part of whites but were necessary to provide equity to black citizens. At first, most Southern federal judges were reluctant to impose these remedies but became convinced of their necessity when less effective measures failed. While these remedies remain somewhat controversial today, it is important to remember that they were not derived from some abstract notion of social engineering but emerged from the experience of scores of cases in which lesser solutions failed to eradicate the effects of past discrimination.

Despite the changes that have taken place, elements of the past persist in Mississippi. Voting in Mississippi elections remains racially polarized. Most white voters generally continue to refuse to vote for black candidates, regardless of qualifications. Openly racist rhetoric no longer prevails in political campaigns, but in some instances white voters continue to respond to the same messages in coded form.[48] Although the attitudes of most white Mississippians regarding integrated education have changed greatly, many of the all-white private schools begun in the 1960s to avoid public school desegregation are flourishing today. In the 1987 election in which Mississippi's current progressive governor, Ray Mabus, was elected, the voters finally repealed Mississippi's constitutional prohibition against interracial marriage in a statewide referendum. Nonetheless, 48 percent of the voters voted to retain the ban even though it had long been declared unconstitutional by the U.S. Supreme Court. The changes that have been achieved provide a firm basis for future progress. Whether these changes will continue in Mississippi and elsewhere in the South, or whether the society will regress, depends on the commitment by the courts and the federal government to the legal principles and legal remedies that have produced these changes. If this commitment becomes eroded and these remedies are lost, as appears to be happening, the progress in achieving racial justice that has been made thus far will be reversed. If that occurs, the promise of a living Constitution will remain unfulfilled.

NOTES

From 1968 to 1981 the author was an attorney in the Jackson, Mississippi, office of the Lawyers' Committee for Civil Rights under Law and was chief counsel of that office from 1976 to 1981. Parts of this chapter, particularly the section on voting, are adapted from the author's book, *Black Votes Count: Political Empowerment in Mississippi After 1965* (Chapel Hill: University of North Carolina Press, 1990). The views expressed herein are solely those of the author and do not necessarily reflect those of the Lawyers' Committee for Civil Rights under Law.

1. Anthony Lewis and the New York Times, *Portrait of a Decade: The Second American Revolution* (New York: Random House, 1964), 204.

2. H. R. Rept. 439, 89th Cong., 1st sess. (1965), reprinted in U.S. Code Cong. & Ad. News 2437 (1965).

3. David Garrow, *Protest at Selma: Martin Luther King, Jr., and the Voting Rights Act of 1965* (New Haven, Conn.: Yale University Press, 1978), 84.

4. U.S. Commission on Civil Rights, *Political Participation* (Washington: Government Printing Office, 1968), 12–13.

5. U.S. Commission on Civil Rights, *Political Participation*, chaps. 1 and 2.

6. *Connor v. Johnson*, 386 U.S. 483 (1967), affirming, 279 F. Supp. 619 (S.D. Miss. 1966) (three-judge court).

7. See Frank R. Parker, "The Mississippi Congressional Redistricting Case: A Case Study in Minority Vote Dilution," *Howard Law Journal* 28 (1985): 397–415.

8. See *Connor v. Coleman*, 440 U.S. 612, 614–24 (1979).

9. 393 U.S. 544 (1969).

10. 393 U.S. at 569.

11. U.S. Department of Justice, Voting Section, Civil Rights Division, *Number of Changes to Which Objections Have Been Interposed by State and Year, 1965–December 31, 1987; Complete Listing of Objections Pursuant to Section 5 of the Voting Rights Act of 1965,* April 30, 1988.

12. 412 U.S. 755 (1973).

13. 412 U.S. at 766.

14. Even then, black voters were not successful in challenging at-large city council elections, particularly after the Supreme Court's 1980 decision in *City of Mobile v. Bolden*, discussed below. See *Kirksey v. City of Jackson*, 461 F. Supp. 1282 (S.D. Miss. 1978), vacated and remanded, 625 F.2d 21 (5th Cir. 1980), on remand, 506 F. Supp. 491 (S.D. Miss. 1981), aff'd, 663 F.2d 659 (5th Cir. 1981). Black voters were not successful in eliminating at-large elections until after the 1982 amendment to Section 2 of the Voting Rights Act. *Kirksey v. Danks*, 608 F. Supp. 1448 (S.D. Miss. 1985).

15. 446 U.S. 55 (1980).

16. See Frank R. Parker, "The 'Results' Test of Section 2 of the Voting Rights Act: Abandoning the Intent Standard," *Virginia Law Review* 69 (May 1983): 715–64.

17. U.S. Department of Justice, Civil Rights Division, *Enforcing the Law* (Washington: Government Printing Office, 1987), Voting Rights, 2.

18. See, for example, *Chisom v. Roemer*, 115 L.Ed. 2d 348 (1991); *Houston Lawyers' Association v. Attorney General of Texas*, 115 L.Ed. 2d 379 (1991) (at-large judicial elections); *Thornburg v. Gingles, State Chapter, Operation PUSH v. Mabus*, 932 F.2d 400 (5th Cir. 1991) (discriminatory voter registration procedures); *Jordan v. Winter*, 604 F. Supp. 807 (N.D. Miss. 1984) (three-judge court), aff'd mem., 469 U.S. 1002 (1984) (congressional redistricting); *McNeil v. City of Springfield*, 658 F. Supp. 1015 (C.D. Ill. 1987) (northern at-large city council elections).

19. Peter J. Boyer, "The Yuppies of Mississippi; How They Took the Statehouse," *New York Times* Magazine (February 28, 1988), 24, 40.

20. Joint Center for Political and Economic Studies, *Black Elected Officials: A National Roster* (Washington, D.C.: Joint Center for Political and Economic Studies Press, 1990).

21. Quoted in Barbara Gamarekin, "One Woman's Chronicle of the Civil Rights Struggle," *New York Times*, August 31, 1987.

22. Joint Center for Political and Economic Studies, *Black Elected Officials*, ix.

23. In 1950 Mississippi employed more than 700 black teachers who had not completed high school, although every white teacher was at least a high school graduate. In the 1963–64 school year, there were more than 1,900 white teachers with graduate degrees, but fewer than 500 black teachers had graduate degrees. U.S. Commission on Civil Rights, *Voting in Mississippi* (Washington, D.C.: Government Printing Office, 1965), 44–45.

24. Southern Education Reporting Service, *Statistical Summary, State by State, of School Segregation-Desegregation in the Southern and Border Area from 1954 to the Present* (Nashville, Tenn., 1967), 43.

25. Melvyn R. Leventhal, *Agencies Responsible for Desegregation of Mississippi School Districts* (n.d.), photocopy.

26. U.S. Commission on Civil Rights, *Southern School Desegregation, 1966–67* (Washington, D.C.: Government Printing Office, 1967), 47–69, 94.

27. 391 U.S. 430 (1968).

28. *United States v. Hinds County School Board*, 417 F.2d 852 (5th Cir. 1969).

29. 396 U.S. 19, 20 (1969).

30. Gary Orfield, *Public School Desegregation in the United States, 1968–1980* (Washington: Joint Center for Political Studies, 1983), 1.

31. *United States v. Hinds County School Board*, 423 F.2d 1264 (5th Cir. 1969).

32. Luther Munford, "Black Gravity: Desegregation in 30 Mississippi School Districts" (unpublished senior thesis, Princeton University, 1971), 20–21.

33. Orfield, *Public School Desegregation*, 6, Appendix A.

34. "Across the USA: News from Every State," *USA Today*, July 28, 1987.

35. Robert B. Frary and Thomas M. Goolsby, "Achievement of Integrated and Segregated Negro and White First Graders in a Southern City," *Integrated Education* 8 (July-August 1970): 48–55; Glenn Abney, "Legislating Morality; Attitude Change and Desegregation in Mississippi," *Urban Education* 11 (October 1976): 336 et seq.

36. Stephen D. Shaffer, "A Traditionalist Political Culture in Transition: The Case of Mississippi," paper delivered at the 1987 annual meeting of the American Political Science Association, Chicago, 1987, Figure 1.

37. U.S. Bureau of the Census, *1980 Census of Population: General Social and Economic Characteristics, Mississippi*, PC80-C26 (Washington, D.C.: Government Printing Office, 1983).

38. A lawsuit for damages was unsuccessful, among other things, because of the difficulty of determining who shot whom. See *Burton v. Waller*, 502 F.2d 1261 (5th Cir. 1974), cert. denied, 420 U.S. 964 (1975).

39. *Morrow v. Crisler*, 4 CCH Employment Practices Decisions 7541, 7563 (S.D. Miss. 1971).

40. *Morrow v. Crisler*, 491 F.2d 1053, 1056 (5th Cir. 1974) (en banc).

41. 491 F.2d at 1061–64.

42. *Morrow v. Dillard*, 412 F. Supp. 494, 502–04 (S.D. Miss. 1976).

43. Patrol's Semi-Annual Report of April 30, 1988.

44. *Wade v. Mississippi Cooperative Extension Service*, 372 F. Supp. 126 (N.D. Miss. 1974), aff'd, 528 F.2d 508 (5th Cir. 1976).

45. *Wade v. Mississippi Cooperative Extension Service*, Civil No. EC70-29-K (N.D. Miss. Revised Supplemental Order of August 11, 1978).

46. See, for example, *Johnson v. Transportation Agency*, 480 U.S. 616 (1987) (affirmative action plan to hire women held not to violate Title VII of the Civil Rights Act of 1964); *United States v. Paradise*, 480 U.S. 149 (1987) (upholding quota hiring plan to increase the number of black Alabama Highway Patrol officers); *Sheet Metal Workers v. Equal Employment Opportunity Commission*, 478 U.S. 421 (1986) (upholding affirmative action plan to hire nonwhites); but see, *Wygant v. Jackson Board of Education*, 476 U.S. 267 (1986) (teacher layoff provisions favoring retention of minorities over more experienced whites held to violate Fourteenth Amendment).

47. 426 U.S. 229 (1976).

48. See, for example, Parker, "The Mississippi Congressional Redistricting Case," 408.

PART II

RACE AND THE POLITICS OF CONSTITUTIONAL CHANGE

THE EXECUTIVE AND THE CONGRESS

MATTHEW HOLDEN, JR.

RACE AND CONSTITUTIONAL CHANGE IN THE TWENTIETH CENTURY

THE ROLE OF THE EXECUTIVE

Presidential action ("leadership") is often needed to introduce decisions into the "living Constitution." At such times, the president may acquire "license systematically to intervene in or to preempt the customary spheres of other institutions—private and public—thereby effecting national actions that could not otherwise be effected easily or at all."[1] This may happen under conditions of war, for example, as it did when Abraham Lincoln issued the Emancipation Proclamation of 1863 to deal with the inherited social situation of chattel slavery.[2] Since there is no inequality greater than that between master and slave, there could be no other presidential action remotely comparable to the termination of slavery.

This model remains alive in some imaginations. In the vigorous days of the civil rights movement in the early 1960s, a few scholars adopted the symbolism of a "second Emancipation Proclamation."[3] Their theme was that the president had sufficient law-making power to cope with the urgent needs of the nation.[4]

This chapter examines the extent, manner, and effect of executive decision making in matters pertaining to race and constitutional change in the twentieth century. As the following paragraphs show, whether presidents have intervened in or abstained from such issues has depended primarily on *the interest of groups in the presidential entourage, membership of the presidential coalition, and the electoral or support base behind the executive.* My interpretation is based upon a political theory of constitutions.[5] Whereas most discussions of "constitutions" begin with the idea of "law, and often . . . with philosophical or moral 'ideals,'" this discussion focuses on the organization of power in human groups. That is what I mean by a "political" theory of constitutions.

THE REAL CONSTITUTION

In our popular culture, in the teachings of law schools, and often in the pronouncements of our courts, the Supreme Court is taken as the "final" interpreter of what the Constitution means. However, it is important to recognize that the president (as well as the Congress, and even arguably the bureaucracy, neither of which is discussed here) plays a vital role in what the Constitution "does."[6] In political theory, the notion that "the Constitution protects the rights" of weaker parties, for example, is considered incomplete. Although the words of written constitutions may indicate that, if applied logically, they would protect weaker parties, such words do not ring true if there are no strong parties prepared to sustain the rights claimed by the weaker parties. Ideas, ideals, and values are not to be discounted; but they have no force in politics unless they respond to some "interest," in the sense of need.[7] Interests in society will conflict, of course, and in politics that conflict will sometimes end with a negotiated settlement, but more often than not the result will be a victory on one side and a defeat on the other. The function of governmental decision making is to resolve these conflicts of interest.[8]

From this perspective, constitutions in the most general sense stipulate which members of the political community are entitled to all available measures of deference and material benefit, which members can claim only partial benefits, which strangers to that community are to be received on favorable terms, which subjects are to be ruled, and which are mere resources to be used.[9]

The "constitution is the *behavior of the dominant groups* manifest in the operation of the [political system]."[10] The behavior of the dominant groups—"the constitution of usage . . . and not of text alone"—is an agreement among the powerful.[11] It deals with how the powerful will act toward each other, as well as which weaker parties they will reinforce in the distribution of constitutional benefits, and which they will ignore or override.[12] The American Constitution "of usage," the real Constitution," has reflected a racial hierarchy. The dominant group, defining itself mystically as "the white race," has sought to achieve, maintain, and reinforce an hegemony or hierarchy over other persons and groups defined as not white.[13]

Decisions must be made in the present about how to act in the future. The problems requiring a decision, however, are the outcome of past choices; they can be described as the inherited social situation. Executive decision making in matters of race and constitutional change is therefore concerned with the inherited social situation. The central figure involved in executive decision making in the United States—though not the only one—is the president.

THE CONTEXT OF PRESIDENTIAL DECISION MAKING

The office of president bestows enormous prestige on the individual holding it, and at times this individual can exercise extraordinary power. The question of interest here is how the holder of that office uses, or tries to use, that power. To understand presidential decision making, we must examine the president's formal authority and scope of power. Political scientists often begin so, and lawyers almost always begin so. It is also possible to begin with "motivation," with the president's "values" or the president's "sincerity." Because the personal role of each president is important in America, we may be compelled to ask about the president's attitude toward race. The presumption may sometimes be that action is controlled by these personal attitudes. It is common, and by no means foolish, to believe that attitudes motivate decisions.[14]

The historian's methodological canon appears to be that the attitudes of individual presidents can be inferred from the words they use.[15] But what words? The official words or the unofficial words? Harry Truman, for example, made civil rights a page-one political issue, no doubt calculating that it served his own political agenda. In doing so, he changed presidential political habits for the next quarter century: Kennedy and Johnson broadened and deepened the channel he had cut. Yet in private Truman used the hostile and contemptuous words for blacks that would be expected from virtually any white Missourian of his generation. It would be worthwhile, had we the time and the data, to compare the public and private attitudes of Theodore Roosevelt and Taft, Harding, Coolidge, Hoover, and of all the presidents who followed them.

If presidents were entirely clear-minded, language would still be used, as other people use it, to gain social acceptance with the audience. Their words, too, unwittingly express fear, hope, anger, hostility, delusive self-satisfaction, and all the other attitudes that might make us think we could arrive at a better understanding if we were psychoanalysts. The words that presidents choose are mainly from others. The objective of nearly every other person is to enter in the mind of the presidential person. The contest for the mind of the president is part of the biopsychological pressure that is inherent in the presidential role.[16] Indeed, the president might be regarded as a coalition, and not simply as a person.

Nevertheless, the president is a figure of authority imbued with "executive power" by Article II of the Constitution. Article I names him commander-in-chief of the armed forces, puts him in charge of appointing executive officers and judges, and charges him with taking "care that the laws be faithfully executed" and with advising Congress on the State of the Union. According to some, there resides in the presidency the residues of a "royal prerogative," which survived the American Revolution.[17] In constitutional law and statutes, nearly three hundred pages are devoted to elaborating presidential authority.[18]

In practice, the president is both the leader of a political party and the center of a political coalition whose policy decisions often move beyond party lines. Furthermore, today the president is also the presumptive leader of the legislative process, the implication being that he will have a legislative program and that he should have the political skill and power to see that it is enacted. The administrative role of the president, though erratic and sometimes indirect, can also be significant, even though a good many decisions may be in the hands of the president's subordinates and the organizations over which they preside. That is why the executive is considered to be more than the holder of the office of president.[19] When an issue is important enough, the president may direct or encourage a certain course of action, as John F. Kennedy did with civil rights litigation. In such situations, the president may be obliged to bargain, overtly or implicitly, with civil servants who do not agree with his approach.[20] Or the president may act through politically chosen subordinates who then take it upon themselves to implement programs that the civil servants would not choose by themselves. In addition, the president is the symbol of national unity and as such has become highly visible through the medium of telecommunication. Another important role of the president is to articulate issues, and to mobilize public opinion on one side or another of those issues.[21]

Through these roles and the resources available to the president, the individual who holds that office can exert great influence on what people think and can wield enough power to block actions of Congress or the Supreme Court or to carry out actions that Congress or the Court might wish to proscribe. Considerable controversy has surrounded presidential claims to broad authority, often to authority inherent in the office. Particularly in connection with war and national security, but also in the realm of economics, presidential claims have contributed substantively to the meaning of the real constitution.[22] Indeed, war and economics have been two great sources of strain in the U.S. constitutional system. Another has been race, on which even the most adventurous presidents have generally been cautious about making claims to authority. The question of presidential authority was raised in 1961–62 when President Kennedy equivocated on his role in broad civil rights policy. The concept of presidential discretion was apparently viewed with caution, even by the civil rights interests that advanced it. So broad a view had not yet been accepted in policy making except, possibly when arguments of national security were mixed with racial animus and economic interest to secure the relocation of Japanese Americans from the California coast after the attack on Pearl Harbor.[23]

RACIAL STRATIFICATION: EXECUTIVE RETREATS

The Emancipation Proclamation, as mentioned earlier, was the most decisive demonstration ever of presidential power in the constitutional system. Subsequently, executive decision making retreated from the task of achieving effective, and not merely formal, freedom for the slaves of the country. The Civil War, as confirmed by the emancipation, turned racial stratification into an issue that had not existed before. Was white over black to be the organizing principle for all aspects of life? Those who accepted Chief Justice Roger B. Taney's doctrine as expressed in the 1857 *Dred Scott* opinion (19 Howard 393) would have said there was no issue. To them, the simple answer was "yes." Unquestionably, racism was intense in the North. But Justice Benjamin R. Curtis's dissent argued that Taney was wrong in law and history. Nonetheless, there appeared little to discuss. The issue was imperatively transformed into a constitutional problem, now that slaves were legally freed. The issue was national because its resolution rested in the Constitution. But it was located in the South, simply because it had to be made real in the lives of the freed blacks. Under what real, in contrast to merely formal, conditions would they live?

The executive retreated from the defense of black rights, yielding to a social situation in which there was no doubt. By the end of the nineteenth century, the issue was closed. The inherited social situation of the 1960s was the indirect result—the "great grandchild"—of executive retreats in the nineteenth century. The executive did not stop, or the retreats take full effect, all at once. Andrew Johnson's escape negated the executive role. The Department of Justice seems to have been the main vehicle for enforcing civil rights in the nineteenth century.[24] In 1876, Attorney General Alphonso Taft issued instructions to U.S. marshals as "the chief executive officer in [their] district."[25] Those instructions covered a broad charge:

> In elections at which members of the House of Representatives are chosen, which by law include elections at which the electors for President and Vice President are appointed, the United States secure voters against whatever in general hinders or prevents them from a free exercise of the elective franchise, extending that care alike to *the registration lists, the act of voting,* and *the personal freedom and security of the voter at all times as well as against violence on account of any vote that he may intend to give as against conspiracy because of any that he may already have given.*[26]

The attorney general instructed the marshals on their authority to summon a posse comitatus and to take other action related to the election process. Correlative instructions were issued to the United States attorneys.[27] The Hayes-Tilden settlement of 1877 and the early removal of federal troops from the South did not mean that U.S. attorneys and marshals abandoned their efforts. There was substantial effort to use the Reconstruction statutes and policies well into the 1880s, arguably into the 1890s.[28] Nonetheless, there was an off-and-on ratcheting downward, similar to the ratcheting downward that occurred in denazification and in the military government in Japan after 1945.[29] From the 1890s, the Department of Justice had no significant role, with the exception to some degree of peonage cases in the early 1900s.[30]

As a result of the executive retreat, a new political order based upon white violence came into being. The white South kept its arms, revived its old network of slave "patrolers," adapted its four years of military discipline to the current situation, and demonstrated its capacity for massacre.[31] All other explanations of black political weakness in the South are *trivial compared with white violence, from which blacks had no effective defense.* The process is revealed in the extreme at Colfax, in Grant Parish, Louisiana, in 1873. In Grant Parish, the sheriff, chosen by the governor, had convened a posse comitatus in an intense local struggle. At the time, a plantation warehouse was serving as a courthouse.[32] The courthouse was defended by the posse, by black men, some of whom were Union veterans. Local whites, in possession of artillery field pieces, conquered the courthouse. The victors killed fifty-two men of the posse, chiefly by executing them in the night, two by two.

Simple arithmetic tells the story. There was a massacre. In the Grant population of about 5,000 (4,816 in the 1870 census), fifty-two were killed. The resultant Supreme Court case is designated *U.S.* v. *Cruikshank*.[33] In this case, the U.S. attorney got one Cruikshank convicted in federal court on grounds of violating the civil rights of the persons who had been killed. Justice Joseph P. Bradley sat with the district judge in the trial in New Orleans. Bradley wrote the opinion on appeal. According to William A. Dunning, "No circumstance was lacking that could appeal to the sympathy of the judges for the misguided freedmen."[34] The Court had no grounds for ignoring the social facts. In straining to invalidate the convictions, the Court even said that the indictments had not stated that these persons were killed because they were black.[35] As Dunning says, "the court coldly declared that it was not the duty or the right of the United States government to protect its citizens against their fellow citizens; that was the function of the state governments."[36]

If the Court could so reason in this case, where the men killed were a body acting under official instructions, what could be expected in other, less extreme cases, where killing rates were, when one can find the details, sometimes as low as one in five thousand or as high as one in one thousand? The Court knew full well what it was doing.

At the same time, the Court sanctioned the refusal of state and local officials to accept ballots from blacks. It thus accepted racial stratification in the electorate. Having control of the electoral process meant having control over the choice of officials and thus over the use of force, money, or information. Violence reduced, but never eliminated, black participation in any state. A few black politicians continued to present themselves for Congress, for state legislatures, and even for county office in so tough a place as Bolivar County, Mississippi.[37] When office-holding was not possible, blacks sometimes tried to throw their support behind whichever white man seemed more favorable under the circumstances.[38]

White political elites were divided on what to do about black participation. Some wanted to protect such participation, either on philosophical or pragmatic grounds. Their fundamental concern was to defend an electorate that would support Republicans in the South. The majority in the North found it acceptable to tolerate exclusion. The most aggressive white leadership in the South was dedicated to exclusion. The chief support for blacks came from conservative Republicans in Congress. But Congress, with Democrats in control after 1875, retreated even more than the executive did. When the Republicans got control in 1890, they tried federal legislation (the Federal Elections Bill of 1890) to provide direct federal administration of elections for federal offices. The House passed the bill, but the Senate let it die. The same year Mississippi began the parade of Southern state constitutional reform, ruthlessly excising blacks from the electoral process.

Constitutional restructuring in the South, uninhibited by any federal obstacles, married public to private power, to ensure white over black in virtually every aspect of Southern life. This result had never before been achieved since 1865. White supremacy was the "grandchild" of the executive retreats of the nineteenth century. After so long and bitter a fight, it seems that white Southerners would tolerate no uncertainty. Candidates serious about being elected president and presidents serious about governing had to show that they accepted racial stratification (white supremacy) as policy. The twentieth century saw the United States turned into a semiapartheid society. It remained so at least until the time of Pearl Harbor. This semiapartheid society began to show the faintest cracks in the 1930s. The civil rights movement knocked the wall of discrimination down in the 1960s.

REVIVING RACIAL STRATIFICATION: UNWILLING EXECUTIVE ENTRY

By the time World War II began, stratification policy was, almost unbeknownst to most political leaders, already being revived. Since the depression, all presidents have had to confront racial stratification in some degree. Sometimes they behaved as if they were being guided by Hirschman's "principle of the hiding hand."[39] They shifted course, silently, as if disguising from themselves the logical implications of what they were doing.

Sometimes, presumably, the action of presidents was motivated by free choice. Sometimes, more clearly, it was a response to organizational demand from within the government. Most of all, if we accept the premises of this essay, it was motivated by external demand. The most important source of external demand was the civil rights movement. This movement was a long time coming, however, and the action of the executive was correspondingly sluggish.

The change in external demand has, in the main, been connected with three rights: the right to participate in choosing decision makers (or the right to vote); the right to be in the reservoir from which public officials are chosen; and the rights relating to substantive policy. The reopening of debate on all these issues was a product less of "movement" politics in the South than of conventional interest group politics in the North. Northern politicians were sensitive to the small, but marginal, block of votes in the North.

Altering the Rule of Participation:
The Executive and the Right to Vote

The idea of altering the rule of participation became attractive on a national scale because specific political groups acquired an interest in supporting it, and because it is the one right hard to deny in principle under American concepts of legitimacy. The executive did not purposely revive the issue, and, indeed, did not appear to be aware of it. But it was one vital element in the fight over the nomination of John J. Parker to the Supreme Court. Herbert Hoover had, no doubt, given no thought to reopening debate on this subject. Nor, in all likelihood, had Hoover ever heard of George White of North Carolina (a Republican), the last black congressman of the nineteenth century, who had delivered a peroration in the Committee of the Whole on January 29, 1901: "This, Mr. Chairman, is perhaps the [N]egroes' temporary farewell to the American Congress; but let me say, Phoenix-like he will rise up some day and come again."[40] Two decades later, John J. Parker was the Republican candidate for governor in North Carolina. "The participation of the Negro in politics," said candidate Parker, "is a source of evil and danger to both races and is not desired by the wise men in either race."[41]

Here and there throughout the country, blacks were even then challenging this exclusion in the courts. Hence, they could not but take alarm at the idea of a justice who found their participation a source of evil. The National Association for the Advancement of Colored People (NAACP) was vigorous in its opposition to the nomination of Judge Parker to the Supreme Court.[42] With voting rights cases just beginning to come to the Supreme Court, how could the NAACP not oppose him? Labor unions, many practicing the most severe racial exclusion, opposed Parker for other reasons. And Southern Democratic senators, who could not have been supposed to disagree with Parker on the merit of black voting, also opposed him. Coalitions often have incompatible elements, and this was so with the de facto anti-Parker coalition. This explains the Senate vote of 41 to 39. The *Christian Science Monitor* said, "While it was doubtful that more than three or four senators [were influenced by anxiety about the black vote], 'the occasion furnished the first national demonstration of the Negro's power since Reconstruction days.'"[43]

From that time onward, Congress became the forum in which some member would always have the incentive to advocate the black right to vote. The latent issue was once more active, though usually far from being forceful enough to be a front-page issue. It took the intervention of presidents to make it a front-page issue. Thereafter, black voting rights never ceased to be a congressional question, which was usually settled on technical grounds by out-lawing the use of the poll tax. The challenge to the poll tax was thought to appeal to Northern blacks, in sympathy with their Southern relatives. It also appealed to New Dealers. The reason? Southern Democrats were frequent partners with Republicans in the conservative coalition that blocked so much of the New Deal. New Deal supporters, like the Republican conservatives in 1890, needed an expanded electorate, to increase their national strength.[44] They thought blacks, and poor whites, would form the base of their coalition if the poll tax were eliminated. Black voting would go up, and conservative Democrats would change their habits or lose their offices. No president was ready for such an attack upon Southern Democrats' own power base. But events were taking place that presidents could not evade. The courts, in various cases brought by black litigants, struck down virtually all the specifically racial barriers, though the poll tax still remained. One of the points emphasized in the report of the President's Committee on Civil Rights was that action was needed to make it possible for people to exercise the right to vote.[45]

Harry S Truman made the right to vote an explicit issue for presidents to debate, and the issue has remained on the table since then. The Eisenhower administration, following Truman, eventually deemed it necessary to support legislation that became the Civil Rights Act of 1957. The important fact was that *the Senate broke a filibuster and adopted a civil rights bill.* This was the real measure of political change. The act of 1957 authorized the Department of Justice to bring injunctive suits to enforce voting rights. Suffice it to say that suits on a case-by-case basis, in the hundreds of counties and thousands of other local governments in the former Confederacy would have taken many years into the future to go through the courts. The Eisenhower administration brought very few cases under the new bill.

The Kennedy administration would have been satisfied if it could have constrained itself to the enforcement of voting rights. Moreover, the Justice Department, under Robert Kennedy, laid great stress on such cases. Southern resistance was so intense, however, that this strategy could not work.[46] By this time, the civil rights movement had taken to nonviolent mass protests. These protests concerned matters that, years after the fact, can all too easily be thought small: drinking fountains, lunch counters, bathrooms, waiting rooms, and so on. They were the most intimate matters of personal dignity. Mass protest (nonviolent direct action) spilled over to massive attempts to register voters in the rural South, and to mass protests against suppression. Southern governmental and civic leaders proved unable or unwilling to control the hostile whites who turned to violence on a large scale, in full view of the television cameras. But the administration found itself drawn in by the visible public protests, by the criticism from abroad, by disputes that penetrated the White House and the operating agencies.

The administration's increasing engagement drew admiration and loyalty from many blacks. It also brought the Kennedys into utter disrepute in many parts of the South.[47] This "white backlash," led ultimately to a white Republican party in the South, many supporters of which rejected the Democratic party because of the civil rights movement. The Nixon administration, taking office in 1969, was the first political beneficiary of the 1964 Goldwater strategy. At that time, however, the Nixon administration had not made a commitment to oppose a forward-moving civil rights program per se. The administration would argue that it accepted the principle of civil rights. However, it would provide for some mode of enforcement that the civil rights coalition would see as too diffuse or ineffective. In the end there would be some compromise approximating the legal status quo, or on occasion a legislative stalemate.

The initial proposal was for a simple five-year extension of the Voting Rights Act of 1965. The Nixon administration proposed amendments to the law that made it applicable nationwide. The objection of the civil rights community was that this would spread the government's limited enforcement resources rather thin, reducing the attention that could be paid to the places in which they felt most vulnerable, namely the states of the old Confederacy. Ultimately, President Richard Nixon must have deemed it more prudent to sign a bill extending the act until 1975, rather than allow his expressed dissatisfaction to become the basis for a veto. A similar process was perceptible in the Ford administration, only the details of draftsmanship were different.

The process was also similar in the Reagan administration. Because the civil rights coalition held considerable strength in the Congress, the enforcement section was given a longer life than the president advocated. Even more, the statute explicitly adopted a "results" test rather than the "intent" test for the proof of violations.

The change in the franchise pattern has been very important, and is not primarily symbolic. It has constituted a source of danger that some presidents have wished to avoid. Presidents have also been able to cope with changes in the underlying rules of voting, once the first decisions were made. Once it became imperative to attack the restricted voter base in the South in order to satisfy the demands of a larger portion of the Democratic voter base in the North, Democratic presidents could not have withheld, if they had wished.

Altering the Reservoir of Decision Makers:
The Executive and Executive Appointments

If racial stratification also means the automatic precedence of white over black, appointments are a clue to how much an administration accepts or rejects the principle. An administration may signify, by the people it puts behind desks, that the government is a white government. The president can also become an instructor to the nation. By the appointments that an administration makes, the president teaches the citizens to think of blacks as presumptively "qualified" for public leadership.

The narrowing of federal jobs of blacks, under Theodore Roosevelt, William Howard Taft, and Woodrow Wilson was one of the indicators of the acceptance of stratification into the constitution of usage. The turn toward a more open degree of black employment and away from segregation was evident in Franklin Delano Roosevelt's administration. In each succeeding administration, some change in personnel occurred, whereby at least a few blacks secured jobs from which they would before have been excluded.

Why did this begin with Franklin Delano Roosevelt? The president was not a racial reformer. His nomination depended on his being a conventional Democrat, and his entourage included intensely racist persons. The answer comes of organizational demand. Roosevelt's entourage had learned, while he was still seeking the presidency, if not before, the necessity of observing social niceties in dealing with blacks while avoiding stances that might agitate Southerners. Moreover, he could also tolerate about him a faction that would urge him to adopt policies later called "liberal." Some of these subordinates began to bring blacks into their agencies. This was the first visible and sizable set of African American bureaucrats. Harold Ickes, the secretary of the interior, was one of these liberals. Ickes appointed the young Robert C. Weaver, an economist, his "race relations adviser." Ickes soon let his friends know that he wanted to appoint a black lawyer in the solicitor's office. When Ickes had barely been in office seven months, he appointed William H. Hastie an assistant solicitor. Aubrey Williams made President Mary McLeod Bethune of Bethune-Cookman College director of Negro affairs in the National Youth Administration. Similar persons were in other agencies, a few on general assignments; others were "advisers on Negro affairs," and still others had a variety of functional subordinate positions.[48]

The black press soon christened this group "the Black Cabinet." There is little in the public record of this group and how it functioned.[49] The key chairs of committees, when chairs were more powerful than they are today, were mostly Southern members of Congress who could not have been very friendly to the group. They probably had little acceptance by most of the press. The black Democratic politicians were barely emerging in national affairs. William L. Dawson's influence was reputedly far reaching in the Truman administration. But Dawson did not switch from the Republican to the Democratic party until 1939.[50] He was merely an alternate delegate to the Democratic National Convention of 1940.[51] He did not make it to Congress until 1942. Adam Clayton Powell, Jr., was a young minister and local politician in New York City. The chances are that most of the new black administrators probably were most effective when their sponsors inside the administration were effective. Some sponsors, notably Ickes, had great staying power in the volatile world of executive politics. Others, such as Aubrey Williams, were themselves often at the margins of the president's decision making. For these reasons, the group must have been at the margin of executive decision making. On the whole, their overall role was to keep before agency staffs some claims about the needs of blacks.

In 1949, black appointments were taken to a new level, though the change was so small that today it seems a mere crack in the face of a glacier. Oscar Ewing, the administrator of the Federal Security Agency (later rechristened Department of Health, Education, and Welfare) brought into his office a black woman named Anna Arnold Hedgeman. Just after World War II, Hedgeman had been a lobbyist for "fair employment" legislation, later rechristened "equal employment opportunity" legislation. Her testimony is that she had gone into the 1948 campaign because she had been impressed by Truman's strong support of such legislation. She had worked with Dawson in the campaign, and Dawson had recommended her appointment to the administration.[52] Hedgeman was an "assistant to the administrator," not yet an "assistant administrator." But to be an "assistant-to" was a major step.

The Eisenhower administration, after negotiations, brought E. Fredric Morrow to the White House staff. Morrow had, by his account, been recruited into the Eisenhower campaign from his job at the Columbia Broadcasting System with the promise of an appointment at the White House. The White House job he was promised seemed to elude him, but he was finally appointed to the Commerce Department. After a while, Morrow was moved to the White House, yet he was sensitive that he was still carried on the Commerce payroll. After he got to the White House, he still did not know where he fit in. He wrote of sitting alone in the office, "bewildered," not knowing where to turn for information on such simple things as how to get a secretary, to get his office furnished, or how to make reports and to whom. But he was determined not to take it up with Chief of Staff Sherman Adams. "This may be part of a test to see whether I can take it."[53] Eisenhower also appointed a Chicago lawyer, J. Ernest Wilkins, an assistant secretary of labor. Such an appointment crossed a political threshold, that of Senate confirmation. Wilkins was the second black person in history to have even a subcabinet appointment, the first being William H. Lewis, an assistant attorney general under President Taft. Kennedy widened the pattern still more, appointing a black man as associate press secretary, a black man deputy assistant secretary of state, and at least one black appointee a major regulatory commissioner. His appointees in turn made a variety of hitherto unexpected appointments of their own.[54]

Lyndon Johnson expanded the appointments still further and in 1966 he appointed Robert Weaver secretary of HUD. By Nixon's presidency, the black appointee at the subcabinet level was no longer a novelty, though still unusual. Jimmy Carter was the most aggressive of the recent presidents before Clinton. Those who watched the administration were more compelled with the presence of blacks at cabinet or subcabinet level in 1980.[55] At least 7 percent (19/270) of such appointees were black. This number would be supplemented by the discretionary civil service appointments that department heads and other subordinates can make.

Presidents have found it increasingly easy to deal with appointments. They can make their own choices, yet often they can explain to those who object that the appointees are under their control and can do nothing not authorized. They can explain to those who want a new policy that the appointee is in a position to make sure that it gets consideration. There is a certain lag involved in making appointments when they have not been made before, and appointments by themselves represent a lag on policy. The presence of these men and women showed, if nothing more, that blacks were no longer simply the American equivalent of untouchables. "The government" was no longer simply "the *white* government."

Altering Basic Substantive Policy: The Role of the Executive

The idea of "substantive policy" elements in the Constitution has been in disfavor in recent political science, critical of the Supreme Court of the early 1930s. "Substantive due process" is the doctrine that the Constitution requires legislation to "be fair and reasonable in content as well as application."[56] Content was the means by which the Supreme Court negated New Deal economic legislation. Substantive due process went into decline in the New Deal. Yet a political system cannot be all procedure and no more. Perhaps everyone recognizes that protection against preventable death is an even more critical concern. Nothing can be more substantive than to mandate that people shall die. *If this protection against the illegal imposition of death is absent, little else matters.* Until quite recently, a serious constitutional question was whether blacks have the same imperative right to life as others.[57] In a formal sense, the answer was "yes." The reality test, rather than the formal test, was lynching, remnants of which remained until the late 1950s.[58] Lynching was a critical element of the *white* control structure, which meant that a black man was the natural sacrificial victim. The film *Places in the Heart*, released several years ago, illustrates, in the fate of Moses, what can happen to those who live in a lynch-mob culture. Moses was not killed, but he was severely beaten and fled with the knowledge that he could be killed at whim.

Under mob control, the authority of government to protect life, and prevent or punish murder, might by common consent be withheld if the victim were black. Lynching, based on opinion and informal structure, was a more powerful ultimate threat than capital punishment under law. Some, even among those who had given active verbal support, found occasion to oppose particular lynchings. The threat to public authority sometimes had to be contained. Often, however, opposition entailed too high a political cost and some public officials acceded to lynching with virtually no resistance.[59] Presidents passively accepted lynching as a normal part of life. Presidents sought successfully to keep their distance from this subject. Warren G. Harding, for whom hardly a good word is said by students of the presidency, was an exception. Harding did, indeed, urge Congress to take action on the subject. He did not live to see any action, and his administration was so afflicted with corruption that he might well have been incapacitated politically in any case. (We are told that Hoover "favored an antilynching law" but this did not appear to enter into his official activity.)[60] From the enforcement standpoint, the same federal statutes that are in existence today were in existence from the 1870s. But it would appear that no administration even evaluated the potential use of those statutes until the Civil Rights Section was created under Attorney General Frank Murphy.[61] This must have been a departmental matter, or the particular interest of Murphy, who did know about racial violence from his days in Michigan, but whose main interest was in the civil liberties of union organizers.[62]

Franklin Roosevelt was persuaded to use some critical language in a speech transmitted by radio to the Federal Council of Churches. But when he was asked to send a courtesy message to the opening of the National Urban League's convention, the draft message had to be negotiated to make sure that it contained no references to lynching. When a coalition of congressional Democrats and Republicans (some sixty in number), sponsored an anti-lynching bill in 1937, Roosevelt refused to offer the public support that anti-lynching lobbyists wanted. Walter White, the executive secretary of the NAACP, carried his case to the president in person. Roosevelt expressly would not intervene. His rationale was that he could not let his economic program be held hostage.[63]

Truman was drawn into the lynching issue after World War II, and through the lynching issue into the broader civil rights issue. After World War II, as after World War I, there was notorious maltreatment of returning black veterans. There were widespread reports that some black soldiers had been lynched in Louisiana and Georgia. In South Carolina, one veteran, Isaac Woodward, had been blinded—his eyes beaten out. Truman said, "My God! I didn't know things were as bad as that. We've got to do something."[64] It was then that Truman decided to create the President's Committee on Civil Rights. When his black visitors asked how to prevent its funds from being blocked in Congress, he said he would pay for it out of his contingency fund. When they expressed fear that it would become bogged down, and lost as one more committee report, he said he would have it reported to him in three months. Truman's clarity suggests that the advice of his internal staff, which was to take the civil rights issue up strongly in order to preempt Henry Wallace, had been heard and accepted. The committee did report rapidly, and its report was a landmark in the evolution of civil rights policy. One of the legislative proposals eventually put forward was that measures be taken to guarantee "the right of security of persons," which was a different way to propose anti-lynching.

Some political friends of Truman's whose sympathies were Southern had written that he would get Southern support, but that he needed to deemphasize his civil rights program. Truman replied that his own family history was also Southern in sympathy, but "My very stomach turned when I learned that Negro soldiers just back from overseas, were being dumped out of army trucks in Mississippi and beaten." He continued, "Whatever my inclinations as a native of Missouri might have been, as President I know this is bad [and] I shall fight to end evils like this."[65]

Beyond protection against death, one of the fundamental rights society grants its citizens is the ability to enter into the economy. Constitutional theory of a conservative sort, although it does focus on "economic liberties," overlooks the basic human concern with earning a living.[66] Indeed, when a constitution encompasses only some members of the society, or acceptable

aliens, they are most often likely to be people who have the freedom to participate in the economy, even if they lack other citizenship rights. In this sense,
the foreign investor within recent times had in practice rights that were only
theoretically available to the American black. Until recently, the real Constitution provided the American black no assurance of entry into the competitive
workplace. Racial discrimination in the workplace was the accepted norm.

If the American economy is vastly integrated, whatever may be said about
"affirmative action," "the glass ceiling," and "quotas," the roots of that integration may be traced in part to executive decisions. Presidential subordinates
began to touch on this problem during the New Deal. Robert C. Weaver and
William Hastie opened up some additional job opportunities in the construction industry. Their superior (and sponsor), Secretary Ickes, had some housing
programs under his control. Weaver and Hastie sought to increase black hiring on the construction sites under these programs. Contractors and unions
would each blame the other for the absence of blacks. Weaver and Hastie
worked out an early affirmative action plan under which 5 percent of the
skilled jobs, 15 percent of the semiskilled, and 40 percent of the unskilled
would have to be filled by blacks. Failure to meet those requirements would
constitute prima facie evidence of racial discrimination.[67]

This move marked a critical change in that it allowed the government to
alter the basic terms of the mythology surrounding freedom of contract. No
longer could the principle that an employer could hire (or refuse to hire) any-
body on any terms be maintained without limit. Yet the concept was far from
being implemented in official action at the time.

The job discrimination issue was forced upon, and taken up by, President
Franklin Delano Roosevelt, and it turned into a national policy debate on the
eve of World War II in 1941. The question was whether blacks could now be
assured of being hired in defense plants. A black coalition, in which the most
prominent figure was A. Philip Randolph, promised to lead many thousands
of people in a march into Washington, in protest against employment discrimination by defense contractors.[68]

President Roosevelt decided to enter negotiations with Randolph and others personally. This direct involvement was unusual for any president, and
Roosevelt apparently had not seen black spokespersons for protracted periods. Although the negotiations were eventually canceled, they were followed
by Executive Order 8802 (1941). The order, arising from the president's emergency powers, forbade discrimination in defense industries.

The executive order established the President's Committee on Fair Employment Practice as the administrative entity, thus setting "in train a precedential

process which in 1961 gave us the basis for today's affirmative action programs."[69] The concept of executive intervention in the economy remained even in the Nixon administration. The Nixon administration's major initiative was its Philadelphia Plan to increase minority employment on federal construction projects. The underlying concept of this kind of plan, which took effect in September 1969, was rejected by the presidential surrogates in the Reagan administration. The effect of the new approach is to sanctify the enjoyment of benefits and opportunities granted under previously discriminatory situations.

If the human being has earned something, he or she also needs to be able to go into the market and buy what is offered. Many things are offered without which one would rather not do. But exclusion from some opportunity to buy is a severe privation, as is exclusion from the right to earn. Few privations can be as severe as a limit on one's ability to buy (or rent) a place to lay one's head. It was a measure of some change in the atmosphere of policy relating to blacks that the Department of Justice could adopt the practice of filing amicus briefs in private civil rights actions in the 1940s, and especially that it could agree to file a brief opposing the enforceability of covenants that forbade the sale of real property to blacks, or the use of such property by them.[70] The practice was so extensive that, according to data cited in the Department's brief, about 80 percent of the rental apartments in Chicago were under such restrictions. As far as I know, the character of the policy discussion in the department has not been reported, although the issue was a significant one. One account treats the action as almost fortuitous. Philip Elman, then an attorney in the solicitor general's office, persuaded his superiors that such a brief should be filed.[71]

The role of blacks in military service is slightly different from the problem of entry into the economy, though it does involve the crucial question of how the population of the country is to be utilized at a time when personnel are in short supply. The military approach could be characterized chiefly as of the use of some "resource" that did not have to be considered in human terms. During World War II, the administration had to decide, whether to admit blacks to combat units or to use them only for noncombat work duty. Another question was how far to permit the training of black officers. In the case of the navy, the issue was whether to readmit blacks to the navy, since the navy had not been fully segregated before World War I.[72] As blacks retired, or otherwise left the navy after World War I, their replacements were few. Throughout World War II, there were intense struggles to get the military services to change their policy toward the use of blacks, the dominant tendency still being to use them in segregated labor or service units. There were, as well, numerous complaints of simple abuse and mistreatment of black service personnel in all sorts of circumstances. As a result of black complaints, Judge William Hastie was appointed civilian aide to Secretary of War Henry L. Stimson. He found that he never had rapport with Stimson. Not only were most of the professional soldiers opposed to change, so was the secretary. Stimson apparently believed that blacks were essentially equipped to be farmers, and that the blacks who had insisted on becoming officers in World War I had made fools of themselves. Hastie was left out of the information loop.Such a department head obviously would not be able to perform a leadership role among his subordinate professionals. After a little over two years, Hastie resigned and wrote a series of newspaper articles criticizing the department.[73]

When, toward the end of the war, the War Department began to thinking about a new approach, it found field implementation extremely slow, so that by the end of the war the army was in effect still segregated. Although in practice segregation had sometimes been overcome during the war, it remained the dominant policy until the Truman administration and the Korean War.[74] (The situation was somewhat different in the more segregated navy, partly because James V. Forrestal, Stimson's navy counterpart, took the issue in a different light. Forrestal was more willing to authorize, and even direct, subordinates to break with the older patterns.)[75] In any event, if the American military is today the most integrated institution in the country, it is partly due to a change in public opinion, but largely due to a change in military personnel requirements (especially in the Korean War), and in directions from the president of the United States acting as commander in chief of the armed forces.

School segregation is perhaps the substantive issue that recent presidents have found least manageable. Presidents were pulled into this controversy unwillingly. Lincoln Caplan recites extensive claims from an oral history archive that Philip Elman was the source of the department's decision to file a brief attacking the basic concept of the legality of racial segregation. If Caplan is correct, that decision was made almost idiosyncratically when James P. McGranery was attorney general. (The account also claims that Elman was in constant communication with Justice Felix Frankfurter while he was shaping what the department ought to argue.)[76]

By the time Richard Nixon became president, executive support appeared to have swung behind the white majority and the status quo. Many whites in the North also opposed busing. This caused a split that is still present, though sometimes papered over, within the Democratic party in Congress, and that continues to put pressure on Democratic presidents.

Republicans have had no reason to be ambivalent. Not the least is the role of the Internal Revenue Service (IRS) and its decision-making criteria as to the tax-exempt status of private institutions created as segregated alternatives to desegregated public school systems.[77] Blacks and their legal representatives in Mississippi had wanted the IRS to move against the segregated private academies. They had sued. Apparently anticipating defeat in the courts, IRS entered into a settlement under which exemptions would be denied. Evidently, the settlement had been accepted by the IRS during the Nixon administration, over the objection of Attorney General John Mitchell. In *Bob Jones University* v. *U.S.*, a 1983 case, the IRS was challenged for withholding tax-exempt status to a private school practicing discrimination.

President Ronald Reagan personally entered, arguing that he was not sure that it was legal for the IRS to be making social policy judgments. The practices complained of had been reviewed before the Reagan administration took office and more than once accepted by other federal courts. Hence the administration's exercise of its rights, in choosing to rethink the matter, if it wished, could better be interpreted as a willingness to see the privately funded academies operate under public sanction with the benefit of what is technically called a "tax expenditure." Outcomes will depend, in large measure, on whether the presidents themselves have a strong interest and whether there is conflict or agreement within the president's circle.

THE INTERPRETATION OF THE EXPERIENCE
THE DYNAMICS OF A SEPARATION OF POWERS SYSTEM

Presidential action ("leadership") is often called for to introduce necessary decisions into the "living Constitution." As a rule, presidential leadership has been restrained in matters relating to race. Since the depression, presidents have confronted racial stratification almost silently, and with great caution. Policy relevant to racial stratification has oscillated, generally in accord with the political coalition that dominates at any given moment. As mentioned earlier, the change that has taken place is in the area of electing public officials, standing for public office, and revising substantive policy.

Presidents are not merely leading actors. In the use of the resources described, they often become lagging leading actors. They lag behind the courts and behind active nuclei in Congress for protracted periods, but they also lead. They have led at certain crucial moments, making latent issues into active issues, active issues into front-page issues, and have been decisive in making front-page issues winning issues. Presidential interest has been necessary to convert the work of the active minority into a legislative majority. Some scholars have suggested that the president has his own powers of legislation that could be applied to the civil rights situation.[78] The interesting phenomenon is that the black leadership of the civil rights movement never adopted such a theory. The "Second Emancipation Proclamation" was decidedly second best. "If we were to be reduced to executive action, I meant to get Kennedy to do more than he was doing."[79] Roy Wilkins, one of the great strategists of the century, seemed to comprehend intuitively or from experience that overreliance on presidents is dangerous. *A minority, racial or otherwise, is also a political minority; it will lose out if it cannot discover a means of putting leverage on the presidency itself.* The objective is to exact from an administration a high price for negligent or adverse action.

How has executive energy been generated? Principally by external demand. The black interest group leadership had a distinct effect in gaining presidential interest when there was a high level of energy within the black population, relative clarity in presumptive black leadership elites, a broad public situation that requires attention, and a reasonably friendly internal coalition in the administration. There is some element of free choice, or of doing what the president personally wants to do. But free choice is likely to be uninformative, at least by itself. While free choice may sometimes have been relevant, the president is more likely to be substantially influenced by organizational demand, or the aggregate of demands from formally subordinate officials. Presidents will also be influenced by external demand, which means demand from those whose claims come from within the society but outside the government, and from the others in the "rest of the world" whose judgments, fears, demands, and threats are also relevant.[80] There is also some element of the president's doing, or allowing to be done, what agencies want to do. And there is the large element of external demand, or incentives that come into the process from the world outside the government.

If presidents deem themselves to represent the effective political majority, one should expect their racial policies to be in accord with what they imagine the effective political majority to support. If the active political majority should be deemed to support more egalitarian policies, the president's course is easy. Therefore, when the effective political majority is thought to support stratification, presidential advocacy of stratification is entirely predictable.

The situation is more complex when the disposition of the effective political majority is uncertain. Then the choice open to the president is at once freer and more dangerous. It is also more complex if the political "coalition" over which the president presides is divided. Finally, the situation is even more complex when the personal disposition of the president and the objective political indicators are in conflict with respect to racial stratification.

It appears that the theory of interest group politics does not yet articulate the circumstances under which interest groups can mobilize and induce new decisions under adverse conditions. As initially conceived, the Constitution states who has actual membership in the political community that is entitled to all available measures of deference and material benefit.[81] The problem is that the status of African Americans under the purely legal theory of the Constitution does not yet accord with the operative political reality of the Constitution. Moreover, if we *assume* (what may be contrary to fact) that the demography and economics of the next two to five presidential elections are not necessarily going to favor a constitutional politics of racial equality, then the practical situation demands serious intellectual effort, and the intellectual problem is far more than a curiosity for the seminar room.

NOTES

This chapter draws on material previously published in Matthew Holden, Jr., *Racial Stratification as Accident and as Policy* (Charlottesville: University of Virginia, Center for Public Service, 1989); and lectures on the president, Congress, and racial stratification. See also Matthew Holden, Jr., *The Challenge to Racial Stratification*, National Political Science Review Set, vol. 4 (New Brunswick, N.J.: Transcription Publications of Rutgers University, 1993).

1. James Sterling Young, *On Nation Leading in America: Thinking about the Presidency, Political Culture, and the Culture of Nation in a Nation of Many Cultures*, Miller Center of Public Affairs Occasional Paper 07/93 (Charlottesville: University of Virginia, 1993), 6.

2. Edward S. Corwin, *The President: Office and Powers, 1787–1957* (New York: New York University Press, 1957), 230, n.7. The discussion in the note is quite detailed. See also LaWanda Cox, *Lincoln and Black Freedom: A Study in Presidential Leadership* (Columbia: University of South Carolina Press, 1987).

3. See Harry Kranz, "A 20th Century Emancipation Proclamation: Presidential Power Permits Withholding Federal Funds from Segregated Institutions," in *The Presidency*, ed. Aaron Wildavsky (Boston: Little, Brown, 1969), 741–69.

4. Ruth P. Morgan, *The President and Civil Rights Policy-Making by Executive Order* (New York: St. Martin's Press, 1970), 86.

5. Charles E. Merriam, *The Written Constitution and the Unwritten Attitude* (New York: Richard R. Smith, 1931). This set of depression-era lectures deserves new attention.

6. Norton E. Long, *The Polity* (Chicago: Rand McNally, 1960), 64–76; Jerry L. Mashaw, *Bureaucratic Justice* (New Haven, Conn.: Yale University Press, 1983); and John A. Rohr, *To Run a Constitution* (Lawrence: University of Kansas Press, 1986).

7. The most influential exposition of this approach can be found in David B. Truman, *The Governmental Process* (New York: Knopf, 1953).

8. Richard C. Snyder, "A Decision-Making Approach to the Study of Political Phenomena," in *Approaches to the Study of Politics*, ed. Roland A. Young (Evanston, Ill.: Northwestern University Press, 1985), esp. 15–36.

9. James Bryce, *Studies in History and Jurisprudence* (New York: Oxford University Press, 1901). This concept is in contrast to constitutions conceived as political ideals or principles, whether practiced or not, or as were similar to business contracts or "working memoranda of association." Cf. Frank M. Coleman, *Politics, Policy, and the Constitution* (New York: St. Martin's, 1982), 22. See also Charles McIlwain, *Constitutionalism Ancient and Modern* (Ithaca, N.Y.: Cornell University Press, 1940).

10. Charles B. Hagan, "The Group in a Political Science," in *Approaches to the Study of Politics*, ed. Roland A. Young (Evanston, Ill.: Northwestern University Press, 1958), 46.

11. Eugene V. Rostow, *President, Prime Minister, or Constitutional Monarch?* (Washington, D.C.: Institute for National Strategic Studies, National Defense University, 1989), 4.

12. Merriam, *The Written Constitution*, 15.

13. The question, sorely neglected in social science, as to why the phenomenon called "race" should have become so vital a part of the definition of social organization in modern history, as a phenomenon of European and American thinking and culture, is beyond the scope of this chapter. Intergroup differences are virtually universal, but the mysterious attachment to the presumptive virtue of "race" is peculiar to recent times. See Michael D. Biddiss, *Father of Racist Ideology: The Political and Social Thought of Count Gobineau* (New York: Weybright and Talley, 1976), 103–9. In this chapter I am focusing on African Americans, and there is evidence of the particular anxiety that the Founders had about African Americans. See, for instance, Coleman *Politics, Policy, and the Constitution*, 68, n. 12. However, it is worthwhile for all who would think carefully about the matter of race and politics to consider the relations of other population groups. On attitudes toward the Chinese in California, for example, see Carl Brent Swisher, *Motivation and Political Technique in the California Constitutional Convention, 1878–79* (New York: DaCapo Press, 1969). On attitudes toward the Japanese in California, see Roger Daniels, *The Politics of Prejudice:The Anti-Japanese Movement in California and the Struggle for Japanese Exclusion* (New York: Atheneum, 1968); and on other groups, see Morton Grodzins, *Americans Betrayed: Politics and the Japanese Evacuation* (Chicago: University of Chicago Press, [1949] 1974). See also William A. Brophy et al., *The Indian, America's Unfinished Business* (Norman: University of Oklahoma Press, 1966).

14. Snyder, "A Decision-Making Approach," 31–33.

15. On Presidents from Lincoln to Theodore Roosevelt, see George Sinkler, *Racial Attitudes of American Presidents* (New York: Vintage, 1972).

16. Matthew Holden, Jr., "Why Entourage Politics Is Volatile," in *The Managerial Presidency*, ed. James Pfiffner (Pacific Groves, Calif.: Brooks-Cole, 1990), 61–77.

17. Rostow, *President, Prime Minister, or Constitutional Monarch?* is perhaps the strongest advocate of prerogative in the presidency. For another discussion of presidential authority, see Snyder, "A Decision Making Approach," 25–26.

18. Edward S. Corwin, *The President: Office and Powers* (New York: New York University Press, 1957); John H. Kessel, "The Structures of the Carter White House," *American Journal of Political Science* 27 (August 1983): 431.

19. Matthew Holden, Jr., "Bargaining and Command by the Heads of U.S. Government Departments," *Social Science Journal* 25 (1988): 255–76.

20. Joel Aberbach and Bert F. Rockman, "Clashing Beliefs within the Executive Branch: The Nixon Administration Bureaucracy," *American Political Science Review* 70 (June 1976): 456–68.

21. Regarding presidential action through subordinates, see Marissa Martino Golden, "How Reynolds Beat the Bureaucrats with Brains, Zeal, and Long Hours," *IGS Public Affairs Report* 32 (November 1991): 8–9. Concerning the president as symbol of national unity, see President's Committee on Administrative Management, *Report* (Washington, D.C.: Government Printing Office, 1937).

22. For material on this topic, see Howard E. Shuman and Walter R. Thomas, eds., *The Constitution and National Security* (Washington, D.C.: National Defense University Press, 1990).

23. Grodzins, *Americans Betrayed*.

24. Stephen Cresswell, *Mormons, Moonshiners, Cowboys & Klansmen: Federal Law Enforcement in the South & West, 1870–1893* (Tuscaloosa: University of Alabama Press, 1991), chaps. 1 and 6; and Homer Cummings and Carl McFarland, *Federal Justice: The History of Justice and the Federal Executive* (New York: DaCapo Press, 1970), 230–49.

25. "Instructions to Marshals and United States Attorneys," *Annual Report of the Attorney General of the United States* (Washington, D.C.: Government Printing Office, 1877), Exhibit M, 77.

26. "Instructions to Marshals and United States Attorneys," Exhibit M, 77.

27. Posse comitatus refers to the power or force of the county, or the population of a certain county, to aid the sheriff in keeping the peace, in pursuing and arresting felons., *Black's Law Dictionary*, 6th ed. (St. Paul, Minn.: West, 1990), 1162. This power is based in English precedent and is interpreted by the United States marshal to be within the scope of that office. See "Instructions to Marshals and United States Attorneys," Exhibit N.

28. Cresswell, *Mormons, Moonshiners, Cowboys & Klansmen*.

29. In the South, the Reconstruction authorities were even more constrained than were those in the occupation of Germany and Japan after World War II. Energy in the population of the North turned to other matters. Other interests, needs, and ambitions took precedence. Robert Wolfe, ed., *Americans as Proconsuls: United States Military Government in Germany and Japan, 1944–1952* (Carbondale: Southern Illinois University Press, 1964).

30. Pete Daniel, *The Shadow of Slavery* (Urbana: University of Illinois Press, 1972).

31. Cummings and McFarland, *Federal Justice*, 233; Allen Trelease, *White Terror: The Ku Klux Klan Conspiracy and Southern Reconstruction* (New York: Harper & Row, 1971), xliv.

32. Cummings and McFarland, *Federal Justice*.

33. 92 U.S. 542 (1875).

34. William A. Dunning, *Reconstruction: Political and Economic* (New York: Harper and Brothers, 1907), 264.

35. Cummings and McFarland, *Federal Justice*, 243–44.

36. Dunning, *Reconstruction*, 264.

37. Florence Warfield Sillers, and others, comp., *History of Bolivar County, Mississippi,* edited by Wirt A. Williams (Jackson, Miss.: Hederman Brothers, 1948), 35, 36, 37.

38. James Weldon Johnson, *Along This Way: The Autobiography of James Weldon Johnson* (New York: Viking Press, 1968), 140–41.

39. Albert O. Hirschman, *Development Projects Observed* (Washington, D.C.: Brookings Institution, 1967), 9–34.

40. *Congressional Record,* January 29, 1901, 1638. The speech is also printed in Carter G. Woodson, ed., *Negro Orators and Their Orations* (Washington, D.C.: Associated Publishers, 1950).

41. The language is reprinted in NAACP, *20th Annual Report for 1930* (New York: 1931), 8.

42. Kenneth W. Goings, *The NAACP Comes of Age: The Defeat of Judge John J. Parker* (Bloomington: Indiana University Press, 1990).

43. Editorial, *Christian Science Monitor,* May 9, 1930, 21

44. See note 11.

45. Harry S. Truman, *Memoirs of Harry S. Truman: Years of Trial and Hope* (New York: DaCapo Press, 1956), 181.

46. For a detailed recitation of the forms of resistance even to voting rights in the South, see Burke Marshall, *Federalism and Civil Rights* (New York: Columbia University Press, 1963).

47. Arthur M. Schlesinger, Jr., *Robert F. Kennedy and His Times* (Boston: Houghton Mifflin, 1978), vol. 1.

48. T. H. Watkins, *The Righteous Pilgrim* (New York: Henry Holt, 1990); Gilbert Ware, *William Hastie: Grace under Pressure* (New York: Oxford University Press, 1984), 81. Some persons who might have been considered "advisers on Negro affairs" as of 1941 are included in "A List of Negroes Holding High Positions in the Federal Government As of December 31, 1941," in Florence Murray, comp. and ed., *The Negro Handbook* (New York: Wendell Malliett and Company, 1942), 173–75. However, the list cited there contains more than a hundred names. It is unlikely that there were one hundred black persons exercising authority or influence at a high level at that time. Most of the persons who are identified in black political folklore as even mildly significant are listed and are identified in jobs of apparent significance. However, many persons on this list would not have been so considered.

49. William J. Trent, Jr., once urged the importance of a good historical and analytical account. Conversation with the author in the later 1960s. Trent is listed as a staff member at the Federal Works Administration in Murray, *The Negro Handbook,* 173–75. It may, perhaps, no longer be feasible to secure much of the most relevant material since most of the participants are no longer active, and few may still be alive. What the state of documentation is, I would be unable to guess.

50. Harold F. Gosnell, *Negro Politicians* (Chicago: University of Chicago Press, 1935); and James Q. Wilson, *Negro Politics: The Search for Leadership* (Glencoe, Ill.: Free Press, 1960), 78.

51. Murray, *The Negro Handbook,* 169.

52. Anna Arnold Hedgeman, *The Gift of Chaos* (New York: Oxford University Press, 1977), 22–23.

53. E. Fredric Morrow, *Black Man in the White House* (New York: Macfadden Books, 1963), 11.

54. For example, see Roger Wilkins, *A Man's Life: An Autobiography* (New York: Simon and Schuster, 1982), chap. 9.

55. Office of Louis Martin, The White House, *Fact Sheet 115, Revised Appointees List* (Washington, D.C.: The White House, August, 1980). Clinton's appointments have exceeded Carter's.

56. *Black's Law Dictionary,* 6th ed. (St. Paul, Minn.: West, 1990), 1428.

57. Mary Frances Berry, "Do Black People Have a Constitutional Right to Life: A Consideration of Federal and State Concern about the Murder of Black People," unpublished paper, n.d., copy in my files, by courtesy of Dr. Berry.

58. Howard Smead, *Blood Justice: The Lynching of Mack Charles Parker* (New York: Oxford University Press, 1986).

59. For some illustrations of acceding, see Arthur Bushnell Hart, *The Southern South* (New York: D. Appleton and Company, 1910), 208–16.

60. William Starr Myers, ed., *The State Papers and Other Public Writings of Herbert Hoover* (Garden City, N.Y.: Doubleday, Doran, 1934), 54.

61. Robert K. Carr, *Federal Protection of Civil Rights: Quest for a Sword* (Ithaca, N.Y.: Cornell University Press, 1957), 24–32; Cummings and McFarland, *Federal Justice,* chap. 12.

62. Sidney Fine, *Frank Murphy: The Washington Years* (Ann Arbor: University of Michigan Press, 1984), 76–80.

63. Walter F. White, *A Man Called White* (New York: Viking Press, 1948), 168–70.

64. See White, *A Man Called White,* 325–27. I recall the Isaac Woodward episode as it was reported in the *Chicago Defender* at the time. The quotation is on p. 331 of White.

65. Margaret Truman, *Harry S. Truman* (New York: Pocket Books, 1974), 429.

66. James A. Dorn and Henry G. Manne, *Economic Liberties and the Judiciary* (Fairfax, Va.: George Mason University Press, 1987), xi–xxii.

67. Gilbert Ware, *William Hastie: Grace under Pressure* (New York: Oxford University Press, 1984), 82.

68. Herbert Garfinkel, *When Negroes March* (New York: Atheneum, 1959), 38.

69. James E. Jones, Jr., "The Genesis and Present Status of Affirmative Action in Employment: Economic, Legal, and Political Realities," paper presented at the 1984 Annual Meeting of the American Political Science Association, Washington, D.C., August 30–September 2, 1984.

70. Philip B. Perlman with Tom Clark, *Prejudice and Property* (Washington, D.C.: Public Affairs Press, [1948]). (Published brief of the United States against restrictive covenants.)

71. Lincoln Caplan, *The Tenth Justice* (New York: Alfred A. Knopf, 1987).

72. Bernard C. Nalty, *Strength for the Fight: A History of Black Americans in the Military* (New York: Free Press, 1986), 85.

73. See Richard M. Dalfiume, *Desegregation of the U.S. Armed Forces: Fighting on Two Fronts, 1939–1953* (Columbia: University of Missouri Press, 1975), esp. 42, 84.

74. Dalfiume, *Desegregation of the U.S. Armed Forces,* chaps. 5, 9, and 10.

75. Nalty, *Strength for the Fight,* 193–94. James E. Jones, Bascom Professor of Law, University of Wisconsin, responded to a draft of this manuscript that if Forrestal had this approach, it did not seep down to the point at which an enlisted seaman at the time could experience it in daily life.

76. Nalty, *Strength for the Fight*, 25–30.

77. Augustus J. Jones, Jr., *Law, Bureaucracy, and Politics: The Implementation of Title VI of the Civil Rights Act of 1964* (Washington, D.C.: University Press of America, 1982).

78. Morgan, *The President and Civil Rights Policy-Making*.

79. Roy Wilkins, with Tom Matthews, *Standing Fast: The Autobiography of Roy Wilkins* (New York: Viking Press, 1982).

80. Richard Rose, *The Post-Modern President*, 2d ed. (Chatham, N.J.: Chatham House, 1990).

81. Harold D. Lasswell and Abraham Kaplan, *Power and Society* (New Haven, Conn.: Yale University Press, 1950).

GARY ORFIELD

CONGRESS AND CIVIL RIGHTS

FROM OBSTACLE TO PROTECTOR

mericans tend to view the Constitution and the nation's laws as if they were self-interpreting and self-enforcing, but they are not. Many Americans also tend to describe their history in terms of constitutional progress toward a resolution of society's problems. Prominent among these problems has been racial injustice. All sides in the political debate praise the Supreme Court's great 1954 civil rights decision, *Brown* v. *Board of Education*, as an expression of that progress and of the Court's special role in protecting the rights of minorities. In actuality, the Supreme Court played this critical role for only a brief, albeit important, period of time before changing direction. From the 1940s to the 1960s, the leadership came from the presidency, but in the next generation it shifted to the institution that was long considered the graveyard of civil rights, the Congress.

Although some aspects of its structure, particularly lifetime appointments and isolation from direct political pressure, provide broad discretion for the Supreme Court, it is dominated by the appointees of previous presidents and is normally reluctant to change precedent. As a result, the Court tends to be biased toward the past and toward the ideologies of the administrations that put justices in office. The fierce struggles over Supreme Court appointments during the Johnson, Nixon, Reagan, and Bush administrations indicate that the selection of justices has great influence on the evolution of the Court's role.

One of the most important and widely criticized periods of American constitutional history was that in which the Supreme Court nullified the interpretation of much of the force of the Civil War amendments on race relations. It was the Supreme Court's earlier sweeping defense of slavery in the *Dred Scott* decision that helped drive the nation into a civil war. During recent generations these decisions have been seen as the by-products of a time before the Supreme Court assumed its modern role as protector of minority interests and helped put civil rights issues on the national agenda.

In a democratic society, however, no set of institutions can permanently protect the rights of minorities against determined majorities. The enforcement of controversial legal protections ultimately depends not only on institutions but also on public beliefs and political leadership working through party and governmental institutions. Although courts may delay and diffuse the effects of these forces, they will eventually be reconstituted by them.

Throughout the twentieth century, many American scholars have argued that various institutions in the federal government have special missions and orientations in the enforcement of civil rights, missions that derive from the structural differences among those institutions. This view was particularly evident in public understanding of the role of the Supreme Court after 1954. At a time when no civil rights law had been enacted for more than three-fourths of a century, the Court acted and had to withstand a decade of brutal controversy before the elected branches of government provided strong support. The Court, through a series of decisions, had brought back to life the laws and constitutional changes of the Reconstruction period, generations after their virtual nullification by all branches of government.

Congress had long been seen as the principal barrier to civil rights. Even after the Supreme Court's 1954 *Brown v. Board of Education* school desegregation decision challenged the entire system of segregation laws in the seventeen Southern and border states, there seemed little possibility that the representative branch of government could take significant action. While the Court was hailed as the special protector of unpopular minority rights, reflecting its solemn responsibility to enforce the Constitution's limits even against those forms of discrimination supported by popular majorities, Congress was seen as the stronghold of segregationist power.

It was no accident that the civil rights groups turned to the courts when the popular branches of government failed to answer their entreaties or that the first breakthrough in the civil rights era was the 1954 Supreme Court decision on the desegregation of Southern schools. For many years the Supreme Court was the only institution that would even give serious consideration to the claims of the minority groups.

The inability of the federal government to act on even the clearest civil rights issues was long blamed on Congress. Although almost a century earlier Congress had been the radical force in Reconstruction, far to the left of the president and the Supreme Court, it had long since become the burying ground of even the most modest civil rights proposals and of laws that had even an indirect possibility of upsetting the racial status quo in the states that mandated segregation.

It was a commonplace notion of political science in midcentury that several of the basic institutional and political features of Congress constituted almost insurmountable barriers to any significant civil rights action.[1] Even laws with only indirect effects on civil rights, such as federal aid to education, were often blocked because opponents feared their possible impact on race relations.

The strong focus on congressional barriers was not unreasonable. It was a basic reality that given the distribution of power within Congress and the rules under which power was exercised, significant positive action on civil rights was virtually impossible. Forces supporting civil rights controlled few of the key committees, civil rights bills would be blocked in the Senate unless they had a two-thirds majority, and representatives of the states with legal segregation occupied many of the critical leadership positions. The Southerners were better organized than civil rights forces and determined to resist. While Southerners felt intense constituency pressure against civil rights, Northerners usually faced little serious pressure on behalf of civil rights legislation except for the brief period from mid-1963 to mid-1965, when churches and many other organizations across the nation mobilized for civil rights change. The South, where most blacks have always lived, offered no black perspectives in a region where overwhelmingly white electorates returned conservative Democrats to office with monotonous regularity. It seemed that changes of the most profound sort would be needed if Congress were to contribute to civil rights policy.

THE IMPACT OF THE FILIBUSTER SYSTEM

Under the nation's system of equal representation, the seventeen states with segregation laws accounted for more than a third of the members of the Senate, and more than the region's share of the national population. The Senate's filibuster system, prohibiting cutoff of debate unless two-thirds of the members voted for cloture, meant that the thirty-four votes from states with apartheid laws were sufficient to block all possibility of a vote on a civil rights bill even if all other senators favored it. Other senators, particularly those from some of the small states, almost always voted against debate limits on principle and thus further strengthened the position of civil rights opponents.

To overcome the filibuster system, and the South's determination to use it to preserve the racial status quo, meant a civil rights law needed an extraordinary majority—more than two-thirds of the members. In other words, some votes had to come from the states where segregation was required by law; civil rights needed the support of almost all those outside the segregation region who opposed debate limits on principle. For generations, the filibuster barrier stood firm against even the most limited civil rights law. So long as the states with segregation laws were united and could mobilize the thirty-four votes needed to block Senate action, it did not matter how big the majority in favor of civil rights among the American public might be; there was an absolute block to a change.

The filibuster system and the willingness of Southern leaders to use it when they could not kill civil rights measures in committee not only defeated any such measures but also created such a sense of futility that the issues were usually simply ignored. Why invest a great deal of energy in a struggle that one was certain to make powerful enemies over and was certain to lose? Even though Americans opposed the lynching of blacks by white mobs, for instance, the issue was rarely brought to the Senate floor. Filibusters killed anti-lynching laws twice in 1938; killed anti–poll tax measures in 1942, 1946, and 1948; and blocked a voting rights measure in March of 1960 and the enactment of a strong law against job discrimination in 1972. Many other measures never even got that far.

Civil rights forces never succeeded in beating a filibuster until 1964. The barrier was so strong that President Truman's civil rights proposals went nowhere in Congress in spite of their endorsement in the 1948 Democratic National Convention.[2] When President Dwight Eisenhower called for bipartisan action on a more limited civil rights bill in 1956 and 1957, after the Supreme Court's school decision had greatly increased the attention given to the issue, the threat of filibuster led to the dropping of the most important portion of the bill, the provision authorizing the Justice Department to initiate civil rights cases, and to a critical weakening of another provision. Even then, only the masterful leadership of Senate majority leader and future president, Lyndon B. Johnson, was able to win enactment of the first bill of any significance in eighty-nine years.[3]

It was only at the peak of the vast civil rights movement and with the strong leadership of two successive presidents, John Kennedy and Lyndon Johnson, that the congressional deadlock was finally broken and Congress passed the two most important civil rights laws of the twentieth century—the 1964 Civil Rights Act and the 1965 Voting Rights Act. Organized civil rights forces led by Senator Hubert Humphrey, strongly supported by President Johnson, persisted through months of Congress's longest recorded debate and finally succeeded in breaking the filibuster. Liberal strength in Congress, however, reached its high point after the 1964 election and would soon decline. President Johnson's 1966 fair housing bill, for example, was badly defeated. As the civil rights movement decayed in the late 1960s and a large reaction to the civil rights revolution helped bring President Richard Nixon into power on an anti–civil rights platform, it still seemed that little could be expected from Congress. Indeed, Congress was busily passing a variety of "antibusing" measures and punitive measures against "crime in the streets." It seemed as if the filibuster system would once again protect the racial status quo.

SENIORITY AND COMMITTEE POWER

The seniority system in Congress was another impediment to civil rights. When the Democrats seized a firm hold on Congress in 1930, their party was dominated by the Southern faction. Even though blacks and liberals were also concentrated in this party, the power over policy making rested in the House Rules Committee and the Senate Judiciary Committee, which were dominated by Southern civil rights opponents with high seniority. The Senate was a "Southern club" that treated outsiders advocating civil rights very harshly.[4] The one-party South, which continually reelected Democratic senators and representatives, relied on the seniority system to select committee chairmen from its ranks and to guarantee the South strategic control over a disproportionate number of committees. After Reconstruction, the South had virtually excluded the Grand Old Party of Lincoln, the GOP, from congressional representation and excluded many blacks from voting for the Democrats who would hold congressional power. Southern leaders traditionally kept key committees related to civil rights staffed with reliable civil rights opponents.

As the 1960s began, civil rights supporters found Judge Howard Smith (Democrat of Virginia), head of the Southern caucus and a bitter civil rights opponent, chairing the House Rules Committee. His Mississippi counterpart, Senator James O. Eastland, was chair of the Senate Judiciary Committee. Getting a civil rights bill in regular order through the Senate Judiciary Committee, past a filibuster, and onto the floor of the House seemed about as probable as the Pope embracing Protestantism—all it would take would be a triple miracle. It was no wonder that reformers looked to other institutions. Congressional action seemed probable only when the Supreme Court, the president, and public opinion were aligned on the side of a reform and a coalition could be assembled covering much of the political spectrum.

The electoral system that produced presidents was believed to produce leaders much more responsive to racial minorities since it magnified the importance of minority voting in the largest states. Before he was elected president, Senator John F. Kennedy actively opposed electoral college reform on these grounds, and his election was, in fact, decided in Chicago. For decades, political strategists had pointed out that minorities, if their numbers were large enough, had great influence in closely divided states, where changes in the votes of a small group of voters could swing large numbers of electoral votes.[5] Harry Truman's early civil rights initiatives, for example, were often explained in terms of this political reality.[6] The leading political science study of presidential elections in the 1960s concluded:

> In fact, the present method of electing the President tends to give greater power to the large, urban states . . . because the large states can deliver to the winner large blocks of the votes he needs to win. Consequently, Presidential nominees tend to come from big states and tend to run on platforms likely to appeal to big city interests. . . .
>
> This feature . . . is the mirror image of the situation in Congress. . . . [T]he seniority rules of Congress and the rules allocating jurisdiction of Congressional committees have over the years worked to give one-party areas the most power.[7]

For a long time, the only real hope for action outside the courts was concentrated on the White House. Since the end of the anti–civil rights administration of Woodrow Wilson, who approved open segregation within the federal bureaucracy, the presidency had been the branch more favorably inclined. One of the few memorable positive acts of President Warren G. Harding, for example, was his 1921 call for antilynching legislation, something that was blocked on Capitol Hill until 1968.[8] Franklin Delano Roosevelt did not propose legislation on civil rights, but he did create a more favorable climate and he did appoint a more responsive Supreme Court. The New Deal brought blacks into significant governmental positions and sought equal treatment of blacks and whites in some of the economic programs of the period.[9] During World War II, FDR responded to black protests by using his wartime emergency powers to institute the Fair Employment Practices Committee, but Congress eliminated it shortly after the war ended.

The presidents from World War II until the late 1960s all demonstrated either substantial civil rights leadership or, at least, a willingness to uphold the law. Harry Truman, a president from a state with segregation laws, launched a White House Committee on Civil Rights, which issued a path-breaking report in 1947. Truman proposed civil rights legislation, but it died in Congress.[10] His Justice Department took a more active stance in civil rights cases and urged the Supreme Court to outlaw segregated education in the South. President Eisenhower, though distinctly unenthusiastic about the *Brown* decision, integrated the armed forces, organized policies against job discrimination in federal contracts, enforced the school desegregation decision with military force in Little Rock, and proposed the first successful civil rights bill of the twentieth century. (The Eisenhower-Nixon ticket in 1956 received more than 40 percent of the black vote.) President Kennedy took little action in his first years; when he sent up his sweeping 1963 civil rights bill, it was blocked on Capitol Hill until after his assassination. Lyndon Johnson was the most important advocate of racial change to sit in the White House since Abraham Lincoln, and he presided over the "second reconstruction" of Southern society.

Until Richard Nixon took office, it had been decades since there had not been a president supporting racial progress, endorsing more change than Congress was prepared to enact. Nixon himself had been the head of the Presidential Committee on Government Contracts, intended to ensure nondiscrimination by federal contractors.[11] It is hardly surprising that Congress was seen as the ultimate barrier to civil rights progress.

When John F. Kennedy took office, civil rights advocates asked for presidential action through executive orders, something that Kennedy had promised in his campaign.[12] This seemed the only viable strategy in the face of congressional deadlock. Even as late as 1966, President Johnson's decision to send a fair housing bill to Congress rather than to issue a broad executive order forbidding housing discrimination in all housing affected by federal housing or lending programs, was attacked as a sellout, showing that the president was not really serious about the issue.

The analyses about the civil rights orientation of Congress, the White House, and the courts were correct then, as they had been for a long time. Until 1964, Congress had not been able to take any decisive action on behalf of civil rights for almost ninety years. The error was not in describing the situation but in concluding that it was inherent in the institutions themselves rather than result of the political history of the period.

NEW POLITICAL COALITIONS AND THE TRANSFORMATION OF INSTITUTIONAL ROLES

As it turned out, the role of all the institutions of government changed rapidly from the late 1960s on. The changes took place not in institutional structure, but in politics and were eventually reflected in the parties and in each of the branches of government in quite different ways. The most striking change was that by the 1980s, the institution that had been least supportive to civil rights, Congress, became the most positive. The presidency and the Supreme Court worked to dismantle existing civil rights policies in several areas.

A change in the nature of successful presidential coalitions necessarily changed the Supreme Court, since presidents choose justices and since the new coalition was based, in good part, on an altered stance toward racial issues. As the political base of the presidency changed, and the Court, along with the president, moved to the right, what had been long-term features of congressional representation also changed. As the Republicans built a successful Southern presidential strategy that partly rested on strongly identifying with the white South, Republicans became much more competitive in Southern congressional elections. When Republicans defeated Democratic incumbents or captured vacant seats, they cut the accumulation of Southern seniority and helped break the region's hammerlock on committee chairmanships. A growing share of the South's seniority was going to Republicans. Since Republicans had not controlled the House of Representatives for three decades, this meant that seniority was largely wasted in terms of real power in the House. In the Senate, the GOP majority between 1981 and 1986 gave powerful positions to some Southern Republicans, including Strom Thurmond (Republican of South Carolina), who became chairman of the Judiciary Committee, controlling civil rights policy and judicial appointments. By the 1986 election, however, the Senate majority became Democratic again, as it had been from 1956 to 1980.

As Southern politics became competitive and conservative whites increasingly Republican, there was much more incentive for Democrats to seek black support. A basic requirement for strong black support was a different position on civil rights. A change in the grand structure of national political coalitions, in other words, set the stage for an alteration in the role of each of the branches of government in protecting minority rights.

THE POWER OF CONGRESSIONAL ACTION

Although the Supreme Court raised the curtain on the civil rights era, rapid change awaited the break in the congressional deadlock. It was Congress that eventually enacted the decisive measures that made possible rapid change on the basic Southern civil rights questions—public accommodations, school and public facility desegregation, and voting rights. It was when Congress acted decisively, and the new laws were vigorously enforced, that the most clear and rapid changes took place. The rapid impact of congressional action on the segregation of hotels and restaurants, on the number of black voters in the Deep South, and on the integration of Southern public schools and colleges was far more dramatic than the effect of any court decision or presidential action.

When Congress first acted, in the mid-1960s, it was amid a great social movement and strong support for civil rights progress from both the Supreme Court and President Lyndon Johnson. Congress had to act for the laws to change, but Congress was the last of the major institutions to change its role in civil rights policy.

Although the South had spent a decade assailing the Supreme Court's *Brown* decision as illegitimate and trying, with considerable success, to delay or prevent its enforcement, the response to the Southern defeat in Congress on the 1964 Civil Rights Act was very different. Southern leaders had insisted that the Court had no authority to prohibit school segregation and had passed a variety of measures purporting to invalidate the *Brown* requirements. There was no such response to the Civil Rights Act or the Voting Rights Act, even though Congress certainly had the right to adopt a new law and the South had been defeated by a very powerful coalition that even included some Southerners. In many places in the South there was peaceful voluntary compliance with the laws, though resistance would later grow. There was no doubt that Congress disposed of every power when it acted and that its role as the representative institution of government gave its actions a greater legitimacy. The problem was that it was so difficult to get Congress to act.

STAGES IN THE TRANSFORMATION OF INSTITUTIONAL ROLES

As the 1960s came to an end, the roles of Congress and the president began to be reversed in ways inconsistent with the previous model. The White House was captured by a candidate who ran in opposition to civil rights enforcement and promised a more conservative Supreme Court, Richard Nixon. It was the beginning of a generation of White House domination by conservative Republicans.

Beginning in 1964, and with great success since 1968, Republican presidential candidates greatly expanded their electoral base in the South with a powerful conservative appeal, including an attack on the civil rights decisions of the Supreme Court.[13] The civil rights program of the Great Society had broken a century-long tie between the white South and the Democratic party and changed Southern whites from a secondary part of the Democratic coalition to a decisively important part of a new Republican majority. Apart from the first Jimmy Carter campaign, in 1976, no Democratic candidate carried the South after 1964. Hubert Humphrey, in 1968, carried only one of the eleven states of the old Confederacy. In the next election, President Nixon carried all eleven, as did Ronald Reagan in 1984 and George Bush in 1988. In 1980, Ronald Reagan showed the degree of consolidation of Southern presidential Republicanism in this period by carrying ten of the eleven Southern states against Jimmy Carter, the first president elected from the Deep South since the Civil War.[14]

The Republicans won five of the six presidential elections from 1968 to 1988 and the sole Democratic victory was by a Southern moderate who was nominated after the eruption of the Watergate scandal, which made Nixon the first president forced to leave in the face of certain impeachment. No Democrat after Lyndon Johnson, including Jimmy Carter, managed to carry the majority of white voters. The white South had become a central element in presidential politics and a key part of the increasingly conservative party dominating the White House and reshaping the Supreme Court.

Under Nixon and under Reagan and Bush, it was Congress that protected the civil rights laws against attacks and extended the voting rights act when the White House and executive branch were opposed. With the exception of the Carter years, the president consistently took a more conservative position than Congress on civil rights from 1968 through 1991.

Nor did the old understanding of the role of the judiciary as the special protector of civil rights hold. The pattern became much more complicated. It was Congress that delayed conservative control of the Supreme Court, as it repeatedly blocked or fought Supreme Court nominees with records of hostility to civil rights—defeating the nominations of Judges Clement Haynsworth, G. Harold Carswell, and Robert Bork—perhaps preventing major legal reversals that would otherwise have occurred.

When conservative control of the Court was nonetheless consolidated by a long series of appointments and the Supreme Court did narrow the interpretation of the 1964 Civil Rights Act and the 1965 Voting Rights Act, it was Congress that enacted new legislation strengthening the coverage of both laws and reversing the limits imposed by the Supreme Court. After the Supreme Court issued a series of 1989 decisions severely weakening affirmative action, it was Congress that enacted a 1990 bill designed to strengthen the legal base of affirmative action. It was Presidents Reagan and Bush who strongly fought against and vetoed two of those measures, the Civil Rights Restoration Act of 1988 and the 1990 civil rights bill. This was almost an exact reversal of what until recently had been considered the function of the Supreme Court, the president, and Congress.

CIVIL RIGHTS INFORMATION

Even when there had been a deadlock on policy, the executive branch had played a crucial role in gathering and disseminating basic facts about racial conditions, a precondition for mobilization and policy change. Various agencies of the New Deal era, for example, had gathered invaluable information about social and economic conditions in the South. Traditionally, one of the most important roles of the administrative agencies of government is the provision of reliable basic statistics, data that permit citizens to know about the basic trends in the nation and information than can be used by all sides in policy debates. Those favoring government action almost always benefit if there are reliable official data documenting the problem they wish to correct.

The federal government greatly expanded the preparation and publication of civil rights research and data during the 1950s and 1960s, following the creation of the U.S. Civil Rights Commission in 1957 and the great expansion of social research and data collection engendered by the programs of the Great Society. Serious enforcement of the 1964 Civil Rights Act's prohibition against discrimination in all programs receiving federal aid required, for example, a collection of statistics on race from all major programs receiving federal aid. Many governments and nonprofit institutions had never collected or released racial data before. Federally funded research in the 1960s placed central emphasis on questions of poverty and race.[15] There was a flood of information on racial problems and urban conditions. Though research funds were largely directed elsewhere after the 1960s, the government continued to produce a great deal of data through the 1970s.

The Reagan administration brought reduced information, drastic limits on data collection and publication in a number of executive branch agencies, and White House control over the previously independent Civil Rights Commission. It was Congress that unsuccessfully fought the president's effort to take political control of the fact-finding machinery of the created by the 1957 Civil Rights Act. Individual subcommittees and committees of Congress provided virtually the only active supporting constituency for unpopular kinds of civil rights enforcement and carried out the fact-finding investigations that spotlighted retreats in civil rights enforcement. And Congress developed the case and assembled the coalitions that permitted extensions of civil rights law during a conservative era with little support from the president or the courts.

Inherent Limitations of Congress

The fact that Congress has become the most responsive branch of government does not mean that its policies are adequate or effective or that it responds at all to some basic problems. Congressional action is not always constructive and Congress normally quickly reflects intense public pressures, whatever they may be. It is in the nature of the organization of Congress, a representative institution with a highly decentralized and fragmented system of power, that there are many points at which policy initiative can be attacked and vetoed and that powerful legislative action on highly divisive and visible issues can only come under extraordinary circumstances, typically at the climax of a generation or more of debate. Important new policies often come after those rare electoral shifts that significantly change Congress.

Although it is difficult for Congress to act, it is easy to obtain a forum for a new policy idea in Congress. Even when neither public opinion nor political leadership has focused attention on a new issue, it is often possible to find a subcommittee in which the still unpopular question can be discussed in public.

156

Durability, Significance, and Impact of Congressional Policy

Some of the same institutional features of Congress that seemed to hurt civil rights in the 1960s often worked to benefit civil rights law in the 1970s and 1980s. While the barriers to major new congressional action are widely understood, the implications of these barriers for the durability of law, once a fundamental change is enacted, are not. Sometimes the congressional struggle itself becomes a force in convincing people that the society has changed, that the ultimate battle has been lost, and that it is best to accommodate to the new reality.

The extraordinary power of congressional action after an epic legislative struggle was apparent after the enactment of the two great civil rights acts, the 1964 Civil Rights Act and the 1965 Voting Rights Act. The largest fight over the 1964 bill concerned the provisions against discrimination in restaurants, hotels, and other public accommodations. There were fierce debates concerning whether Congress possessed the constitutional authority to regulate the racial practices in small private businesses all over the South. Almost as soon as the law was enacted, however, the struggle was over. Generations of segregationist policies changed almost immediately with very little action required by the federal government to enforce the law. The leaders of the South recognized that they had lost a legitimate political struggle and that they would have to change. When Congress acted, the battle was over. By the time Congress acted on these issues, there was an overwhelming consensus in the country on the policy, and the segregationists at the local level recognized that they had been overwhelmingly defeated. Local resistance crumbled almost immediately once Congress acted.

Senator Richard Russell (Democrat of Georgia), leader of the Southern opposition, noted the great importance of congressional action in 1964 after a thirteen-week filibuster battle, the longest in the history of Congress. Pointing out that floor leader Hubert Humphrey (Democrat of Minnesota) had allowed a full and fair debate, he said that Southerners seeing clear defeat in an epic legislative battle conducted fairly would obey it. He advised constituents to comply and to "refrain from violence."[16] On some issues, the voluntary compliance was overwhelming. Southern political leaders had no such regard for Supreme Court decisions or executive orders.

Changes were by no means so rapid in fields where public opinion was more divided, but congressional action and enforcement had a large impact there as well. White colleges began to integrate on a significant scale after the

1964 Civil Rights Act. School desegregation increased far more in the first year after enactment of the 1964 law than in the decade following the *Brown* decision. Hospitals changed basic racial practices. In voting rights, black registration rapidly soared in a number of areas of the South even before the Supreme Court sustained the constitutionality of what was a very radical change in state and local election law, and long before the effect of Justice Department litigation could be felt. These changes were made possible by broad congressional action, although some also required determined executive branch enforcement.[17]

Except on the most difficult racial questions, those of urban school and housing segregation, the simple fact that Congress has acted is itself a major force for change. It is seen as a legitimate action, probably in a sense that executive action or court decisions never can be. Lyndon Johnson had an acute sense of the importance of this fact, evident in his explanation of why he insisted on a law rather than an executive order on fair housing:

> Most of my advisers, black and white, argued for abandoning the legislative struggle in favor of an Executive order. . . .
> [NAACP lobbyist Clarence Mitchell] knew how difficult it would be, even with legislation, to induce the people in the heartlands and the suburbs, the cities and the countryside, to change their deep-seated sense of individualism in buying and selling their homes. . . . Without the moral force of congressional approval behind us, the struggle for open housing would be lost before it had ever begun.[18]

Many people and institutions do obey an unambiguous provision of federal law without being forced to.

Once Congress acts, it is difficult to repeal an important law, as long as it retains any significant support. The same inertia and the same process of multiple vetoes requiring extraordinary majorities that long block enactment of the policy later make it very difficult to repeal a policy that has been written into the U.S. Code. It is far more difficult to reverse a principle that is embedded in law by Congress than it is to change an order issued by a president or even to change a Supreme Court decision under some circumstances. A new majority on the Supreme Court has the full authority to reverse or distinguish away a previous policy by a simple majority vote; it is constrained only by its own sense of respect for precedent. Changing a policy in Congress, on the other hand, requires much more than a majority in favor—a policy change can be blocked by a hostile committee or subcommittee in either house, by the Rules Committee, by the floor leadership, by a filibuster, or by a hostile majority in either house. Congressional policy has been far more consistent than that of the White House or the courts on some major areas of civil rights policy. This does not mean, of course, that the congressional policies were consistently enforced, but only that they remained in place for possible enforcement by the courts and by more sympathetic future administrations.

In twenty-two years of political conflict from 1968 to 1990, most of it dominated by conservative opponents of civil rights, none of the basic civil rights laws of the 1960s have been weakened by Congress in a major way—with the single exception of the busing issue—and there have been significant strengthening provisions enacted in voting rights, fair employment, and open housing laws, as well as affirmative action and minority set-aside programs.

In striking contrast, the body supposedly more independent and free of political control, the Supreme Court, narrowed its interpretation of many of the basic provisions of civil rights law during this period, particularly in its decisions on voting rights, affirmative action, and the nondiscrimination in institutions receiving federal aid. In each of these cases, a well-established civil rights policy was seriously limited by judicial decisions, some of them representing rather sudden changes of interpretation.

The conservative movement never got firm control of Congress on racial issues, in part because Congress is so well insulated from any dramatic change in representation. During the last forty years, with recessions, wars, scandals of all sorts, and huge landslide presidential victories for both liberal and conservative presidents, nothing has changed the partisan control of the House of Representatives. With very few exceptions, 90 to 95 percent of the incumbents running for reelection win, regardless of the changes in the larger political issues. It may well be that Congress, particularly the House, is actually more insulated from sharp political change than is the Supreme Court.

Congressional action is extremely important for civil rights. It is consequential, legitimate, and long-lasting. The fact that Congress has debated and decided an issue has an effect on public behavior. In contrast to the bitter debates over the legality and appropriateness of action by the courts, apart from the substantive merit of those actions, there is little doubt about the legitimacy of Congress passing a law. When Congress has written a major new statute, that policy is likely to remain on the books for a long time. (In fact, one of the interesting facts of civil rights law in the last generation is that some important court decisions have been based on provisions of law from the Reconstruction statutes, provisions that survived generations of reaction against Reconstruction ideology.)

WHY THE ROLE OF CONGRESS HAS CHANGED

There have been no fundamental changes in the structure of Congress as an institution during the period in which it has changed from a negative to a relatively positive force in the resolution of civil rights issues. The major changes took place in the politics and attitudes outside of Congress, in some cases as a result of civil rights laws and of the very fact that Congress had enacted civil rights laws in the 1960s. These changes, together with a series of crucial civil rights decisions by the Supreme Court, meant that civil rights policy in the last generation has by and large been concerned with defending a legal status quo, not with enacting new policy. This is a task for which Congress is ideally suited.

If this analysis is correct, there is nothing inevitable about Congress continuing to occupy its present position as the most favorable of the branches of government in the making of civil rights policy. If the policy focus once again turns toward major new expansions of civil rights policy and if the public in the country moves strongly in that direction, it is quite possible that a future president or the federal courts could again lead in the creation of the new issues. Congress as a whole would probably require more time to adapt to the new situation. Before the president or the Supreme Court acted, however, there would almost certainly have to be a serious examination of the issue in some subcommittees or committees of Congress, where the civil rights agenda is often articulated. Major legislation might well be blocked until a large popular majority came out in favor of the change and until the leaders of both the executive and legislative branches moved together on the issue and put it on top of the agenda.

If public opinion turned against civil rights, those attitudes would almost immediately be reflected in parts of Congress. After the courts began to issue busing orders, for example, there were many efforts to limit the policy in Congress. Nevertheless, the major proposals that would have put Congress in direct conflict with the Supreme Court over this issue were consistently blocked in Congress over two decades, in spite of strong public opposition to busing and the support of both the Nixon and Reagan administrations for such efforts.[19]

Much of the resistance to negative civil rights policy is led by liberal Democrats chairing key committees and subcommittees. Should the GOP win control of both houses, something that has not happened since the party moved into opposition to civil rights in 1964, Congress could become a seriously negative force. Reapportionment, suburbanization, and continuing migration to the Sunbelt might eventually make this possible.

The Changing Significance of the Seniority System

One significant reason for Congress's new role in civil rights policy is that the distribution of power produced by the seniority system has been substantially altered since the early 1960s. By the 1980s the system was providing bastions of strategic power to liberals even in the midst of the strongest conservative movement in a half-century. Three basic changes account for this new trend. Since the mid-1960s, in good part because of the changes created by the civil rights legislation, Republicanism has grown greatly in the South, particularly in statewide elections. There are fewer Southern Democrats in Congress, and those who remain are less certain to hold their seats for a long enough time to accumulate the seniority needed to chair a committee. In 1960 all Southern Senators were Democrats; in 1982 half were Republicans. In the House, 94 percent of Southerners were Democrats in 1960 but only 64 percent twenty years later.[20]

The Republican party became a real competitor in Southern politics, thanks in part to the white reaction to civil rights legislation and the GOP's move to the right on the issue. Competition means less secure accumulation of seniority, and it means that more of the South's seniority is on the minority side of the aisle, where it will never lead to committee chairmanships.

The Voting Rights Act and the
Reconstruction of Minority Representation

The other vital change produced in large measure by the Voting Rights Act is that many Southern states now have a much larger black electorate. The loss of conservative white votes makes the black support vital for Democrats in many congressional elections. Democrats have learned how to build successful biracial coalitions to hold seats in Congress. Because key civil rights votes are highly visible to blacks, there is now a Southern constituency of real political power for civil rights votes in Congress.

TABLE 9.1.
Committee Chairmen and Civil Rights Support Scores,
99th Congress, 1986 (percent)

Committee	LCCR Score	Chairman
Senate Judiciary	96	Biden (Delaware)
House Judiciary	90	Rodino (New Jersey)

Note: Score is percentage of "correct" votes, as rated by Leadership Conference on Civil Rights, the lobbying coalition of civil rights organizations (LCCR).
Source: JCPS Congressional District Fact Book, 3d ed., 1988.

The old "inner circle" of conservative Southern Democratic leaders in the Senate who saw to it that Southerners started building their seniority on the key committees while liberals did not, no longer exists.[21] An important part of Lyndon Johnson's consolidation of power as Senate Majority Leader in the 1950s was that he broke with this tradition, giving liberals fair access to good committee assignments. The results were not evident for some time, but are apparent now.

One key committee for civil rights, Senate Judiciary, symbolizes the changes. The last two Democratic chairs of the Senate Judiciary Committee have been Northern liberals, Senators Edward Kennedy (Democrat of Massachusetts) and Joseph Biden (Democrat of Delaware), both with an markedly different view from that of long-time chairman, James O. Eastland, a segregationist planter from Mississippi who chaired the committee into the 1970s, or Republican Chairman Senator Strom Thurmond, who became famous for leading the Dixiecrat walkout on the Democratic party following the adoption of a civil rights plank at its 1948 convention. Since the 1960s one or both of the judiciary committees in Congress have always been chaired by liberals who were prepared to use their power as chairmen to block anti–civil rights measures when public opinion moved in a negative direction (see Table 9.1).

The dominant wing of the Democratic party in each chamber is composed of Northern liberals. The House leadership has had strong control of the Rules Committee for two decades, and it has not blocked any civil rights legislation since the early 1960s. One of the most interesting effects of the seniority system, together with the expansion of black representation and the development of the Black Caucus and the Hispanic Caucus in the House of Representatives, has been the accumulation of strategic positions by minority members ideologically located on the left of the congressional policy spectrum. In some key positions today, the seniority system amplifies the views of the minority members in much the same way it used to give added weight to Southern conservatives.

Black and Hispanic members have worked closely with the Democratic leadership to gain broad representation on powerful committees, particularly those of special interest to their communities. Since all represent districts with a large minority population and overwhelming Democratic majorities, and since they have little hope of achieving a higher office, because of white prejudice, they are like the old Southern Democrats in the security of their electoral base, remaining in office as long as they want to continue to run and very unlikely to leave to run for something else.

Almost all black and Hispanic seniority is accumulating within the party that has run the House almost without interruption for nearly six decades. Two of the three chairmen of the House Education and Labor Committee since 1961 have been black. In 1988 there were senior blacks and Hispanics in a number of key positions in the House, including chairman of the crucial Budget Committee, and their power is likely to increase further with time (see Table 9.2). Minorities still have far fewer representatives than their proportion of the population but the number will grow with the requirements of the 1982 Voting Rights Act for drawing congressional district boundaries in the 1990s that provide fair representation of minority voters. The enormously rapid growth of the Hispanic population and its extreme concentration in a limited number of metropolitan areas should produce a particularly rapid growth in Hispanic membership as the number of voting-age Hispanic citizens grows and registration and turnout levels increase. Much of the Hispanic population is concentrated in rapidly growing states that will be gaining representation in Congress.

By the late 1980s the members of the Black and Hispanic caucuses in the House of Representatives were both highly visible national leaders and very important figures in their own communities. Moreover, the twenty-three members of the Black Caucus and the eleven members of the Hispanic Caucus occupied strategic positions, including the chair of one of the most powerful committees in Congress, the House Budget Committee. Augustus Hawkins, a member representing the Los Angeles ghetto, knows and cares about urban minority programs and has a hammerlock on education and jobs legislation as chairman of the House Education and Labor Committee. A number of minority members of Congress are now in important positions to initiate new policies, to fight effective guerrilla wars against policy retreats during conservative periods, and to exercise great leverage in policy bargaining.

TABLE 9.2.
Committee and Subcommittee Chairmanships,
Black and Hispanic Chairs, 100th Congress, 1988

Chairperson	Committee/Subcommittee
Gray (Pa.)	Budget Committee
Hawkins (Calif.)	Education and Labor Committee
DeLaGarza (Tex.)	Agriculture Committee
Dellums (Calif.)	District of Columbia
Rangel (N.Y.)	Select Committee on Narcotics Abuse
Stokes (Ohio)	Select Committee on Intelligence
Leland (Tex.)	Select Committee on Hunger
Roybal (Calif.)	Select Committee on Aging
Dixon (Calif.)	Committee on Standards of Official Conduct
Dellums (Calif.)	Subcommittee on Military Installations
Fauntroy (D.C.)	Subcommittee on International Development
Fauntroy (D.C.)	D.C. Subcommittee on Fiscal Affairs
Savage (Ill.)	Subcommittee on Economic Development
Dixon (Calif.)	Appropriations Subcommittee on D.C.
Hawkins (Calif.)	Subcommittee on Elementary, Secondary, and Vocational Education
Hawkins (Calif.)	Subcommittee on Investment, Jobs, and Prices
Dymally (Calif.)	D.C. Subcommittee on Judiciary
Dymally (Calif.)	Subcommittee on Census and Population
Roybal (Calif.)	Subcommittee on Appropriations
Collins (Ill.)	Subcommittee on Government Activities and Transportation
Conyers (Mich.)	Subcommittee on Criminal Justice
Crockett (Mich.)	Subcommittee on Western Hemisphere Affairs
Clay (Mo.)	Subcommittee on Labor-Management Relations
Rangel (N.Y.)	Ways and Means Subcommittee on Select Revenue
Ford (Tenn.)	Ways and Means Subcommittee on Public Assistance and Unemployment Compensation
Leland (Tex.)	Subcommittee on Postal Operations
Roybal (Calif.)	Appropriations Subcommittee on Treasury-Postal Service
Roybal (Calif.)	Subcommittee on Retirement Income and Employment
Martinez (Calif.)	Subcommittee on Employment Opportunities
Garcia (N.Y.)	Subcommittee on International Finance, Trade, and Monetary Policy
Gonzalez (Tex.)	Subcommittee on Housing and Commercial Development

164

The Voting Rights Act and the Changing Positions
of White Southern Democrats in Congress

Legal requirements for racial change always meet with resistance, and that resistance is always fed back through the political process. This was true in the case of all the basic civil rights laws, including the Voting Rights Act, which vastly extended federal authority over elections in the Deep South. Unlike the other basic civil rights laws, the Voting Rights Act was not permanent legislation but was set to expire in five years unless extended by Congress. This meant that Congress had to take action again, and perhaps to face another filibuster, under the much more conservative Nixon administration and after the collapse of the civil rights movement, which by the end of the 1960s had lost its key leaders and had fragmented into various groups.

The Voting Rights Act survived because it worked. Its goal was to change the political process rapidly, and it did. The filibuster system was no longer decisive for voting rights because the law had sufficiently transformed politics that a number of senators from the very states that had resisted most strongly felt that they now had more to lose from black voters by opposing renewal of the act than they had to gain from whites by attacking it. Blacks intensely favored the voting rights law while its elimination was not a top priority for whites. Even in the South, surveys showed that many whites supported voting rights. The congressional base of opposition was severely eroded, and Republican leaders were not ready to pay the possible political costs of moving to the right of Southern Democrats by opposing voting rights protections that were widely accepted outside the South. Thus there was simply not sufficient manpower for a successful filibuster. Even in the most conservative periods, civil rights advocates were able to not only forestall attacks but actually strengthen and lengthen the Voting Rights Act.

The act greatly increased black political participation (Table 9.3). The 1970s amendments strengthened the provisions protecting voters who were not English-speaking and helped create a strong Hispanic constituency for the law. Because of the movement of the national Republican party against civil rights policies and the identification of the Democratic party with minority interests, almost all of the new black voters came into the Democratic electorate, where they soon became an extremely important part of the party's vote. This meant that for Democrats who wished to receive nominations and be elected to Congress, it was important not to alienate the black voters while attempting to appeal to white voters to the greatest possible extent. As a result, Southern Democrats in Congress became much more sensitive to black

TABLE 9.3.
Black and White Voting in the South,
1966–86 (percent)

Year	Whites	Blacks
1966	45.2	32.9
1968	61.9	51.6
1970	46.4	36.8
1972	57.0	47.8
1974	37.4	30.0
1976	57.1	45.7
1978	41.4	33.5
1980	57.4	48.2
1982	42.9	38.3
1984	58.1	53.2
1986	43.5	42.5

Source: U. S. Census Bureau.

issues, particularly those not crucial to the white voters not already firmly in the Republican column. Since a great many of the leading white opponents to civil rights were now Republicans, there was little political value for Democrats in an anti–civil rights posture.

Within a few years, the Voting Rights Act dramatically altered traditional expectations about the voting of Southern Democrats on some civil rights issues. Much to their surprise, the administration leaders attempting to follow a "Southern strategy" of anti–civil rights policy during the Nixon and Reagan administrations found themselves facing some hostile Southern senators and representatives. This pattern first emerged in 1970, when a number of Southern senators broke ranks to support extension of the Voting Rights Act and to defeat the nomination of a Southern conservative judge, G. Harrold Carswell, for the Supreme Court. Only half of the Southern senators voted against the extension bill and four actually voted in favor. Other senators from the Deep South refused to participate in a filibuster that could hurt them with black constituents.[22] On the Carswell vote, the nominee, who was assailed for his harsh anti–civil rights record on the bench, lost the decisive votes of four Southern senators in spite of intense pressure from the White House, which tried to brand opponents as "anti-Southern."[23]

The pattern was much more dramatic in 1987, when Southern Democrats played a crucial role in the defeat of President Reagan's effort to put Judge Robert Bork on the High Court over the determined opposition of the civil rights lobby and other critics. The fifty-eight negative Senate votes against confirmation included all but one Southern Democrat and also one of the Southern Republicans.[24] During 1988 the great majority of Southern Democrats voted for the two major civil rights measures of the year, the Civil Rights Restoration Act and the new fair housing law. Eight Southern Senators had a voting record rated 75 percent or more correct by the civil rights lobby and 15 voted to override President Reagan's veto of the Civil Rights Restoration Act.[25]

This change in the position of the Southern Democrats in the Senate has had extremely important consequences. As long as the South could be considered a unit, the possibility of breaking a filibuster on civil rights was extremely dim. The senators from the states directly affected had enough strength to prevent a vote on passage of a civil rights measure in most cases by filibustering. With the southern Senators split, there is no automatic blocking vote and a filibuster will be successful only when it receives substantial Republican support.

The Changing Presidential and Congressional Electorates

Several major developments have radically changed the political influences shaping both presidential and congressional elections, with the net result that the presidency has become much more susceptible to radical change on racial policy while Congress has become strongly disposed against negative civil rights changes. The presidential electorate and presidential campaign strategy has shifted. The minority vote is no longer a key swing vote but is a basic part of the Democratic party's coalition, a part that is highly influential when the Democrats are in power but has had very little access to Republican presidents since the 1950s. The electoral college contests now focus on swing states in the South and West, where the swing voters are whites. The suburbs of the large cities in the biggest states are another clear target of presidential contests. The basic situation is currently unfavorable for the representation of minority interests in the executive branch when it is in GOP hands.

Congress is quite different. In the first place, the House of Representatives has little turnover. More than nine-tenths of those seeking reelection normally return to Washington, and party control in the House has not changed for more than a third of a century. House seats have not changed to any extent since the 1960s. Districting for House seats has been changed to increase minority representation because of the requirements of the 1982 voting rights legislation and the fact that blacks and Hispanics were increasing far more rapidly than whites.

The only federal requirements for congressional districts, in fact, are those coming from the Supreme Court, which specify that each district in a state must represent approximately the same number of voters and the Voting Rights Act requirement that the districts should be drawn to permit the election of minority representatives where there are concentrated minority populations that have not historically had representation.

While Southern congressional seats have become much more competitive and much more of the seniority has been invested in the GOP, where it rarely produces real congressional power, exactly the opposite has happened for minority representatives. Black and Hispanic representation has been concentrated almost exclusively in the Democratic party and, once elected, minority politicians face few obstacles to reelection and to the accumulation of power and position within the majority party. Thus, even as the Southerners were historically overrepresented in critical chairmanships in the House, it is likely that minority members will be substantially overrepresented in the future.

Senate campaigns are much more like the presidential races, with the significant exception that many of the Republican senators representing the major industrial states have not followed the move of the national GOP platform and administrations into opposition on civil rights measures. In fact, Republican senators from these states have been instrumental in defeating a number of the key civil rights initiatives of conservative GOP presidents since the 1960s. Republican senators from California, Pennsylvania, Connecticut, and Rhode Island, for example, had a relatively liberal voting record on civil rights in the 100th Congress. A number of Republican senators have, in turn, maintained a significant nonwhite voting constituency even as the black Republican vote for president has almost disappeared. In highly competitive states, candidates can seldom afford to write off major groups in advance in the hopes of profiting from racial polarization.

THE CHANGING SIGNIFICANCE OF THE FILIBUSTER SYSTEM

The most obvious barrier to civil rights legislation and the one that made it virtually impossible to enact serious bills from 1875 until 1964 was the Senate's tradition of unlimited debate, which prevented any vote on significant civil rights legislation. Only three major pieces of civil rights legislation won cloture votes in the 1960s. Filibusters reemerged the very year after the triumph of the Voting Rights Act in 1965. A fair housing bill was summarily killed in the Senate in 1966, and only an extremely skillful effort in 1968 was able to win Senate passage of the fair housing law. That bill might well have been blocked in the House Rules Committee were it not for the assassination of Martin Luther King, Jr., and the riots in Washington just before the vote.

During the coming years, filibusters were used effectively both against civil rights measures and against measures intended to limit civil rights enforcement. Relatively few major civil rights proposals came up for a vote in the Senate and a substantial share were disposed of by minorities using the filibuster to block any vote or using the threat of a filibuster to critically weaken any proposed bill.

The first modern pro–civil rights filibuster came in 1972, shortly before the presidential election, as President Nixon attempted to win congressional passage of legislation intended to limit the ability of the courts to order school desegregation in urban areas where busing was necessary to put students into integrated schools. The liberals fought off three efforts to end debate and force a vote just a month before the landslide reelection victory of President Nixon. The highly unusual liberal filibuster in October 1972 succeeded in defeating three attempts to end debate and force a vote; it was successful in preventing passage of legislation that commanded a popular majority at the time, in spite of its probable unconstitutionality.[26]

A variety of stalling techniques, legislative hearings designed to produce positive information, and other strategies were used to blocked anti–civil rights proposals, particularly antibusing bills, early in the Reagan era, when they might have been enacted. These strategies, together with the inherent constitutional difficulties of any policy attempting to limit the courts, protected the unpopular policy until attention shifted to other issues.

Filibusters also continued to have negative effects, of course, blocking congressional action on bills providing stronger remedies for job and housing discrimination. A filibuster in 1972 against a bipartisan bill resulting from a three-year struggle to strengthen enforcement against job discrimination succeeded in weakening the bill by eliminating key enforcement tools.[27] Later, in 1980, filibusters killed the effort to enact a fair housing enforcement bill that doubtless had the support of a majority of the senators. Although there was a 54-43 majority to end debate and enact the law, that was short of the 60 votes needed and the measure died.[28] The recollection of a bitter filibuster and the massive efforts of one of the nation's largest lobbies and sources of campaign funds, the National Association of Realtors, blocked another effort to enact enforcement legislation until nearly the end of the decade. Even then, the only way to get any legislation enacted in the face of this threat was for the civil rights organizations to work out a bargain with the real estate lobby for a modest expansion of enforcement authority during the 1988 presidential campaign.

The filibuster system remained a serious obstacle to major civil rights legislation throughout recent history. Even though the Nixon busing episode showed that it was also possible to use this tactic to prevent civil rights reversals, it remained much more a barrier to positive change. In contrast to the situation in the early 1960s, however, when civil rights supporters faced a barrier that had never been breached, it is now clear that the barrier is far from absolute.

NEGATIVE EXECUTIVE INITIATIVES

Civil rights reversals do not often require positive action by Congress. Many can come in a simple refusal to enforce existing law. The executive branch can render most provisions of civil rights law that remain controversial virtual dead letters, at least for a time, by refusing to apply them. The federal courts will intervene to overrule administrators only in highly unusual circumstances, and even when they have found administrators violating civil rights enforcement duties, the courts have had great difficulty in controlling the federal administrative processes. Another important presidential strategy toward weakening civil rights law without congressional action is to appoint federal judges and administrators in civil rights agencies who come from conservative backgrounds and are inclined to interpret civil rights law narrowly.

One striking fact about the anti–civil rights policies of the Reagan and Bush administrations is that they never went to Congress asking for legislation on their civil rights goals. They attempted to achieve them in the same way the liberals did before they had a congressional majority—by executive action and by decisions from an increasingly sympathetic judiciary.

THE CHANGED ROLE OF CONGRESS AND THE COURTS

Anyone writing about the making of civil rights policies in the 1940s or 1950s would have to describe the federal courts as the most important avenue of expanding governmental protection of equal rights. Usually, all other paths were closed.

U.S. SUPREME COURT MEMBERSHIP

During the Johnson administration, in the mid-1960s, the elected branches of government took decisive leadership. By the end of the decade, with the negative policies of the Nixon presidency, the Supreme Court had again become the crucial pro–civil rights force. From 1969 through the early 1970s, the Court was particularly forceful in rejecting political pressure against school desegregation and initiating busing orders in the face of intense public opposition and strong criticism from the president. The Court made clear that actual desegregation had to be achieved rapidly and that district-wide busing was an appropriate remedy.[29] Between 1968 and 1972, for example, the fraction of Southern blacks in intensely segregated schools fell from 78 percent to 25 percent as the new court orders were implemented.[30]

A central goal of the conservative movement, however, was to change the Supreme Court by changing its membership. The decisions on race, on the rights of accused criminals, and on abortion were particular targets of attack. A conservative judiciary was sought with great intensity by Presidents Nixon, Reagan, and Bush. By 1974, the Nixon administration had appointed four justices and produced a much more conservative court, ending the period of substantial forward movement of civil rights decisions. For instance, the Court's 5-4 decision of 1974 against city-suburban school integration, *Milliken* v. *Bradley* (418 U.S. 717), ended progress in school desegregation. Four of the five negative votes were cast by Nixon justices. The Court's negative decisions on school finance cases and on litigation attempting to end exclusionary zoning in suburbs blocked off change in other key areas of urban inequality. Since that time, there has been no gain in integration for black students in the United States and Hispanics have become far more segregated.[31]

President Reagan had three Supreme Court appointments, including a new chief justice. Reagan appointed William Rehnquist, the most conservative Nixon justice with the strongest record of opposition to civil rights issues, to the position.[32] As a Supreme Court clerk, Rehnquist had opposed overturning the *Plessy* doctrine of "separate but equal" and he had been a leading opponent of civil rights on the Court. President Bush followed directly in the Reagan model, nominating strong conservatives, including Clarence Thomas, a black conservative who had served the Reagan administration by dismantling much of the civil rights enforcement process at the U.S. Department of Education and then at the Equal Employment Opportunities Commission.[33] By the early 1990s the great majority of federal judges had been appointed by Presidents

Reagan and Bush and there had not been an appointment by a Democratic president to the Supreme Court for a quarter century.

Fierce battles were waged over the Supreme Court nominees of all three presidents, battles that produced three of the four Senate defeats for nominees in this century and forced the withdrawal of other nominations even before they could be considered. Civil rights issues were prominent in all of these battles as well as in the fight over both Rehnquist's initial nomination to the Court and his selection as chief justice, which produced the largest negative vote received by any successful nominee in the century. In these instances it was the president who was attempting to move the Court toward a more conservative posture on civil rights and Congress that resisted and slowed the process.

U.S. SUPREME COURT AND INTERPRETATION OF CIVIL RIGHTS LEGISLATION

Even though some of the basic established civil rights principles did not change fundamentally under the more conservative court, the Reagan administration did win two major Supreme Court victories concerning the meaning of the most important civil rights measures of the 1960s, the Voting Rights Act and the 1964 Civil Rights Act. The Supreme Court, in the *Bolden* case, greatly increased the burden of proof on civil rights groups in voting rights cases and interpreted the 1964 provision forbidding discrimination in institutions receiving federal assistance so narrowly in the *Grove City College* case that institutions could accept federal aid without incurring any general civil rights responsibilities. These cases could have been first steps toward the kind of judicial nullification of civil rights reforms that appeared in the *Slaughter House* cases of 1873 and culminated in the 1896 "separate but equal" decision in *Plessy* v. *Ferguson*, which stood as a great justification for the South's apartheid laws until the *Brown* decision fifty-eight years later. Even later, four decisions in 1989 dramatically curtailed affirmative action policies relating to employment and state and local government contracting.

Battles on the issue of interpretation of civil rights legislation had begun in early 1985, with the introduction of the Civil Rights Restoration Act, finally approved by both houses in 1988. It won overwhelming passage in the face of strong opposition and a threatened veto from the White House. When President Reagan became the first president in 120 years to veto a civil rights bill, Congress promptly enacted the law over his veto by a 73-24 vote.[34] Congress was once again showing its willingness to close large gaps in civil rights coverage opened by court decisions resting on claims that Congress had intended narrow enforcement policies. Congress did not have the necessary votes, however, to override President Bush's veto of the affirmative action legislation in 1990. The president and some GOP congressional candidates carried the issue to the nation, claiming that affirmative action legislation would actually require "quotas" and thereby would discriminate against whites, even though the bill explicitly forbade quotas.

The Supreme Court's limits on the reach of civil rights responsibilities in institutions receiving federal aid also brought a rapid counterattack on Capitol Hill. Although the House passed the Civil Rights Act of 1984 just months after the Supreme Court's *Grove City College* decision, the bill faced opposition from both the committee and the majority leader in the GOP-controlled Senate. The bill was killed by parliamentary strategies preventing a vote even after cloture had been invoked.[35]

Limiting U.S. Supreme Court decisions were not accepted by Congress, which had the power to reverse them because they turned on the Court's interpretation of congressional intent, not of the Constitution. The decisions created large new issues in Congress, stimulating proposals to strengthen the acts and to reverse the Supreme Court's narrow interpretations. The voting rights problems were reversed and the law strengthened by Congress in 1982. Title VI coverage was expanded greatly in the 1988 Civil Rights Restoration Act. Only a presidential veto blocked the expansion of federal affirmative action policy by Congress in 1990. Bush continued to vigorously attack the measure in 1991, denouncing it as a quota bill even though it explicitly forbade quotas. Nonetheless, the House of Representatives passed the bill, 273-158, knowing that members might be subject to racial scare advertising about whites losing jobs to blacks like that used by Senator Jesse Helms (Republican of North Carolina) in his 1990 campaign.[36]

DEVELOPING THE AGENDA: HEARINGS AND POLICY

One of the most important roles of Congress is to bring to light new issues. Congressional committees are incubators of issues not yet prominent on the national agenda. In an area so extremely visible and sensitive as racial policy, major changes typically require support from the general public and the executive branch, media focus on the issues, and a variety of other special conditions that are far beyond the reach of committee or subcommittee chairs. Any major change reflects years of work on many fronts.

The committees can collect and publicize extremely important information about racial issues, independent of the executive or whatever happens to be the prevailing attitude of the time. At times when the executive branch is reversing civil rights policy, committees can expose the problems and call into question the data and justifications of policy changes used by the executive branch. Serving three purposes, some congressional hearings have been critical: putting the civil rights issue before the public; increasing public understanding of it; and building pressure against not only weak enforcement policies, but also anti–civil rights actions of the past generation.

The most controversial civil rights issue in Congress after the late 1960s was the busing question. Three large series of hearings were very important in limiting the negative initiatives of President Nixon and President Reagan and in creating a base for limited positive action. The largest set of hearings, and one of the most far-reaching ever on any racial issue, were those of the Senate Select Committee on Equal Education, created in response to the busing crisis and chaired by Senator Walter Mondale (Democrat of Minnesota). In dozens of hearings across the country, the committee explored all aspects of the issue and the conditions that led the courts to order desegregation. It ended up not only diffusing the efforts of the Nixon administration for legislative action or a constitutional amendment to limit the courts but also contributing substantially to the shaping of the only positive federal action on urban desegregation yet to emerge from Congress—the Emergency School Aid of 1972.[37]

Two sets of extensive hearings by the House Judiciary Committee played an important role in defusing initiatives to limit school desegregation. The 1972 hearings on constitutional amendment proposals against busing demonstrated the severe legal and practical problems with the proposals and provided an important review of the facts at the heart of the busing controversy.[38] Hearings in 1981 by the House Subcommittee on Civil and Constitutional Rights provided a similar examination of the objectives of the Reagan Justice Department in this area and the basic facts of the controversy in the early 1980s.[39]

The fair housing enforcement effort was kept alive legislatively primarily by hearings in the House and Senate Judiciary Committee. In addition, voting rights hearings helped build the record and the consensus that led to substantive expansions of the laws in the Nixon and Reagan periods. Senate judiciary hearings played a dominant role in gathering opposition to the three Supreme Court nominees defeated during the past two decades.

Particularly since the change in the role of the U.S. Civil Rights Commission in the 1980s, congressional committees have become both the principal monitors of civil rights enforcement and proponents of civil rights issues. If there is to be another period of expansion of federal civil rights policy, its direction will almost surely be foreshadowed in the activities of a few committees and subcommittees on Capitol Hill.

WHAT CONGRESS HAS NOT DONE: STASIS AND POLICY

Although Congress has become a relatively progressive force in civil rights policy in the last generation, much of this record rests merely on blocking executive policy and judicial policy changes that would have reversed civil rights gains. The key term for Congress is "relatively progressive."

Very little progress has been made in strengthening civil rights law except in the area in which there is the greatest consensus, voting rights. The law has been extended even when under attack from the administration, its coverage has been expanded, and it has been transformed from a temporary to a quasi-permanent statute. The Supreme Court decision limiting the law's power has been reversed by an amendment making clear the requirement for positive action to ensure minority representation.

Dealing with deep-seated racial problems, however, requires much more than blocking negative moves or expanding relatively noncontroversial policies. It also requires positive actions to extend civil rights protections where necessary, particularly for problems of urban racial inequality on which real progress has been almost nonexistent. In striking contrast to the far-reaching and drastic laws that changed the South, we have no laws requiring a clear goal of integrating urban communities and schools. We do not even have an effective process for investigating and correcting individual violations of housing and job rights against discrimination.

The underlying assumption of public policy against housing discrimination is that the problem can readily be addressed through weak enforcement machinery capable of dealing with only a small number of individual cases of discrimination each year. The best research indicates, however, that there are millions of violations each year. Even modest changes to slightly increase the effectiveness of the fair housing law were blocked from 1980 to 1988, when a modest strengthening amendment, accepted by the real estate industry, finally became law. The enforcement process is still highly limited.

Even less has been done to make possible larger changes. There has been no serious discussion in Congress of the racial effects of suburban exclusion of low-income and working-class families. The requirement in the 1974 community development and housing legislation for "spatial deconcentration of the poor" was not seriously enforced. Federal civil rights law was amended in the mid-1970s to explicitly forbid federal education officials from requiring busing, even though the courts had recognized that it is the only way to achieve desegregation in urban communities with serious residential segregation. Congress prohibited Legal Services lawyers from handling cases for minority children requesting desegregation or urban schools.

The fundamental political problem is that although the public opposed the Southern system of official segregation, no similar conclusion emerged concerning the causes of or solutions for urban racial segregation and inequality. Public opinion has always been divided even on some of the issues already embodied in federal law, such as fair housing, to say nothing of those not yet faced. The white public does not accept either the responsibility for current racial inequalities or the argument that there must be drastic changes to repair the damage caused by the ghetto system and ghetto education. The surveys show, for example, that although most Americans accept the principle of fair housing, there has never been a significant majority in favor of government efforts to enforce that right. A depressingly high fraction of the public still believes that owners should have the right to discriminate in selling their homes.

When Congress is described as a more progressive institution than the presidency in terms of civil rights, this means that it seldom moves backward and sometimes takes strategic steps to block reversals or to take small steps forward on relatively noncontroversial issues. Very occasionally, as on the affirmative action issues in 1990 and on the various voting rights amendments since 1970, have there been major changes.

Compared with the presidency, which has varied wildly in orientation toward civil rights in the post-*Brown* period, this is a very important role. It means that once important reforms are enacted they are, to a considerable degree, insulated from hostile changes in national opinion and from political tactics attempting to exploit racial fears, both of which have occurred in the presidency.

The Supreme Court can be significantly altered by consistently ideological appointments, and all of the justices appointed by Presidents Nixon, Reagan, and Bush were selected with such a goal in mind. As already mentioned, this was, of course, a central reason for the fierce Senate battles over four of the appointees and for pressures from the Senate that led to the exclusion of others from consideration. There have been clear civil rights consequences of those Nixon and Reagan appointees that were confirmed, primarily in terms of blocking further development of civil rights law and in strictly limiting the enforceability of other rights.

Congress protected the basic legacy of the civil rights reforms of the 1960s and avoided the temptation to enter into confrontation with the courts over the most controversial issues such as busing. It has not been able, however, to take even small positive steps of any sort on sensitive urban racial issues in the 1980s. It has not even begun the serious work of understanding where the burgeoning Hispanic population fits into the civil rights equation. Apart from small bilingual education programs, language discrimination provisions of the Voting Rights Act, and some protections against discrimination in the immigration reform law, which was opposed by many Hispanic leaders, there has been a policy vacuum regarding what will be the nation's largest minority community in another generation. For black Americans, Congress has served primarily as a bulwark of the status quo in a period when the status quo has come to include some important civil rights laws.

THE TRENDS AND THE FUTURE: CONGRESS AND POLICY CHANGE

In a society where blacks and Hispanics constitute a rapidly increasing share of the young people and where there are profound signs of inequality and social and educational decay in the concentrated urban minority areas, it may be vital for some branch of government to be able to take quick and decisive action to deal with severe and basic problems by attacking central elements of the system of inequality. There is no evidence that Congress or any other political institution is prepared to do this at present. The domination of, first, the executive branch and, then, the federal judiciary by strong opponents of civil rights is clear. One of the ultimate questions for a democracy is whether it is capable of acting on an issue of discrimination by its majority group, discrimination that that group refuses to recognize.

The problem is exacerbated by the fact that Congress requires a super-majority for major actions, but it is rooted in more fundamental characteristics of American politics. Although many of the serious political conflicts in American history have turned on questions of race, the elected branches of government have generally been unable or unwilling to take significant action on racial problems except in times of great crisis or social and political change.

In all of American history, major initiatives extending federal power to protect civil rights have been put forth only twice, during the Reconstruction and during 1964–72. The first was the product of an immensely costly civil war and some of the changes were imposed by a Congress without representatives from the South. The second was the product of major social change, several of the most important Supreme Court decisions in American history, and one of the country's greatest social movements. The reforms of the 1960s wrote into law large changes in the Southern apartheid system that grew out of generations of protest, research, litigation, and changing public attitudes. Even under those extraordinary circumstances, the powerful measures were focused overwhelmingly on the South, and there was a huge political price for the political party that imposed them—the party lost all but one of the Southern states in the next election and precipitated a historic political realignment of white Southern voters, breaking a pattern that had held since the Civil War.

Decisive action by the president and Congress has been limited largely to the classic problems of the South—slavery and the Jim Crow system. Neither Congress nor the president has ever acted strongly against the remaining source of racial inequality, the ghetto system of metropolitan America. Nor have the courts shown any willingness to significantly alter the systems that produce segregated housing and schools in the metropolitan areas where two-thirds of our population lives.

Even conceding that serious civil rights action by any branch of government is rare, Congress still played an extremely important function during the periods of general stalemate or reaction. First, it participated in the struggles over the maintenance, interpretation, and application of the principles enacted in the major reform eras, and second, it contributed to the gradual development of public understanding and consensus within the political system concerning the central issues that have not been addressed. It is well to remember that Reconstruction ended primarily not through repeal of the constitutional amendments and laws of the Reconstruction Congresses, but through political decisions not to enforce them, later confirmed by the courts. The laws remained, and it was the judicial decisions culminating in *Brown* that brought them back to life and helped spur the great social movement of the 1960s.

Since the triumphs of the civil rights movement in the 1960s, Congress and the president have battled over the enforcement or abandonment of existing policies, over appointments to the Supreme Court and other agencies that may decisively affect racial policy, and over efforts to limit or reverse court decisions. Congress has been able to preserve the civil rights laws of the 1960s and to maintain some pressure for their enforcement. Whenever the Supreme Court has narrowed the readings of the laws, Congress has responded by enacting amendments to clarify its intent for broader enforcement policies. Congressional hearings have helped to keep issues alive and set the agenda for the next period of more rapid reform. These have been invaluable contributions, though their short-term impact is usually hard to detect. Through a series of political changes, the institutions seen a generation ago as the decisive forces in civil rights protection have receded or reversed direction. Congress, often denounced as the great obstacle, has become a central protector of the legacy of civil rights reform.

The congressional system is still not well adapted to cope with new civil rights issues. Some of its old institutional problems no longer have the same consequences, but important political trends, particularly the reorientation of the Republican party against civil rights, mean that the congressional requirements for extraordinary majorities will create serious problems, as they did for the proposals to modestly expand job and housing antidiscrimination enforcement in 1972 and 1980. The filibuster system remains a key barrier, not because of the South but because of its much more frequent use by the conservative movement. For the foreseeable future, the seniority system, particularly in the House, may have a strong positive bias toward minority issues.

The root of the problem with contemporary civil rights policy is not our institutions; rather, it is the fact that most Americans do not think there are any serious problems. Yet, few leaders in any branch of government are challenging this belief. Until they do, it will be the task of Congress to protect the structure of the law and to keep alive one of the most important debates for the future of our society.

NOTES

1. Howard E. Shuman, "Senate Rules and the Civil Rights Bill," *American Political Science Review* (December 1957): 995–75. See also Joseph Clark, *The Senate Establishment* (New York: Hill and Wang, 1963); and James MacGregor Burns, *The Deadlock of Democracy* (Englewood Cliffs, N.J.: Prentice-Hall, 1963).

2. See William C. Berman, *The Politics of Civil Rights in the Truman Administration* (Columbus: Ohio State University Press, 1970).

3. See J. W. Anderson, *Eisenhower, Brownell and the Congress: The Tangled Origins of the Civil*

Rights Bill of 1956–1957 (University: University of Alabama Press, 1964); and Myron W. Orfield, Jr., "Lyndon Johnson and the Senate: The Battle to Pass the 1957 Civil Rights Act" (Ph.D. diss., University of Minnesota, 1983).

4. William S. White, *Citadel* (New York: Harper, 1957), 67–94; and Hubert H. Humphrey, *The Education of A Public Man: My Life and Politics* (New York: Doubleday, 1976), 123–31.

5. See Burns, *The Deadlock of Democracy.*

6. Berman, *The Politics of Civil Rights,* 124–35.

7. Nelson W. Polsby and Aaron B. Wildavsky, *Presidential Elections: Strategies of American Electorial Politics,* 2d ed. (New York: Charles Scribner's Sons, 1968), 31–32.

8. Berman, *The Politics of Civil Rights,* 137.

9. Ralph J. Bunche, *The Political Status of the Negro in the Age of FDR* (Chicago: University of Chicago Press, 1973), 608–31.

10. See Berman, *The Politics of Civil Rights.*

11. Samuel Krislow, *The Negro in Federal Employment: The Quest for Opportunity* (Minneapolis: University of Minnesota, 1968), 35.

12. Carl M. Bauer, *John F. Kennedy and the Second Reconstruction* (New York: Columbia University Press, 1973), 43, 205–19.

13. See Harry S. Dent. *The Prodigal South Returns to Power* (New York: John Wiley and Sons, 1978); see also Wayne Greenhaw, *Elephants in the Cottonfields: Ronald Reagan and the New Republican South* (New York: Macmillan, 1982).

14. Paul R. Abramson, John H. Aldrich, and David W. Rohde, *Change and Continuity in the 1984 Elections* (Washington, D.C.: Congressional Quarterly Press, 1986), 83; and Gerald Pomper and others, *The Election of 1988: Reports and Interpretations* (Chatham, N.J.: Chatham House, 1989), 132.

15. See Henry J. Aaron, *Politics and the Professors: The Great Society in Perspective* (Washington, D.C.: Brookings Institution, 1978).

16. Charles Walen and Barbara Walen, *The Longest Debate: A Legislative History of the 1964 Civil Rights Act* (Cabin John, Md.: Seven Locks Press, 1985), 204–5.

17. See Gary Orfield, *The Reconstruction of Southern Education: The Schools and the 1964 Civil Rights Act* (New York: John Wiley, 1969).

18. Lyndon Baines Johnson, *The Vantage Point: Perspectives on the Presidency, 1963–1969* (New York: Holt, Rinehart, Winston, 1971), 176ff.

19. See Gary Orfield, *Must We Bus? Segregated Schools and National Policy* (Washington, D.C.: Brookings Institution, 1978), chap. 8.

20. Norman J. Ornstein, et al., *Vital Statistics on Congress, 1984–1985* ed. (Washington, D.C.: American Enterprise Institute, 1984), 12–16.

21. See White, *Citadel.*

22. *Congressional Record,* March 13, 1970; and *Chicago Daily News,* March 14, 1970.

23. *New York Times,* April 21, 1970.

24. *New York Times,* October 24, 1987.

25. See Leadership Conference on Civil Rights, "A Civil Rights Voting Record for the 100th Congress" (October, 1988).

26. Orfield, *Must We Bus?* 225.

27. Gary Orfield, *Congressional Power: Congress and Social Change* (New York: Harcourt Brace Jovanovich, 1975), 88–90.

28. *Congressional Quarterly Almanac*, 1980, 14, 373–77.

29. *Green* v. *New Kent County*, 391 U.S. 430 (1968); and *Swann* v. *Charlotte-Mecklenburg Board of Education*, 402 U.S. 1 (1971).

30. See Gary Orfield, "Public School Desegregation in the United States, 1968–1980" (Washington, D.C.: Joint Center for Political Studies, 1983).

31. See Myron Willard Orfield, Jr., "The Congressional Response to the Supreme Court's Decision in *Grove City College* v. *Bell*" (copy of unpublished manuscript, University of Chicago Law School, 1986).

32. Sue Davis, "Justice Rehnquist's Equal Protection Clause: An Interim Analysis," *Nebraska Law Review* 62 (1984): 288.

33. *Washington Post Weekly Edition*, September 1991, 16–22

34. See *Washington Post*, March 23, 1988.

35. See *Congressional Record*, October 2, 1984; see also Myron Willard Orfield, "The Congressional Response to the Supreme Court's Decision in *Grove City College* v. *Bell*."

36. See *New York Times*, May 31, June 6, 1991.

37. See Senate Select Committee on Equal Educational Opportunity, *Hearings Toward Equal Educational Opportunity*, Report 92–000, 92d Cong., 2d sess., 1972.

38. See U.S. House of Representatives Committee on the Judiciary Subcommittee, *Hearings—School Busing*, 92d Cong., 2d sess., 1972.

39. See U.S. House of Representatives, Subcommittee on Civil and Constitutional Rights, *Hearings—School Desegregation*, 97th Cong., 1st sess., 1981.

PART

THE LEGACY OF
RACIAL DISCRIMINATION

WHO PAYS THE COST?

DERRICK BELL

THE REAL COSTS
OF RACIAL DISCRIMINATION

Racial discrimination lives! Even the most conservative critics of civil rights policies will concede the continued existence of racial bias and acknowledge the heavy burden of discrimination borne by this nation's people of color. It is difficult to deny the obvious. Despite oft-repeated pledges of equal opportunity, discriminatory policies continue to facilitate the exploitation of black labor and bar access to benefits and opportunities that would otherwise be available. As has been the case since the slavery era, all the manifestations of exclusion-bred despair are explained on the asserted inferiority of the victims.

Two other interconnected political phenomena emanate from the widely shared belief that whites are superior to blacks. Both serve critically important stabilizing functions in the society.

First, whites of widely varying socioeconomic status, employ white supremacy as a catalyst to negotiate policy differences, often through compromises that sacrifice the rights of blacks.

Second, even those whites who lack wealth and power are sustained in their sense of racial superiority and thus rendered more willing to accept their lesser share by an unspoken but no less certain property right in their "whiteness." This right is recognized and upheld by courts and the society like all property rights under a government created and sustained primarily for that purpose.

The compromise-catalyst role of racism in American policy making has ancient roots. When the Constitution's Framers finished their summer's work in
Philadelphia, it was clear that their compromises on slavery were the key that
enabled Southerners and Northerners to work out their economic and political differences. The slavery compromises set a much-followed but never-
acknowledged precedent under which black rights have been sacrificed
throughout the nation's history to further white interests. But those compromises are far more than an embarrassing blot on our national history. Rather,
they are the original and still definitive examples of the ongoing struggle between individual rights reform and the maintenance of the socioeconomic
status quo.

Why did the Framers do it? Can we account for compromises with the
traditional rationalizations that the slavery provisions in the Constitution
were merely unfortunate concessions pressured by the crisis of events and
influenced by then prevailing beliefs? Such beliefs did include (1) slavery was
on the decline and would soon die of its own weight, or (2) Africans were
thought a different and inferior breed of beings and their enslavement carried
no moral onus.

The insistence of Southern delegates on protection of their slave property
was far too vigorous to suggest that the institution would soon be abandoned.
And the antislavery statements by slaves and white abolitionists alike were
too forceful to suggest that the slavery compromises were the product of men
who did not know the moral ramifications of what they did.[1]

The question of what motivated the Framers remains. My 1987 book, *And
We Are Not Saved*, contains several allegorical stories intended to explore various aspects of American racism using the tools of fiction.[2] In one of these
stories or "Chronicles," the book's heroine, Geneva Crenshaw, a black civil
rights lawyer who is gifted with extraordinary powers, is transported back to the
Constitutional Convention. Her mission is to use her knowledge of the next
two centuries to convince the Framers that they should not incorporate recognition and protection of slavery in the document they are writing.

To put it mildly, her sudden appearance in the locked meeting room and the
protection she is provided when the delegates try to eject her are sufficiently
startling to intimidate even those men, some of the outstanding figures of their
time. Some of the more vigorous delegates, outraged at the sudden appearance in their midst of a woman, and a black woman at that, charged toward
her. As Geneva described the scene:

> Suddenly, the hall was filled with the sound of martial music, blasting trum-
> pets, and a deafening roll of snare drums. At the same time—and as the dele-

gates were almost upon me—a cylinder composed of thin vertical bars of red, white, and blue light descended swiftly and silently from the high ceiling nicely encapsulating the podium and me.

To their credit, the self-appointed eviction party neither slowed nor swerved. As each man reached and tried to pass through the transparent light shield, there was a loud SssZap, quite like the sound electrified bug zappers make on a warm, summer evening. While not lethal, the shock the shield dealt each attacker was sufficiently strong to literally knock him to the floor, stunned and shaking.[3]

This phenomenon evoked chaos rather than attention in the room, but finally during a lull in the bedlam, Geneva tries for the third time to be heard.

"Gentlemen," she began again, "Delegates"—then paused and, with a slight smile, added, "fellow citizens, I have come to urge that, in your great work here, you not restrict to white men of property the sweep of Thomas Jefferson's self-evident truths. For all men (and women too) are equal and endowed by the Creator with inalienable rights, including, 'Life, Liberty and the pursuit of Happiness.'"[4]

The debate that ensues between Geneva and the Framers is vigorous, but despite the extraordinary powers at her disposal, Geneva is unable to alter the already reached compromises on slavery.

She tries to embarrass the Framers by pointing out the contradiction in their commitment to freedom and liberty and their embrace of slavery. They will not buy it:

"There is no contradiction in our compromise," replied one delegate. "Life and liberty are generally said to be of more value, than property, . . . [but] an accurate view of the matter would nevertheless prove that property is the main object of Society."

"A contradiction," another added, "would occur were we to follow the course you urge. We are not unaware of the moral issues raised by slavery, but we have no response to the Southern delegates who admonish us that 'property in slaves should not be exposed to danger under a Govt. instituted for the protection of property.'"

"Government, was instituted principally for the protection of property and was itself . . . supported by property. Property is the great object of government; the great cause of war; the great means of carrying it on. The primary protection the Southerners seek is that their government not take their slaves from them. After all, Negroes are their wealth, their only resource."[5]

Where, Geneva wondered, were those delegates from Northern states, many of whom abhorred slavery and had spoken out against it in the convention?

She found her answer in the castigation she received from one of the Framers who told her:

> "Woman, we would have you gone from this place. But if a record be made, that record should show that the economic benefits of slavery do not accrue only to the South. Plantation states provide a market for Northern factories, and the New England shipping industry and merchants participate in the slave trade. Northern states, moreover, utilize slaves in the fields, as domestics, and even as soldiers to defend against Indian raids."

> "Slavery has provided the wealth that made independence possible," another delegate told her. The profits from slavery funded the Revolution. It cannot be denied. At the time of the Revolution, the goods for which the United States demanded freedom were produced in very large measure by slave labor. Desperately needing assistance from other countries, we purchased this aid from France with tobacco produced mainly by slave labor. The nation's economic well-being depended on the institution, and its preservation is essential if the Constitution we are drafting is to be more than a useless document. At least, that is how we view the crisis we face."[6]

At the most dramatic moment of the debate, a somber delegate got to his feet and walked fearlessly right up to the shimmering light shield. Then he spoke seriously and with obvious anxiety:

> Woman. The contradiction of which you speak is real. Surely we know, even though we are at pains not to mention it, that we have sacrificed the freedom of your people in the belief that his involuntary forfeiture is necessary to secure the property interests of whites in a society espousing, as its basic principle, the liberty of all. Perhaps we, with the responsibility of forming a radically new government in perilous times, see more clearly than is possible for you in hindsight that the unavoidable cost of our labors will be the need to accept and live with what you call a contradiction.[7]

Realizing that she was losing the debate, Geneva intensified her efforts, but the imprisoned delegates' signals for help had been seen and the local militia summoned. Hearing some commotion beyond the window, she turned to see a small cannon being rolled up and aimed at her. Then, in quick succession, a militiaman lighted the fuse; the delegates dived under their desks; the cannon fired; and, with an ear-splitting roar, the cannonball broke against the light shield and splintered, leaving the shield intact, but terminating both the visit and all memory of it.[8]

The Framers felt—and likely they were right—that a government committed to the protection of property could not have come into being without the
race-based, slavery compromises placed in the Constitution. It is surely so
that the economic benefits of slavery and the political compromises of black
rights played a major role in the nation's growth and development. In short,
without slavery, there would be no Constitution to celebrate.

The point here—that the slavery compromises set a precedent under which
black rights have been sacrificed throughout the nation's history to further
white interests—is almost self-evident. Consider only a few examples:

- The long fight for universal male suffrage was successful in several states
  when opponents and advocates alike reached compromises based on their
  generally held view that blacks should not vote. Historian Leon Litwack
  reports, that "utilizing various political, social, economic, and pseudoan-
  thropological arguments, white suffragists moved to deny the vote to the
  Negro. From the admission of Maine in 1819 until the end of the Civil
  War, every new state restricted the suffrage to whites in its constitution."[9]

- By 1857, the nation's economic development had stretched the initial slavery compromises to the breaking point. The differences between planters
  and business interests that had been papered over seventy years earlier by
  greater mutual dangers could not be settled by a further sacrifice of black
  rights in the *Dred Scott* case.[10]

  Chief Justice Roger B. Taney's conclusion in *Dred Scott* that blacks had no
  rights whites were bound to respect—a view rather clearly reflecting the
  prevailing belief in his time as among the Founding Fathers—represented
  a renewed effort to compromise political differences between whites by
  sacrificing the right of blacks. The effort failed, less because Taney was
  willing to place all blacks—free as well as slave—outside the ambit of constitutional protection, than because he rashly committed the Supreme
  Court to one side of the fiercely contested issues of economic and political
  power that were propelling the nation toward the Civil War.

- When the Civil War ended, the North pushed through constitutional
  amendments, nominally to grant citizenship rights to former slaves, but
  actually to protect its victory. But within a decade, when another political
  crisis threatened a new civil war, black rights were again sacrificed in the
  Hayes-Tilden Compromise of 1877. Constitutional jurisprudence fell in
  line with Taney's conclusion regarding the rights of blacks vis à vis whites
  even as his legal opinion was condemned. The country moved ahead, but

blacks were cast into a status that only looked positive when compared with slavery itself.

I hope these examples suffice to make my first point. Throughout our history, whites of widely varying socioeconomic status have employed deeply set beliefs in white supremacy as a catalyst to negotiate and resolve policy differences, often through compromises that sacrifice the rights of blacks.

My second and connected point is that even those whites who lack wealth and power are sustained in their sense of racial superiority and thus rendered more willing to accept their lesser share, by an unspoken but no less certain property right in their "whiteness." This right is recognized and upheld by courts and the society like all property rights under a government created and sustained primarily for that purpose.

According to historians, including Edmund Morgan and David Brion Davis, most white laborers did not oppose slavery when it took root in the mid-1660s.[11] Although white laborers were and would remain economically subordinate to whites able to afford slaves, identification of whites as sharing a bond in their racial difference from and superiority over blacks mitigated against divisions based solely upon economic status. The creation of a black subclass enabled poor whites to identify with and support many of the policies of the upper class. Moreover, large landowners, with the safe economic advantage provided by their slaves, were willing to grant poor whites a larger role in the political process.[12] Thus, paradoxically, slavery for blacks led to greater freedom for poor whites, at least when compared with the denial of freedom to African slaves. Slavery also provided mainly propertyless whites with a property in their whiteness.

The upper classes were not unaware of the class-stabilizing role slavery played. In 1832, when the Virginia legislature convened to consider ending slavery in the wake of the South Hampton revolt, Thomas Roderick Dew argued that despite its economic limitations via capital/wage-labor, (and presumably its dangers), slavery should be retained because it afforded an ideological basis to resolve conflict between propertied and unpropertied whites, with the Negro as low man on the totem pole. And thus slavery was consistent with the spirit of republicanism in its ability to promote freedom and community among whites.

In the post-Reconstruction era, the constitutional amendments, initially promoted to provide rights for the newly emancipated blacks, were transformed into the major legal bulwarks for corporate growth. The legal philosophy of that era espoused liberty of action untrammeled by state authority, but the only logic of the ideology—and its goal—was the exploitation of the working class, whites as well as blacks.

As to whites, consider *Lochner* v. *New York*, where the Supreme Court refused to find that the state's police powers extended to protecting bakery employees against employers who required them to work in physically unhealthy conditions for more than ten hours per day and sixty hours per week.[13] Such maximum-hour legislation, the Court held, would interfere with the baker's inherent freedom to make their own contracts with the employers on the best terms they could negotiate. In effect, the Court simply assumed in that pre-union era that employees and employers bargained from positions of equal strength. Liberty of that sort legitimated the sweat shops in which men, women, and children were quite literally worked to death.

For blacks, of course, we can compare *Lochner* with the decision in *Plessy* v. *Ferguson*, decided only eight years earlier.[14] In *Plessy*, the Supreme Court upheld the state's police power to segregate blacks in public facilities even though such segregation must, of necessity, interfere with the liberties of facilities' owners to use their property as they saw fit.

Both opinions are quite similar in the Court's use of Fourteenth Amendment fictions: the assumed economic "liberty" of bakers in *Lochner*, and the assumed political "equality" of blacks in *Plessy*. Those assumptions required the most blatant form of hypocrisy. Both decisions, however, protected existing property and political arrangements while ignoring the disadvantages to the powerless caught in those relationships: The exploited whites (in *Lochner*) and the segregated blacks (in *Plessy*).

The effort to form workers' unions to combat the ever-more powerful corporate structure was undermined because of the active antipathy against blacks practiced by all but a few unions.[15] Excluded from jobs and the unions because of their color, blacks were hired as scab labor during strikes, a fact that simply increased the hostility of white workers that should have been directed toward their corporate oppressors.

The Populist Movement in the latter part of the nineteenth century attempted to build a working-class party in the South strong enough to overcome the economic exploitation by the ruling classes. But when neither Populists nor the conservative Democrats were able to control the black vote, they agreed to exclude blacks entirely through state constitutional amendments, thereby leaving whites to fight out elections themselves. With blacks no longer a force at the ballot box, conservatives dropped even the semblance of opposition to "Jim Crow" provisions pushed by lower-class whites as their guarantee that the nation recognized their priority citizenship claim, based on their whiteness.

Southern whites rebelled against the Supreme Court's 1954 decision declaring school segregation unconstitutional precisely because they felt that the long-standing priority of their superior status to blacks had been unjustly repealed. In 1988 we celebrated the thirty-fourth anniversary of the Court's rejection of the "separate but equal" doctrine of *Plessy* v. *Ferguson*.[16] But in the late twentieth century, the passwords for gaining judicial recognition of the still viable property right in being white include "higher entrance scores,"[17] "seniority,"[18] and "neighborhood schools."[19] There is as well the use of impossible-to-hurdle intent barriers to deny blacks remedies for racial injustices where the relief sought would either undermine white expectations and advantages gained during eras of overt discrimination (see *Washington* v. *Davis*);[20] or where such relief would expose the deeply embedded racism in a major institution, such as the criminal justice system (see *McCleskey* v. *Kemp*).[21]

The continuing resistance to affirmative action plans, set-asides, and other meaningful relief for discrimination-caused harm is based in substantial part on the perception that black gains threaten the main component of status for many whites: the sense that as whites, they are entitled to priority and preference over blacks. The law has mostly encouraged and upheld what Mr. Plessy argued in *Plessy* v. *Ferguson* was a property right in whiteness, and those at the top of the society have been benefited because the masses of whites are too occupied in keeping blacks down to note the large gap between their shaky status and that of whites on top.

Blacks continue to serve the role of buffers between those most advantaged in the society and those whites seemingly content to live the lives of the rich and famous through the pages of the tabloids and television dramas, like "Dallas," "Falcon's Crest," and "Dynasty." Professor Manning Marable points out that all of our institutions of education and information—political and civic, religious and creative—either knowingly or unknowingly "provide the public rationale to justify, explain, legitimize or tolerate racism." In his view, a collective consensus within the social order of the United States gives rise to the result that

> the media play down potentially disruptive information on the race question;
> inferior schooling for black children denies them necessary information and
> skills; cultural and social history is rewritten so that racial conflict and class
> struggle are glossed over and the melting pot ideal stressed; religious dogmas

such as those espoused by fundamentalist Christians divert political protest
and reaffirm the conservative values on which the white middle class' traditional illusions of superiority are grounded.[22]

Caught in the vortex of this national conspiracy that is perhaps more effective because it apparently functions without master plans or even conscious
thought, the wonder is not that so many blacks manifest self-destructive or
nonfunctional behavior patterns, but that there are so many who continue to
strive—and sometimes succeed—despite all.

The cost to black people of racial discrimination is high, but beyond the
bitterness that blacks understandably feel, there is the reality that most whites
too are, as Jesse Jackson puts it, victims of economic injustice. Indeed, allocat-
ing the costs is not a worthwhile use of energy when the need now is so
clearly a cure.

There are today—even in the midst of outbreaks of antiblack hostility on
our campuses and elsewhere—some indications that an increasing number of
working-class whites are learning what blacks have long known: that the rhetoric of freedom so freely voiced in this country is no substitute for the economic justice that has been so long denied.

True, it may be that the structure of capitalism, supported (as was the Framers' intention) by the Constitution, will never give sufficiently to provide real
economic justice for all. But in the beginning, that Constitution deemed those
who were black as the fit subject of property. The miracle of that document—
too little noted during its bicentennial—is that those same blacks and their
allies have in their quest for racial justice brought to the Constitution much
of its current protection of individual rights.

The challenge is to move the document's protection into the sacrosanct
area of economic rights—this time to ensure that opportunity in this sphere
is available to all. Progress in this critical area will require continued civil
rights efforts, but may depend to a large extent on whites coming to recognize
that their property right in being white has been purchased for too much and
has netted them only the opportunity, as C. Vann Woodward put it, to hoard
sufficient racism in their bosoms to feel superior to blacks while working at a
black's wages.

The cost of racial discrimination is levied against all. Blacks feel the burden
and strive to remove it. Too many whites believe that it is in their interests
to resist black freedom efforts. Those beliefs, despite the counterindicators
provided by history, logic, and simple common sense, remain strong. But the
efforts to achieve racial justice have already performed a miracle of trans-

forming the Constitution—a document primarily intended to protect property rights—into a vehicle that provides a measure of protection for those whose rights are not bolstered by wealth, power, and property. The challenge is to further this reform, a task that will require whites to learn what black people have long known about the real costs of racism.

NOTES

In addition to its presentation at the Smithsonian Institution's symposium on "Afro-Americans and the Evolution of a Living Constitution," the author has published versions of this essay in *Villanova Law Review* 33 (1988), and in the American Bar Association's *Human Rights Journal* 15 (1988).

1. The vigor of this insistence is illustrated by how adamant were Southern delegates even on the subject of the importation of slaves. Delegate John Rutledge from South Carolina warned: "If the Convention thinks that N. C., S. C. & Georgia will ever agree to the plan, unless their right to import slaves be untouched, the expectation is vain. The people of those States will never be such fools as to give up so important an interest." Max Farrand, ed., *The Records of the Federal Constitution of 1787*, vol. 1 (New Haven: Yale University Press, 1911), 373. In regard to slavery as a moral question, the debate over the morality of slavery had raged for years with influential Americans denouncing slavery as a corrupt and morally unjustifiable practice. See, for example, William Wiecek, *The Sources of Antislavery Constitutionalism in America: 1760–1848* (Ithaca, N.Y.: Cornell University Press, 1977); and Herbert Aptheker, ed., *A Documentary History of the Negro People in the United States*, vol. 1 (New York: Citadel Press, 1968), 5–12.

2. Derrick Bell, *And We Are Not Saved: The Elusive Quest for Racial Justice* (New York: Basic Books, 1987).

3. Derrick Bell, "White Superiority in America: Its Legal Legacy, Its Economic Costs," *Villanova Law Review* 33 (September 1988): 767–79. See also Bell, *And We Are Not Saved*, 27ff.

4. Bell, "White Superiority," 768.

5. Bell, "White Superiority," 768.

6. Bell, "White Superiority," 769.

7. Bell, "White Superiority," 769–70.

8. See Bell, "White Superiority," and *And We Are Not Saved*, 41–42.

9. Leon Litwack, *North of Slavery: The Negro in the Free States, 1790–1860* (Chicago: University of Chicago Press, 1961), 79.

10. *Dred Scott* v. *Sandford*, 60 U.S. (19 How.) 393 (1857).

11. See Edmund Morgan, *American Slavery, American Freedom: The Ordeal of Colonial Virginia* (New York: W. W. Norton, 1975); and David Brion Davis, *The Problem of Slavery in the Age of Revolution: 1770–1820* (Ithaca, N.Y.: Cornell University Press, 1975).

12. Morgan, *American Slavery, American Freedom*, 380–81.

13. 198 U.S. 45 (1905).

14. 163 U.S. 537 (1896).

15. See, for example, William B. Gould, *Black Workers and White Unions: Job Discrimination in the United States* (Ithaca, N.Y.: Cornell University Press, 1977); and Herbert Hill, *Black Labor and the American Legal System* (Washington, D.C.: Bureau of National Affairs, 1977).

16. *Brown v. Board of Education*, 347 U.S. 483 (1954);

17. *Regents of the Univ. of California v. Bakke*, 438 U.S. 265 (1978).

18. See, for example, *Wygant v. Jackson Bd. of Educ.*, 106 S. Ct. 1842 (1986).

19. See, for example, *Milliken v. Bradley*, 418 U.S. 717 (1974).

20. See *Washington v. Davis*, 426 U.S. 229 (1976).

21. See *McCleskey v. Kemp*, U.S. Law Week, 55 (April 22, 1987): 4537. See also *McCleskey* 481 U.S. 279 (1987).

22. Manning Marable, "Beyond the Race-Class Dilemma," *The Nation* (April 11, 1981): 428, 431.

CHARLES LAWRENCE III

LISTENING TO THE LESSONS
OF OUR HISTORY

AFRICAN AMERICANS, HATE SPEECH,
AND THE FIRST AMENDMENT

In the early morning hours of June 21, 1990, long after they had put their five children to bed, Russ and Laura Jones of St. Paul Minnesota were awakened by voices outside of their house. Russ got up, went to his bedroom window, and peered into the dark. "I saw a glow," he recalled. There in the middle of his yard, was a burning cross. The Joneses are black. In the spring of 1990 they had moved into their four-bedroom three-bath dream house on 290 Earl Street. They were the only black family on the block. Two weeks after they had settled in this predominantly white neighborhood, the tires on both their cars were slashed. Several weeks later, the windows on one of their cars were shattered, and a group of teenagers had walked past their house and shouted "nigger" at their nine-year-old son. And now this burning cross.

TRUE LIFE FIRST AMENDMENT STORY:
A CONTEXT FOR DISCUSSION

Russ Jones did not have to guess at the meaning of this symbol of racial hatred. There is no black person in America who has not been taught the significance of this instrument of persecution and intimidation, who has not had emblazoned on his or her mind the image of black men's scorched bodies hanging from trees. One can only imagine the terror that Russell Jones must have felt as he watched the flames and thought of the vulnerability of his family and of the hateful cowardly viciousness of those who would attack him and those he loved under cover of darkness.[1]

This assault on Russ Jones and his family begins the story of the Supreme Court case entitled *R.A.V. v. City of St. Paul, Minnesota*.[2] The assailants who had burned the cross in the fenced yard of the Jones home were identified and prosecuted under a local hate crime ordinance. In the course of the prosecution one of the defendants challenged the constitutionality of the ordinance. He claimed that his assault on the Jones family was protected by the First Amendment: Burning a cross is political speech, he argued, and any ordinance directed against such speech is unconstitutional.

The Minnesota Supreme Court rejected this argument. It held that the ordinance did not violate the First Amendment because it only regulated "conduct that itself inflicts injury or tends to incite immediate violence." Therefore the ordinance only reached expression that the First Amendment does not protect. The state court also concluded that the ordinance was not impermissibly content-based because the ordinance was "a narrowly tailored means toward accomplishing the compelling government interest in protecting the community against bias motivated threats to public safety and order." "Burning a cross in the front yard of an African American family's home is deplorable conduct that the City of St. Paul may without question prohibit," said the state high court.[3]

The U.S. Supreme Court reversed the state court. Justice Antonin Scalia, writing for the Court's majority, found the St. Paul ordinance unconstitutional on its face. He argued that while certain modes of speech such as fighting words or libel may be regulated because of their "non-speech elements," the government may not regulate speech "based on hostility—or favoritism—towards the underlying message expressed." Scalia held that the conviction of the cross burners under this ordinance violated the First Amendment because the ordinance prohibited cross burning that conveyed a message of virulent racial supremacy but did not prohibit cross burning that conveyed some other message.[4]

Near the end of his opinion Justice Scalia conceded that the ordinance "helps to insure the basic rights of members of groups that have been historically subjected to discrimination, including the right of such group members to live in peace where they wish," but there is little else in this opinion that indicates a recognition or understanding of the injury to the Jones's constitutional rights: the right to live where they please, the right to associate with their neighbors, the right to be treated as full and valued participants in the political community, or the right to free speech. The Jones family's terror at finding a cross burning in their yard is nowhere described in this opinion. We are told nothing about the hostility they experienced upon moving into the neighborhood.

The Ku Klux Klan, lynching, and night riders are never mentioned. Nor are recent hate crime statistics showing the increasing racial harassment of ethnic minorities. Justice Scalia proceeds as though we know nothing about the origins of the practice of cross burning or about the meaning that a burning cross carries for both those who use it and those whom it terrorizes. It is a completely ahistorical opinion characterized by abstract legal analysis divorced from the experience of American racism.

It is not my purpose here to consider the rather complex legal issues that are present in the *R.A.V.* case. I begin with the story of this cross-burning case because it demonstrates how our view of what the First Amendment means, and how it ought to be interpreted, is shaped in large part by our history and life experience. More specifically, it provides an example of how the historical experience of African Americans is instructive in constitutional interpretation.

THE FALSE DICHOTOMY IN THE HATE SPEECH DEBATE

There is an ongoing and heated debate among constitutional scholars, civil libertarians, and civil rights activists concerning the proper response to racial assaults in the form of words or symbols such as the cross burning in the *R.A.V.* case. Many people believe that any regulation of speech constitutes a grave danger to First Amendment liberties. They argue that even when the government seeks to insure equal rights to a family like the Joneses it may not do so by restricting speech. Others have argued that there are times when the regulation of speech is necessary to protect the rights of those who have been and continue to be denied the full benefits of citizenship.

Those of us who favor restrictions on assaultive hate speech are in a distinct minority within the legal academy and the civil liberties community. Our commitment to free speech has been questioned. We have been called "First Amendment revisionists" and "thought police." Because African Americans and other people of color have often been among those who have called for the regulation of racist hate speech, the debate has sometimes been perceived as a controversy between civil libertarians and civil rights activists.

First Amendment absolutists have been particularly critical of African Americans and other people of color who have called for the regulation of assaultive racist speech. They feel we have deserted the cause of free speech. "Where would the civil rights movement be today without the First Amendment?" they ask rhetorically. "Don't you realize that if freedom of speech is weakened for one person, group, or message, then it will no longer be there for others?"

These arguments misunderstand and misrepresent the still tentative position that many of us are struggling to define and articulate on the question of cross burning and other assaultive racist speech.[5] Our stance is a pro- not antispeech one. We are attentive to that part of our experience that makes us intuitively suspicious of any regulation of speech, but we have also learned to be suspicious when it is argued that a commitment to free speech requires that we maintain a white supremacist status quo. We ask whose speech is silenced by whom? We challenge simple answers based on abstract and ahistorical First Amendment theories. As African Americans, we must ask and answer questions about free speech in the context of the history of American racism. We believe that racial justice and free speech are interconnected goals.

While it is true that one cannot think about the problem of hate speech without recognizing the tension that sometimes exists between our coexisting constitutional commitments to free speech and equality, it is neither useful nor accurate to frame the debate as it has been framed—as one in which the liberty of free speech is in conflict with the elimination of racial oppression. I claim a deep commitment to the values that motivate both sides of the debate, and I do not experience them as in conflict. True free speech requires the elimination of structures of subordination, and true equality requires equal speech. A truly liberating First Amendment theory must recognize privatized censorship in the form of violence and economic coercion. It must understand that when we condemn children to schools where they cannot learn, they are being denied the right of free speech. It must know that homelessness and poverty deny First Amendment rights.

OUR "SECOND SIGHT": HOW HISTORY
INFORMS OUR VIEW OF THE FIRST AMENDMENT

I believe that the origin of such a theory can be found in the historical experience of the African American community and in that community's tradition of political resistance to racial oppression. W. E. B. Du Bois called the gift and burden inherent in the dual, conflicting heritage of African Americans our "second sight".[6] The "double consciousness" that comes from our sense of belonging and not belonging is evident in our historical relationship to the First Amendment and free speech.

African Americans have always known that free speech is vital to a people fighting for freedom. The institution of slavery could not tolerate dissent, and the African who dared to speak his or her mind was a dangerous person. No punishment was too severe for the slave who raised his or her voice against the master. To challenge the system of slavery in any way was an act of rebellion.

Ours is a history of sustained resistance to this systematic and violent suppression of our voices. Escape routes and clandestine gatherings were disguised in the texts of spirituals and Sunday sermons. African Americans, both slave and free, risked life and limb to spread abolitionist tracts and news of insurrections among their brothers and sisters. Our forbears experienced an insatiable thirst for literacy and for the forbidden words that showed the way to freedom. Our voices have been our weapons of choice and necessity: Frederick Douglass through his *North Star*, David Walker in his *Appeal*, Sojourner Truth, Ida B. Wells, W. E. B. Du Bois, William Monroe Trotter, Mary Church Terrell, Marcus Garvey, Malcolm X, Martin Luther King, Jr., Angela Davis, Fannie Lou Hamer, George Jackson. Our poets and our politicians have looked to "the word." to the moral power of ideas, as they have waged the battle for a freedom that would make us whole persons and full participants in a more humanized world.

Perhaps more than any other group of Americans, African Americans have relied upon the power of their words to transform the nation. We have used our voices to petition both our government and our neighbors for redress of grievances. We have been a vital and vocal opposition to a dominant politics of racism, and we have been a primary force in the creation of this country's vital culture of tolerance and dissent.

African Americans have likewise played a central role in shaping the jurisprudence of the First Amendment. It was an African American organizer arrested for "attempting to incite insurrection" by distributing a leaflet calling for "equal rights for Negroes and self determination in the Black Belt" whose conviction was reversed in the landmark case of *Herndon* v. *Lowry*.[7] Demonstrators seeking integrated public facilities, demanding equal access to the ballot, staging boycotts for economic justice, and protesting the arrest of fellow civil rights workers were the subjects of hundreds of cases that required the courts to consider the scope of First Amendment protections for all Americans. *New*

York Times v. *Sullivan,* a case growing out of black student protests at Alabama State College, may be the most important case protecting the freedom of the press.[8] Many First Amendment scholars believe that this case defined the "central meaning" of the First Amendment, the right to criticize public officials. When the Alabama chapter of the National Association for the Advancement of Colored People refused to submit its membership list to the state attorney general, the Supreme Court held, in *NAACP* v. *Alabama,* that such a requirement violated the First Amendment, and the right of association was firmly established for all.[9]

These are but a small sampling of the thousands of cases through which the lives of African Americans have shaped the First Amendment. This is the part of us that knows the experience of belonging. We know that we are benefited when our society is more tolerant of difference and dissent. We know that the First Amendment rights of others, even racists, are inseparable from our own. We do not need white people to tell us that a tyrannic majority, uninhibited by the First Amendment, would turn first on us. Our history has taught us that lesson.

Our history has also taught us the lesson of not belonging. We have known what it means to stand on the outside of the First Amendment's shelter and to fight with our voices nonetheless. The framers excluded us from the protection of the First Amendment. The same Constitution that established rights for others endorsed a story that proclaimed our rightlessness. In the infamous words of Chief Justice Roger B. Taney's decision in the *Dred Scott* case, "blacks had no rights which a white man was bound to respect."[10]

Historian Vincent Harding tells this eloquently illustrative story of how even free blacks stood outside of the First Amendment's guardianship.

In 1800 the outspoken black community of Philadelphia, under the leadership of Absol[a]m Jones, sent a petition to Congress calling for legislative action against the African slave trade as well as for laws which would gradually abolish slavery. It was put forward in a respectful tone, a quiet call for justice. In Congress the usual treatment for all antislavery petitions from white constituents was to refer them to a committee and kill them. However, in response to this black petition Harrison Gray Otis, a Massachusetts congressman, opposed even that negative form of recognition. To acknowledge this word from black people he said, "would have an irritating tendency and must be mischievous to America very soon. It would teach them the art of assembling together, debating and the like, and would soon . . . extend from one end of the Union to the other." After a two-day debate, devoted largely to the promulgation of views like those of Otis, the House voted 85–1 to offer "no encouragement or countenance" to such messages from the children of Africa in America.[11]

When the Thirteenth, Fourteenth, and Fifteenth amendments were enacted, African Americans found that the formal rights of citizenship did little to protect them from the night riders, the lynch mobs, or the economic stranglehold of the white men who owned the land they worked. The First Amendment prohibited the government from abridging their speech, but the law of the Klan, the mob, the hiring boss, and the white ladies they cooked and cleaned for were beyond the reach of the First Amendment, and these were the laws that mattered. When the night riders came to a black man's house and said, "Shut your mouth, boy, if you want to keep living," the First Amendment was nowhere to be found. We continued to raise our voices in protest and resistance, but we did so with the outsider's knowledge that there is a difference between the abstract world of formal rights, where all speech is equal and equally valued, and the real world, where there is speech that silences and speech that is silenced.

BRINGING OUR HISTORY TO THE CONTEMPORARY HATE SPEECH DEBATE

For the past several years I have been struggling to find a way to talk to my colleagues in the academic world and my friends in the civil liberties community about what this history teaches me about the First Amendment. I have tried to explain how a fourth-generation political activist and constitutional scholar, who has spent the better part of his life as an outspoken dissenter, can believe that we should restrict racist assaults when those assaults are "only words."

I begin by asking them to recognize and take seriously the harm that assaultive racist speech, like the cross burning in the R.A.V. case, does to its victims. I think that part of what makes it difficult for many First Amendment absolutists to hear those of us who argue for a more complex approach to free speech is that they have never experienced the injury and therefore do not fully understand it. This is why we so often hear the argument that we must learn to tolerate "offensive" speech. The word "offensive" is used as if we were speaking of a difference in taste, as if we should learn to be less sensitive to words that "offend" us. But the burning cross in the Jones's yard does much more than offend. It inflicts a real harm that is far from trivial. Moreover it is a harm of constitutional dimension.

The injury inflicted by assaultive racist speech extends beyond that which it does to its immediate victims. It harms us all, white and black alike, by undermining core values in our Constitution. The first of these is the value of full and equal citizenship expressed in the Fourteenth Amendment's Equal Protection Clause. The second constitutional value threatened by assaultive racist speech is the value of free expression itself.

How Assaultive Racist Speech Undermines the Constitutional Value of Equality

When racist speech is employed with the purpose and effect of maintaining established systems of caste and subordination, it violates the core constitutional value of equal citizenship. Racist hate speech often prevents its victims from exercising rights guaranteed by the Constitution and by state and federal civil rights statutes: the right to vote, the right to fair housing, the right to equal employment and equal educational opportunity.

My first efforts to articulate what was missing in the traditional legal discourse about racism and free speech came in the context of the debate over whether and how universities ought to regulate hate speech on campus. As I lectured at universities throughout the United States, I learned about increasing numbers of serious racist hate incidents. Students who had been victimized told me of racist tracts and threatening notes shoved under their doors. Stories of campus cross burnings, racial slurs spray-painted on dorm walls, and vicious verbal assaults made me cringe even as I heard them second hand. Universities, long the home of institutional and euphemistic racism, were witnessing the worst forms of gutter racism. In 1990, the *Chronicle of Higher Education* reported that approximately 250 colleges and universities had experienced serious racial incidents since 1986, and the National Institute against Prejudice and Violence estimated that 25 percent of all minority students are victimized at least once during an academic year.

I urged my colleagues to hear these students' voices and argued that *Brown v. Board of Education* and its antidiscrimination principle identified an injury of constitutional dimension done to these students that must be recognized and remedied.[12] We do not normally think of *Brown* as being a case about speech. Most narrowly read, it is a case about the rights of black children to equal educational opportunity. But *Brown* teaches us another very important lesson: that the harm of segregation is achieved by the meaning of the message it conveys. The Court's opinion in *Brown* stated that racial segregation is unconstitutional not because the physical separation of black and white children is bad or because resources were distributed unequally among black and white schools. *Brown* held that segregated schools were unconstitutional primarily because of the message segregation conveys—the message that black children are an untouchable caste, unfit to be educated with white children. Segregation stamps a badge of inferiority upon blacks. This badge communicates a message to others that signals their exclusion from the community of citizens.[13]

The "Whites Only" signs on the lunch counter, swimming pool, and drinking fountain convey the same message. The antidiscrimination principle articulated in *Brown* presumptively entitles every individual to be treated by the organized society as a respected, responsible, and participating member. This is the principle upon which all our civil rights laws rest. It is the guiding principle of the Equal Protection Clause's requirement of nondiscriminatory government action. It has also been applied in regulating private discrimination.

The words "Women Need Not Apply" in a job announcement, the racially exclusionary clause in a restrictive covenant, and the racial epithet scrawled on the locker of the new black employee at a previously all-white job site all convey a political message. But we treat these messages as "discriminatory practices" and outlaw them under federal and state civil rights legislation because they are more than speech. In the context of social inequality, these verbal and symbolic acts form integral links with historically ingrained systems of social discrimination. They work to keep traditionally victimized groups in socially isolated, stigmatized, and disadvantaged positions through the promotion of fear, intolerance, degradation, and violence. The Equal Protection Clause of the Fourteenth Amendment requires the disestablishment of these practices and systems. Likewise, the First Amendment does *not* prohibit our accomplishment of this compelling constitutional interest simply because those discriminatory practices are achieved through the use of words and symbols.

The primary intent of the cross burner in *R.A.V.* was not to enter into a dialogue with the Joneses, or even with the larger community, as it arguably is when the Klan holds a rally on main street. His purpose was to intimidate—to strike fear in the hearts of his victims, to drive them out of the community, to enforce the practice of residential segregation, and to encourage others to join him in the enforcement of that practice.

The discriminatory effect of this speech, or what it does, is of even more importance than the speaker's intent. When the government passes a law in order to protect victims of discrimination, there is a compelling governmental interest that is unrelated to the suppression of the speaker's political message. When that interest is enforcing the antidiscrimination principle, it is especially compelling because it is a constitutional interest.

Those opposed to the regulation of hate speech often view the interest involved as the maintenance of civility, the protection of sensibilities from offense, or the prohibition of group defamation. This analysis misconstrues the nature of the injury. Defamation—injury to group reputation—is not the same as discrimination—injury to group status and treatment. The former is more ideational and less material than the latter, which recognizes the harm of second-class citizenship and inferior social standing with the attendant deprivation of access to resources, voice, and power.

The Title VII paradigm of "hostile environment" discrimination best describes the injury to which victims of racist, sexist, and homophobic hate speech are subjected.[14] When plaintiffs in employment discrimination suits show they have been subjected to racist or sexist verbal harassment in the workplace, courts have recognized that such assaultive speech denies the targeted individual equal access to employment. These verbal assaults most often occur in settings where the relatively recent and token integration of the workplace makes the victims particularly vulnerable and where the privately voiced message of denigration and exclusion echoes the whites-only and males-only practices that were all too recently official policy.

The speech that Title VII's "hostile environment" provision makes unlawful, like the burning cross in *R.A.V.*, does more than communicate an idea. It interferes with the victims's right to work at a job free from degradation because of her gender or race. Likewise the African American college student has a right to an equal educational opportunity. The university is that student's place of work, and the right to an equal education is denied when that student must attempt to learn while being subjected to racist assaults.

How Assaultive Racist Speech Undermines the Constitutional Value of Free Speech

It is not sufficient to describe the injury occasioned by assaultive hate speech only in terms of the countervailing value of equality. There is also an injury to the First Amendment. Hate speech frequently silences its victims, who, more often than not, are those who are already heard from least. When Russ Jones looked out his window and saw that burning cross, he heard a message that said, "Shut up, black man, or risk harm to you and your family." It may be that Russ Jones is especially brave, or especially foolhardy, and that he may speak even more loudly in the face of this threat. But it is more likely that he will be silenced, and that we will lose the benefit of his voice.

First Amendment scholars have identified two underlying values that are implicated in the First Amendment's protection of speech. The first is the intrinsic value of speech, which is the value of individual self-expression. Speech is intrinsically valuable as a manifestation of our humanity and our individuality. The second is the instrumental value of speech. The First Amendment protects dissent to maximize public discourse and to achieve the great flowering of debate and ideas that we need to make our democracy work. Both of these values are implicated in the silencing of Russ Jones by his nocturnal attacker.

For African Americans, the intrinsic value of speech as self-expression and self-definition has been particularly important. The absence of a "black voice" was central to the ideology of European American racism, an ideology that denied Africans their humanity and thereby justified their enslavement. African American slaves were prevented from learning to read and write, and they were prohibited from engaging in forms of self-expression that might instill in them a sense of self-worth and pride. Their silence and submission was then interpreted as evidence of their subhuman status. The use of the burning cross as a method of disempowerment originates, in part, in the perpetrators' understanding of how, in the context of this ideology, their victims are rendered subhuman when they are silenced. When, in the face of threat and intimidation, the oppressors' victims are afraid to give full expression to their individuality, the oppressors achieve their purpose of denying the victims the liberty guaranteed to them by the Constitution.

When the Joneses moved to Earl Street in St. Paul, they were expressing their individuality. When they chose their house and their neighbors, they were saying, "This is who we are. We are a proud black family and we want to live here." This self-expression and self-definition is the intrinsic value of speech. The instrumental value of speech is likewise threatened by this terrorist attack on the Joneses. Russ and Laura Jones brought new voices to the conversations in this St. Paul community. Ideally, they will vote and talk politics with their neighbors. They will bring new experiences and new perspectives to their neighborhood. A burning cross not only silences people like the

Joneses, it impoverishes the democratic process and renders our collective conversation less informed.

Typically, the targets of assaultive racist speech have been outspoken political activists or brave individuals who have dared to challenge discrimination and injustice: the local field secretary of the NAACP, the first black family to register to vote or enroll their children in the all-white schools, the tenant farmers who pool their resources to buy land and start a cooperative farm, the worker who testifies before a legislative committee investigating job discrimination. These are the targets of the burning cross's message and of the bomb or bullet that often makes good on the threat. Those who deliver the message to the black man or woman who dares to speak know it is a silencing message delivered to all African Americans.

CONCLUSION

On the occasion of the bicentennial celebration of the U.S. Constitution, Justice Thurgood Marshall delivered a speech entitled "Celebrating the Constitution: A Dissent."[15] Justice Marshall distanced himself from the flag-waving fervor and celebratory spirit that had characterized so much of the Constitution's 200th birthday. His speech questioned the efficacy of the practice of interpreting the Constitution by inquiring into the "original intent" of the white men who participated in the constitutional convention. The Constitution was "defective from the start," Justice Marshall argued, noting that when the framers used the words "We the People" in the Constitution's Preamble, they had neither African Americans nor women in mind.

Justice Marshall called for a different vision of the Constitution, a vision "nurtured through two turbulent centuries of our own making."[16] The power of Marshall's vision is that it includes *us*—all of us. It calls upon each of us to be active participants in making the Constitution; in deciding how the constitutional values of free speech and equal citizenship should be reflected in our laws. Marshall's vision calls upon all of us to be the Constitution's framers.

The historical experience of African Americans has taught us that the constitutional rights of free speech and equality are interdependent and inseparable. We know that there is a relationship between the epithet "nigger" and the fact that a disproportionate number of the children who go to bed hungry every night in this country are African American. We know that schools in which black children cannot learn to read or write deny them freedom of speech, even as did the legal codes that made it a crime to teach a slave to read.

The law of the First Amendment, as it is interpreted and applied in the vast majority of our courts and law schools, proceeds as if it does not know these things. It invokes the ideal of the "marketplace of ideas" as if all voices have equal access to that market. It speaks of the need to protect all speech as if there is not speech that silences and speech that is silenced, as if those who are silenced are not always less powerful than those who are silenced.

In 1787 African Americans were formally excluded from the discourse that gave content and meaning to the Constitution and its First Amendment. But our forbears insisted that their voices be heard in the constitutional conversation nonetheless. This history of belonging and not belonging has defined the special responsibility of African Americans as framers of the Constitution. That responsibility has been to constantly challenge this nation to bring the ideals of equality and free speech face to face with the realities of racism. African Americans must insist on a First Amendment that knows our history and listens to its lessons.

NOTES

1. This description is taken from a news report. See Tamar Lewin, "Hate-Crime Law Is Focus of Case on Free Speech," *New York Times*, December 1, 1991, sec. 1, 1.

2. 464 N.W. 2d 507 (Minn. Sup. Ct. 1990), cert. granted U.S. Sup. Ct. No. 90-7675, 1991 Term.

3. *In the Matter of the Welfare of R.A.V.*, 464 N.W. 2d 507 at 508 (Minn. 1991).

4. *R.A.V. v. City of St. Paul*, MN, 112 S. Ct. 2538 (1992).

5. For a more complete discussion of the First Amendment and assaultive hate speech, see Mari J. Matsuda, Charles R. Lawrence, Richard Delgado, and Kimberlé W. Crenshaw, *Words That Wound: Critical Race Theory, Assaultive Speech, and the First Amendment* (Boulder, Colo.: Westview Press, 1993).

6. See W. E. B. Du Bois, *The Souls of Black Folk* (New York: Bantam Books Reprint 1989), 16–17.

7. 301 U.S. 242 (1937).

8. 403 U.S.713 (1971).

9. 357 U.S. 449 (1958).

10. *Dred Scott v. Sanford*, 60 U.S. (19 How.) 393, 407 (1857).

11. Vincent Harding, *There Is a River: The Black Struggle for Freedom in America* (New York: Harcourt, Brace, Jovanovich, 1981), 54.

12. 347 U.S. 483 (1954).

13. For a full discussion of this analysis of the *Brown* case, see Charles R. Lawrence III, "If He Hollers Let Him Go: Regulating Racist Speech on Campus," *Duke Law Journal* 1990 (1990): 431.

14. See for example, *Meritor Savings Bank* v. *Vinson,* 477 U.S. 57 (1986), where the Supreme Court held that sexual harassment that creates a hostile or abusive work environment constitutes a violation of Title VII's prohibition against sex discrimination in employment.

15. This speech was later published under another title in the *Howard Law Journal.* Thurgood Marshall, "The Constitution: A Living Document," *Howard Law Journal* 30 (1987): 623. It also appears in this volume, Part V, chap. 16, pp. 314–18. Also see *infra,* p. 318.

16. See Marshall, "The Constitution," 627.

W. H. KNIGHT AND ADRIEN WING

WEEP NOT, LITTLE ONES

AN ESSAY TO OUR CHILDREN ABOUT AFFIRMATIVE ACTION

Do not be conformed to this world, but be transformed by the renewing of your minds.

Romans 12:2

Many of the authors in this volume have forcefully argued for a broad interpretation of the Constitution as a means of giving that document fuller meaning, particularly for those who find themselves at the lowest rungs of America's social and economic ladder. Although many different racial and ethnic groups are at this low end of our society, no group has waited as long as African Americans to gain admission and to be treated as recognized equals. People of African descent were on these shores for more than 150 years before this nation's founding, only since the Supreme Court's 1954 decision in *Brown v. Board of Education* have we as African Americans been a part of the constitutional discourse on how ideals such as equal protection, due process, and freedom of expression could become more inclusive.[1] As we approach the twenty-first century, the problem of the color line remains *the* problem for America.[2]

In this essay we attempt to describe how race continues to permeate America's societal fabric and how negative connotations of color blur our collective vision of the purpose of affirmative action. We dedicate the chapter to all children, but especially to our own children, respectively, as they come of age.[3] We are sure that they will face pain and despair because of their race, and, that at times race will affect both their opportunities and their achievements. However, we hope that through these words they will better understand this nation's schizophrenia over race as it affects affirmative action. We also hope that they will be capable of leading lives that will help this society perceive race, ethnicity, and difference as positive rather than negative attributes.

While color-blindness, theoretically, might well lead this nation closer to the constitutional goal of equality, the facts remain that color-consciousness and race-based action continue to persist at the forefront of the American psyche.[4] To illustrate the magnitude of this point, let us recount a brief experience that we are sure all African American parents have had.

In considering what we might say in this essay, we both observed that shortly after our children turned three years old, each of them began to ask questions about skin color. It seemed that race had become an issue at day care even among children at that tender age. "Why are you different?" "Can you rub that brown off?" "Black people aren't as smart as white people." At the precious age of three, our children were forced to ask questions about, and to deal with, negative comments concerning their race. By the time one child reached the age of four, he asked, "Why do black people have to have it so hard?" The so-called innocence of childhood had vanished.

As parents, our initial desire is to shield our children from the potential harm that words can and do cause (even if that harm was unintended). Each of us sought to reassure them by saying, "Sometimes kids say things they don't mean." But we could not help thinking, "Why or how is it that children become so aware of the power of race so early in life?"

While many parents are successful in teaching their children to protect themselves from many of life's physical dangers, how do parents of African American children protect them from the dangers caused by racism? We use the term "protect" because racially charged language and race-based perceptions and actions in fact harm our children in ways that demand that we shield them. We believe that it is vital to teach our children about the history and use of race not only to protect them, but also to enlarge our understanding of race in this society. Perhaps if they are equipped with a historical understanding of affirmative action and the impact of race in this society, our children will be able to treasure their own and racial differences, as well as those of others. Perhaps they will be able to see beyond the limitations that racialism now places on America.

WHAT IS AFFIRMATIVE ACTION?

Simply put, affirmative action is the name given to an array of policies designed to create greater equality of opportunity in American society.[5] Many people think of the term in two principal arenas, employment and education. One author has described the concept as "actions appropriate to overcome the effects of past or present policies or other barriers to equal employment [and educational] opportunity."[6] The long-range goal of affirmative action programs is twofold: first, to address the effects of past discrimination by affording greater opportunities to those who have been discriminated against; and second, to create a community that values racial, ethnic, and gender diversity to a point that discrimination based on these characteristics ceases to occur.[7] These policy goals are reflected in both governmental and private initiatives that encourage parties to consider race, ethnicity, and gender as *positive* factors both in admissions decisions in higher education and in employment hiring and promotion. The addition of race or ethnicity to the decision-making calculus does not suggest that other factors are excluded; instead, the equation recognizes race as an element that should also receive weight.

Affirmative action differs from equal employment opportunity, which requires employers to treat everyone equally in employment activities; employers are not to discriminate on the basis of race, creed, color, national origin, gender or disability. Put another way, employers are not to let personal characteristics become *negative* factors in the employment decision. Affirmative action, on the other hand, requires people to go beyond mere efforts not to discriminate. The concept dictates that employers use good faith efforts to provide opportunities for African Americans and other protected class groups who either have been denied such chances historically, or who have been competitively disadvantaged by the lack of such fortune.

A number of people have the misconception that affirmative action is a recent policy designed to help "unqualified" people of color (and Caucasian women) get positions that they don't deserve at the expense of the "qualified" (Caucasian males).[8] Critics argue that affirmative action programs lower the standards and reputations of those institutions that make such efforts.[9] These arguments are wrongly based on a vision of affirmative action as a means by which Caucasians will be discriminated against. However, common sense, court decisions, and the Equal Employment Opportunity Coordinating Council's policy statement on affirmative action all provide evidence that affirmative action does not require employers to dispense positions to unqualified job applicants.[10] Race or gender is taken into consideration only when an applicant, who happens to be a woman or a person of color, already meets the basic, stated qualifications for a job position.[11] Employers therefore, may continue to have specific needs that are tailored to fit certain job requirements.[12] Thus, the concept of affirmative action does not lower standards, since such programs only require employers to look at race or gender as additional qualifying criteria.

Despite attempts to emphasize the need for qualifications first in affirmative action decisions, for many the perception remains that qualifications are somehow ignored when race is also used as a factor to favor a person of color. We find this perception odd given this nation's historical use of racial preference. Some Americans seemingly want to ignore the history of preferences that have been given Caucasian males in this country. Decisions often have been made to provide opportunities on the basis of some preferred set of characteristics. Education, alma mater, family history, wealth, political affiliation—all have served as criteria for selecting one person or group over others.[13] Race, however, has been foremost among the characteristics used to grant or to *deny* opportunity. The most vivid example, of course, is slavery. The history of human bondage in the United States can be distinguished from that in virtually every other society by the fact that here, race was the principal determining factor.[14] Commenting on this fact, Professor J. Clay Smith has noted:

> Our nation's founding persons proclaimed that "all men are created equal" but they also gave us a Constitution which accorded to black slaves the fractional status of three-fifths of a free person, and provided a fugitive slave clause to preserve the white master's control over his slaves. Until the arrival of the third decennium in this century, women citizens of this Republic were denied the basic political right, the right to vote. Until the middle of this century, the Equal Protection Amendment to the Constitution, enacted at the close of a civil war, meant only that blacks were entitled to separate but manifestly unequal treatment.
>
> We cannot lay claim to a tradition of color and sex blind administration of our laws. In view of this, it does not behoove us to suddenly make the Constitution color and sex blind.[15]

Being Caucasian has been and often remains a prime basis for granting an opportunity; being of African, Latino, Indian, or Asian ancestry has been and often remains a basis for denying that same opening. Discriminatory attitudes toward non-Caucasians denied such people the very chance to compete on the basis of their actual abilities and led to preferential actions based on race that benefited Caucasians. Throughout this long period of Caucasian preference, questions about qualification were rarely raised.

Today, affirmative action represents an attempt to address this historical fact of unequal access to opportunity by opening competitive fields through the expansion of opportunities for protected classes of people.[16] "In order to get beyond racism, we must first take account of race. . . . And in order to treat some persons equally, we must treat them differently. We cannot—we dare not—let the Equal Protection Clause perpetuate racial supremacy."[17]

The myths surrounding affirmative action clearly need debunking. Many Americans do not appreciate the value of affirmative action because they are afraid of the word "preference." People are exasperated by the word because they believe it conflicts with the concept of qualification. As Patricia Williams has noted, "Qualifications are nothing more than structured preferences"— beliefs we have come to hold about how society should go about classifying or categorizing someone.[18] Moreover,

> Categorizing is not the sin; the problem is the lack of desire to examine the categorizations that are made. The problem is not recognizing the ethical worth in attempting to categorize with not only the individual *but also social goals* in mind as well. The problem is in the failure to assume responsibility for examining how or where we set our boundaries.[19]

Affirmative action *starts* with both a societal goal of equal opportunity and a pool of capable people. The theory then asks on what basis, if any, should we prefer one able person over another?[20] In a world of limited opportunities, people must make difficult decisions about what factors to emphasize in choosing someone to hire or to admit to an educational program. Usually, there are more people with the basic capabilities to do a particular job than there are available positions. The task for both employers and educational institutions is to select from among these individuals. Affirmative action is the one way to ensure that those who have been historically discriminated against and traditionally excluded can now be included in educational and employment opportunity. Equal competition among all people cannot exist until we include all groups of people.

THE DEVELOPMENT OF AFFIRMATIVE ACTION

Civil rights for the African American had already begun to emerge during the early years of the Roosevelt administration. The number of African American federal employees tripled during the 1930s. Roosevelt also began the desegregation of federal rest rooms, cafeterias, and secretarial pools. In addition, the U.S. labor movement began to reach out toward the African American community by emphasizing the damage done to individuals and the nation by bigotry and prejudice.[21]

The advent of World War II "stimulated blacks to demand a better deal" from American society; African Americans rushed to fill the employment void caused by the war.[22] Union membership also steadily increased during the period. The concept of affirmative action developed in response to this change in the work force. In 1941, President Franklin Roosevelt's Executive Order 8802 established the Fair Employment Practices Committee (FEPC) in the Office of Production and Management. The executive order was a direct result of pressure levied on the administration by A. Philip Randolph, president of the Brotherhood of Sleeping Car Porters. Randolph had threatened a historic march on Washington unless the executive branch stopped employment discrimination by military contractors. The establishment of FEPC was based upon two presidential precepts: (1) the power of the commander-in-chief to guarantee military supplies, and (2) the president's power, as administrative head, to establish conditions under which the government is to be run. Roosevelt's order marked the first presidential directive concerning race since Reconstruction. A vocal minority's threat to march was effective.

The establishment of the FEPC was an important turning point because it provided a means to investigate grievances. The mere fact that such an agency had been started by the executive branch signaled a change in the federal government's approach toward employment discrimination.[23] On a national level, there was the possibility that the government would be more scrutinizing of employment practices.

Despite this prospect, America moved slowly. During the war, the nation focused on defeating the German and Japanese enemies. Even among African Americans, racial equality took a back seat to winning the war. A wartime poll conducted by the Pittsburgh *Courier* revealed that 71 percent of African Americans opposed a march on Washington to protest racial discrimination.[24] By the end of the war, America's economic boom began in earnest. More than six million new civilian jobs were created between 1945 and 1950—and African Americans were among the prime beneficiaries. Given the prospect of good-paying factory jobs, it seemed that the vast majority of African Americans did not want to "rock the boat" of employment opportunity that the postwar economy brought. The absence of a mass public outcry for racial reform meant that the Truman administration felt little pressure to enact measures that would move the nation away from its culture of racial division.

America's postwar fear of Communism was also cleverly linked to civil rights calls for racial equality. White supremacists frequently charged that challenges to the racial status quo were un-American. "The fear of McCarthyism so inhibited blacks that they failed to use the Korean War as a lever for racial reform, as they had World War II. At mid-century, direct action had ceased being a tactic in the quest for racial justice."[25]

Civil rights activists thus concentrated on eradicating segregation through court challenges. The rise of black economic fortunes since World War II led many people to believe that educational opportunity was the best path toward racial acceptance. In ruling that separate schools for black and Caucasian children were inherently unequal and therefore unacceptable, the Supreme Court's 1954 decision in *Brown* v. *Board of Education* acknowledged the prime importance of education in providing black people with the very opportunity to compete in a society dominated by Caucasians.[26] *Brown*, many thought, marked the beginning of a new period of race relations, a period that would erase nearly a century of professed but unrealized freedom. With the abolition of "Jim Crow" in the school system, blacks would finally obtain equality and recognition as full citizens.[27]

But the promise of educational equality proved just that, a promise. Scarcely more than a year after the outlawing of separate but unequal public schools, the Supreme Court rejected the NAACP's request for immediate and complete school desegregation.[28] The Court refused to set a deadline and instead adopted a "go-slow" approach that had been advocated by the Justice Department. "For the first time, the Supreme Court had vindicated a constitutional right and then deferred its exercise."[29]

The administration of Dwight D. Eisenhower provided little assistance in affirming the rights enunciated by the Supreme Court. The president refused to endorse the *Brown* decision because he feared that forced and rapid integration would lead to social upheaval and conflict. Eisenhower also believed that the executive branch of government should be more administrative than proactive. This restricted view of presidential authority coupled with the Court's own go-slow attitude hindered racial progress and cast another eight-year shadow on the development of affirmative action.[30]

It was not until 1962 and President John F. Kennedy's Executive Order 10925 that the idea of "affirmative action" became a major part of governmental action. The principal provisions of the executive order included (1) a directive not to discriminate against traditionally disfavored minorities, (2) a requirement that job advertising describe the federal government as an "equal opportunity employer," and (3) a call for special efforts to recruit black Americans for admission and training programs.[31] Kennedy's order was stirred, in part, by the growing national attention to the demands of African Americans. Student sit-ins, freedom bus rides, and nonviolent protest marches received widespread media attention and necessitated an administration response. With massive direct action throughout the nation, African Americans responded to the calls for protest by organizations like the Student Non-Violent Coordinating Committee, the Southern Christian Leadership Conference, and the Congress for Racial Equality. Even after Kennedy's order—the first executive command to consider race and ethnic origin as positive factors in the employment decision-making process—the protests did not stop. The violent Southern responses to protesters demanded that the federal government act. By the summer of 1963, the administration asked Congress to pass a civil rights law that would desegregate public facilities and move America toward racial equality. To show both black America's impatience at the slow pace of integration and support for the president's bill, a broad coalition of people at last began to trumpet A. Philip Randolph's twenty-two-year call for a march on Washington.

The August 1963 gathering of nearly a quarter of a million people demanding congressional action ultimately led to the passage of the Civil Rights Act of 1964.[32] While often hailed as a major step, the decision to afford other races an affirmative classification was much more pragmatic than radical.[33] At the time of passage of the 1964 act, the nation had experienced an unprecedented long-term economic expansion. Race-based affirmative action programs did not present the problem of choosing to take jobs or educational opportunities away from Caucasians. The vision of an ever-expanding economic pie made it easier to offer a slice to those who previously had been denied a seat at the table.[34]

The modern use of the actual phrase "affirmative action" came with President Lyndon Johnson's Executive Order 11246. That directive required federal contractors to adopt and implement affirmative action to ensure the hiring of blacks, women, and other minorities in the work force through the use of hiring goals.[35] "In its early form affirmative action was seen as a temporary intervention into the processes of various competitions to insure that all individuals were treated fairly regardless of factors such as race, ethnicity, religion or sex."[36] The use of affirmative action was not limited to federal contractors, however. After the executive order, affirmative action programs grew rapidly as governments, schools, and private employers actively sought to expand opportunities for African Americans.

At first, the very promise of equal opportunity was enough to satisfy a large majority of African Americans and was not sufficiently threatening to most of the principal managers of business and government. Although working-class

Caucasians may have felt threatened, the reality of seniority systems and so-called race-neutral qualification requirements worked to ensure that affirmative action would not pose a risk to their livelihoods. Consequently, affirmative action programs grew and prospered between 1965 and 1972, despite opposition in some corners. Even the Supreme Court seemed to acknowledge the importance of recognizing the long-term effects of past discrimination.

In *Griggs* v. *Duke Power*, the Court observed that job selection criteria had not been shown to predict job performance:

> The objective of Congress in the enactment of Title VII is plain from the language of the statute. It was to achieve equality of employment opportunities and remove barriers that have operated in the past to favor an identifiable group of white employees over other employees. Under the Act, practices, procedures, or tests neutral on their face, and even neutral in terms of intent cannot be maintained if they operate to "freeze" the status quo of prior discriminatory employment practices.[37]

The justices thus prohibited Duke Power from requiring job applicants to have a high school diploma and subjecting them to a general intelligence test where the effect was to put black applicants at a disadvantage. *Griggs* may have represented the high-water mark for affirmative action, however. Even before the case was decided in 1971, America had already begun to change both economically and politically.

Politically, the 1967 and 1968 race riots in numerous U.S. cities, the assassinations of Robert Kennedy and Martin Luther King, Jr., and, the growing anti-Vietnam war movement pushed the nation toward a conservative ideology. Many Americans embraced the law-and-order rhetoric of presidential candidates Richard Nixon and George Wallace in 1968. Noting this change, historian Harvard Sitkoff writes:

> Appealing to those weary of protest, Richard Nixon rode the backlash into the White House. He campaigned against open housing and busing for racial balance. He promised to slow federal efforts at school integration and to appoint only conservative justices to the federal courts. Nixon particularly solicited the support of traditional Democratic voters disgruntled with the excesses of the black struggle. Many responded to the appeal. The Democratic nominee, Hubert Humphrey, long associated in the public mind with the civil-rights movement, won just one out of every three white votes. The ethnic working class that deserted Humphrey largely rallied to the banner of George

Wallace, whose American Independent Party made the fear and resentment of blacks the central thrust of its campaign. . . .

Immediately after entering the White House, President Nixon began wooing the Wallace constituency to insure his reelection in 1972. He deliberately pursued a "Southern strategy," conceding the votes of blacks and those committed to liberalism and going after those of white Southerners, suburbanites, and ethnic workers troubled by the specter of racial equality. Rather than follow the course counseled by his domestic advisor, the sociologist Daniel Patrick Moynihan, to behave with "benign neglect" on the race issue, the President intentionally focused public attention on the matter, and in a manner hardly benign to blacks.[38]

By 1971, the twenty-five-year, postwar economic boom also had run its course. The same opportunities for economic progress—manufacturing jobs—were less available to African Americans as seniority systems worked to preserve the status of long-term workers while the number of new jobs diminished. The nation's switch to a service economy began in earnest.

The fading of America's producer base meant that fewer factory or other semiskilled positions were available. This fact was particularly devastating for African Americans who had come to realize their part of the economic American dream through factory work.[39] Many jobs were exported to developing nations where the cost of labor was substantially less. These corporate moves were often made with only the short-term goal of higher profit margins in mind. The longer-term question of what happens to the displaced worker was rarely asked. Today, nearly two-thirds of all employment in America consists of providing services rather than producing goods. Many of these service jobs require special training in science, mathematics, and economics—training that is attained principally in colleges and universities.

Threatened by the prospect of smaller economic growth, more Caucasians began to oppose affirmative action programs. This time the opposition did not come from just those who felt threatened in the manufacturing workplace; resistance also came from the governing elite. Watergate, the OPEC oil crisis, the rise of feminism, and increasing civil rights militancy all combined to threaten the political fabric of America. With both the working class and the business and government elite threatened by the future, the federal response to affirmative action took a noticeable turn. Government support for affirmative action began to diminish.

Without a forceful government voice to lead the debate on affirmative action during less than stable economic times, opponents increased their attacks through a series of clever and deceptive myths. Foremost among them was the notion of *reverse discrimination*. The term "reverse discrimination" first appeared in the popular media in 1974 after the Supreme Court issued its decision in *DeFunis* v. *Odegaard*. In that case the plaintiff, Marco DeFunis, argued that the admissions committee at the University of Washington Law School had discriminated against him on account of race and thus violated the Equal Protection Clause of the Fourteenth Amendment. The Court held that the issue was moot on the grounds that DeFunis would graduate with his law class regardless of his legal action. The case, however, raised a new whipping post in efforts to broaden access to higher education.[40]

Because higher education opportunities were available to only a relatively small number of African Americans (and principally through historically black institutions), a number of predominantly Caucasian colleges and universities sought to increase the number of African Americans on campus through preferential admissions policies. To combat this problem of access, schools began to take race into account positively, in their admissions decision-making process. In some instances, a specific number of seats were reserved for black and other applicants of color. In making comparisons among applicants, most schools used only two quantifiable factors: (1) an applicant's grade point average in high school; and (2) that person's college entrance examination score. Neither of these two factors are accurate predictors of a student's performance or success in college. Few, if any, schools fill their classes solely on the basis of those factors. However, the consideration of race in the admissions process permitted Caucasian applicants denied a seat in a particular school to claim victim status.

The seminal case regarding affirmative action in university admissions is *Regents of the University of California* v. *Bakke*.[41] In *Bakke*, a Caucasian medical school applicant sued the University of California at Davis, claiming that its minority set-aside program violated both the Equal Protection Clause of the Fourteenth Amendment and Title VI of the Civil Rights Act. Bakke successfully contended that his grade point average and medical entrance examination scores were higher than those of some persons accepted for the minority slots. No majority opinion emerged from the Supreme Court's consideration of the case. The justices wrote six separate opinions, with no more than four justices agreeing about the reasoning. Four justices gave the Davis plan intermediate review and found it completely constitutional. Four found the plan unlawful on statutory grounds but did not reach the equal protection claim. It therefore fell on the ninth justice, Lewis Powell, to form a majority. Justice Powell concurred with Justices Harry A. Blackmun, William J. Brennan, Thurgood Marshall, and Byron R. White that a university should be permitted to take race into account when considering whether to admit a candidate. However, Powell believed that any racial classification must be subjected to strict constitutional scrutiny; thus, there must be a compelling state interest in order for the program to stand.[42] In his view, the Davis special admissions program was unconstitutional because applicants like Bakke were placed at a disadvantage, even though they were not responsible for "whatever harm the beneficiaries of the special admissions program are thought to have suffered."[43] The "principal evil" of the program, Powell wrote, was the denial of Bakke's right to "individualized consideration without regard to race."[44]

In cases like *Bakke* and *DeFunis*, the legal challenges focused on the relatively few seats set aside for minorities rather than on the general admissions process that historically favored elite white males over everyone else. As a result of such reverse discrimination challenges, colleges began to retreat from their affirmative action efforts. A vast number of African Americans were simply excluded from even taking advantage of these limited educational opportunities. But the college admissions process contains a number of variables that extend beyond grade point and entrance examination scores. The process is not one that can be applied mechanically.

> Moreover, use of a pool defined exclusively by a high school G.P.A. and S.A.T. results would itself disguise the fact that the substandard, segregated education of many parents of the current generation of African-American students directly impacts the G.P.A.s and S.A.T. scores of . . . current black applicants. Education is a continuous and expanding process in which knowledge, skills and attitudes towards learning are communicated from one generation to another. Unfortunately, we still live in a time when many African-Americans of college age are disadvantaged in this respect because their forbears received an inferior education.[45]

Recognition of the long-term and far-ranging effects of educational discrimination is the message that proponents of affirmative action programs are trying to help people understand. "Reverse discrimination" is itself an inaccurate and misleading term. It misleads by focusing attention away from affirmative action as an effective remedy to discrimination. It is inaccurate because such programs are *not* taking something away from one group (Caucasians), but instead are varying the calculus so that others might also partake in the opportunity.

Like educational programs, affirmative action efforts in the work force met similar challenges.[46] Instead of supporting measures that called for specific outcome-focused goals with respect to racial composition, opponents successfully argued that good-faith affirmative action efforts should suffice. The problem with good-faith efforts in this area is that they permit institutional inertia—the employer simply goes through the motions of searching for someone to hire. Stiffer job or admission requirements permitted institutions, "in good faith," to tell African American and other candidates with clear potential for success in the classroom or in the work force that they did not quite measure up to the revised standards. The shifting away from stated numerical goals that were linked to timetables for their achievement to good-faith efforts rarely resulted in anything more than the hiring of a token number of people of color.[47]

Underlying the reverse discrimination myth is the concept of tipping—the psychological notion in the minds of many Caucasians that the addition of more African Americans will change the essential nature of the institution.[48] The words "essential nature" are nothing more than doublespeak for the unstated assumption that most people fundamentally conceive of their workplace, their schools, and even *our* nation as an essentially white country.[49] Alex Aleinikoff notes that

> the stories that African Americans tell about America—stories of racism and exclusion, brutality and mendacity—simply do not ring true to the white mind. Whites have not been trained to hear it, and to credit such accounts would be to ask whites to give up too much of what they "know" about the world. It would also argue in favor of social programs and an alteration in power relations that would fundamentally change the status quo. . . . [I]t is the white version that becomes the "official story" in the dominant culture.[50]

In his book *And We Are Not Saved*, Derrick Bell tells the parable of the seventh minority candidate for a law school faculty, who despite having a superior vitae is denied a position because Caucasian faculty had reached their racial tipping point. Thus, an African American with superior credentials was still denied acceptance because of race.[51]

Though there have been few studies of the early successes of such programs, one might assume positive results because of the subsequent growth of affirmative action programs to encompass many other people in American society. Women, Hispanics, Native Americans, and many new immigrant groups have come within affirmative action's inclusive umbrella. Perhaps because so many more people from many different groups now seek affirmative action recognition, or, perhaps because others became threatened by it, affirmative action soon came under increasing attack. "Quotas," "reduced standards," "special interest politics," and "reverse discrimination" are just some of the invectives cast at programs that seek to include African American and other historically underrepresented people. Even some African American scholars, many of whom have been the principal beneficiaries of affirmative action, now suggest that affirmative action has no place in America's societal discourse because of the stigmatizing harm caused to participants.[52] These and other writers suggest that the truest constitutional principle is that of a color-blind society.[53]

The idea of constitutional color-blindness was first articulated in Justice John Marshall Harlan's famous dissent in *Plessy v. Ferguson*:

> In respect of civil rights, common to all citizens, the Constitution of the United States does not, I think, permit any public authority to know the race of those entitled to be protected in the enjoyment of such rights. Every true man has pride of race, and under appropriate circumstances, when the rights of others, his equals before the law, are not to be affected, it is his privilege to express such pride and to take such action based upon it as to him seems proper. But I deny that any legislative body or judicial tribunal may have regard to the race of citizens when the civil rights of those citizens are involved. Indeed such legislation as that here in question is inconsistent, not only with that equality of rights which pertains to citizenship, national and state, but with the personal liberty enjoyed by every one within the United States.
>
> [I]n view of the Constitution, in the eye of the law, *there is in this country no superior, dominant, ruling class of citizens. There is no caste here. Our Constitution is color-blind, and neither knows nor tolerates classes among citizens. In respect of civil rights, all citizens are equal before the law.* The destinies of the two races in this country are indissolubly linked together, and the interests of both require that the common government of all shall not permit the seeds of race hate to be planted under the sanction of law.[54]

Harlan's powerful language should perhaps be recast by changing the word "is" throughout the second paragraph to "should be"—*there should be in this country no superior, dominant, ruling class of citizens. There should be no caste here. Our Constitution should be color-blind.* Such an interpretive phrasing would force us to ask the all-important question of whether we have indeed reached a point where race does not matter.

It appears that a growing number of people have come to believe that race does not matter. The present Supreme Court has attempted to narrow the definition of permissible affirmative action programs.[55] Contrary to these claims, America is and has always been a color-conscious and not a color-blind society. Race is such a powerful aspect of our lives that overcoming it may well be impossible; however, to claim that race should be ignored, simply disregards the American reality.

The ultimate goal of affirmative action programs is to create a community that values racial, ethnic, and gender diversity to a point that discrimination based on these characteristics ceases to occur. Clearly, this aspiration is a long-term dream. Opponents of affirmative action often focus on this goal to support their claims that the only way to achieve a society that values all of its members is to ignore race completely. These critics argue that it is immoral, unprincipled, and paradoxical to have a goal of color-blindness, yet seek to reach that goal by color-conscious actions.[56] They refuse to acknowledge the breadth and depth of the continuing legacy of racism in this country. Even though segregation is no longer the expressed law of the land, the aftermath of nearly two centuries of race-based denials of opportunity lingers to this day as disproportionate numbers of African Americans realize less of America's promise than members of any other racial or ethnic group.[57]

EFFECTS OF ATTACKS ON AFFIRMATIVE ACTION

As African Americans, we are caught between a rock and a hard place. While some few of us who have benefited from affirmative action can be pointed to as success stories, this fact cannot mask the bitter reality that the majority of our people languish economically and, even worse, spiritually.[58] In particular, the effect on young African Americans has been devastating. Unlike those of us who benefited from these programs in the 1960s and 1970s, the generation and a half of young people who have grown up since then have seen opportunities shrink and their own accomplishments either unrecognized or minimized. The effect on their self-esteem is undeniable.

Those of us who have been the beneficiaries of affirmative action have parlayed the opportunities offered us into respectable middle- and upper middle-class lifestyles. Now, so many of us are unwilling to speak out not only in favor of continuing but also of expanding affirmative action efforts. A number of our own best and brightest have begun to question the basic underpinnings of affirmative action. Indeed, some beneficiaries even claim that "America is a meritocratic nation that permits people to rise or fall according to their quality." Hearing such declarations from our own may be even more debilitating than hearing the same from Caucasians. Disagreement over the worth of affirmative action within the African American community not only sends mixed signals to the governing elite, but, what is more important, such disagreement divides and confuses the African American community itself.

The nomination of Justice Clarence Thomas to the Supreme Court is a prime example of community division. Despite Thomas's own condemnation of affirmative action, his academic and professional career attainments were due, in large measure, to the very programs he opposed. Confronted with this irony, African Americans found ourselves split between supporting or opposing his nomination. Writing about this episode, Cornel West notes,

> Bush's choice of Thomas caught most black leaders off guard. Few had the courage to say publicly that this was an act of cynical tokenism concealed by outright lies about Thomas being the most qualified candidate regardless of race. Thomas had an undistinguished record as a student (mere graduation from Yale Law School does not qualify one for the Supreme Court); . . . and his performance during his short fifteen months as an appellate court judge was mediocre. The very fact that no black leader could utter publicly that a black appointee for the Supreme Court was *unqualified* shows how captive they are to white racist stereotypes about [African American] intellectual talent.[59]

In reality, Thomas's appointment was the quintessential *anti*–affirmative action case because it went to the very core of the conservative critique—namely, that a less-than-best-qualified person received a position through preference. This situation confused many in the African American community because we viewed the Thomas nomination as forcing us either to support someone solely because of race, or, to admit that an African American candidate was not the best-qualified. Either position arguably would confirm the conservative claims about affirmative action.

The reluctance to dispute the expected qualifications of an African American judicial nominee reflects the degree of internalized oppression that exists in our community. Instead of leading the debate about how to refine, revitalize, and reconfigure affirmative action, African Americans have permitted critics to monopolize the discussion and to call into question our own sense of self-worth. Were we like Clarence Thomas—perhaps positioned where we were because of someone's benevolence; or, were we at a particular life station because of our accomplishments, because we were the best? Even among the most educated and most successful African Americans, personal doubts still exist about our place within institutions.[60]

But African Americans have no need to doubt ourselves or our accomplishments. Our successes stand on their own. Instead of harboring doubts about our achievements, let us focus on the tasks that remain. Affirmative action continues to be a misunderstood concept. We agree that society should ask whether any person can meet the basic criteria for a position. But the word "qualified" means competent or eligible; it does not mean best. Despite this fact, most people, African Americans included, believe that decisions are and should be made to favor that "best" person. Rarely if ever can one say that the person chosen is the best of all choices that could have been made. Many are differently qualified. The selection of any person of color who is comparable with, or even better than, a Caucasian is too often seen as an injustice to that Caucasian. But too often we accept the false claim that affirmative action programs result in the selection of incompetent persons.

American institutions have never operated on a completely merit-based system. There are few, if any, positions that demand that the *most* capable or credentialed person be selected. It is mere folly to suggest that capabilities can be measured so as to determine who has the most or who is the best. Race-based affirmative action merely opens doors that have been closed despite our possessing comparable or even superior credentials. It gets us to the starting gate. Where each of us then finishes is a function of our own grit and determination as well equal employment opportunity. Thus, there is no need for us to shy away from or to question the role of affirmative action.

THE CHALLENGE FOR THE FUTURE

But what can we say to our children about the challenges awaiting us and them in the future with respect to affirmative action? One solution is to tell them to look at affirmative action over the past twenty-five years not as a failed policy, but as one that was never really tried. The Great Society programs of the 1960s were never fully funded and were insufficient to begin addressing the legacy of slavery and ongoing discrimination. We are just now coming to the point of funding programs like Head Start, an idea that Republicans and Democrats alike believe works. Imagine the result if such resources had been allocated to Head Start from 1965 to now! Perhaps more young African American children and their families would be able to overcome the social and economic woes through greater classroom successes.

We might also tell our children that another way of regarding affirmative action is to see it as a band-aid on the cancer of racism. Racism may well be a permanent phenomenon, and African Americans may never have true equality. "Even our most successful efforts will produce no more than 'temporary peaks of progress'."[61] A band-aid may provide some minor relief or protection from outside infection. Thus affirmative action may frustrate and retard some of the infectious manifestations of racism.[62]

Either of these alternatives may be too pessimistic to convey to our children. Instead we need to give them hope. We can give them hope by teaching them the history of this centuries-long struggle for racial equality and just opportunity. We can give them hope by teaching them about all those African Americans who came before them, who suffered and even died without losing sight of this quest. We can give them hope by telling them that their and our efforts must continue to be directed at reconfiguring this society in a way that will lead us and others to see race, ethnicity, and difference as positive rather than negative attributes. Such a society, we must tell them, will permit all of us to be confident in ourselves, our capabilities, and in those same attributes we find in others. We must tell the children that affirmative action should be one of many tools that help us grow beyond "the accumulated effect of the black wounds and scars suffered in a white dominated society . . . a deep seated anger . . . a boiling sense of rage, and a passionate pessimism regarding America's will to justice."[63] Like Cornel West, we believe in the politics of conversion, politics that emphasize love, care, and the rebuilding of African Americans and all society.[64]

In the next century our children will become part of the majority as America becomes a nation principally comprised of people of color. If this country is to survive and perhaps even flourish in the future, it must overcome, or at least honestly confront, its fear of race. We must be bold enough to utilize tools such as affirmative action as sources of growth and reconciliation that will spirit-warm rather than spirit-assault.[65] The memory of our ancestors should hearten us for this effort; their hopes and dreams have not yet been realized. The sweet faces of our children will inspire us; what legacy will we leave for them? We are a nation inextricably bound together—black, brown, red, and white. We must work together to build a tomorrow filled with hope. We must work now, and we must not fail.

NOTES

1. "As early as 1501, Spain relinquished her earlier ban and permitted Africans to go into the Spanish lands in the New World." John Hope Franklin and Alfred A. Moss, *From Slavery to Freedom* (New York: Alfred Knopf, 1987), 30. See also Mary Frances Berry and John W. Blassingame, *Long Memory: The Black Experience in America* (New York: Oxford University Press, 1982), 7, which states that "[t]he First Africans arrived in the New

World in 1502." Franklin and Moss note that "[t]hirty Negroes . . . were with Balboa when he discovered the Pacific Ocean. Cortes carried blacks with him into Mexico and one of them planted and harvested the first wheat crop in the New World. . . . As the Spanish and Portuguese explorers moved into the interior of North America, Negroes assisted in the undertakings. They were with Alarcon and Coronado in the conquest of New Mexico. They accompanied Navarez on his expedition of 1527 and were with Cabeza de Vaca in the exploration of the southwestern part of the present United States." Franklin and Moss, *From Slavery to Freedom*, 30.

As early as 1797 persons of African descent petitioned Congress for freedom and rights, arguing that racial oppression was a "direct violation of the declared fundamental principles of the Constitution." Herbert Aptheker, ed., *A Documentary History of the Negro People in the United States* (New York: Citadel Press, 1951), 43. However, the year 1954 remains the date that persons of African descent were able finally, to persuade the U.S. Supreme Court that the Constitution's protective cloak should be opened for all citizens, regardless of their race or color, to seek refuge.

2. W. E. B. Du Bois, *The Souls of Black Folk* (Chicago: A. C. McClurg, 1903), 1. See also Walter R. Allen and Reynolds Farley, *The Color Line and the Quality of Life in America* (New York: Russell Sage Foundation, 1987).

3. Michael and Lauren Knight, ages eight and six; and, Che and Nolan Wing Melson, ages ten and five.

4. For a helpful discussion on the issue of color-blindness and race awareness, see also T. Alexander Aleinikoff, "A Case for Race-Consciousness," *Columbia Law Review* 91 (1991): 1062–63, 1075–76.

5. George LaNoue, The Demographic Premises of Affirmative Action, *Population and Environment: A Journal of Interdisciplinary Studies* 14 (1993): 421.

6. J. Clay Smith, "Symposium: Perspectives on Equal Employment Opportunity Litigation: Review: Affirmative Action," *Howard Law Journal* 27 (1984): 496. Though Professor Smith's definition did not include education, we believe that his explanation is equally well-suited for the educational context. For another often-used definition, see also Bernard R. Boxill, *Blacks and Social Justice*, rev. ed. (Lanham, Md.: Rowman and Littlefield, 1992), 148, 168 (defining affirmative action as "preferential treatment for minorities which provides compensation for wrongs committed in the past which resulted from racist practices and attitudes. The goal of affirmative action is to allow for greater equality and an elevated sense of social utility"). We disagree with the Boxill definition because of its singular focus on compensation for past discrimination as the justification for affirmative action programs. A compensatory model is subject to criticism when calls for affirmative measures are made in the absence of direct proof of past and direct discrimination. Instead, we prefer a theoretical model of affirmative action based upon notions of distributive justice. . . . that a fair and just society should afford opportunity to all of its citizens. It is precisely because of past and present discrimination that many people in this society are not able to compete in a relatively objective manner with others for such opportunities. Given this view, we regard our modification of Professor Smith's definition as a more accurate depiction of our impression of the concept.

7. Boxill, *Blacks and Social Justice*, 148. See also Smith, "Symposium," 496. Boxill states that affirmative action can be seen in two ways, either through a "backward looking"

argument that aims at compensation for past wrongs or through a "forward looking" argument that seeks to achieve greater status, education, and income for blacks. As noted above, we embrace this forward-looking model as a means to achieve greater distributive justice and not simply a method of compensation that will elevate the status of some select few.

The underlying philosophical basis for affirmative action goes beyond a mere compensatory justice model. It includes distributive justice concerns. The present distribution of disadvantaged groups in the work force suggests that factors other than capability have led to a maldistribution of certain groups within the work force. Historically, people of black, Latino, American Indian, and Asian descent have been among the least educated as a group and have occupied unusually large numbers of the lowest-earning jobs in American society. A distributive model of justice encourages a forward-looking policy that seeks to achieve an improved work force distribution through actual redistribution of these affected groups by means of expanded employment and educational opportunities. Kathanne W. Greene, *Affirmative Action and Principles of Justice* (New York: Greenwood Press, 1989), 170.

With a compensatory model, a person injured by discrimination will be compensated for the harm caused. Under this model, victims would be expected to prove the actual harm caused by the discriminating party. Often, proving such harm is difficult, if not impossible. This situation has led some advocates of affirmative action to argue group injustice as a basis for providing a remedy; mere membership in a group is sufficient (thus, all African Americans have been actual psychological victims of discrimination because of this country's history of slavery and segregation laws). While we subscribe to this view, we are aware of the criticisms leveled against it, namely, that not all African Americans (or other designated groups) have been discriminated against and thereby disadvantaged; thus, it would be inappropriate to provide compensation on the basis of the group characteristic.

It is precisely because of this criticism that we emphasize the forward-looking concept of distributive justice. Under this idea, affirmative action becomes the means by which society can achieve a distributive principle of equal opportunity—that all individuals should have an equal chance to compete for societal benefits. See Greene, *Affirmative Action*, 171–72.

8. In this essay we use the phrase "people of color" in a limited manner to encompass only those groups specifically defined by the Office of Federal Contract Compliance Programs as protected class persons: blacks, Hispanics, Asian and Pacific Islanders, and Native Americans.

9. See Allan Bloom, *The Closing of the American Mind* (New York: Simon and Schuster, 1987); Stephen Carter, *Reflections of An Affirmative Action Baby* (New York: Basic Books, 1991); Dinesh D'Souza, *Illiberal Education: The Politics of Race and Sex on Campus* (New York: Free Press, 1991); and Shelby Steele, *The Content of Our Character: A New Vision of Race in America* (New York: St. Martin's Press, 1990). See also, Thomas Sowell, "Are Quotas Good for Blacks?" and Harvey C. Mansfield, Jr., "The Underhandedness of Affirmative Action," in *Racial Preference and Racial Justice: The New Affirmative Action Controversy*, ed. Russell Nieli (Lanham, Md.: University Press of America, 1990), 129.

10. See Equal Employment Opportunity Coordinating Council Policy Statement on Affirmative Action Programs for State and Local Government Agencies, 41 Fed. Reg. 38,

814 (1976). See, for example, *Griggs* v. *Duke Power Co.*, 401 U.S. 424 (1971); *Wright* v. *National Archives & Records Service*, 609 F.2d 702 (4th Cir. 1979).

11. In an interesting twist, Alan Goldman and Thomas Nagel have criticized the arguments for affirmative action that are based on the concept that minorities deserve compensation for past wrongs that caused harm through racist attitudes and practices. See Boxill, *Blacks and Social Justice*, 148. Their argument proceeds on the notion that in the job market, affirmative action requires people of color (and women) to have qualifications relative to those of Caucasian males with whom they are competing for a position. Thus, since these people are indeed qualified, they are not the ones who deserve preferential treatment, which should be reserved for those who are the most unequal in comparison with Caucasian males. This criticism seems to make little sense to us. While it may be true that an applicant who is less qualified because of prior racist practices should be the most deserving of compensation, that fact alone does not necessarily lead to the conclusion that those people of color who are more qualified should not receive any additional preference at all. Indeed, one of the essential points of this essay is that the effects of explicit and implicit racial discrimination go far beyond standard measuring instruments. The fact that one grows up in a middle- or upper-income household, for example, does not mean that person has been unaffected by her or his race. See Boxill, *Blacks and Social Justice*, 148 (Boxill's reply to Goldman and Nagel).

12. See Smith, "Symposium," 500–1.

13. Historically, the word "qualified" has been used to describe outright race-based decisions. In universities, for example, affirmative action was used for more than a century to fill classrooms with Protestant Caucasian males and their children. Subsequently, Caucasian females and even non-Protestants were also included. Even now, children of alumni in Ivy League schools have approximately a 50 percent acceptance rate, as compared with a 17 percent acceptance rate for the children of nonalumni. But Caucasian alumni children do not suffer a stigma because of their preferred treatment; indeed, many regard it as their birthright to matriculate at the institution that their parents attended.

Another example of the use of the word "qualified" concerns test scores. Somehow people have come to believe that a lower test score indicates that the person is less qualified or even unqualified to attend the institution. Test scores and grade point averages are but two indications of a person's potential. There are many other factors involved in an admissions decision, including an applicant's curriculum, the institution attended, residency status, geographic diversity, work or life experiences. No school has ever filled its entire class solely on the basis of test scores and grade point averages. Yet, the issue of qualification arises most frequently when race is also a factor. This situation leads to people of color being socially and intellectually stigmatized as inadequate.

14. Chief Justice Taney's opinion in *Dred Scott* v. *Sanford*, 60 U.S. (19 How.) 393, 404–5 (1857) reflects a part of this history: "[Negroes] . . . were at that time [the founding of the nation] considered as a subordinate and inferior class of beings, who had been subjugated by the dominant race, and whether emancipated or not, yet remained subject to their authority, and had no rights or privileges but such as those who held the power and the Government might choose to grant them." Taney went on to note that "[Negroes] had for more than a century before been regarded as beings of an inferior order; and altogether unfit to associate with the white race . . . and so far inferior, that

they had no rights which the white man was bound to respect; and that the negro might justly and lawfully be reduced to slavery for his benefit. He was bought and sold, and treated as an ordinary article of merchandise and traffic, whenever a profit could be made by it" (p. 407).

15. Smith, "Symposium," 518.

16. On this point Professor Smith writes: "A thorough understanding of affirmative action is not possible without reference to the problem it seeks to cure. Affirmative action is a remedy for the disease of discrimination which still exists in epidemic proportions in America." Smith, "Symposium," 503–4. As stated in a U.S. Commission on Civil Rights' publication, "Discrimination has become a process that builds the discriminatory attitudes and actions of individuals into the operations of organizations and social structures (such as education, employment, housing and government). Perpetuating past injustices into the present, and manifesting itself through statistically measurable inequalities that are longstanding and widespread, this discriminatory process produces unequal results along the lines of race, sex, and national origin, which in turn reinforce existing practices and breed damaging stereotypes which then promote the existing inequalities that set the process in motion in the first place." *Affirmative Action in the 1980's: Dismantling the Process of Discrimination* (1981), 5. Also, "When such a discriminatory process is at work, insistence upon neutrality and color-blindness insures the continuation of current inequitable practices. It is this ongoing cycle of discrimination permeating our society which affirmative action seeks to remedy. When this discriminatory process has been dismantled, affirmative action will no longer serve any legitimate social purpose and will no longer be justifiable." *Affirmative Action in the 1980's*, 503–4.

17. *Regents of the University of California v. Bakke*, 438 U.S. 265, 407 (1978) (opinion of Blackmun, J.).

18. Patricia J. Williams, *The Alchemy of Race and Rights* (Cambridge, Mass.: Harvard University Press, 1991), 103.

19. Williams, *The Alchemy of Race and Rights*, 102 (emphasis added).

20. While it is true that some affirmative action efforts also employ a strategy for training people who are less qualified or less experienced than others within the same pool, the fact remains that employers can and do begin such programs with an assumption that those people selected possess at least a basic capability that qualifies them for training or for a specific job. Often, the employer's decision to emphasize race or gender occurs because of some belief that there has been historic discrimination in the development of the specific employee work force. Historic discrimination is often the driving force behind employer programs that emphasize the selection of persons with less seniority than others in a particular work setting.

Still other employers adopt voluntary programs that seek to take corrective steps before costly litigation alleging discrimination ensues. In these cases, there may or may not be historic discrimination; instead of entertaining a court challenge, these employers seek to institute programs to diversify the work force before problems develop. In *United Steelworkers of America v. Weber*, 443 U.S. 193, 201–4 (1979), the Court made it clear that voluntary affirmative action plans were indeed permissible when based upon an employer's self-assessment that underrepresentation among certain groups in the potential work force existed. The Court found that such employers may voluntarily seek to correct such imbalances, irrespective of the cause, whether by the employer's own discriminatory acts or by those of society in general.

The Equal Employment Opportunity Commission has promulgated specific guidelines by which affirmative action programs should be based. They include: (1) a reasonable self-analysis by a business regarding whether its practices exclude the disadvantaged or whether such practices have a disparate impact on previously discriminated groups; (2) a reasonable basis for the employer's affirmative action; and (3) reasonable action to alleviate any problems disclosed as a result of the self-analysis. See J. Clay Smith (former Commissioner of the EEOC), "The Three R's of the Affirmative Action Guidelines, a speech delivered to the Texas Association of Business, February 27, 1979, San Antonio. Under these criteria, affirmative action programs are not just based on mere preferences or blind and subjective whims.

Professor Williams aptly summarized this idea when she wrote: "Preferential treatment isn't inherently dirty; seeing its ubiquity, within and without racial politics, is the key to the underground vaults of freedom locked up in the idea of whom one likes. The whole historical object of equal opportunity, formal or informal, is to structure preferences for rather than against—to like rather than dislike—the participation of black people. Thus affirmative action is very different from numerical quotas that actively structure society so that certain classes of people remain unpreferred. "Quotas," "preference," "reverse discrimination," "experienced," and "qualified" are con words, shiny mirror words that work to dazzle the eye with their analogic evocation of other times, other contexts, multiple histories. As a society, we have yet to look carefully beneath them to see where the seed of prejudice are truly hidden. Williams, *The Alchemy of Race and Rights*, 103.

21. Harvard Sitkoff, *The Struggle for Black Equality 1954–1992*, rev. ed. (New York: Hill and Wang, 1993), 11.

22. Sitkoff, *The Struggle for Black Equity*, 11. Some two million blacks found employment in defense-related industries.

23. James E. Jones Jr., "The Development of Modern Equal Employment Opportunity and Affirmative Action Law: A Brief Chronological Overview," *Howard Law Journal* 20 (1977): 75–77.

24. Jones, "The Development," 13.

25. Jones, "The Development," 17.

26. 347 U.S. 483 (1954). It is important to remember that the concept of separate but equal was not being dismantled as much as the concept that schools for African American and Caucasian American children should be on an equal footing. The idea of an equal starting point was key to the idea of a fair competition. See 347 U.S. 493 (1954).

27. *Brown* expressly repudiated the blatantly racist doctrine promulgated in *Plessy* v. *Ferguson*, 163 U.S. 537, 538, 542–51 (1883). In *Plessy*, Homer Plessy, a black man, was convicted of violating a local Louisiana statute that mandated that whites and blacks could not share train compartments. The Court ruled that the state statute did not violate the Thirteenth or Fourteenth amendments because the statute represented a valid exercise of police power by the state. The upshot of this decision was a judicial reaffirmation of the belief that blacks did not have rights similar to those of whites, that blacks were, in essence, less than full citizens.

The *Brown* decision reflected a judicial acknowledgement of the constitutional existence of blacks as full citizens entitled to share in the benefits provided under that document with respect to access to education.

28. *Brown* v. *Board of Education* (No. 2), 349 U.S. 294 (1955).

29. Under the go-slow approach, local school authorities were given the responsibility for drawing up desegregation plans and federal judges were to determine whether school districts were making progress toward desegregation "with all deliberate speed." Both quotations are from Sitkoff, *The Struggle for Black Equality*, 23.

30. For a description of part of this eight-year history of opposition to desegregation, see Sitkoff, *The Struggle for Black Equality*, 25–36.

31. Steven J. Witosky, "Beyond Reverse Discrimination: The Quest For a Legitimizing Principle," *Nova Law Journal* 4 (1980): 63.

32. 42 U.S.C. § 2000d, 45 C.F.R. §§ 80.1 et seq. The two most important provisions of the act were Titles VI and VII. Title VI prohibited race discrimination in any program that received federal funds. The law applied to both educational admissions programs and to actual job employment. Title VII prohibited employment discrimination based on race, color, religion, sex, or national origin by any employer with fifteen or more employees.

33. See, for example, Sitkoff, *The Struggle for Black Equality*; and Franklin and Moss, *From Slavery to Freedom*, 436–94.

34. Though rarely stated in this fashion, it seems clear that the Kennedy and Johnson administrations believed that the experience of integrating returning World War II and Korean War veterans into the socioeconomic mainstream could be duplicated for African Americans. The Johnson and Kennedy years also marked a time of struggle for America's place in world affairs. During the 1960s, European colonialism disintegrated; in many parts of the world, there was an effort to replace European dominance with either the Communist influence of the Soviet Union and China or a democratic influence spearheaded by the United States. As America struggled for supremacy in world authority, it was clear that international appeals for democracy had to find some domestic examples of democratic egalitarian principles at work. America's attempt at providing equal opportunity for the African American would support U.S. calls for democratic rule in a number of newly emerging nations, particularly those on the continent of Africa. Thus, race-based affirmative action programs also served America's own international agenda. For a discussion of America's international agenda as it related to the *Brown* decision, see Mary L. Dudziak, "Desegregation as a Cold War Imperative," *Stanford Law Review* 41 (1988): 61.

35. Executive Order 11,246, 41 C.F.R. §§ 60–1 et seq. (1965), as amended in Executive Order 11,375 (1967). A number of laws were passed to govern affirmative action program efforts. The unifying principle among these laws is an inquiry into whether targeted recruitment goals are designed to remedy the effects of current or past discrimination. See U.S. Constitution, Amendment 14, Titles VI and VII of the Civil Rights Act of 1964, 42 U.S.C. §§ 2000d and 2000e (with regulations at 45 C.F.R. §§ 80.1 et seq. and 29 U.S.C. §§1604–6, 1608.1 et seq.).

36. LaNoue, *The Demographic Premises*, 421.

37. 401 U.S. 424, 429–30 (1971).

38. Sitkoff, *The Struggle for Black Equality*, 212.

39. Andrew Hacker, *Two Nations: Black and White, Separate, Hostile, Unequal* (New York: Scribner's, 1992), 101. In 1960, 62.8 percent of all employed African American men worked in blue-collar jobs; the figure for Caucasian men was 54.2 percent. Only 87.3 percent of adult African American men were employed in 1960 (the figure for Caucasian men was 95.6 percent). By 1990, only 48.3 percent of African American men were employed in blue-collar jobs. Although the percentage for Caucasian men showed a similar decline to 39.4 percent, the overall percentage of employed adults showed a 13.5 percent decline in the number of employed African American men (the percentage decline for Caucasian men was only 6.4 percent). In other words, 26.2 percent of eligible African American men were unemployed while only 10.8 percent of Caucasian men were similarly without work of any kind. Hacker, *Two Nations*, 233.

40. 416 U.S. 312, 319–21 (1974) (Douglas, J., dissenting).

41. 438 U.S. 265 (1978).

42. 438 U.S. 265, 289 (1978). For Justice Powell, the curing of past intentional discrimination on the part of an institution using such a plan would be the only interest the Court should find sufficiently compelling. However, Powell's opinion also recognized that educational benefits could flow from a racially and ethnically diverse student body and that such a goal is constitutionally permitted as long as race is not the sole factor considered in the admissions process.

43. 438 U.S. 265, 310 (1978).

44. 438 U.S. 265, 318, n. 52 (1978).

45. *Podberesky v. Kirwan*, 838 F. Supp. 1075 (1993). 1993 WL 482923 (D. Md. Nov. 18, 1993), 10. *Podberesky* had to do with the University of Maryland's use of race-based scholarships. In finding that the specific program withstood constitutionally strict scrutiny, Judge Motz also suggested that it might well be appropriate to consider the employment and education contexts differently: "The various restrictions that the Court has applied to affirmative action programs in the employment context—particularly the prohibition against remedying the effects of "societal discrimination," or discrimination that was done by another "governmental unit"—appear inappropriate in the education context where the effects of past discrimination are obviously societal in scope. Indeed, the Court emphasized the broad social effect of education in *Brown*: '[Education] is required in the performance of our most basic public responsibilities, even service in the armed forces. It is the very foundation of good citizenship. Today it is a principal instrument for awakening the child to cultural values, in preparing him for later professional training, and in helping him to adjust normally to his environment. In these days, it is doubtful that any child may reasonably be expected to succeed in life if he has been denied the opportunity of an education.'" 347 U.S. at 493. A fire department's discriminatory hiring practices have little or no effect on the society at large. But discrimination in the nation's educational institutions has created a ripple effect that necessarily touches every aspect of our economy and society. Accordingly, it seems entirely proper that in order to cure these effects, legislatures and educational administrators be given more leeway in fashioning remedies that take into account the vast extent of the damage that has been done by our shameful legacy of involuntary segregated education. 1993 WL 482923, at 17.

46. See, for example, *Martin v. Wilks*, 490 U.S. 755 (Oct. Term, 1988) (permitting Caucasian firefighters to sue the city of Birmingham alleging that "less qualified" African Americans were promoted).

47. While the expansion of affirmative action to include non–African Americans should be applauded, one cannot ignore the adverse effect on African Americans as a group. With even more people coming within the protective scope of affirmative action, employers could show good faith by hiring other people of color. Thomas Boston's book *Race, Class and Conservatism* (Boston: Unwin Hyman, 1988) traces part of the international migration of people from other countries. Boston suggests that many of these new arrivals enter this country with skills and education levels far higher than many Americans, including African Americans. Some of these immigrants also arrive with economic resources and support from their homeland. Given these initial advantages, it should not surprise observers that such immigrants often achieve significantly more success than many African Americans.

48. For a description of the tipping phenomenon, see Ankur Goel, "Recent Developments," *Harvard C.R.-C.L. Law Review* 24 (1989): 561. See also, John M. Goering, "Neighborhood Tipping and Racial Transition: A Review of Social Science Evidence," *Journal American of the American Institute of Planners* 44 (January 1978): 69–78.

49. Derrick Bell, *Race, Racism, and American Law*, 3d ed. (Boston: Little, Brown, 1992), 7.

50. Aleinikoff, "A Case for Race-Consciousness," 1069.

51. Derrick Bell, *And We Are Not Saved: The Elusive Quest for Racial Justice* (New York: Basic Books, 1987). 140. We also remember the famous words of Paul Robeson in the pre-affirmative action era, when he applied to Princeton in 1914, after being both the number-one student and a top athlete at Somerville, New Jersey, High School: "Well the best people from Princeton sat down with us and talked, and they convinced my family and I that it would be better for us, for our people, and for Princeton University, if I applied for a scholarship to Rutgers." Paul Robeson speaking to sculptor Joe Brown, as quoted in Howard Waxwood, "Paul Robeson," *Daily Princetonian*, February 6, 1976, 7. See also Richard Delgado, "Approach-Avoidance in Law School Hiring: Is the Law a WASP?" *St. Louis University Law Journal* 34 (1990): 631.

52. See note 9.

53. See note 6 (Smith quote) and accompanying text.

54. 163 U.S. 537 (1896) (emphasis added).

55. In *Wards Cove Packing Co.* v. *Antonio*, 490 U.S. 642, 659 (1989) the Court stated that even if employer standards had a disproportionate impact on minorities, the standards did not have to be essential to the employer's business to justify their use. In *Martin* v. *Wilks*, 490 U.S. 755, 766–68 (1989), the Court permitted Caucasian workers to challenge a court-approved settlement establishing numerical goals and preferential treatment for minorities even though they were not part of the earlier proceeding. In *City of Richmond* v. *J. A. Croson Co.*, 488 U.S. 469, 507–8 (1988), the Court invalidated numerical set-aside provisions for minority contractors who sought work with the city. Fortunately, Congress rebuked the Court through passage of the 1991 Civil Rights Act, which restored affirmative action law to its pre-1989 status.

56. Note 9 and accompanying text.

57. Nationally, the high school dropout rate of African Americans is twice that of Caucasian American school children. See Gerald D. Jaynes and Robin M. Williams, Jr., eds., *A Common Destiny: Blacks and American Society* (Washington, D.C.: National Academy Press, 1989), 20. In nearly every economic or social measure, African Americans are significantly worse off than their Caucasian American counterparts. The median income for African American families is 57 percent of that for Caucasian American families.

In 1987, the median income for an African American family was $18,098 a year, as compared with $32,274 for a Caucasian American family. Harry A. Ploski and James Williams, eds., *The Negro Almanac: A Reference Work on the African American* 5th ed. (Detroit: Gale Research, Inc., 1989), 482. Fully one-third of all African Americans live below the poverty level (compared with only one out of every ten Caucasian Americans who occupy the same economic level). African American unemployment rates are double those of Caucasian American individuals; life expectancies for African American men and women are less than those for Caucasian American men and women. Ploski and James, *The Negro Almanac*, 503.

With respect to crime and punishment, the statistics are even more bleak. African Americans also constitute one-half of all prison inmates, despite the fact that we make up only 13 percent of the population. African Americans are six times more likely to be victims of violent crime than our proportion in the general population, and seven times more likely to be the victims of murder (the leading cause of death among African American men between the ages of fifteen and twenty-five). See Jaynes and Williams, *A Common Destiny*, 464–65, 498.

58. For a general discussion concerning discontent among successful African Americans, see Ellis Cose, *The Rage of a Privileged Class* (New York: Harper Collins, 1993).

59. Cornel West, *Race Matters* (Boston: Beacon Press, 1993), 23.

60. See Carter, *Reflections*; and Cose, *Rage*.

61. Bell, *Race, Racism, and American Law*, 62, n. 56. See also Derrick A. Bell, *Faces at the Bottom of the Well: The Permanence of Racism* (New York: Basic Books, 1992).

62. While we disagree about this characterization, one might also tell our children that affirmative action should be characterized as a policy that in fact did what it was supposed to do. It was never intended to raise all blacks to the level of Caucasians. Developed as a response to the civil rights movement and the black power struggle, its purpose was to coopt the black talented tenth, who might otherwise lead the black masses in revolution, and incorporate them into the system. This was a dynamic of colonialism as well. The indigenous elites were often coopted into the system by being given access to superior education, jobs, and so on. Those who feel part of the system, even if somewhat shaky in their feelings, are less likely to want to overthrow it. Yesterdays Black Panthers are today's members of Congress. If this was one of the purposes of affirmative action, it has succeeded very well indeed. Black lawyers, bankers, doctors, firefighters, abound.

Furthermore, affirmative action will always be paternalistic at its core since it requires the selected few African Americans deemed at least marginally qualified to assimilate into a potentially or overtly hostile environment that remains under white control. See Rhonda Magee, "The Master's Tools, from the Bottom Up: Responses to African-American Reparations Theory in Mainstream and Outsider Remedies Discourse," *Virginia Law Review* 79 (1993): 863, 914.

63. West, *Race Matters*, 18.

64. West, *Race Matters*, 18–19.

65. Professor Patricia Williams has coined the term "spirit assault or murder." Patricia Williams, "Spirit-Murdering the Messenger: The Discourse of Fingerpointing as the Law's Response to Racism," *University of Miami Law Review* 42 (1987): 127.

CHARLES J. OGLETREE

BLIND JUSTICE? RACE, THE CONSTITUTION, AND THE JUSTICE SYSTEM

The significance of race in the justice system in the United States is sad and disappointing. In his classic study of race relations in America, Gunnar Myrdal observed: "The subordinate position of Negroes is perhaps the most glaring conflict in the American conscience and the greatest unsolved task for American democracy."[1] Those who have incurred the wrath of our system have taken a more partisan view of the problem. More than a century ago, Frederick Douglass noted the disparity in the treatment of the various races in America, particularly in the area of criminal justice. Douglass, himself a former slave, was a constant source of encouragement for those who sought a better life in America, despite his painfully accurate observations about the justice system:

> Justice is often painted with bandaged eyes, she is described in forensic elo-
> quence as utterly blind to wealth or poverty, high or low, white or black, but a
> mask of iron, however thick, could never blind American justice when a black
> man happens to be on trial. It is not so much the business of his enemies to
> prove him guilty, as it is the business of himself to prove his innocence. The
> reasonable doubt which is usually interposed to save the life and liberty of a
> white man charged with crime, seldom has any force or effect when a colored
> man is accused of crime.[2]

The available evidence regarding the impact of race confirms Douglass's worst fears. The history of discrimination against minorities, particularly black Americans, in the justice system is well known. While much of it focuses on the way blacks were treated as defendants, it also shows that, until recently, they were denied the full benefits of citizenship. Despite the existence of seemingly race-neutral laws, the criminal justice system achieved the vulgar goals of racism. In 1931, for example, nine black youths were indicted in Alabama as a result of the alleged rape of two white women in what was known as the infamous Scottsboro boys case. Although the defendants were being tried in Alabama, they were denied the opportunity to have blacks serve on their jury. At his second trial, one of the defendants, Clarence Norris, challenged this practice and, through counsel, attempted to present evidence showing that blacks were systematically eliminated from service on both grand and petit juries in Alabama. The Alabama jury commissioner acknowledged that the jury selected contained no blacks, but justified such an exclusion:

> I do not know of any Negro in Morgan County over 21 and under 65 who is generally reputed to be honest and intelligent and who is esteemed in the community for his integrity, good character and sound judgment, who is not an habitual drunkard, who isn't afflicted with a permanent disease or physical weakness which would render him unfit to discharge the duties of a juror, and who can read English, and who has never been convicted of a crime involving moral turpitude.[3]

The jury commissioner's findings were accepted by the Alabama trial judge, as well as the Alabama appellate courts, but the U.S. Supreme Court disagreed. In a ruling designed to bring an end to racial discrimination against blacks serving on juries, the Court strongly condemned the practice:

> We think that the evidence that for a generation or longer no Negro had been called for jury service on any jury in Jackson County, that there were Negroes qualified for jury service, that according to the practice of the Jury Commissioner, their names would normally appear on the preliminary list of males citizens of the requisite age, but that no names of Negroes were placed on the jury roll and the testimony with respect to the lack of appropriate consideration of the qualifications of Negroes, established the discrimination which the Constitution forbids.[4]

This practice, which was quite prevalent in the early part of the twentieth century, regrettably continued, albeit in an attenuated form, up to the present day. In 1986, Thurgood Marshall, in *Batson* v. *Kentucky*, condemned the prosecutor's use of peremptory challenges, a device used to exclude jurors without stating any reason, as further evidence of continuing discrimination against blacks in the justice system.[5] Although the Supreme Court established a stringent standard in *Batson*, requiring prosecutors to give racially neutral reasons for striking black jurors, Justice Marshall felt that merely setting guidelines or a standard was not enough. He feared that racial discrimination would continue, notwithstanding *Batson's* prohibition against jury discrimination:

> The decision today will not end the racial discrimination that peremptories inject into the jury selection process. That goal can be accomplished only by eliminating peremptory challenges entirely. . . . Misuse of the peremptory challenge to exclude black jurors has become both common and flagrant. . . . The prosecutor can easily assert facially neutral reasons for striking a juror, and trial judges are ill-equipped to second guess those reasons. . . . Nor is outright prevarication by prosecutors the only danger here. . . . A prosecutor's conscious or unconscious racism may lead him easily to the conclusion that a prospective black juror is "sullen" or "distant," a characterization that would not have come to his mind if a white juror had acted identically. A judge's own conscious or unconscious racism may lead him to accept such an explanation as well supported. . . . Even if all parties approach the Court's mandate with the best of conscious intentions, that mandate requires them to confront and overcome their own racism in all levels—a challenge, I doubt, all of them can meet.[6]

While Justice Marshall lamented the risk of discrimination against blacks in the jury selection process, a more significant danger was posed by racial discrimination in capital punishment. The very painful history of discrimination against blacks through the application of the death penalty is well documented.[7]

In light of experiences like *Batson*, many African Americans believe that there are two systems of justice in the country: one for white Americans and one for people of color. The resulting hopelessness and despair within the criminal justice system unfortunately has not diminished through time. The existence of institutionalized measures of race discrimination have led many blacks to lose faith in the system's ability to protect their rights. Rather, many African Americans accept, without question, the racial injustices as a part of the system: "Most black defendants in American courts do not expect equal justice, and even black lawyers are seldom moved either by disappointment or outrage to protest violently a courtroom procedure or decision that, no matter how unfair, was at least predictable, given the realities of race in America."[8]

Racial discrimination is practiced not only in jury selection, but also in capital sentencing and prosecutorial discretion, noncapital sentencing, jury summations by prosecutors, the exercise of police discretion, Fourth Amendment intrusions on racial minorities, and jury deliberations.[9] Furthermore, the application of certain criminal statutes has been shown to have a adverse impact on racial minorities. Some examples include the potential for racial bias in fetal endangerment cases, the growing reliance on curfews, and the disparate use of lease forfeitures in public housing for racial minorities.[10] Sadly, few remedies are afforded to victims of such practices and only modest relief is available.

Instances in which racially discriminatory conduct may influence criminal prosecutions range from the investigatory stage through the post-conviction stage. While many challenges to race discrimination focus on trial activities, it is important that the challenges be made much earlier in the process. This chapter considers the breadth of the problem, and where appropriate, suggests remedies.

SENTENCING AND PROSECUTORIAL DISCRETION

Claims of racial discrimination against people of color in criminal cases are not recent phenomena and its opponents have been particularly vocal in response to the application of the death penalty in the United States.

Capital Sentencings

In 1972 in *Furman* v. *Georgia*, the Supreme Court declared the death penalty, as applied in Georgia, to be unconstitutional.[11] Of the multiplicity of reasons available to support this conclusion, several justices focused on the disparity in the imposition of capital punishment on African Americans. Justice William O. Douglas noted the evidence of apparent discrimination against blacks in a study of capital cases tried in Texas from 1924 to 1968: "In several instances where a white and a Negro were co-defendants, the white co-defendant was sentenced to life imprisonment or a term of years and the Negro was given the death penalty. Another ethnic disparity is found in the type of sentence imposed for rape. The Negro convicted of rape is far more likely to get the death penalty than a term sentence, whereas whites and Latinos are far more likely to get a term sentence than the death penalty."[12]

In voting to reverse the death penalty convictions in *Furman* v. *Georgia*, Justice Marshall noted the degree of discrepancy in prosecutions of minorities in contrast to that of other groups:

> Indeed, a look at the bare statistics regarding executions is enough to portray much of the discrimination. A total of 3,859 persons have been executed since 1930, of whom 1,751 were white and 2,066 were Negro. Of the executions, 3,334 were for murder; 1,664 of the executed murders were white and 1,630 were Negro; 455 persons, including 48 whites and 405 Negroes, were executed for rape. It is immediately apparent that Negroes were executed far more often than whites in proportion to their percentage of the population.[13]

Despite this rather convincing evidence of racial disparity, the Supreme Court declared in 1976 that the death penalty, as applied in the various states, met constitutional standards.[14] Scarcely a year later the Court had to consider the obvious question of the disparate application of death penalty on African Americans. In *Coker* v. *Georgia*, the Supreme Court was faced with the question of whether the imposition of a penalty of death was disproportionate to the criminal offense of rape.[15] Although it ultimately concluded in *Coker* that the penalty of death was a disproportionate sentence for rape, it did not weigh in its analysis the evidence of race discrimination in the application of the death penalty as discussed in *Furman* v. *Georgia*.

Nearly a decade earlier, a challenge was made to the Arkansas rape statute that permitted the penalty of execution. In *Maxwell* v. *Bishop*, the defendant presented expert testimony regarding the application of the death penalty for the crime of rape in the state of Arkansas and several other states.[16] A comprehensive study prepared by Dr. Marvin Wolfgang, a criminologist and statistician from the University of Pennsylvania, revealed that a disproportionate number of African Americans were given the death penalty for the crime of rape.

The prevalence of racial discrimination in the criminal justice system is vividly illustrated in the case of *McCleskey* v. *Kemp*.[17] Warren McCleskey, an African American, was convicted in Fulton County, Georgia, of killing a white police officer. McCleskey was convicted and sentenced to die in the Georgia death chambers.[18]

In a challenge to the imposition of capital punishment in Georgia, McCleskey submitted the most comprehensive statistical analysis ever done on the relationship of race to the imposition of capital punishment in Georgia. McCleskey argued, among other things, that his death sentence should be reversed because his race and the race of his victim played a significant role in the decision to sentence him to death. In supporting McCleskey's arguments, Dr. David Baldus noted that his examination of more than 2,000 murder cases between 1973 and 1979 indicated that persons convicted of murdering whites were eleven times more likely to be condemned to death than those convicted of murdering blacks. Moreover, Dr. Baldus found that the prosecutor sought the death penalty in 70 percent of cases involving black defendants and white victims, 32 percent of cases involving white defendants and white victims, 19 percent of cases involving white defendants and black victims, and 15 percent of cases involving black defendants and black victims.[19]

In his study, Dr. Baldus took into consideration more than 230 nonracial variables that might have influenced the pattern of death sentences for blacks who kill whites in Georgia. He concluded that even after discounting every nonracial variable, the race of the victim continued to have a statistically significant correlation to the imposition of capital sentences.[20] In a 5–4 ruling, the Supreme Court rejected McCleskey's argument and affirmed the imposition of the death sentence. Justice Lewis F. Powell, noting the significance of McCleskey's challenge to the system, observed that "McCleskey's claim, taken to its logical conclusion, throws into serious question the principles that underlie our entire criminal justice system."[21] The Court in effect acknowledged that McCleskey had to confront the difficult proposition that racial discrimination is inevitable in the criminal justice system.

Although McCleskey made every effort to prove discrimination in his case, the burden of proving purposeful discrimination on the basis of race is clearly a substantial one, and the Court was not willing to examine unconscious ways in which such discrimination may influence the outcomes on criminal cases.[22]

Despite statistical arguments showing compelling evidence of discrimination against blacks in the application of the death penalty, that proof has provided little comfort to those who face the ultimate punishment. In his poignant dissent in *McCleskey* v. *Kemp*, Justice William Brennan imagined the conversation that the attorney representing Warren McCleskey to explain why he had been selected for the death penalty, while others with equally egregious crimes were not chosen for such an punishment:

At some point in this case, Warren McCleskey, doubtless, asked his lawyer whether a jury was likely to sentence him to die. A candid reply to this question would have been disturbing. First, counsel would have to tell McCleskey that few of the details of the crime or of McCleskey's past criminal conduct were more important than the fact that his victim was white. Furthermore, counsel would feel bound to tell McCleskey that defendants charged with killing white victims in Georgia, are 4.3 times as likely to be sentenced to death as defendants charged with killing blacks. In addition, frankness would compel the disclosure that it was more likely than not that the race of McCleskey's victim would determine whether he received a death sentence: 6 of every 11 defendants convicted of killing a white person would not have received a death penalty if their victims had been black, while among defendants with aggravating and mitigating factors comparable to McCleskey's, 20 of every 34 would not have been sentenced to die if their victims had been black. Finally, the assessment would not be complete without the information that cases involving blacks defendants and white victims are more likely to result in a death sentence in cases featuring any other racial combination of defendant and victim. The story could be told in a variety of ways, but McCleskey could not fail to grasp its essential narrative line that there was a significant chance that race would play a prominent role in determining if he lived or died.[23]

Whether McCleskey's counsel had that conversation or not, we can only speculate.In any event, he was ultimately executed while the issue of race discrimination in the imposition of capital punishment in the state of Georgia remained by and large unresolved. These disparities, which are alarming enough in the area of capital punishment, are as prevalent, and troubling , in noncapital cases.

Noncapital Sentencings

Two comprehensive studies have established the existence of disparate treatment based upon race in noncapital cases. In the first study, it was found that more than one million Americans were incarcerated at the end of 1988, and the prospects of any significant decline in these numbers, given our focus on prison construction rather than on alternatives to incarceration, was remote.[24] A subsequent study revealed the impact that this incarceration mentality has on racial minorities in general and black males in particular. The results were unsettling and depressing:one out of every four black men between the ages of twenty and twenty-nine were under the control of the criminal justice system.[25] This mindless incarceration mentality has given the United States the sad distinction of having the highest rate of incarceration of any industrialized nation in the world, surpassing both South Africa and the former Soviet Union.[26]

What these empirical data suggest is that law enforcement officials, state and federal prosecutors, and state and federal judges should be made aware of the disproportionate impact of our current incarceration policies on racial minorities. The racial disparity in the criminal justice system is abundantly clear from other data as well, particularly concerning arrests, bail decisions, and sentencing decisions.[27]

Both state and federal courts have considered claims of racial disparity regarding the disproportionate impact of criminal statutes on racial minorities.[28] In *State v. Russell*, for example, the Minnesota Supreme Court agreed with a trial judge that the penalties for crack cocaine, in contrast to powdered cocaine, had a disproportionate, and unconstitutional, impact on African Americans.[29] In *Russell*, five African American defendants, all prosecuted for possession of crack cocaine, challenged the Minnesota criminal sentencing statute that permitted judges to sentence those charged with possessing crack cocaine more seriously than those charged with possessing powdered cocaine. The defendants presented evidence establishing that 96 percent of defendants charged with possession of crack cocaine were African Americans, while nearly 80 percent of those charged with possession of powdered cocaine were whites.

The defendants were also able to establish notable disparities in the sentences for possession of crack and powdered cocaine. Under the Minnesota statute, the possible penalty for three grams of powdered cocaine was up to five years imprisonment, but the *likely* sentence was probation. In contrast, the possible penalty for three grams of crack cocaine was up to twenty years imprisonment, but the *likely* sentence was four years. The Minnesota Supreme Court concluded that there was no rational basis for the distinction in penalty for powdered and crack cocaine, and that the statutory distinctions had a discriminatory impact on African Americans, observing: "There comes a time when we cannot and must not close our eyes when presented with evidence that certain laws, regardless of the purpose for which they were enacted, discriminate unfairly on the basis of race."[30]

While other courts considering similar or related objections have been reluctant to follow the Minnesota decision, a federal district court judge ruled that, in circumstances where undercover police officers induce suspects to convert powdered cocaine into crack cocaine, because the officers are aware that the suspects will, as a result, be subject to more severe penalties, the Eighth Amendment prohibition of cruel and unusual punishment is violated.[31] The absence of a compelling justification to permit racial disparities in capital cases is as apparent in noncapital cases.

IMPROPER PROSECUTORIAL SUMMATIONS

Prosecutorial misconduct in closing arguments have frequently provided a basis for new trials and dismissals.[32] In *United States* v. *McKendrick*, the Second Circuit affirmed the grant of habeas corpus where racially prejudicial remarks by a prosecutor in summation constitutionally deprived the defendant of a fair trial. The racist remarks to the all-white jury included:

> I know that [defendant's counsel], in his experience, he has dealt with people for many years of the colored race. There is something about it, if you have dealt with colored people and have been living with them and see them you begin to be able to discern their mannerisms and appearances and to discern the different shades and so on . . . . What I am getting at is those who are living with them, dealing with them, and working with them in a sense, have a much better opportunity to evaluate what they see to identify what they see. . . .
>
> Now, counsel for the defendants told you, and Attorney Gold is probably as well versed with the colored race as any man I know in the legal profession. He knows their weaknesses and inability to do certain things that maybe are commonplace for the ordinary person to do or remember or know certain things.[33]

The prosecutor also referred to African American men as "young bucks" and implied that blacks are more promiscuous than whites. The Court of Appeals, stating that a prosecutor may not summon the thirteenth juror, prejudice, concluded that "the prosecutor's remarks introduced race prejudice into the trial and thereby denied petitioner his constitutional right under the due process clause to a fair trial."[34] The court cited not only the harm to the defendant, but also the harm to the judicial system, which is disparaged by even the appearance of racial bias. The court also cited the Fourteenth Amendment as a restriction on the conduct of state district attorneys: "If there is anything more antithetical to the purposes of the Fourteenth Amendment than the injection against a black man of race prejudice—whether in a procedure underlying, the atmosphere surrounding, or the actual conduct of a trial—so that he . . . is deprived of the right of 'being tried the same way as a white man,' we do not know what it is."[35] Because of the probability that racism substantially prejudiced the outcome of the trial, the defendant was granted a new trial.[36]

Such discriminatory conduct has been experienced by other racial minorities as well. In *Villacres* v. *United States*, the prosecutor substituted the English pronunciation for the Spanish pronunciation of the name of the victim of a homicide, a Hispanic man named "Jesus," and drew an analogy between the murder and the crucifixion of Jesus, claiming in essence that the Hispanic defendant, Villacres, had executed "Jesus" (English pronunciation).[37] The District of Columbia Court of Appeals concluded that the prosecutor's conduct was improper and reversed the conviction.

EXERCISE OF POLICE DISCRETION

Some of the most damning conduct has been that of police officers, often in circumstances out of the public's view. On March 3, 1991, the world watched the shocking videotape of the beating of Rodney King, an African American, by several white members of the Los Angeles Police Department. The incident was quickly followed by hundreds of claims by African Americans, and members of other minority groups, that racially motivated conduct like the beating of Rodney King was not unusual.[38] In city after city and case after case, minorities have presented claims of various forms of police abuse of power and authority. In evaluating these claims, courts have attempted to maintain an appropriate balance between the lawful exercise of discretion by police officers and the rights of citizens to be treated with dignity.[39] The available empirical studies tell a compelling story of disparate treatment based on race. A number of studies have documented the comparatively high arrest rates for blacks suspected of crime.[40] Some studies have also documented the frequent use of deadly force by police officers against both armed and unarmed black suspects.[41] One reported that blacks were ten times more likely than whites to be shot at by police officers, eighteen times more likely to be wounded, and five times more likely to be killed.[42] This use of deadly force by police officers against racial minorities is corroborated by other data revealing a propensity by the police to focus on minorities in criminal investigations.[43]

Even in cases where the courts have determined that particular police practices were unconstitutional, little attention has been given to the race of the suspects.[44] Accordingly, federal courts have sustained challenges to police stops despite obviously racially discriminatory aspects to the case being heard. Where police officers have used generalized prejudices regarding blacks to stop automobiles operated by blacks with out-of-state license plates or made arbitrary stops of Mexican Americans or become suspicious merely because two black men were sitting in parked cars, the courts have confined their holdings to a determination that the police's use of such was inconsistent with the parameters of the Fourth Amendment.[45]

Beyond the reported decisions by state and federal courts are numerous examples of public testimony by minorities, in every section of the country, recounting instances of racially motivated police abuse. The incidents consist of verbal and physical abuse, as well as unlawful arrests. Although only a small percentage of these reported instances of abuse lead to either some form of compensation for the alleged victims, or some form of discipline for the offending officer, cases are continually reported. Any effort to eliminate racial discrimination in our legal system must take special note of the problem of improper police conduct.

IMPACT OF FOURTH AMENDMENT INTRUSIONS ON RACIAL MINORITIES

Racially discriminatory practices by law enforcement officers are providing a predicate for further abuses of minorities. Even as it decided *Terry*, the Supreme Court was aware that the power to stop and frisk on the basis of a reasonable suspicion could be used as a tool for harassment against minorities. Alluding to police practices that "can only serve to exacerbate police-community tensions in the crowded centers of our Nation's cities," the Court seemed to recognize the grave implications of its decision.[46] Justice Earl Warren quoted at length from a report of the President's Commission on Law Enforcement and the Administration of Justice, which concluded that in "many communities, field interrogations are a major source of friction between the police and minority groups."[47] "This is particularly true," the Court added, "in situations where the 'stop and frisk' of youths or minority group members is 'motivated by the officers' perceived need to maintain the power image of the beat officer, an aim sometimes accomplished by humiliating anyone who attempts to undermine police control of the streets.'" Yet, having raised the "race question," the Court chose to ignore its consequences, believing that it was impossible to forestall racial discrimination in this context.[48]

More than twenty years after *Terry*, the day-to-day experience of minority residents of many urban areas shows that the policeman's power to "stop and frisk" is still applied discriminatorily against African Americans and other people of color. Studies reveal that African Americans are more likely than whites in similar situations to be stopped by the police.[49] Even though courts have never condoned the use of race or ethnicity as the sole basis for an investigative stop, "there is substantial evidence that many police officers believe minority race indicates a general propensity to commit crime. The evidence further suggests the police weigh race in their decisions to detain."[50] It should be noted that, as with any claim regarding covert racial discrimination, the role of race in the police officer's decision to stop is a difficult factor to measure or research. In the first place, police officers and judges seldom acknowledge that race had any effect on the decision-making process. Often, courts will omit any discussion of race in their evaluation of the propriety of a *Terry* stop and will go so far as to omit the defendant's race from the discussion of the case, making it impossible to draw any reliable generalizations from the cases or to identify particular instances of abuse. In addition, no field studies have been conducted in recent years to document the scope of race based police stops and judicial evaluations of the same. However, research conducted in the 1960s and 1970s sheds some light on the current practices. The law regarding *Terry* stops has not significantly changed since that decision was handed down, nor have there been substantial changes in other relevant variables, such as the racial demographics of cities, the racial composition of police forces, and the stereotypes that generally influence racial perceptions.

As already noted, people of color and others have been disparately victimized by police officers conducting *Terry* stops. Typical of this treatment is the treatment of an African American man with a Rastafarian hair style who has a penchant for wearing doctors' surgical clothes. He was stopped and detained by police officers more than fifteen times during his evening walks because he struck officers as suspicious and out of place.[51] In Long Beach, California, a police task force, formed to "clean up" the downtown center, has been criticized for its harassment of poor people and people of color. Officers reportedly questioned and searched a man sitting on a bench in a downtown plaza and dressed in torn jeans and a black leather jacket. The police officers stopped the man because they "wanted to question [him] for possibly loitering. [He and his companion] were sitting there, kind of shabbily dressed. Not that people don't have the right to sit there shabbily dressed. But [they were people] we wanted to talk to, with the emphasis of cleaning up the mall and ridding it of people who have no business being there." One Long Beach officer explained that he stops "anyone you see who you wouldn't want your wife, mother or daughter coming in contact with."[52]

The infamous case of *Davis* v. *Mississippi* illustrates the role race plays in police decisions regarding whom to stop. This case was decided only one year after *Terry*. In *Davis*, Mississippi state police officers were searching for a rape suspect, of whom the only description they had been provided was that he was a "Negro youth." During the course of their search, they indiscriminately stopped, interrogated, and fingerprinted young black men without any rational or reasonable suspicion that these persons were implicated in the rape. In the course of this apparent police dragnet, officers interrogated forty to fifty black children and fingerprinted at least twenty-four more black boys. The fingerprint evidence seized from a fourteen-year-old black youth was ultimately excluded as the product of an unlawful arrest, although the Court did not consider the racial issues raised by the police officers' conduct.[53]

Similarly, in *United States* v. *Mallides*, an officer relied on racial criteria as the sole basis for stopping motorists of apparent Hispanic origin. The officer observed six Mexican-appearing men in a moving car and signaled the car to stop. There was nothing suspicious about the driver's operation of the vehicle, and no traffic violation was noted. Instead, "the suspicion [of illegal alienage] was based entirely on the officers' fleeting observation of the Mexican-appearing men who sat stiffly in the car and did not look at the patrol unit as it passed. One officer testified that he made it a practice to stop 'all cars with Mexicans in them that appear to be sitting and packed in like people in [Mallides'] car.'" In ruling that the stop was illegal, the Court found that "tested by any objective standard, there is nothing suspicious about six persons riding in a sedan. The conduct does not become suspicious simply because the skins of the occupants are nonwhite."[54]

Police officers are seldom made to answer to the Equal Protection Clause of the Fourteenth Amendment for racially motivated stops. Rather, such claims are heard under the Fourth Amendment, which has not been interpreted to include a special recognition of the harms of racially motivated police conduct.[55]

In its command that no state "deny to any person within its jurisdiction the equal protection of the laws," the Fourteenth Amendment requires that "all persons similarly circumstanced shall be treated alike."[56] A police officer's decision to detain a suspect violates the Constitution if it "make[s] unjust and illegal discriminations between persons in similar circumstances."[57] Because one of the guiding principles of the Fourteenth Amendment is the prevention of unjustified official distinctions based on race, racial classifications are subject to "the most rigid scrutiny." Classifications that put a racial minority at a disadvantage therefore must be "precisely tailored to serve a compelling governmental interest if it is to survive scrutiny."[58] If white people are similarly situated to people of color with regard to their likelihood to commit a crime, the Equal Protection Clause demands that police officers not distinguish between individuals on the basis of race in conducting stops.[59] A police officer may base a decision to detain a suspect on racial criteria only if there is a compelling basis for differential treatment—which requires, at a minimum, an empirical showing that people of color are more likely to commit crimes than white people.

While courts have recognized that flawed premises based upon race could not justify detention, they have declined to bar its use for all purposes. In *United States* v. *Nicholas,* the Supreme Court reversed the conviction of two black defendants detained out of a "generalized suspicion that any black person driving an automobile with out-of-state license plates may be engaged in criminal activity." The Court found race to be too "scant" a basis to justify even momentary detention, but did not condemn the racial prejudice as an independent constitutional wrong.[60] Furthermore, courts seem to consider race probative to some extent and will validate police decisions as long as the totality of circumstances gives rise to a reasonable suspicion.[61]

Under either the Fourth or Fourteenth amendments, judicial review proceeds as follows. If the victim of police discrimination raises an inference that race influences the officer's decision to conduct the stop, the burden shifts to the government to show that (1) race did not play a role in the officer's action, or (2) there was a reasonable or compelling basis for the racial classification. An inference of discrimination arises from the officer's acknowledgment that race influenced his or her decision to conduct the stop or from the officer's failure to articulate a nonracial, objective basis for the stop; the officer's use of racial epithets or references during the stop; the stop's conformity with a pattern of police conduct (repeated stops of the individual or of other individuals of the same race); or evidence that the stop was based on a profile incorporating racial factors.

In order to rebut an inference of discrimination, the government must demonstrate the validity of the suspicions upon which police officers act.[62] The requirement that racial criteria have an empirical basis is simply *Terry's* requirement that officers act upon objective and articulable factors. It is difficult to understand what the justices in *Terry* intended by demanding that officers articulate the basis of their decision to stop if not to prevent reliance on un-proven assumptions produced by bias or ignorance.

The ability of the government to meet its burden of showing a nondiscrimi-nation basis for its action depends on the probity of the statistics it produces and the relation of these statistics to the crime of which an individual is sus-pected. Police officers may not act on "questionable racial and sociological grounds" or "an unwarranted use of circumstantial evidence."[63] Instead, the government must offer empirical data proving that race is a statistically sig-nificant correlate of the likelihood that a particular person will commit a spe-cific crime. The government has never come forward with statistics support-ing racial distinctions as a basis for predicting criminal behavior, and it is frankly inconceivable that any set of data will offer a satisfactory basis for concluding that there is a nexus between race and crime. In the first place, such statistics must be sufficiently tight-fitting to avoid problems of overinclu-sion or underinclusion. Reliance on race is almost always unconstitutionally overinclusive and underinclusive because it includes an overwhelmingly large number of people who have no propensity to commit crimes while excluding a significant number of whites who may be worthy of suspicion.[64] In addition, almost every conceivable measure—from arrest rates to conviction rates—are tainted by existing discrimination at every level of the criminal justice system. Therefore, statistics would have to be adjusted to account for the influence of past unwarranted discrimination. Furthermore, the government must show that it is race, and not factors often associated with race (such as poverty, education, or area of residence), that enhances the likelihood of un-lawful activity. For if it is poverty or location that causes the increased proba-bility of crime, reliance on race offends the Fourth and Fourteenth amend-ments, since race is not itself a probative basis for action but a proxy for other, more closely tailored criteria.[65] In addition, the government must offer data that a suspect, because of his or her race, is more likely to commit the particu-lar crime of which he or she is under suspicion. Statistics showing that Latinos are more likely than white people to be illegal aliens does not provide a basis for heightened suspicion of Latinos for robberies.[66]

"Racial incongruity" is another questionable factor in the officer's decision to conduct a stop of a suspect.[67] People of color in white areas are stopped by police officers because their presence is suspicious in the context of the neighborhood. Police officers act upon the assumption that a person of color would have no legitimate business in an area that is predominantly white. One officer, testifying as to why he had stopped a defendant, stated: "You know, when we first observed him we could tell that something wasn't correct. He just didn't look, I mean—he was a Mexican male in a predominantly white neighborhood of—oh, middle- to upper-middle class people."[68] Despite this racially based rationale, the court concluded that the stop satisfied Fourth Amendment standards and authorized the consideration of racial incongruity in determining whether detention is lawful.[69]

In an extreme example of how racial incongruity is employed in decisions to detain, a sheriff of Parish County, Louisiana, announced that blacks in white neighborhoods would be stopped and searched.[70] The sheriff stated:

> If there are some young blacks driving a car late at night in a predominantly white area, they will be stopped. . . . We will stop everybody that we think has no business in the neighborhood. It's obvious that two young blacks driving a rinky-dink car in a predominantly white neighborhood—I'm not talking about on the main thoroughfare, but if they're on one of the side streets and they're cruising around—they'll be stopped.[71]

Other areas of racial bias permitted under the guise of pursuing legitimate Fourth Amendment jurisprudence include the use of drug courier profiles. The drug courier profiles, permitted by the Supreme Court as a basis for reasonable suspicion of drug trafficking, often include racial and ethnic factors—focusing on blacks and Latinos as having "group characteristics" making them ideal targets for drug surveillance.[72] For example, the Florida Highway Patrol for a period of time relied on a profile that cautioned troopers to be suspicious of drivers who "did not fit the vehicle," or who belonged to "ethnic groups associated with the drug trade."

Moreover, drug profile cases have consistently incorporated clear race and class bias stereotypes. The drug courier profile, designed to single out those persons likely to be traveling with illicit narcotics, include factors such as travels with little luggage, travels to or from a source city (defined as almost any urban center in the United States), dresses differently, pays in cash, appears nervous, uses public transportation, and appears to be Latino.[73] While these factors may identify a drug courier, it is equally likely that they indicate a person of color without financial resources. The profile identifies as suspicious all those who cannot afford luggage, do not dress neatly or "tastefully," do not have a checking account or credit card, are inexperienced or uncomfortable with air travel, and do not have a car or money for a taxi.[74] It should be noted that these factors are listed in drug courier profiles even though they do not, in the vast majority of cases, point to actual drug-traffickers.[75]

Because drug profiles are so manipulable, they are particularly susceptible to abuse and the exercise of racial bias. These profiles allow officers, post hoc, to adapt almost any set of facts to justify the stop. Justice Thurgood Marshall was wary of drug profiles because of their "chameleon-like way of adapting to any particular sets of observations."[76] Drug courier profiles trigger suspicion whether the target deplaned first, last, or in the middle of the group; whether he or she had one-way or round-trip tickets; whether the target traveled alone or with a companion; whether he or she acted nervous or too calm.[77] One Drug Enforcement Agency (DEA) agent admitted that "the profile in a particular case consists of anything that arouses his suspicions."[78] "The one constant," notes one commentator, "according to a few statistical analyses and a lot of anecdotal evidence, is that you are far more likely to be scooped into the police net . . . and asked to submit to a search if you are black or Hispanic."[79]

In the past several years, police have also begun to develop and rely upon gang profiles, which also incorporate race-conscious factors.[80] In the one case in which an officer acknowledged the use of a gang profile, the Ninth Circuit Court of Appeals nevertheless upheld the detention as reasonable. The defendant, who was arriving at the Seattle Airport on a flight from Los Angeles, attracted the attention of DEA agents assigned to the airport because he fit the "L.A. gang-member" profile. The DEA created the gang-member profile used at airport, train, and bus stations in Seattle because Los Angeles street gang members allegedly had been transporting drugs into Seattle. Factors included in the profile were a certain type of sneaker, a blue or red scarf or handkerchief, gold jewelry, and hand signals. The accused was a young black man wearing a blue jacket (a color favored by one Los Angeles gang) and traveling on Continental Airlines (an airline allegedly favored by gang members transporting drugs).[81]

The agents' suspicion that the defendant was carrying illegal drugs was apparently corroborated by other factors: defendant's nervousness and furtive glances, the fact that defendant carried no luggage although he claimed to be on a three-day trip, and defendant's inability to explain the purpose of his trip. Considering the totality of the circumstances, the court found that there was a reasonable suspicion to detain the defendant.[82]

In United States v. Grant, the Sixth Circuit found a racially motivated stop to be unreasonable under the Fourth Amendment.[83] The government had argued that it was justified in seizing the defendant because he was originally from Belize and his appearance differed from the photograph on his immigration card. However, the significance of his national origin evaporated as soon as he produced a valid green card. The court found that the agents had originally decided to question Grant because they observed that he wore dreadlocks and suspected that he might be Jamaican. The assumption that a man of color wearing dreadlocks and arriving from Los Angeles is an illegal alien from Jamaica or a drug courier, the court wrote, is racially biased and insufficient to support a stop. The court worried that if race, ethnic identity, or flight-origin furnishes reasonable grounds for a stop, many black and Latino men "would be subject to virtually random seizures." Therefore, the court ordered that the drugs seized during a search of Grant's bag be suppressed and the case dismissed.

Three plainclothes officers of the Memphis Police Department stationed at the Memphis International Airport stopped an individual arriving on a flight from Miami.[84] Their decision to detain the suspect was based on their observations that he was a black man and "appeared much different from the other deplaning passengers." Whereas other passengers were dressed in business or vacation attire, this man was clad in dark slacks, "a work shirt" and hat.[85] The accused carried what appeared to be a new designer travel bag. He was apparently the only black on the flight. One officer testified the suspect, Eddie Taylor, "appear[ed] nervous and constantly look[ed] over his shoulder," walking rapidly through the terminal.

The officers followed Taylor and ordered him to stop. Taylor answered the officers' questions and produced a Missouri driver's license and airline ticket (the names on which matched). The officers then asked Taylor if they could look into his bag. Taylor unzipped the bag, shuffled papers around in it, and said "There's nothing that you are looking for here." The officers did not observe anything suspicious, but took the bag and searched it themselves, discovering two packages wrapped in brown plastic tape—wrapping typically used for cocaine. At that point, the officers arrested Taylor. Although Taylor refused to sign a consent form and no warrant was produced, the officers opened the packages. The substance in the packages field-tested positive as cocaine. The officers then searched Taylor and found $1,000 in cash hidden in his socks.

Noting that "the valiant effort of our law enforcement officers to rid society of the drug scourge cannot be done in total disregard of an individual's constitutional rights," the Court of Appeals suppressed the evidence seized from Taylor. Finding that none of the behaviors cited by the officers—walking quickly, being dressed "differently," appearing nervous, or arriving from Miami—were probative bases for a stop, the court determined that "agents were more apt to stop Taylor because of his race." "The mere fact that a black man

is observed walking quickly through an airport terminal," the court concluded," does not raise the suspicion of criminal activity."

The danger of such profiles is that they legitimize reliance on factors that—
individually or as a whole—do not create a reasonable suspicion. The DEA
gang profile described above subjects any black man wearing blue and flying
on a particular commercial airline—ostensibly a large group of people—to
forced detention by law enforcement officials, even though the person has
done nothing even arguably illegal. This imposition was allowed in *Malone*
even in the absence of any empirical proof that blacks wearing blue and traveling on Continental Airlines are more likely to be involved in criminal conduct
than any other group. Because officers subjectively believe that men of color
wearing a color adopted by a gang are more likely to commit crimes, courts
grant the officers free reign to act upon these racially influenced hunches.

Novel Race-Based Fourth Amendment Challenges

Professor Tracey Maclin of Boston University Law School, a prolific scholar
on Fourth Amendment jurisprudence, identifies another area of police practices that falls more harshly upon minority citizens. Maclin argues that the
Supreme Court's failure to define as "seizures" those encounters that do not
involve the exercise of some degree of physical control over the suspect ignores the practical reality of most people of color. The Supreme Court has
presumed that the reasonable person will feel free to walk away from an officer
who approaches to ask questions. But overreaching by the police against
people of color, deep distrust and fear of police by people of color, and a
general sense of disempowerment mean that many people of color will be
coerced into consenting to an encounter that white persons would refuse. As
a result, the Fourth Amendment jurisprudence systematically undervalues the
intrusion by officers into the lives of people of color and fails to provide a
remedy for those situations that are legitimately felt by people of color to be
seizures. Maclin's solution: "The Court should dump the notion that there is
a hypothetical, average, reasonable person out there in which to judge the
constitutionality of police encounters. When assessing a challenged police
practice, the Court should explicitly consider the race of the citizen and how
the citizen's race might have influenced his attitude toward the encounter."[86]

Victims of racially motivated stops have challenged such police practices
through federal civil rights actions. In *Buffkins v. Omaha*, an African American
woman claiming to have been illegally stopped by narcotics agents brought a

claim under sections 1981 and 1983 of the Civil Rights Act.[87] Officers received a tip that cocaine would be imported by an African American person or persons arriving on a flight from Denver. Ms. Buffkins was the only African American person exiting a plane from Denver. Police officers claimed that she appeared nervous and carried a teddy bear whose seams appeared to have been resewn. The Eighth Circuit Court of Appeals rejected her claim under 42 U.S.C., section 1981, on the ground that Buffkins had failed to show purposeful discrimination. Instead, it found that the police officers' identification was reasonable and nondiscriminatory because her race matched the racial description of the suspect. However, the court found that her seizure was illegal as a matter of law and therefore violated her right to be free from unreasonable searches and seizures under 42 U.S.C., section 1983. The sole credible basis for the stop, according to the Court, was Buffkins's race, which could not create a reasonable and articulable suspicion of criminal activity.

Racially Discriminatory Arrests and Prosecutions

Statistical data indicate that blacks are more likely to be arrested than white persons, and are disproportionately arrested.[88] In 1984, 46 percent of those arrested for violent crime were blacks, even though blacks constitute slightly more than 12 percent of the national population. Data from the Federal Bureau of Investigation (FBI) indicate that blacks make up an increasing percentage of drug arrests, having increased from 30 to 38 percent of the total between 1984 and 1988. Separate studies by the FBI and the National Institute for Drug Abuse in 1988 came to the identical conclusion that African Americans constitute only 12 percent of the nation's drug users.[89]

Data also indicate that prosecutors are more likely to pursue full prosecution, file more severe charges, and seek more stringent penalties in cases involving minority defendants, particularly where the victim is white.[90] In response to these options, defendants have increasingly responded by challenging racially selective prosecution through federal civil rights actions under 42 U.S.C., sections 1981, 1982, 1983, and 1985.

JURY DELIBERATIONS

The Rodney King incident also had an impact on jury deliberations, although not on African American defendants. In the state court prosecution of the four police officers charged with beating Rodney King, all were acquitted. Many

African Americans condemned the verdicts, decrying that it was impossible for an African American who was a victim of a crime at the hands of white police officers to receive a fair trial.

More frequently, courts have been asked to consider whether the apparent racial prejudices on the part of jurors against black defendants or black witnesses rise to the level of a deprivation of protected constitutional rights. In most of these cases, the courts have concluded that relief is not warranted. The existence of racial bias by jurors involved in the process of deliberation raises the question of fairness in the criminal justice system and is a cause of concern where examples of such racially discriminatory conduct by jurors have been documented.[91] Since it is practically impossible to impeach jury verdicts because of the public policy favoring the inviolability of jury verdicts, challenges to racially biased jury deliberations have largely been unsuccessful.[92]

RACIAL DISPARITY IN THE APPLICATION OF STATUTES

Although much of the discussion of race and the criminal justice system focuses on black males, it should be noted that black women have significantly experienced difficulties in its system.

Race-Based Claims in Fetal Endangerment Prosecution

Since 1987, at least fifty "fetal abuse" cases have been brought in nineteen states and the District of Columbia.[93] The majority of these prosecutions have been against women of color. Pregnant substance abusers are incarcerated in order to protect the fetus from further drug exposure or are prosecuted after the child's birth for charges ranging from distributing drugs to a minor, child abuse or neglect, and manslaughter to assault with a deadly weapon. In an eloquent and persuasive article in the *Harvard Law Review*, Professor Dorothy Roberts details the history of these prosecutions and opines that the prosecutions amount to a denial of racial equality and invasion of privacy.[94]

Of fifty-two defendants prosecuted, thirty-five were African American, two were Latino, one was Native American, and fourteen were white.[95] Furthermore, most of the prosecutions arise from use of crack, a drug that is disproportionately used by people of color, rather than from other conduct that can injure the fetus, such as smoking and drinking.[96]

The government detects and prosecutes more poor African American women, who are subject to greater official supervision through public health care institutions, welfare agencies, and probation departments, than any other racial grouping.[97] Hospitals, many of which now screen newborns for evidence of drugs in their urine and report positive results to child welfare authorities, disproportionately report African American patients.[98] Often, hospitals do not rely on formal screening protocols, but depend solely on the suspicions of health care professionals. These suspicions often derive from stereotype assumptions regarding the characteristics of drug addicts. Doctors, too, are more likely to report African American women to the government than their wealthy white patients.[99] A study published by the *New England Journal of Medicine*, however, reveals little difference in the prevalence of substance abuse by pregnant women by race or by class. Despite similar rates of substance abuse, women of color are ten times more likely than whites to be reported to public health authorities for substance abuse during pregnancy.[100] Twenty-six percent of drug users are African American, yet in Florida, 90 percent of prosecutions for drug abuse during pregnancy involve African American women.[101]

On January 2, 1991, a California judge ordered Darlene Johnson, an African American woman on welfare who was convicted of child abuse for beating her four- and six-year-old children with a belt and an extension cord be implanted with the drug Norplant for three years as a condition of probation.[102] The judge advised Ms. Johnson, whose prior record consisted of fraud and bad check convictions, that she would be incarcerated for two to four years on the child abuse charge. He offered to sentence her to only a few months of jail time and three years probation if she agreed to the Norplant implant. Johnson was pregnant with her fifth child at the time. Johnson, who had not heard of Norplant, asked the judge if it would hurt her. He compared Norplant to the pill and said that it was reversible and had been approved by government regulators. He never explained that the device would be implanted in Darlene Johnson's body through surgery.[103] Johnson agreed to the implant (along with a four-month jail term) at the time, but changed her mind one week later. At her sentencing on January 10, the judge refused to change the conditions, stating: "It is in the defendant's best interest, and certainly in any unconceived child's interest, that she not have any more children until she is mentally and emotionally prepared to do so."[104] Johnson is currently in jail awaiting appeal of the probation condition.

Norplant had been approved by the Federal Drug Administration only weeks before and had not been released to the general public when the judge "offered" it to Darlene Johnson.[105] When news of Norplant's invention was first released, the *Philadelphia Enquirer* ran an editorial exhorting readers to "think about" Norplant as a tool in the fight against African American poverty and declaring it "fair subject for debate" whether use of Norplant should be a precondition for receiving welfare.[106] A storm of criticism caused the newspaper to retract the editorial, but not before commentators assailed Norplant as a threat to the reproductive liberty of poor women and women of color.[107]

The proposed sentencing deal ignited a significant controversy.[108] Some have criticized the racist and sexist nature of the sentence, whereas others have focused on the appropriateness of the sentence for the case at hand.[109] First, preventing Darlene Johnson from having more children is not well-suited to serve the ostensible purpose of the sentence—preventing this potentially abusive woman from abusing her children in the future. Parenting classes and counseling, which had been the original plea agreement, would certainly be a more successful and less invasive means of preventing Ms. Johnson from abusing her children.[110] Furthermore, the state can protect children from future abuse by removing them from the custody of an abusive parent and need not control conception to do so.

Finally, evidence shows that Norplant, like other estrogen-based forms of birth control, can cause uncomfortable and dangerous side effects, including a heightened risk of cancer. Darlene Johnson's medical condition—heart murmur, diabetes, and high blood pressure—could make using Norplant a health risk for her.[111]

Challenges to Curfew Laws

The application of certain statutes to conduct by citizens have frequently had a disproportionate impact on minorities. The enforcement of curfews and the application of public housing lease forfeitures are prime examples of these practices. For example, the enforcement of the District of Columbia's curfew law (the "New Law"), which made it a crime for persons under the age of eighteen to be on the streets between 11:00 p.m. and 6:00 a.m., was temporarily enjoined because of its significant interference with the constitutional rights of minors in *Waters* v. *Barry*.[112] Making a claim of racial discrimination was not without difficulty in this case in that the proponent, Mayor Marion Barry, and the targets of the curfew law, were both African Americans. Yet, the impact of the law on young African Americans, even though the curfew's intent (to reduce crime) was deemed admirable, was found to be unconstitutional. The court concluded that the curfew law was not narrowly tailored and expressed particular concern about the potentially discriminatory impact of the ordinance:[113]

> The Court is further concerned with the potential (the plaintiffs would say inevitable) discrimination inherent in the operation of the New Law. The Court is greatly concerned that the New Law's impact will be felt most severely by the poorer of this city's inhabitants, i.e., those lacking the sumptuous private yards of other recreational areas in which to pass a warm summer evening. As the plaintiffs note, "[i]t appears likely that all of the outdoor areas of public housing projects are 'street[s], sidewalk[s], park[s] or other outdoor public place[s]' within the meaning" of the New Law . . . . Under these circumstances, it appears that the New Law's inevitable operation may well burden the rights of the poor more than the rights of the affluent.[114]

Because of the substantial possibility that the New Law would be found to be unconstitutionally overbroad, the court granted plaintiff's request for a temporary restraining order.[115]

These cases highlight the potential dangers of curfew laws. They provide police with a codified pretext to investigate and detain youths despite the fact that they are unable to establish either reasonable suspicion to conduct a stop or probable cause to arrest. The curfew law allowed officers to intervene without any constitutionally acceptable level of suspicion in any case where the suspect "looked underaged." By creating a broad license, the enforcement of which is completely discretionary, the curfew laws vested enormous authority in police officers. Furthermore, as noted in the *Barry* case, curfew laws are likely to have the greatest impact on residents of the inner city, where there are no shielded backyards to preserve the minors' privacy and freedom, and where police are most likely to intervene.

Racial Bias in Public Housing Lease Forfeitures

The criminal justice process is frequently the vehicle by which the rights of racial minorities in public housing are violated. In 1990, Jack Kemp, then secretary of the Department of Housing and Urban Development, announced the government's intention, in cooperation with the Department of Justice, to seize the leases of public housing tenants suspected of involvement in illicit drug activity—even where the leaseholder has not been indicted or convicted of any crime.[116] Although the policy has been attacked in national class action suits on a case-by-case basis, any equal protection or racial challenges to the forfeiture proceedings have not been manifest.[117]

In considering a public housing forfeiture action, one federal judge did not mince words when expressing his distaste for the procedure:

> But what can be said for the extinction of a low-income public housing in terms of tangible benefit to the United States? And any thought that such activity is worthwhile because it provides a meaningful deterrent to the drug trade betrays an abysmal ignorance of the economics of that illicit business— in which the perceived dollar incentives, even at the lowest levels of distribution, are so much greater than the perceived risks that there are literally people standing in line to replace anyone taken out of business by arrest or conviction. So the net effect of this line of activity will be punitive as to the few individuals involved but purely cosmetic in governmental terms—nice headline-grabbers that mask the failure of the vaunted "war on drugs" to deal with our massive drug problems in any meaningful way.[118]

CONCLUSION

These issues are rarely presented to courts for review of racially disparate treatment but must be considered in light of impact of such practices on minority communities. We live in a society that is committed to a "color-blind" constitution. That blindness, however, obscures this adverse impact of the criminal justice system on minority men and women.

NOTES

1. Gunnar Mrydal, *An American Dilemma: The Negro Problem and Modern Democracy*, vol. 2 (New York: Harper and Row, 1962), 12.

2. See Phillip S. Foner, ed., *The Life and Writings of Frederick Douglass*, 5 vols. (New York: International Publishers, 1950–75).

3. See *Norris v. Alabama*, 294 U.S. 587, 598–99 (1935). During the evidentiary hearing, however, Norris presented evidence documenting that of the 8,801 males over age twenty-one in Jackson County, 666 were black. Norris was also able to document that blacks had never served on any jury in the memory of any person living in that county. For a compelling critique of the impact of peremptory challenges against Hispanics, see Deborah A. Ramirez, "Excluded Voices: The Disenfranchisement of Ethnic Groups from Jury Service," *Wisconsin Law Review* 1993 (May/June 1993): 761.

4. *Norris*, 294, 596 U.S. 587, 596.

5. 476 U.S. 79 (1986). See also C. Ogletree, "Supreme Court Jury Discrimination Cases and State Court Compliance, Resistance, and Innovation," *Toward a Useable Past:*

Liberty Under State Constitutions, ed., Paul Finkelman and Stephen E. Gottlieb (Athens: University of Georgia Press, 1991), 339–67.

6. See J. Marshall concurring. *Batson* v. *Kentucky*, 476 U.S. 79, 102–6 (1986).

7. See, for example, Samuel R. Gross and Robert Mauro, "Patterns of Death: An Analysis of Racial Disparities in Capital Sentencing and Homicide Victimization," *Stanford Law Review* 37 (1984): 27.

8. Derrick Bell, "Racism in America's Courts: Cause for Black Disruption or Despair?" *University of California Law Review* 61 (1973): 165. See also Jewelle Taylor Gibbs et al., eds., *Young, Black, and Male in America: An Endangered Species* (Dover, Mass.: Auburn House, 1988), 8–11.

9. See, for example, *United States* v. *McKendrick*, 481 F. 2d 152 (2d. Cir. 1973); also, *Kelly* v. *Stone*, 514 F. 2d 18 (9th Cir. 1975).

10. These examples are discussed in greater detail later in the chapter.

11. 408 U.S. 238 (1972).

12. *Furman* v. *Georgia*, 408 U.S. 238, 451 (1972), citing Rupert C. Koeninger, "Capital Punishment in Texas 1924–1968," *Crime and Delinquency* 15 (1969): 132, 141.

13. *Furman* v. *Georgia*, 408 U.S. 238, 364 (1972).

14. *Gregg* v. *Georgia*, 428 U.S. 153 (1976).

15. 433 U.S. 584 (1977).

16. 398 F.2d 138 (1968).

17. 107 S.Ct. 1756 (1987). See also Randall L. Kennedy, "*McCleskey* v. *Kemp*: Race, Capitol Punishment, and the Supreme Court," *Harvard Law Review* 101 (1988): 1388.

18. *McCleskey* v. *Zant*, 580 F. Supp. 338 (N.D. Ga. 1984) and 111 S.Ct. 2841.

19. *McCleskey* v. *Kemp*, 107 S.Ct., 1763.

20. *McCleskey* v. *Kemp*, 107 S.Ct., 1764, n. 5.

21. *McCleskey* v. *Kemp*, 107 S.Ct., 1779.

22. See Charles R. Lawrence III, "The Id, the Ego and Equal Protection: Reckoning with Unconscious Racism," *Stanford Law Review* 39 (1987): 317.

23. See J. Brennan, dissenting, *McCleskey* v. *Kemp*, 481 U.S. 279, 321.

24. See Marc Mauer, *America's Prisons Reach 1 Million Mark* (Washington, D.C.: Sentencing Project, January 1989).

25. See Marc Mauer, *Young Black Men and the Criminal Justice System: A Growing National Problem* (Washington, D.C.: Sentencing Project, February 1990).

26. See Marc Mauer, *Americans Behind Bars: A Comparison of International Rates of Incarceration* (Washington, D.C.: Sentencing Project, January 1991).

27. See "Race and the Criminal Process," *Harvard Law Review* 101 (1988): 1465–1641 and Douglas C. McDonald and Kenneth E. Carleson, *Sentencing in the Federal Courts: Does Race Matter? The Transition to Sentencing Guidelines, 1986–1990* (BJS Federal Justice Statistics Program Report, NCJ-145328, December 1993). Also, Norval Morris, "Race and Crime: What Evidence Is There That Race Influences Results in the Criminal Justice System," *Judicature*, 72 (August-September 1988): 111.

28. See, for example, *State* v. *Russell*, 477 N. W. 2d 886 (1991); *United States* v. *Lattimore*, 974 F.2d 971 (8th Cir.) (1992); *United States* v. *Thomas*, 932 F.2d 1085 (5th Cir.) (1991).

29. 477 N.W. 2d 886 (Minn. 1991). In a hearing before the trial judge, it was disclosed that in 1988, 96 percent of all defendants charged with possession of crack cocaine were

African American, while nearly 80 percent of all defendants charged with possession of powdered cocaine were whites. Further, the testimony before the court revealed that the penalties for the possession of three grams of crack cocaine was up to twenty years in prison, with a presumptive sentence of four years incarceration, while the penalty for the same amount of powder cocaine was up to five years, with a presumptive sentence of probation. See p. 887.

30. 477 N.W. 2d 886, 888, n. 2 (Minn. 1991).

31. See, for example, *United States* v. *Thomas,* 932 F.2d 1085 (5th Cir.) 1991; *United States* v. *Turner,* 928 F.2d. 956 (10th Cir.) (1991). See also *United States* v. *Avant,* 907 F.2d 623 (6th Cir.) (1990). Also, Revised Memorandum on Sentencing, *United States* v. *Walls, et al.,* Criminal No. 92-0234-LFO, January 24, 1994, 14–16.

32. See, for example, *Griffin* v. *California,* 380 U.S.609 (1965); *Berger* v. *United States,* 295 U.S. 78, 88 (1935) ("while [the prosecutor] may strike hard blows, he is not at liberty to strike foul ones. It is as much [the prosecutor's] duty to refrain from improper methods calculated to produce a wrongful conviction as it is to use every legitimate means to bring about a just one"). See also C. Ogletree, "Does Race Matter in Criminal Prosecutions?" *The Champion,* July 1991, 7.

33. 481 F.2d 152 (2d Cir. 1973). See also *Kelly* v. *Stone,* 514 F.2d 18 (9th Cir. 1975) (finding that prosecutor's argument that defendant should be convicted because "maybe next time it won't be a little black girl from the other side of the tracks; maybe it will be somebody that you know; maybe it will be somebody I know" constituted a "highly inflammatory and wholly impermissible appeal to racial prejudice" and, with other factors, warrants grant of writ of habeas corpus).

34. *McKendrick,* 481 F.2d, 154.

35. *McKendrick,* 481 F.2d, 159.

36. In a similar circumstance, a New York appellate court reversed a conviction for possession of a weapon where the prosecutor made racially charged comments during the course of the trial. See *People* v. *Thomas,* 129 A.D. 2d 596, 514 N.Y.S. 2d 91 (1987). The defendant, a black male, testified that he believed the white officers who approached him to be muggers. The prosecutor repeatedly questioned the defendant on this point. In summation, the prosecutor returned to this theme, arguing to the jury that an African American in an African American neighborhood cannot conceivably be the victim of a crime committed by a white man. The court concluded that the prosecutor's comments impermissibly encouraged the jury to weigh the credibility of defendant's testimony by considering the race of the arresting officers, and therefore deprived the defendant of a fair trial.

37. 357 A. 2d 423, 427–28 (D.C. 1976).

38. See The Harvard Law School Criminal Justice Institute & The Monroe Trotter Institute, University of Massachusetts at Boston, *Beyond the Rodney King Story: An NAACP Report on Police Conduct and Community Relations,* March 1993, 12–13 ("The beating of Rodney King is part of a long and shameful history of racially motivated brutality and degradation that continues to find expression in powerful places"). For another compelling and fascinating critique of this issue, see M. Shanara Gilbert, "An Ounce of Prevention: A Constitutional Prescription for Choice of Venue in Racially Sensitive Criminal Cases," *Tulane Law Review* 1855 (1993).

39. See *Beyond the Rodney King Story*, 23–60.

40. See E. G. Brown, "Bridges over Troubled Water: A Perspective on Policing in the Black Community," in *Black Perspectives on Crime in the Criminal Justice System*, ed. Robert L. Woodson (Boston: G. K. Hall, 1977), 79; R. L. McNeely and Carl L. Pope, "Race, Crime and Criminal Justice: An Overview," in *Race, Crime and Criminal Justice*, ed. R. L. McNeely and Carl L. Pope (Beverly Hills: Sage, 1981), 13–14.

41. See *Beyond the Rodney King Story*.

42. See James J. Fyfe, "Blind Justice: Police Shootings in Memphis," *Journal of Criminal Law and Criminology* 73 (1982): 707, 718–20.

43. See, for example, *Hall v. Pennsylvania State Police*, 570 F.2d, 86 (3d Cir. 1978); *Davis v. Mississippi*, 394 U.S. 721 (1969); *United States v. Mallides*, 473 F.2d 859 (9th Cir. 1973). See also Sheri Lynn Johnson, "Race and the Decision to Detain a Suspect," *Yale Law Journal* 93 (1983): 214.

44. See, for example, *Papachristou v. City of Jacksonville*, 405 U.S. 156 (1972); *Lindsey v. Normet*, 405 U.S. 56 (1972); *Kolender v. Lawson*, 461 U.S. 352 (1983).

45. See, for example, *United States v. Beck*, 602 F.2d 726, 729 (5th Cir. 1979); *United States v. Carrizoza-Gaxiola*, 523 F.2d 239, 241 (9th Cir. 1975); *United States v. Nicholas*, 448 F2d 622 (8th Cir. 1971).

46. *Terry v. State of Ohio*, 392 U.S. 1, 12 (Oct. Term, 1967).

47. Task Force Report, 183.

48. *Terry*, 392 U.S. 14–15 (noting that "[t]he wholesale harassment by certain elements of the police community, of which minority groups, particularly Negroes, frequently complain, will not be stopped by the exclusion of any evidence from any criminal trial"). See, *Beyond the Rodney King Story*, 23–32.

49. G. Peirson, "Institutional Racism and Crime Clearance," in *Black Perspectives on Crime in the Criminal Justice System*, 111.

50. Johnson, "Race and the Decision to Detain," 236. See also Michael K. Brown, *Working the Street: Police Discretion and the Dilemmas of Reform* (New York: Russell Sage Foundation, 1981), 166 ("Race, the field observations reveal, is one of the most salient criteria to patrolmen in deciding whether or not to stop someone"); model code, 294 U.S. §110.2 (recognizing particular danger to "youths, unconventionally attired persons, Negroes in white areas, whites in Negro areas"); challenge of crime, Myrdal, *An American Dilemma*, 99–103 (noting differential treatment by police on the basis of race); Race and the Criminal Process, Norris, 294 U.S., 1494, 1496.

51. *Kolender v. Lawson*, 461 U.S. 352 (1983).

52. Woodyard, "Long Beach Task Force Told to Act within Law," *Los Angeles Times*, October 1, 1987, Sec. 9, 1.

53. *Davis*, 394 U.S. 721, 722–23 (1969).

54. 473 F.2d 859, 860–62 (9th Cir. 1973). See also *United States v. Pena-Cantu*, 639 F.2d 1228 (5th Cir. 1981) (finding unconstitutional the stop of Latino men who were sitting low in the back seat of a car of the types sometimes used by smugglers); *United States v. Urias*, 648 F.2d 621 (9th Cir. 1981) (approving the stop of a Latino because he turned off the highway just prior to a checkpoint); *United States v. Munoz*, 604 F.2d 160 (9th Cir. 1979) (rejecting stop that was based on the officer's observations of two cars traveling in tandem with a child in each front seat sitting between two Latino adults who did not look at the agent); *United States v. Mallides*, 473 F.2d 859 (9th Cir. 1973) (striking down

stop premised on the fact that the Latino men were sitting "erectly" and did not turn to look at a passing car). But see *United States* v. *Hernandez-Lopez*, 538 F.2d 284, 285 (9th Cir. 1976) (upholding questioning based on the fact that the defendant was "sitting very rigidly in his seat" and "look[ing] like a Mexican cowboy"); *United States* v. *Lopez-Barajas*, 412 F. Supp. 1007 (E.D. N.Y. 1976) (upholding the stop of a Latino on the grounds that he wore two-inch heels, dark green pants, and a blue-and-red checked shirt, and retreated when a plainclothes agent stared at him).

55. "Race and the Criminal Process," 1497.

56. *F.S. Royster Guana* v. *Virginia*, 253 U.S. 412, 415 (1920).

57. *Yick Wo* v. *Hopkins*, 118 U.S. 356, 374 (1886) (invalidating facially neutral laundry ordinance enforced discriminatorily against Chinese persons).

58. *Strauder* v. *West Virginia*, 100 U.S. 303, 307–8 (1880); *Slaughter-House Cases*, 83 U.S. 36, 81 (1873).

59. Even officers' seemingly good-faith reliance on assumptions regarding the correlation between race and crime does not insulate the conduct from review since government action that facially discriminates on the basis of race is unconstitutional regardless of motivation. See, for example, *Village of Arlington Heights* v. *Metropolitan Housing Development Corp.*, 429 U.S. 252, 265–66 (1977).

60. 448 F.2d 622, 625 (8th Cir. 1971).

61. Race and the Criminal Process, 1501–2.

62. There is, though, arguably one set of cases in which race-conscious action by the police is permissible: identification of a known suspect. Because racial designations are neutral and do not rely on invidious racial stereotypes, their use need not be subjected to strict scrutiny. See Johnson, "Race and the Decision to Detain," 242–43. However, even where race is an identifying factor, it may not be the sole basis of a stop. See Johnson, 225–26. Allowing individuals to be stopped solely because they share a racial identity with a suspect enables the police to conduct the sweeps and dragnets discussed earlier. Police are not entitled to stop every African American where they have reason to believe that an African American man has robbed a bank. Instead, police may stop only those African American men about whom they have an individualized suspicion. The most appropriate use of race as an identifying characteristic is not to create suspicion of a particular person, but only to eliminate from suspicion all persons of other races.

63. See, for example, *Korematsu* v. *United States*, 323 U.S. 214, 236 (1944) (Murphy, J., dissenting) (arguing that the military order to evacuate Japanese residents during World War II was unconstitutional because there was "no reasonable relation between the group characteristics of Japanese Americans and the dangers of invasion, sabotage and espionage" and because the basis for the order was "an accumulation of much of the misinformation, half-truths and insinuations that for years have been directed against Japanese Americans by people with racial and economic prejudices").

64. See Johnson, "Race and the Decision to Detain," 221, n. 144.

65. In 1989, five black men filed a class action suit for declaratory and injunctive relief and for damages against the city of Boston and officers of the Boston Police Department. Plaintiffs alleged that "the defendants have instituted and carried out a policy, generally known as 'search on sight,' calling for the warrantless search, without probable cause or lawful justification, of black and Hispanic youths in public areas of Roxbury, Dorchester and Mattapan," in violation of the state constitution and the Fourth and Fourteenth

amendments of the federal Constitution. The class consisted of African Americans and Latinos between the ages of fifteen and thirty who live, work, or travel in the police district subject to the department's special search and seizure policies.

The complainants asserted that the Boston Police Department implemented a policy of stopping and searching all African American and Latino persons suspected of gang membership or in the company of a suspected gang member. Pursuant to this policy, plaintiffs alleged that police officers "have stopped the plaintiffs and the members of plaintiff class without lawful justification and have subjected them to unlawful, intrusive and humiliating searches including, in some cases, being threatened with firearms, being pushed to the ground, being physically and verbally abused, and being required to remove their trousers and underwear in public places." The case was settled before the trial's conclusion for $100,000 to be divided among the five named plaintiffs.

These cases illustrate that *Terry's* highly discretionary nature increases the danger of selective police conduct by allowing police officers to act on subjective stereotypes and assumptions regarding race. In addition, it is apparent that *Terry* has been applied too broadly, permitting a police practice of singling out people of color for interrogations. Reliance by police officers on the suspect's location in a high crime area allows officers to disproportionately stop people of color who live, work, or travel in typically inner-city neighborhoods. Because of patterns of residential segregation, interrelation between race and poverty, and lessened protection for and social investment in communities of color, singling out high crime areas will have the effect of discriminating against blacks and other people of color.

66. Nevertheless, most challenges are mounted in the context of criminal prosecutions. In Boston, two defendants successfully challenged the stop leading to their arrest for unlawful carrying of a firearm and possession of ammunition because the stop was conducted without reasonable suspicion in violation of the Fourth Amendment. The court found the facts leading up to the stop to be as follows: "On July 21, 1989 just prior to 6 p.m., a Boston Police Department cruiser described as a rapid response car was proceeding on Washington Street and approaching Egleston Square at Columbus Avenue in Roxbury. Traffic was heavy in both directions and moving slowly. A 1986 two-tone Nissan Maxima passed the cruiser on Washington Street going in the opposite direction toward Forest Hills. The two officers in the cruiser observed the driver and passenger to be both young and black."

On the basis of a hunch that the car was stolen, the officers determined to reverse their direction and requested a stolen car check. The officers testified that they saw the defendants get out of the vehicle and then back into it. They also allegedly noticed "suspicious body language" by both defendants. On the basis of these observations, the officers approached the car, where they saw a firearm protruding from under a seat.

Judge Mather refused to credit the officer's testimony. He found no credible evidence of any suspicious conduct by the defendants. Instead, the judge believed that, after following the defendants as they walked along the sidewalk, the officers stopped, searched the defendants and their car, discovering the weapon, which was the subject of the case.

Before ruling on the legality of the stop and search, Judge Mather described the "systematic application of a Policy" of the Boston Police Department to search "known gang members" on sight. Mather pointed to Deputy Superintendent William Celester's announcement that of a search on sight policy, which the judge described as a "Machiavellian approach to the problems" and "in effect, a proclamation of martial law . . . for a narrow class of people, young blacks, suspected of membership in a gang or perceived by the police to be in the company of someone thought to be a member." Judge Mather concluded: "I have taken and credit testimony from blacks in the Egleston Square area that they, as individuals and in groups, are forced to open their mouths, placed spread eagle against walks, required to drop their trousers in public places and subjected to under-clothing exams."

The court found a tacit understanding exists in the Boston Police Department that constitutionally impermissible searches will not only be countenanced but applauded in the Roxbury area. Mather ordered that the indictments be dismissed, and a copy of the opinion be furnished to the attorney general.

67. Johnson, "Race and the Decision to Detain," 226–30, n. 144.

68. *State* v. *Dean*, 112 Ariz. 437, 439, 543 P.2d 425, 427 (1975). See also *United States* v. *Williams*, 714 F.2d 777, 780 (8th Cir. 1983) (accepting testimony of arresting officer who stated "that it was 'rare' for black persons to be in the predominantly white neighborhood where the robbery occurred"); *State* v. *Ruiz*, 19 Ariz. App. 84, 86, 504 P.2d 1307, 1309 (1973) (crediting police testimony that the few Chicanos in the area were there to purchase narcotics).

69. *Dean*, 112 Ariz., 439, 543 P.2d , 427.

70. The fact that the sheriff who conceived the policy is an Asian American man makes two additional points. First, the case of Parish County illustrates that *Terry* has a particularly devastating effect on African American men who are most frequently the victims of social stereotyping that depicts them as criminals. In addition, the sheriff's decision to stop all African Americans in white neighborhoods shows how the enormous discretion created by *Terry* and the lack of guidance provided for applying *Terry* enables and encourages racially discriminatory conduct even by those who would be expected to be most sensitive to the racial implications of their conduct.

71. J. Michael Kennedy, "Sheriff Rescinds Order to Stop Blacks in White Areas," *Los Angeles Times*, December 4, 1986, sec. 1, 18. A barrage of criticism caused Sheriff Lee to rescind the order before it was implemented.

72. *United States* v. *Mendenhall*, 446 U.S. 544, 562 (1980) (Powell, J., concurring); *Florida* v. *Royer*, 460 U.S. 491, 502 (1983) (plurality opinion); Race and the Criminal Process, 1503.

73. See, for example, *United States* v. *Sokolow*, 490 U.S. 1 (1988); *Florida* v. *Royer*, 460 U.S. 491 (1983); *Reid* v. *Georgia*, 448 U.S. 438 (1980).

74. In *United States* v. *Sokolow*, for instance, stereotypical assumptions clearly colored officers' interpretation of an individual's conduct. The government argued that reasonable suspicion should be based on the following facts and inferences: "Respondent did not go to Miami for another innocent personal reason, such as a wedding or a funeral. A person is not likely to use an alias when traveling to a wedding or a funeral, and petitioner [who was wearing a black jumpsuit and gold jewelry] was hardly dressed for such an occasion. Nor was it likely that he was carrying more formal dress, since his carry-on bags were not designed to accommodate a suit. Accordingly, an experienced narcotics agent could quite reasonably believe, based on all the facts, that respondent was involved in narcotics

activity." Brief for the United States, *United States* v. *Sokolow*, No. 87-1295 (pagination unavailable).

75. One study concluded that the majority of characteristics identified in drug courier profiles fail to describe 90 percent of drug couriers. Morgan Cloud, "Search and Seizure by the Numbers: The Drug Courier Profile and Judicial Review of Investigative Formulas," *Boston University Law Review* 65 (1985): 876.

76. *Sokolow*, 490 U.S., 13 (1988) (Marshall, J., dissenting).

77. See Cloud, "Search and Seizure," 843.

78. *United States* v. *Chamblis*, 425 F. Supp. 1330, 1333 (E.D. Mich. 1977).

79. Taylor, "Travelers Becoming POWs in Drug War," *Manhattan Lawyer*, May 1990, 16.

80. One interesting facet of the gang profiles is that they have been used—perhaps more frequently—by private actors than by the state. Magic Mountain recently came under fire for its use of gang profiles to determine who would be frisked at the park's entrance and who would be excluded from the park. Richard Colvin, "Theme Park Efforts to Keep Out Gangs Raises Issues of Bias," *Los Angeles Times*, April 2, 1988, sec. 2, 3. Critics allege that the gang profile discriminates against African American and Latino youths. See also, Keith Ervin, "Pact Reached on Mall Security—Guidelines Expected to Prevent Discrimination," *Seattle Times*, January 24, 1991, C2 (discussing shopping mall's use of "police profiles," which rely exclusively on race and clothing to identify, monitor, and bar gang members).

81. *United States* v. *Malone*, 886 F.2d 1162 (9th Cir. 1989); *Malone*, 886 F.2d 1162, 1163 (9th Cir. 1990). See also Timothy Egan, "U.S. Agents Aid Drug Fight in Seattle," *New York Times*, July 15, 1988, sec. A, 10.

82. *Malone*, 886 F.2d, 1163, 1165.

83. 920 F.2d 376 (6th Cir. 1990).

84. *United States* v. *Taylor*, 917 F.2d 1402 (6th Cir. 1990).

85. One officer testified as follows:

Q: All right. Now go ahead now, how did the defendant appear on this occasion?

A: He appeared [in] kind of a grungy type work clothes. He had a dirty black baseball cap with something wrote across the front of it. . . .

A: . . . And he had on, I think it was, a blue shirt with "Pace" or something written across the pocket. A pair of blue trousers, white tennis shoes.

Q: And why do you say he—why did he stick out?

A: Well, the rest of the passengers that usually come from Miami flights is either business people or resort type people, people getting off in real casual nice looking clothes. Like I say, it was just different seeing somebody getting off there looking like Mr. [Taylor] looked that night. (*Taylor*, 917 F.2d, 1408–9)

86. Tracey Maclin, untitled speech, 10, 13–17.

87. 922 F.2d 465 (8th Cir. 1990).

88. According to the most recent census data, African Americans constitute only slightly more than 12 percent of the national population. Bureau of the Census, Statistical Abstract of the United States 25, 106th ed. (Washington, D.C.: Government

Printing Office, 1986). In 1989, 3.5 million out of 11.2 million arrests, or 30.8 percent of all arrests, were of African Americans. See also Brown, "Bridges over Troubled Waters: A Perspective on Policing in the Black Community," in *Black Perspectives on Crime and the Criminal Justice System*, ed. Robert L . Woodson (Boston: G. K. Hall, 1977), 79 ("Studies have revealed . . . that in proportion to their number in the population, blacks are more likely to be arrested than whites"). See also John R. Hepburn, "Race and the Decision to Arrest: An Analysis of Warrants Issued," *Journal of Research in Crime and Delinquency* 15 (January 1978): 54, 59, 66. For instance, all but 2 of the 210 persons arrested in Manhattan Port Authority's drug interdiction program were African American or Latino. A study conducted by the Public Defender's Office in Middlesex, N.J., found that while African American motorists driving out-of-state cars represented only 4.7 percent of the total vehicles traveling on a particular portion of the New Jersey Turnpike, they constituted 80 percent of the cases in which drug arrests were made. Maclin, untitled speech, 18.

89. Sam Meddis, "Drug Arrest Rate Is Higher for Blacks," *USA Today*, December 20, 1989.

90. See, for example, Race and the Criminal Process, 1525.

91. See, for example, *Tobias v. Smith*, 468 F. Supp. 1287, 1289 (W. D. N. Y. 1979) (juror told other jurors that problems with identification of the defendant did not matter because "You can't tell one black from another. They all look alike"); *Smith v. Brewer*, 444 F. Supp. 482, 485 (S.D. Iowa) (juror strutted around the jury room imitating a black minstrel); *State v. Shillcutt*, 119 Wis. 2d 788, 791, 350 N. W. 2d 686, 688 (1984) (juror remarked, "Let's be logical, he's a black and he sees a 17-year-old white girl—I know the type.")

92. See Federal Rule of Evidence 606 (B).

93. Jan Hoffman, "Pregnant, Addicted—and Guilty? *New York Times*, August 19, 1990, sec. 6, 32, 35; Eileen McNamara, "Fetal Endangerment Cases on the Rise," *Boston Globe*, October 3, 1990, 1.

94. See Dorothy E. Roberts,"Punishing Drug Addicts Who Have Babies: Women of Color, Equality, and the Right to Privacy," *Harvard Law Review* 104 (1991): 1419, 1421, n. 6, also 1445, 1481. For a compelling critique of this issue, see Dorothy E. Roberts, "Crime, Race, and Reproduction," *Tulane Law Review* 67 (June 1993): 1945.

95. Paltrow and Shende, "State by State Case Summary of Criminal Prosecutions against Pregnant Women and Appendix of Public Health and Public Interest Groups Opposed to These Prosecutions" (unpublished memorandum to ACLU affiliates, October 29, 1990). See also Gina Kolata, "Racial Bias Seen in Prosecuting Pregnant Addicts," *New York Times*, July 20, 1990, A13 (of 133 women charged with fetal endangerment, 80 percent are minorities and 92 percent had incomes below $25,000 per year).

96. Hoffman, "Pregnant, Addicted—and Guilty?" 35.

97. Molly McNulty, "Pregnancy Police: The Health Policy and Legal Implications of Punishing Pregnant Women for Harm to Their Fetuses," *New York University Review of Law & Social Change* 15 (1988): 319.

98. Moss, "Substance Abuse during Pregnancy," *Harvard Women's Law Journal* (1990): 289–90; Rorie Sherman, "Keeping Babies Free of Drugs," *National Law Journal*, October 16,

1989, 1; Note, "The Problem of the Drug-Exposed Newborn: A Return to Principled Intervention," Stanford Law Review 42 (1990): 753, 782 n. 157.

99. Note, "The Problem of the Drug-Exposed Newborn." 754 and n. 36. See also Ira J. Chasnoff, H. J. Landress, and M. E. Barrett, "The Prevalence of Illicit Drug or Alcohol Use during Pregnancy and Discrepancies in Mandatory Reporting in Pinellas County, Florida," New England Journal of Medicine 322 (1990): 1205 (finding racial bias in the reporting of maternal drug abuse).

100. Chasnoff, Landress, and Barrett, "The Prevalence of Illicit Drug or Alcohol Use," 1202–4 (1990) (finding racial bias in the reporting of maternal drug abuse).

101. Chasnoff, Landress, and Barrett, "The Prevalence of Illicit Drug or Alcohol Use," 1204, Table 2; Paltrow and Shende, "Case by Case State Summary," 3–5.

102. See Michael Lev, "Judge Is Firm on Forced Contraception, but Welcomes an Appeal, New York Times, January 11, 1991, A12; Tamar Lewin, "Implanted Birth Control Device Renews Debate over Forced Contraception," New York Times, January 10, 1991, A20.

103. Mark A. Stein, "Judge to Let Birth Control Order Stand," Los Angeles Times, January 11, 1991, A3.

104. See, for example, Bill Ainsworth, "I Take Away People's Rights All the Time," Legal Times, April 8, 1991, 10; Neuborne, "In the Norplant Case, Good Intentions Make Bad Law," Los Angeles Times, March 3, 1991, M1.

105. See Helen R. Neuborne, "In the Norplant Case," M1; Tamar Lewin, "Implanted Birth Control Device Renews Debate over Forced Contraception," New York Times, January 10, 1991, A20 (announcing the FDA's approval of Norplant as of December 10, 1990).

106. Donald Kimelman, "Poverty and Norplant: Can Contraception Reduce the Underclass," Philadelphia Inquirer, December 12, 1990.

107. See, for example, Faye Wattleton, "Using Birth Control as Coercion," Los Angeles Times, January 13, 1991.

108. See, for example, Ainsworth, "I Take Away People's Rights," 10.

109. See, for example, Neuborne, "In the Norplant Case," M1; Ellen Goodman, "An Old Fix in a New Form," Boston Globe, February 17, 1991, 79.

110. See Stein, "Judge to Let Birth Control Order Stand."

111. Ainsworth, "I Take Away People's Rights," 10.

112. Waters v. Barry, 711 F. Supp. 1121 (D.D.C. 1989).

113. The curfew law, for instance, exempted only youths accompanied by their parents (and not any adult), did not exempt youth occupying the sidewalks in front of their homes, and did not exempt minors exercising First Amendment rights. Waters v. Barry, 711 F. Supp. 1121 (D.D.C. 1989).

114. Waters v. Barry, 711 F. Supp. 1121 (D.D.C. 1989).

115. Having accepted plaintiffs' argument that the ordinance is unconstitutionally overbroad, the court did not address the arguments that the New Law violates minors' equal protection and Fourth Amendment rights, or the liberty and privacy interests of the parents.

116. See, for example, United States v. Leasehold Interest in 121 Nostrand Avenue, Apartment 1-C, Brooklyn, NY, 760 F. Supp. 1015 (E.D. N. Y. 1991); Michael Isikoff and Gwen Ifill, "U.S. Seeks Wider Anti-drug Powers," Washington Post, May 16, 1990, A1. Government seizure of leaseholds is authorized by the Controlled Substance Act, 21 U.S.C. s. 881(a)(7),

which subjects to forfeiture "all real property . . . which is used, or intended to be used . . . to commit, or facilitate the commission of, a violation of this title punishable by more than one year's imprisonment." In 1988, the civil forfeiture provisions of 21 U.S.C. s. 881(a) were amended by section 5105 of the Anti-Drug Abuse Act of 1988 to codify "guidelines granting public housing agencies authority to evict tenants if they, their families, or their guests engage in drug-related criminal activity." 134 *Cong. Rec.* S. 17,360 (daily ed. Nov. 10, 1988). The Department of Housing and Urban Development (HUD) has modified the grounds for denial or termination of housing assistance to emphasize that drug-related criminal activity to members of the household, guests, or other persons under the tenant's control will result in eviction. See 56 *Fed. Reg.* 6248 (1991); 55 *Fed. Reg.* 28538 (1990). Several states, including Arizona, Arkansas, California, Massachusetts, Missouri, Nevada, New York and New Jersey, have enacted laws that mandate a tenant's eviction from public housing if he or she is convicted of a drug offense on the premises. See Office of National Drug Control Policy, *State Drug Control Status Report* 11 (November 1990).

117. In *Richmond Tenants Organization, Inc.* v. *Richmond Redevelopment and Housing Authority,* the District Court for the Eastern District of Virginia found that HUD lease provisions allowing eviction for any drug or weapon offenses committed in the public housing unit were reasonably related to the need to control an overwhelming crime problem in public housing developments. 753 F. Supp. 607 (E.D. Va. 1990). See also, *United States* v. *Leasehold Interest in 121 Nostrand Avenue, Apartment 1-c, Brooklyn, N.Y.,* 760 F. Supp. 1015 (E.D. N. Y. 1991) (upholding civil forfeiture provisions but denying forfeiture of leaseholder's interest under the innocent owner provision, since the owner was not aware of drug distribution on premises); *United States* v. *Leasehold Interest in Property Located at 850 S. Maple, Ann Arbor, Washtenaw County, Michigan,* 743 F. Supp. 505 (E.D. Mich. 1990) (striking down pre-notice seizure of public housing lease on suspicion of cocaine use).

118. *United States* v. *Leasehold Interest in the Property Known as 900 East 40th Street, Apartment 102, Chicago, Illinois,* 740 F. Supp. 540, 541 (N.D.Ill. 1990) (Shadur, J.).

ALICE L. BROWN

ENVIRONMENTAL JUSTICE

CONSTITUTIONAL AND STATUTORY CHALLENGES
TO ENVIRONMENTAL RACISM

We are not saying we want all waste disposal facilities taken out of our
backyards and put in white people's backyards. We are raising a more
fundamental question about the industrial policies of the U.S. The
environmental and industrial policies must be aligned with one another—
they are not contradictory.

Benjamin Chavis, Jr., 1991

What is ultimately at stake in the environmental justice debate is
everyone's quality of life. The goal is equal protection, *not* equal pollution.

Deeohn Ferris, 1992

Recently, the view that minority communities bear a disproportionate
share of society's environmental hazards has gained increased attention and acceptance. This disparate treatment has been called environmental discrimination, environmental injustice, or environmental racism.
Observers in academia, the media, philanthropic organizations, and increasingly, agencies of the federal government, have recognized the need to address this problem.

With this awareness has come the environmental justice movement, born
of a desire on the part of affected communities and other concerned persons
to challenge the discriminatory distribution of environmental risks and locally
unwanted land uses in their backyards. This struggle includes attorneys—ad-

270

vocates for both environmental protection and social justice—who are attempting to mount legal challenges to the disparate treatment of minority communities in the siting of polluting industries and the disposing of noxious wastes.

The Reverend Benjamin Chavis is credited with coining the term "environmental racism," which he defines as "racial discrimination in environmental policymaking." That is to say,

> It is racial discrimination in the enforcement of regulations and laws. It is racial discrimination in the deliberate targeting of communities of color for toxic waste disposal and the siting of polluting industries. It is racial discrimination in the official sanctioning of the life-threatening presence of poisons and pollutants in communities of color. And, it is racial discrimination in the history of excluding people of color from the mainstream environmental groups, decisionmaking boards, commissions, and regulatory bodies.[1]

BACKGROUND

The seeds of the environmental justice movement were sown in 1982 when North Carolina state officials decided to build a toxic waste landfill for soil contaminated with polychlorinated biphenyls (PCBs) in Warren County. The contaminated soil had been illegally dumped along the roadways of fourteen counties in 1978.[2] Warren County, the county with the highest percentage of African Americans and one of the lowest socioeconomic profiles in the state, was chosen to be the official dumping ground. In response, local residents, civil rights activists, and political leaders waged a campaign against the siting of the facility that included litigation, public protest, and civil disobedience.[3] Over the months of demonstrations and meetings that followed, more than 500 people were arrested, including the Reverend Chavis, then executive director of the United Church of Christ (UCC) Commission on Racial Justice (CRJ); Congressman Walter Fauntroy, representative from the District of Columbia and a member of the Congressional Black Caucus; and Dr. Joseph Lowery, president of the Southern Christian Leadership Conference.[4] According to Robert D. Bullard and Beverly H. Wright, two sociologists who have written extensively on this topic, "The protests marked the first national attempt by blacks to link environmental issues (hazardous waste and pollution) to the mainstream civil rights agenda."[5]

In the wake of the Warren County protests, several studies were commissioned. First, in December 1982, Representative Fauntroy requested that the U.S. General Accounting Office (GAO) determine the correlation between the location of hazardous waste landfills and the racial and economic status of surrounding communities in the southern region. The GAO focused its review on offsite landfills located in the eight southeastern states—Alabama, Florida, Georgia, Kentucky, Mississippi, North Carolina, South Carolina, and Tennessee—that constitute the U.S. Environmental Protection Agency's (EPA) Region IV. The GAO report, issued in June 1983, found, among other things, that in three of the four communities where offsite hazardous waste landfills were located, African Americans made up the majority of the population. In addition, at least 26 percent of the population in all four communities had income below the poverty level, and most of this population was African American.[6]

The second study was produced by the CRJ under the instruction of the Reverend Chavis. He had begun to consider the connection between the Warren County incident and other polluting facilities in primarily African American communities such as "the federal government's Savannah River nuclear facility, long a source of radioactive leaks and located in a heavily African-American area of South Carolina, and the 'largest landfill in the nation' in the mainly black community of Emelle, Alabama. 'We began to see evidence of a systematic pattern which led us to a national study.'"[7]

It was in 1987 while describing the findings of the CRJ report entitled "Toxic Wastes and Race in the United States: A National Report on the Racial and Socio-Economic Characteristics of Communities Surrounding Hazardous Waste Sites," that the Reverend Chavis coined the term "environmental racism." That document, which was the first comprehensive national report on the demographic patterns associated with the location of hazardous waste sites, found that race—that is, the racial composition of a community—was the most significant factor among variables tested in association with the location of commercial hazardous waste facilities. In fact, the CRJ study found that although socioeconomic status appeared to play an important role in the location of commercial hazardous waste facilities, race proved to be more significant.

The CRJ report has elicited various reactions. Some have questioned the data and criticized the term "environmental racism," citing numerous cases of whites being exposed to hazardous waste. Instead of environmental "racism," they think a more appropriate term might be environmental "classism." These commentators assert that the reasons for siting environmental waste in low-income areas are both economic and political: "Poorer areas are likely to have less expensive land, and residents often lack the political clout or resources to fight back."[8]

Some in this group also say that blaming racism alone for neighborhood pollution oversimplifies the causes. In their view, many factors, including transportation routes, land values, and other economic considerations, not simply racial prejudice, determine where plants are built and where industrial wastes are taken. Indeed, some observers suggest that singling out racism "only complicate[s] the task of building public support for controlling environmental contamination that ultimately threatens all of us."[9]

At the same time, a number of metropolitan-area studies support the finding of the national CRJ report.[10] For instance, a study of municipal incinerators and municipal and private landfills concluded that although African Americans constituted only 28 percent of the population of Houston, Texas, in 1980, six of the city's eight incinerators, five of the six state-permitted municipal landfill sites, and all five of the unpermitted municipal landfill sites were located in predominantly African American neighborhoods.[11] A survey of the three counties surrounding metropolitan Detroit revealed that minorities were approximately four times more likely to live within one mile of a waste facility than were whites, and an investigation of the hazardous waste incineration facilities in Baton Rouge, Louisiana, found that minority communities had an average of one such site for every 7,349 residents, while white communities had only one site per 31,110 residents.[12]

In September 1992 the *National Law Journal* (NLJ) published the results of an eight-month investigation that examined the relationship between race and the enforcement of environmental laws by the EPA. The NLJ analyzed every U.S. environmental lawsuit concluded between 1985 and 1991 and every residential toxic waste site (1,777 in total) authorized under the Comprehensive Environmental Response, Compensation and Liability Act of 1980, also known as Superfund, or CERCLA and came to the following conclusion: the federal government, under the ambit of the EPA, discriminates against minority communities in the cleanup of hazardous waste sites.[13] In particular, the NLJ investigation found that

Penalties against environmental law violators in minority areas are lower than those imposed for violations in largely white areas.

Under the Superfund cleanup program, abandoned hazardous waste sites in minority areas take 20 percent longer to be placed on the national priority action list than those in white areas.

The EPA chooses "containment" procedures, which entail capping or walling off a hazardous site, 7 percent more frequently at sites in minority communities than the preferred permanent treatment method of eliminating the waste or ridding it of its toxins. The permanent treatment is chosen 22 percent more often at sites in white areas.

The racial imbalances occurs whether the community is wealthy or poor.[14]

Notably, the NLJ investigation confirms the findings of earlier reports—such as the CRJ study—which concluded that minorities, despite their economic status, bear a disproportionate share of the burdens attendant to this country's waste and pollution.[15]

Indeed, the reality is that for many African Americans, race and poverty are inextricably linked. In 1989, for example, 30.7 percent of African Americans lived below the poverty level, in contrast to 10 percent of white Americans; and 43.2 percent of African American children lived below the poverty level in contrast to 14.1 percent of white children.[16]

For those not exposed to, or familiar with, the findings linking race and location, the term "environmental racism" may strike a sensitive chord or appear to exaggerate circumstances. The NLJ and other earlier studies, however, verify that race is a significant factor in both the location of hazardous waste facilities and the enforcement of environmental laws. In light of these findings, the terminology should be comprehensible.

Communities that are primarily minority do indeed suffer disproportionately from environmental insults and undesirable land uses and zoning in and near their homes. Moreover, these communities have received unequal protection under the law. And whether this has occurred because they are African American, Latino American, Asian American, Native American, poor, lacking in political clout, or some combination of the above, the result is environmental degradation, property devaluation, and serious risks to health and safety.

The negative health effects are tangible, costly, and potentially deadly. A case in point is lead poisoning, which the Centers for Disease Control has identified as one of the most common health hazards facing U.S. children today.[17] Although all children are at risk for lead toxicity, minority and poor children are disproportionately injured by harmful lead exposure: in fact, more than two-thirds of African American inner-city children are estimated to be contaminated by levels of lead excessive enough to require medical intervention. The effects of the malady include decreased intelligence, loss of short-term memory, deficits in vocabulary, underachievement in reading and spelling, impairment of visual-motor functioning, anemia, convulsions, hyper-tension, kidney disease, and cancer.[18]

Because of the disparities in siting and the resultant health risks, the environmental well-being of African American and other minority communities has become an issue of first magnitude for a number of national, regional, and local civil rights organizations and environmental groups. According to the Reverend Chavis,

> I think when we define the freedom movement, it now includes the environ-mental issues. . . . We see the struggle against environmental racism as being an ongoing part of the civil rights and freedom movement in this country, something we are going to make part of our agenda, not a side issue but a pri-mary issue. We must be just as vigilant in attacking environmental racism as racism in health care, housing, and schools.[19]

The issue of environmental race discrimination received national attention in October 1991, when the First National People of Color Environmental Leadership Summit was held in Washington, D.C. This event brought to-gether more than 650 people from the fifty states, Puerto Rico, Mexico, and the Marshall Islands to discuss the relationship between environmentalism and racial justice. Those in attendance included, among others, environmental activists, civil rights advocates, academicians, public interest lawyers, labor representatives, farm workers, and representatives from the philanthropic community. According to Charles Lee, research director of the United Church of Christ Commission for Racial Justice and one of the principal orga-nizers of the summit,

> The four-day event provided a forum in which leaders from communities of color could participate with other leaders in shaping an "inclusive" environ-mental agenda. The Summit served to strengthen and empower grassroots leaders and build a broader multiracial environmental and social justice net-work. It addressed three fundamental areas: 1) the environmental/social crisis in general, 2) the particularly problematic forms of environmental pollution impacting communities of color, such as hazardous and solid waste, air pollu-tion, radioactive waste, pesticide exposure, and lead poisoning; and 3) the his-torical experience and cultural perspectives of communities of color in the United States regarding the environment.[20]

Along with methods such as community organizing and lobbying, many af-fected communities have attempted to use the legal process to obtain equal environmental protection. As of December 1993, no court ruling had clearly supported claims of civil rights violations in the selection of sites for operations that produce pollution, although there have been several successful lawsuits that relied on other statutory measures to fight environmental injustice.

CONSTITUTIONAL CLAIMS

Some minority communities have tried to challenge government decisions to site environmental hazards in their neighborhoods by using the Equal Protection Clause of the Fourteenth Amendment to the U.S. Constitution or section 1983 of the Civil Rights Act of 1866. These provisions, however, require proof of intentional discrimination, that is, proof that the defendant acted purposefully or with an intent to discriminate. This is a heavy evidentiary burden, which, thus far in the environmental arena, minority communities have found difficult to meet.

For example, in *Bean* v. *Southwestern Waste Management Corp.*, one of the first cases to deal with civil rights claims in an environmental context, a class of African American plaintiffs alleged that the decision of the Texas Department of Health to permit operation of a solid-waste facility in their community was, at least in part, motivated by racial discrimination.[21] In seeking an order to revoke the permit, the plaintiffs presented statistical evidence to support their claim that the department's decision was part of a pattern and practice of discriminatory placement.

Relying on two U.S. Supreme Court cases, *Washington* v. *Davis* and *Village of Arlington Heights* v. *Metropolitan Housing Development Corp.*, the district court stated that "the plaintiffs must show not just that the decision to grant the permit is objectionable or even wrong, but that it is attributable to an *intent* to discriminate on the basis of race."[22] The court found that although plaintiffs had established that the decision was "insensitive and illogical," they had not established a substantial likelihood that it was "motivated by purposeful racial discrimination."[23] With that, the court denied plaintiffs' motion for a preliminary injunction.

Similarly, in 1991, a federal district court in Virginia denied an equal protection challenge to the siting of a regional landfill in a section of King and Queen County that was populated primarily by African Americans. In that case, *R.I.S.E. (Residents Involved in Saving the Environment) Inc.* v. *Kay*, the court acknowledged evidence that the County Board of Supervisors had sought and obtained an injunction to prevent King Land Corp. from operating its landfill in a majority white area of the county.[24] Moreover, the court found that "the placement of landfills in King and Queen County from 1969 to the present has had a disproportionate impact on black residents." Still, relying on *Arlington Heights* and *Washington* v. *Davis*, the court ruled that an "official action will not be held unconstitutional solely because it results in a racially disproportionate impact. Such action violates the Fourteenth Amendment's Equal Protection Clause only if it is *intentionally* discriminatory."

According to the court, the board's approval of the siting of the proposed landfill in a predominantly African American community was based not on the racial composition of the respective neighborhoods in which the landfills were to be located, but rather on the relative environmental suitability of the sites. On appeal, the Fourth Circuit affirmed the decision of the lower court.[25]

Bean and *R.I.S.E.* illustrate the difficulty that African American communities have had in seeking relief based on a constitutional claim. In at least two other cases, *East Bibb Twiggs Neighborhood Association* v. *Macon-Bibb County Planning & Zoning Commission,* and *NAACP* v. *Gorsuch,* federal courts have similarly rejected the plaintiffs' equal protection claim, pointing to the lack of clear evidence of discriminatory intent on the part of the decision maker.[26] Clearly, the equal protection approach to obtaining environmental justice presents some limitations. Other approaches, such as those using environmental and public health laws or Title VI of the Civil Rights Act of 1964, have held, or may hold, more promise for success.

STATUTORY CLAIMS

Traditional environmental laws can be used to challenge, among other things, the issuance of construction and operating permits, the siting of polluting industries, excessive discharges from existing facilities, and the nonenforcement of cleanup provisions. Superfund, the Clean Air Act, and the Federal Water Pollution Control Act (the Clean Water Act) are just a few of the federal environmental statutes that can be used to protect the health and property of minority communities.[27]

As a practical matter, there may be several advantages to pursuing remedies for minority communities via these avenues. Because race is not the primary issue in lawsuits brought under traditional environmental laws, plaintiffs who bring these claims need not prove that the defendants intended to discriminate on the basis of race or even that the defendants' actions had a disparate impact on minorities. In addition, many federal environmental statutes provide for private rights of action, or "citizens suits," which allow a person injured or threatened by a violation to request a court to enjoin the violation. Moreover, under several of the environmental statutes, courts may assess civil penalties payable to the U.S. Treasury.[28]

The following examples show how various environmental, public health, and civil rights statutes have been used to ensure that environmental hazards in minority communities are addressed.

Medicaid Act

Entitlement statutes can be used to address the disproportionate effects of environmental hazards on minority communities. In 1990, for example, a coalition of legal organizations filed a lawsuit in California using the federal Medicaid law to force the state to screen eligible children for lead poisoning. In the suit, *Matthews v. Coye*, the plaintiffs sought to compel the California Department of Health Services to comply with a provision of the federal Medicaid statute that calls for mandatory blood lead screening of all Medicaid-eligible children younger than age six in the Early and Periodic Screening, Diagnostic and Treatment (EPSDT) program.[29]

The plaintiffs had been denied lead testing as part of the Medicaid protocol administered by the health department. In the year before the lawsuit was filed, California had tested only 28,337 of 570,000 eligible children, principally because the department left the decision of whether to test to physician discretion. After a year of litigation, the department abandoned its claim that testing was an unnecessary expense and agreed to provide lead screening for all eligible children, as required by law.[30]

The goal in *Matthews* was to change a practice that deprived poor children, particularly poor minority children, of Medicaid benefits that could help protect their physical and mental health. After *Matthews*, similar suits were brought in other states to obtain better screening for lead poisoning and to identify those in need of medical intervention.[31] One such case is *Thompson v. Raiford*, a nationwide class action representing both individual clients and organizations based in Texas, New York, California, Colorado, and North Carolina.[32]

The object of *Thompson* was to force the U.S. Department of Health and Human Services (HHS) to require effective screening for childhood lead poisoning in all states participating in the Medicaid EPSDT program. Prior to *Thompson*, federal government guidelines recognized that all children ages six months to seventy-two months were considered at risk and should be screened for lead poisoning, but those guidelines also allowed states "to have the option" of using the less expensive, and less accurate, erythrocyte proto-porphyrin (EP) test, a test that does not detect low, yet harmful, levels of lead.[33] Under a consent decree that settled the case in 1993, HHS, through the Health Care Financing Administration, issued guidelines to the states specifying that the most accurate method for screening lead—the blood lead test—is the only acceptable laboratory screening test for assessing blood-lead levels. "The erythrocyte protoporphyrin test," according to the HFCA guidelines, "is no longer acceptable as a screening test for lead poisoning."[34]

The result in the *Thompson* case will provide benefits for millions of children. Yet, with regard to the environmental toxin lead, other problems still need to be addressed, including the need to clean up, or abate, the sources of contamination.

Lead Contamination Control Act

The LCCA, enacted in 1988, is another avenue through which cases have been brought on behalf of lead-poisoned children. The act, an amendment to the Safe Drinking Water Act of 1974, requires states to establish programs to identify and eliminate lead in school or day-care drinking water and to notify the public of drinking-water analyses.[35]

In January 1992 a lawsuit was brought on behalf of children in day-care centers across Colorado alleging that the state had failed to abide by even the most minimal LCCA requirements. Under a consent decree that settled the case, the state agreed to disseminate EPA documents on lead contamination testing and treatment to every licensed child-care facility in the state and to continue to disseminate the documents to newly licensed facilities annually. The state also agreed to establish a public education program on lead-contaminated drinking water.[36]

Many states have failed to establish the testing and remediation programs mandated by federal law, and therefore the Colorado case could be replicated. The LCCA is a classic example of an underenforced environmental statute that, if aggressively enforced, could provide relief for all children, particularly poor and minority children.[37]

Title VI of the Civil Rights Act of 1964

On a number of fronts, Title VI has been abysmally underenforced by the federal government and underused in litigation. Yet, it could play a central role in the attack against race-based inequities in environmental policy making.[38] The basic provision of Title VI proscribes discrimination in federally funded programs or activities: "No person in the United States shall, on the ground of race, color, or national origin, be excluded from participation in, be denied the benefits of, or be subjected to discrimination under any program or activity receiving federal financial assistance."[39] Title VI applies to agencies, service providers, and states that receive any federal assistance through any federal agency or source, including, but not limited to, the EPA, the Department of Education, the Department of Housing and Urban Development, Medicaid, and Medicare.

Title VI and its regulations can be powerful tools because they forbid not only intentional discrimination but also policies and practices that have a discriminatory impact upon a protected class. In *Guardians Association* v. *Civil Service Commission*, a majority of a sharply divided Supreme Court held that a private party could bring suit for prospective relief to enforce regulations under Title VI embodying a disparate impact standard without having to prove discriminatory intent on the part of the defendants.[40] Thus, Title VI and its regulations, in contrast to Constitutional Equal Protection claims or Section 1983 statutory claims, do not require plaintiffs to prove the subjective intent of the alleged offenders.

Clean Air Alternative Coalition v. *United States Department of Transportation* is a case in which Title VI claims were combined with environmental causes of action.[41] The case, filed in federal district court in San Francisco in March, 1993, challenges plans for rebuilding the Cypress Freeway, which collapsed during the October 1989 Loma Perita earthquake. The proposed route through West Oakland would displace nearly forty-five homes and a dozen local businesses and expose the community to increased levels of noise and air pollution, including carbon monoxide and benzene. The residents of West Oakland are predominantly African American, Hispanic, Asian, and poor. They already live close to several other freeways, a sewage treatment plant, rapid transit lines, and other polluting facilities.

The suit charges that the Cypress Reconstruction Project will expose residents of the surrounding neighborhoods to increased health risks, will decrease property values, and will adversely affect nearby parks and churches. The suit names U.S. Department of Transportation, the Federal Highway Administration, the California Department of Transportation, and officials of those agencies as defendants. It charges that they failed to assess the impact of the project on the community and to fully consider less discriminatory alternatives.

In particular, the plaintiffs allege violations of the community's civil rights under Title VI:

> The brunt of the proposed project's negative social, human health, and environmental impacts—including those associated with noise and air pollution, the dislocation of persons, the condemnation of homes and businesses, the chilling of economic development, as well as the disruption of the life of the community—will be borne by minority residents of West Oakland, including plaintiffs.[42]

In addition, the suit claims violations of the National Environmental Policy Act (NEPA), the Federal-Aid Highway Act, the Department of Transportation Act, the federal Clean Air Act, the National Historic Preservation Act (NHPA), and the California Environmental Quality Act.[43]

The suit seeks a court order prohibiting further development of the mostly federally funded project. It also asks government agencies to prepare new environmental-impact statements on the project to replace the one that allegedly failed to analyze properly the impact on the community. In September, 1993, the parties entered into settlement discussions on this matter.

Houston v. *City of Cocoa* is another example of a case that combined both civil rights and environmental causes of action.[44] In 1989 several residents of an African American community located in Cocoa, Florida, brought a lawsuit challenging the city's plans to rezone, redevelop, and displace their historic neighborhood whose origins went back to the 1880s. The complaint, filed in federal district court against both the city and the Cocoa Redevelopment Agency, combined statutory and constitutional civil rights claims under Title VIII of the Fair Housing Act of 1968; Title VI of the Civil Rights Act of 1964; the Civil Rights Act of 1866; and the Fourteenth Amendment to the Constitution with environmental and historic preservation claims under NEPA and the NHPA.[45]

In addition to the court action, the plaintiffs filed an administrative complaint with the U.S. Department of Housing and Urban Development (HUD). They alleged that the city of Cocoa had violated HUD regulations governing Community Development Block Grant (CDBG) recipients by failing to develop an adequate plan for the relocation of low-income households that would be involuntarily displaced by the expected private development within the redeveloped area.[46]

The defendants moved to dismiss the NEPA and NHPA causes of action alleging that (1) NEPA and NHPA could not apply to the city because it is not a federal agency; (2) NEPA protects only the natural environment; and (3) neither NEPA nor NHPA provided a private right of action. The district court was not persuaded by defendants' interpretation of the reach of these statutes and accordingly, it denied the motion.

The court's decision upholding the claims under NEPA and the NHPA helped lead to a negotiated settlement that included the related HUD complaint. In the end, the African American residents prevailed at protecting their community. Among other things, the city agreed to provide zoning incentives for the development of new low-income housing within the neighborhood, to designate $675,000 of future CDBG grant monies and Redevelopment Agency funds to housing rehabilitation, and to provide grant money to a not-for-profit organization for the development of new owner-occupied low-income housing and a community center. Moreover, in recognition of the historic structures remaining and the significance of the neighborhood to the African American community in Cocoa, the city agreed to designate a section of the neighborhood as a historic district.[47]

CONCLUSION

The African American and other minority residents of communities suffering disproportionately from environmental degradation are entitled to equal protection under the law, and many of them are waging a campaign for environmental justice. That movement includes public education and community organizing, lobbying and legislative activities, civil disobedience and other forms of protest, and litigation.

On the litigation front, the pursuit of environmental justice will require diligence and persistence. A number of scholars and practitioners have asserted that current evidentiary barriers are too high under the Constitution and some civil rights statutes to allow redress in all but the most egregious circumstances. Thus, as one legal scholar has observed, it may "require reform of some civil rights laws to facilitate the bringing of racial discrimination claims."[48]

No citizen should live in an environment that is life-threatening. Concerned individuals and groups will therefore continue to lobby for statutory and legislative reform in order to protect all communities, no matter the color or class, from the degenerative effects of industrial waste and pollution. Attorneys for poor and minority communities must help ensure that these, the most disadvantaged, do not continue to bear a disproportionate share of society's waste.

NOTES

The author is grateful for permission to reprint excerpts from "Environmental Justice: New Civil Rights Frontier," *Trial*, July 1993, and "'Environmental Racism': Fact or Fiction?" *Environmental Law*, ABA (quarterly newsletter of the Standing Committee on Environmental Law) 12 (Fall/Winter 1992–93). Alice L. Brown, assistant counsel at the NAACP Legal Defense and Educational Fund, has been counsel on several of the cases discussed in this chapter. The author wishes to thank Angela Johnson, Bill Lann Lee, Kevin Lyskowski, and Brenda Sutton for their helpful comments and suggestions.

1. The Reverend Benjamin F. Chavis, Jr., Foreword to *Confronting Environmental Racism: Voices from the Grassroots*, ed. Robert D. Bullard (Boston: South End Press, 1993). Dr. Benjamin F. Chavis is an ordained minister and a veteran of the civil rights movement. From April 1993 to August 1994 he served as executive director and chief executive officer of the National Association for the Advancement of Colored People (NAACP). From 1985 to 1993 he was the executive director of the United Church of Christ's Commission for Racial Justice.

2. Robert D. Bullard and Beverly Hendrix Wright, "Environmentalism and the Politics of Equity: Emergent Trends in the Black Community," *Mid-American Review of Sociology* 21 (1987): 32.

3. *NAACP v. Gorsuch*, No. 82-768-CIV-5 (E.D.N.C. Aug. 10, 1982). A federal district court rejected a constitutional challenge to the proposed siting of the PCB facility. The court "denied the plaintiffs' request for preliminary injunctive relief, concluding that there was 'little likelihood that plaintiffs will prevail on the merits.' According to the court, 'There is not one shred of evidence that race has at any time been a motivating factor for any decision taken by any official—state, federal or local—in this long saga.'" Richard J. Lazarus, "Pursuing 'Environmental Justice': The Distributional Effects of Environmental Protection, *Northwestern University Law Review* 87 (1993): 787, 832 (quoting Gorsuch).

4. Karl Grossman, "Environmental Racism," *Crisis*, April 1991, 14, 16.

5. Bullard and Wright, "Environmentalism and the Politics of Equity," 32.

6. U.S. General Accounting Office, *Siting of Hazardous Waste Landfills and Their Correlation with Racial and Economic Status of Surrounding Communities*, GAO/RCEO-83-168 (Washington, D.C.: General Printing Office, 1983).

7. Grossman, "Environmental Racism," 16.

8. Matthew Rees, "The Birth of 'Eco-racism' Black and Green," *New Republic*, March 2, 1992, 15.

9. Tom Arrandale, "Are Minorities Target of 'Environmental Racism'?" *The Island Packet*, March 2, 1992.

10. See Vicki Been, "What's Fairness Got to Do with It? Environmental Justice and the Siting of Locally Undesirable Land Uses," *Cornell Law Review* 5 (1993): 1001, 1011–12.

11. Robert D. Bullard, "Solid Waste Sties and the Black Houston Community," *Sociological Inquiry* 53 (1983): 273.

12. Paul Mohai and Bunyan Bryant, "Environmental Racism: Reviewing the Evidence," in *Race and the Incidence of Environmental Hazards: A Time for Discourse*, ed. Bunyan Bryant and Paul Mohai (Boulder, Colo.: Westview Press, 1992), 163, 172; Harvey L. White, "Hazardous Waste Incineration and Minority Communities," in *Race and the Incidence of Environmental Hazards*, 126, 132.

13. The Comprehensive Environmental Response, Compensation and Liability Act of 1980 (Superfund of CERCLA), was enacted by Congress in response to the discovery of "abandoned" hazardous waste sites, such as Love Canal in New York State. The 1980 statute established a $1.6 billion fund to address the need to clean up abandoned hazardous waste sites. In 1986 Congress adopted the Superfund Amendments and Reauthorization Act, which, among other things, increased the fund to $8.5 billion.

14. "Unequal Protection: The Racial Divide in Environmental Law," *National Law Journal*, September 21, 1992, S1.

15. "Unequal Protection," S1.

16. U.S. Bureau of the Census, Statistical Abstract of the United States, 1991, 111th ed. (Washington, D.C. 1991), Table 748 ("Persons below Poverty Level, by Race, Hispanic Origin, Age and Region: 1989").

17. Centers for Disease Control, Department of Health and Human Services, *Preventing Lead Poisoning in Young Children* (Atlanta, Ga.: The Centers, 1991).

18. Centers for Disease Control, *Preventing Lead Poisoning*. See also Karen L. Florini et al., *Legacy of Lead: America's Continuing Epidemic of Childhood Lead Poisoning* (Washington, D.C.: Environmental Defense Fund, 1990).

19. Grossman, "Environmental Racism," 32.

20. Charles Lee, "Beyond Toxic Wastes and Race," in *Confronting Environmental Racism: Voices from the Grassroots*, ed. Robert D. Bullard (Boston: South End Press, 1993), 41, 51–52.

21. *Bean* v. *Southwestern Waste Mgmt. Corp.*, 482 F. Supp. 673 (S.D. Tex. 1979), aff'd mem., 782 F.2d 1038 (5th Cir. 1986).

22. *Washington* v. *Davis*, 426 U.S. 229 (1976); *Village of Arlington Heights* v. *Metro. Hous. Dev. Corp.*, 429 U.S. 252 (1977). In *Arlington Heights*, the Supreme Court articulated a five-part test for conducting an equal protection analysis: (1) the impact of the official action and if it "bears more heavily on one race than another"; (2) the historical background of the decision; (3) the series of events prior to the decision, which could reveal the decision maker's purpose; (4) any departures, substantive or procedural, from the normal decision making process; and (5) the legislative and administrative history of the decision (429 U.S. at 266–68). The quotation is from *Bean*, 482, F. Supp. at 677 (emphasis added).

23. *Bean*, 482 F. Supp at 681, 680.

24. *R.I.S.E., Inc.* v. *Kay*, 768 F. Supp. 1144, 1149 (E.D. Va. 1991), aff'd without op., 977 F.2d 573 (4th Cir. 1992).

25. *R.I.S.E., Inc.* v. *Kay*, at 1150.

26. *East Bibb Twiggs Neighborhood Association* v. *Macon-Bibb County Planning and Zoning Com'n.*, 706 F. Supp. 880 (M.D. Ga. 1989), aff'd, 896 F.2d 1264 (11th Cir. 1989); *NAACP* v. *Gorsuch*, No. 82-768-CIV-5 (E.D.N.C. Aug. 10, 1982).

27. 42 U.S.C. §§ 7401-7671(a) (Supp. II 1991); 33 U.S.C. § 1251 et seq. There are also numerous state law analogues to these federal statutes.

28. James F. Simon, "Citizen Suits for Environmental Enforcement," *Trial*, September 1991, 30.

29. *Matthews* v. *Coye*, No. C-90-3620 EFL (N.D. Cal. settled Oct. 16, 1991). The Medicaid Act, 42 U.S.C. § 1396d(r)(1)(1992), provides that Medicaid "screening services . . . shall at a minimum include laboratory tests (including blood lead level assessment appropriate for age and risk factors)." Guidelines relevant at the time required states to "screen all Medicaid-eligible children ages 1–5 for lead poisoning. . . . Children with lead poisoning require diagnosis and treatment, which include periodic reevaluation and environmental evaluation to identify the sources of lead." Health Care Financing Administration, Department of Health and Human Services, *State Medicaid Manual*, § 5123.2D (incorporating 1990 revisions).

30. *Matthews*, No. C-90-3620 EFL.

31. See *Ellis* v. *Wetherbee*, No. S92-0529 (R)(R) (S.D. Miss. filed Apr. 9, 1993); *Denver Action for a Better Community* v. *Colo.* (case not reported by Federal District Court). These two cases were mooted by the settlement in *Thompson* v. *Raiford*.

32. *Thompson* v. *Raiford*, No. CIV-3:92-CV-1539-R (N.D. Tex.)

33. Robert Pear, "U.S. Orders Testing of Poor Children for Lead Poisoning," *New York Times*, September 13, 1992, 42.

34. Health Care Financing Administration, Department of Health and Human Services, *Guidelines*, October 1993, 5123.2(D)(1).

35. 42 U.S.C. § 300j-24(d)(1) (West supp. 1993).

36. *Colorado Envtl. Coalition* v. *Romer*, Civ. No. 92-B-625 (D. Colo. Apr. 3, 1992). In a subsequent memorandum and order, the court held that the plaintiffs were the prevailing party and were entitled to reasonable costs and attorney fees. *Colorado Envtl. Coalition* v. *Romer*, 796 F. Supp. 457 (D. Colo. 1992).

37. See Evelyn A. Mauss et al., *The Lead Contamination Control Act: A Study in Non-Compliance* (Washington, D.C.: Natural Resources Defense Council, 1991).

38. See James H. Colopy, "The Road Less Traveled: Pursuing Environmental Justice through Title VI of the Civil Rights Act of 1964," *Stanford Environmental Law Journal* 13 (February 1994); and Lazarus, "Pursuing 'Environmental Justice,'" 834–39.

39. 42 U.S.C. § 2000d (1989).

40. *Guardians Ass'n.* v. *Civil Serv. Comm'n.*, 463 U.S. 582 (1983) (Stevens, J., dissenting) (agreeing that regulations with an "effects" standard are valid means of effectuating Title VI).

41. No. C93-0721VRW (N.D. Cal. filed Mar. 3, 1993).

42. Complaint for Declaratory and Injunctive Relief, at 31.

43. 42 U.S.C. § 4321 (1988); 23 U.S.C. §§ 109(a),(d),(h),(i) (1988); 23 U.S.C. § 128 (1988); 49 U.S.C. § 303(c) (1988); 42 U.S.C.A. § 7506(c) (West Supp. 1992); 16 U.S.C. § 470 (1988); CAL. PUB. RES. CODE § 21000 (Deering 1987).

44. *Houston* v. *City of Cocoa*, No. 89-92-CIV-ORL-19 (M.D. Fla., order dated December 22, 1989).

45. 42 U.S.C. §§ 3601 et seq. (1988); 42 U.S.C. § 2000d (1989); 42 U.S.C. §§ 1981 et seq. (1988); 42 U.S.C. §§ 4321 et seq. (1988); 16 U.S.C. §§ 470 et seq. (1988).

46. 30 C.F.R. Part 570.306. See Karl S. Coplan, "Protecting Minority Communities with Environmental, Civil Claims," *New York Law Journal*, August 20, 1991, 1.

47. Coplan, "Protecting Minority Communities," 1.

48. Lazarus, "Pursuing 'Environmental Justice,'" 857.

PART

V

IDEALS AND COSTLY COMPROMISES

TWO PERSPECTIVES ON
THE BICENTENNIAL OF THE CONSTITUTION

A. LEON HIGGINBOTHAM, JR.

FUNDAMENTAL RIGHTS
AND THE CONSTITUTION

A HEAVENLY DISCOURSE

This chapter explores the theme "African Americans and the Evolution of the Living Constitution" from a slightly different perspective from that of philosophers, political scientists, and historians. To my knowledge, the medium I shall use has never been used before. I call it "a heavenly discourse."

Heaven is populated with so many souls of the departed that they stretch in countless numbers. If we could hear their voices, they would be mingled in a great, unintelligible babel of sound. A single conversation out of these millions that would be particularly interesting to those of us concerned with the living Constitution would be about the strengths and deficiencies in the original Constitution; the kind of job done by framers of the Constitution; and the most enduring values in the Constitution in its present form, including all the post–Civil War amendments.

Some of the Founding Fathers would be in the group debating these issues—including Thomas Jefferson, who though not present at the Constitutional Convention may certainly be regarded as a Founding Father—and from more recent times, perhaps Martin Luther King, Jr. Were we to look in on them, we might hear King saying that this is a golden opportunity to ask some rather pointed questions of the paradoxical Thomas Jefferson, author of the famous Declaration of Independence and owner of slaves; proponent of human dignity, yet believer in racial inferiority. The conversation might go something like this:

King: Good Evening Mr. Jefferson. May I join you?

Jefferson: Please do. I don't seem to recognize you, though your face is familiar. Have we ever met? Are you from Senegal, or Ghana, or somewhere else in Africa? I have been here for 160 years; to be precise, it will be 162 years in July of 1988, and know most of the older residents here. So you must be one of the later arrivals.

King: Yes, I am. My presence here was prompted a bit sooner than originally scheduled, due to an unfortunate incident at the Lorraine Motel in Memphis, Tennessee. My name is Martin Luther King.

Jefferson: Oh, yes, of course I know you. We were just beginning to receive television broadcasts when you were doing your work on Earth, and I followed your activities very closely. I was greatly moved by your March-on-Washington speech in 1963—it was more eloquent than anything I ever heard while I was on Earth—better than anything Patrick Henry or Benjamin Franklin or, indeed even myself, ever said.

King: Thank you, Mr. Jefferson. I value your praise very highly. While I was alive, I read most of the things you had written, as well as the works of others living in the revolutionary period. Now that I am here among you, I appreciate the opportunity to meet and talk with persons such as yourself who had such a profound impact upon America's political beginnings.

Jefferson: Martin, I have great admiration for what you did, too, to bring more justice to America. Yet it's strange that even though you have been here for almost two decades, we've never had the opportunity to talk before. There is really no good reason for it. There's no segregation in Heaven, no North or South, no "separate but [un]equal" here. If it had not been for that broadcast from the Smithsonian in Washington, where they are holding that Conference on African Americans and the Evolution of a Living Constitution, we may still never have met.

King: I have always wanted to meet you, Mr. Jefferson, because I believe that in our lifetimes we shared in some respects a common theoretical ideology, although our pursuit of that ideology was based on far different priorities. And there are similarities in our backgrounds. Both of us grew up in the South. But when I got to Heaven, my first priority was to seek out people here who were opponents of racism and proponents of racial justice.[1] For example, one of my closest friends here has been Mahatma Gandhi, with whom I have spent thousands of hours talking about the power of the nonviolent movement as a liberating force in the world.

I also spend a great deal of time with young people who have come here recently. Young men and women like Stephen Biko, who died in the struggle for freedom in South Africa. Sometimes I visit the more senior people in Heaven, like Sojourner Truth, Harriet Tubman, and Frederick Douglass. I also talk frequently to Ralph Bunche, the Nobel Laureate, who forty years ago was concerned about peace in the Middle East, and about the survival of *both* Israel and the Palestinians. We wonder, after all these intervening years, why peace in that area seems even less probable than Ralph envisioned it in 1949.

I also take time out to talk to old comrades of the 1950s and 1960s, like Mary McLeod Bethune, Roy Wilkins, Clarence Mitchell, Sr., and Whitney Young.

But Mr. Jefferson—Tom (may I call you Tom, now that we are true equals in Heaven together?)—I sought you out tonight because there are many perplexing questions in my mind to which you might have answers.

Jefferson: I'll be glad to help in any way I can.

King: Because you did not at first recognize me, you asked me if I were from Senegal or Ghana or some other African country. No, Tom, I am from America—*your* America, the America created by you and the other Founding Fathers when you hammered out our Constitution by adopting compromise after compromise, some of them very costly indeed to people of my race. We are Americans just like you, Tom, though in your time we were bound in lifelong slavery to you and people like you. Even later, while free, we were doomed to suffer all our lives from the pernicious evils of racist discrimination that were all but built into the Constitution and legal systems of the America you and the other Founders brought forth.

I mentioned that I grew up in the South. I also spent most of my adult years in the South. (Those years were few compared with yours, Tom—my thirty-nine against your eighty-three.) I lived and worked in Atlanta, Georgia, and Montgomery, Alabama. I traveled extensively in the South, visiting places like Selma and Birmingham, Alabama, and my last stop at Memphis, Tennessee. During my travels, I preached the doctrine you yourself expounded in the Declaration of Independence—one about all men being created equal. I don't know whether you meant it when you wrote it, but when I preached it, I did mean it.

Jefferson: What makes you think I didn't mean it, Martin?

King: Because when I went out among the people, the people of *your* America, Tom, those people who celebrate the Fourth of July as the anniversary of your great document, the Declaration of Independence—when I talked to those Americans, and urged them to treat all men and women with dignity, often I was attacked by police dogs, had fire hoses turned on me, and was even imprisoned, all in the name of the law and by officers of the law, such as Sheriff Eugene "Bull" Connor in Birmingham. In the North, it was much the same. I was spat upon in Cicero, Illinois, when I talked about equality; called a "nigger" almost everywhere; and even in Harlem, I was stabbed by a deranged black person.

So much for your brand of equality, Tom. When I was in a Birmingham jail, I wrote my own Declaration of Independence—not against a foreign ruler as you did, but against officials of my own native land: American presidents, American governors, American sheriffs, and in fact against American law. And again, unlike you Tom, I did not urge violence, the creation of armies, or the killing of my enemies. I spoke always on the principles and precepts of nonviolence, even against those who despised me most. I wanted no armed resistance against George Wallace of Alabama, or against Ross Barnett of Mississippi, or even against the officers and members of the Ku Klux Klan.

Jefferson: Martin, all the adversaries you mentioned (except one) are white people; and by implication, even I am an adversary. Since you are familiar with my writings, you must be aware that in my later years I did have serious misgivings about the institution of slavery.[2] Haven't there been any white people joining you in your crusade to secure social justice for your race and for other minorities?

King: Of course, Tom, I have been joined by many, many white people who believe in the importance of human dignity, the commonality of needs, and the brotherhood of all persons. Here in Heaven, I seek out those whites who made an effort during their lifetime to bring about racial equality. Many of them lived after your time on Earth, Tom, so maybe you haven't heard of them. I'll tell you about some of them.

Jefferson: Please do, Martin. I would very much like to discuss these constitutional issues with them.

King: Well, one of the first persons I went looking for when I first got to Heaven was William Lloyd Garrison, an abolitionist and editor of a newspaper called *The Liberator.* Unlike James Madison and other designers of our Constitution, Garrison stated unequivocally that the tolerance of slavery or the advocacy of gradual abolition were compromises that he could not accept.

> I will be as harsh as truth, and as uncompromising as justice. On this subject, I do not wish to think, or speak, to write, with moderation. No! no! Tell a man, whose house is on fire, to give a moderate alarm; tell him to moderately rescue his wife from the hands of the ravisher; tell the mother to gradually extricate her babe from the fire into which it has fallen; but urge me not to use moderation in a cause like the present! I am in earnest. I will not equivocate—I will not excuse—I will not retreat a single inch—and I will be heard. The apathy of the people is enough to make every statue leap from its pedestal, and to hasten the resurrection of the dead.[3]

I have also met and talked with Charles Sumner, that great Bostonian and advocate who argued in the 1850 case of *Roberts* v. *Boston,* that there should not be separate schools for whites and blacks. Sumner went on to become an architect of the 1875 civil rights bill, arguing on the floor of the Senate in support of the bill that "in all of our legislation" there should be "no such word as black or white . . . only . . . citizens." I run across John Brown occasionally, and I know he would be interested in joining our discussions. He led a bold raid at Harper's Ferry for the liberation of slaves, and, I submit to you, that raid was as significant in the annals of freedom as George Washington's crossing the Delaware.

Since you know something about me, Tom, I am sure you are aware that I have always been equivocal about lawyers and even more equivocal about judges. But I do from time to time stop by and talk to some of the great judges in America, who, had they been listened to, would have made a profound difference in our society. I meet regularly with John McLean and Benjamin R. Curtis, those justices who dissented in *Dred Scott* and said that under the Constitution black people were citizens and they should be recognized as such. And I talk to William Cushing of Massachusetts, who said in 1783 that slavery could not be tolerated under that state's Bill of Rights.[4] And we can't leave out Justice John Harlan, who dissented in the infamous *Plessy* v. *Ferguson* decision of 1896 and condemned the "separate but equal" sanction for racial discrimination. I think that Justice Harlan's comments are as relevant today as in 1896. You may remember, he said in his dissent:

> In view of the Constitution, in the eye of the law, there is in this country, no superior, dominant, ruling class of citizens. There is no caste here. Our Constitution is color-blind, and neither knows nor tolerates classes among citizens. In respect of civil rights, all citizens are equal before the law. The humblest is the peer of the most powerful. The law regards man as man, and takes no account of surroundings or of his color where his civil rights as guaranteed by the supreme law of the land are involved. It is, therefore, to be regretted that this high tribunal, the final expositor of the fundamental law of the land, has reached the conclusion that it is competent for a State to regulate the enjoyment by citizens of their civil rights solely upon the basis of race.
>
> In my opinion, the judgment this day rendered will, in time, prove to be quite as pernicious as the decisions made by this tribunal in the *Dred Scott* case.[5]

Tom, I know that you were a lawyer, that you attended the distinguished College of William and Mary, and that you studied law under that gifted teacher and signer of the Declaration of Independence, George Wythe. I have to apologize to you, when I say that the majority opinion in *Plessy* v. *Ferguson* has soured me a little against distinguished law schools. Now there was Justice

Harlan, a Southerner from Kentucky, who went to a nondescript law school, Transylvania, but who wrote one of the all-time great eloquent dissents, in *Plessy* v. *Ferguson*. And what was the background of the lawyers who wrote the majority opinion, which said in effect that under the Fourteenth Amendment to the Constitution, you could treat black people differently from the way you treated everyone else? Well, there was Justice Henry B. Brown, a graduate of Harvard and Yale Law Schools. (He picked up his worst law at Harvard.) Then there were two other Harvard Law School alumni, Melville Fuller and Horace Gray, and George Shirus of Yale.[6] None of those four men are here in Heaven, but they might have been, had they joined John Harlan and refused to support the venal doctrine of "separate but equal."

In my own time, and here in Heaven with us, there is the great chief justice of the 1960s civil rights era, Earl Warren, along with John Kennedy and Robert Kennedy, both of whom were murdered, as I was, for trying to make a difference in our native land.

Jefferson: I am truly impressed, Martin, at your wide circle of acquaintance here in Heaven, among all these great people in history.

King: Don't mistake me, Tom. It is true that, during my brief stay on Earth, I was privileged to walk with some of the great people of the world. And now that I am in Heaven, I sometimes seek out those great men and women of the past who made an important impact on the betterment of society. But I am proud to include in my visits around Heaven those many others who have lived and died in obscurity and anonymity, but whose lives have made a profound difference in the pursuit of liberty and justice throughout the world.

I am thinking particularly of all the young men who have died on foreign soil in the several wars we have had since you were president, Tom. Some of these wars were fought for noble causes, and some not so noble. In World War I, our boys marched willingly onto the battlefields of France and to their early graves because they had been assured by President Woodrow Wilson that the war was necessary in order to make the world safe for democracy.

Jefferson: That is a very noble reason to fight, Martin.

King: Yes, Tom, but President Wilson had a distorted concept of democracy. What he wanted was a racist democracy. He wanted a segregated army and a segregated civil service. He made the federal government more racist and discriminatory than anyone had ever done before, or has done subsequently. Further, Wilson was very ambivalent in his judgment of right and wrong: he took swift and decisive military action against the barbarous German regime four thousand miles away, yet at home, in America, even in his own native state of Virginia, he implicitly tolerated the inhuman practice of lynching, by opposing the passage of antilynching laws.

A generation later, Tom, Heaven again had a rapid growth in population when young soldiers, so many scarcely out of boyhood, gave their lives in battle, not only in France, but in Italy, in Africa, and on the faraway islands of the Pacific. Again, they fought willingly, even gladly, because they believed that Hitler was evil, that they must do something to stop the horrors of the Holocaust and the killing of millions more, all done to enforce his immoral theory that Germans were an Aryan super-race who were endowed with the right to dominate all others. These Americans risked their lives in World War II because they believed that we should no longer tolerate a world where people are denigrated, beaten, killed, and deprived of their human rights simply because they are of a different race, religion, or national origin from those who are in power.

Jefferson: No man could die a nobler death than in fighting and for the defeat of the kind of ideology that Hitler represented. As a Christian minister, Martin, you surely hold to that lofty principle.

King: But for many of those veterans who survived, it was a hollow victory, Tom. When they went back to their homes in Mississippi, in Alabama, everywhere in the South, including your own state of Virginia, Tom, many found that they still could not vote, their children were still denied quality education, and that the threats and intimidation of the Ku Klux Klan still carried more weight than the constitutional assurances of equal justice under the law for all citizens of our America.

Jefferson: Yes, Martin, in the 1960s I followed closely the massive resistance pursued by many Southern governors and legislators to oppose the rights decreed by *Brown* v. *Board of Education.* They closed the Prince Edward County public schools in Prince Edward County, Virginia. In fact, I remember the broadcast of one of President John F. Kennedy's stirring speeches in the 1960s, when he said that there were two places in the world where children cannot get a public education—in Vietnam and in Prince Edward County, Virginia.

King: Yes, Tom, they closed down all public schools in that county, rather than integrate the races. So, many African Americans were forced to migrate, just so that their children could be educated, a basic right that parents in all other parts of America and in the world took for granted.

And even in the North, black veterans found they could not get the same housing benefits under the G.I. Bill that other veterans got. They could not take advantage of the opportunity given in that bill to obtain higher education at many of the better universities and colleges because these institutions refused to accept blacks for admission. And many decent, well-paying jobs were closed to blacks because segregation was the rule in most manufacturing, construction, and skilled labor environments. So is it little wonder that many of these World War II veterans began to question whether what they accomplished in the end was really worth risking their lives for.

Jefferson: But, Martin, surely the world as a whole is a better place for the sacrifices of those lives? Tell me frankly, Martin—do you think our "Noble Experiment" called America has been a failure? Do you think the Constitution is a flawed document? How would you evaluate me and my colleagues who tried to build a more perfect union?

King: Tom, I know that many believe that the United States of America is the fairest land that has ever existed and the Constitution the greatest document ever written by man, and that the Founding Fathers were good, sincere men, who wanted only the best for their country. I think that perception was conveyed by Ronald Reagan's statement for the celebration of the bicentennial of the Constitution. As you may remember, he said: "In these two hundred years of our Constitution, you and I stand on the shoulders of giants, men whose words and deeds put wind in the sails of freedom."

I must confess I question some aspects of President Reagan's sentiments—certainly black people in 1787 got no benefit from the "wind in the sails of freedom."

Jefferson: I do think that President Reagan's phrase, "putting the wind in the sails of freedom" does seem rather flowery and ornate. But who am I to talk—I used quite similar expressions in my own writing, when I got carried away in a burst of creative zeal.

King: Tom, you are considered to be America's leading political philosopher. Let me ask you this: which one of your writings and publications do you think did more than any other to "put wind in the sails of freedom"? Or, put another way, since you are uncomfortable with President Reagan's expression: What in your opinion is the most important human rights document you ever wrote?

Jefferson: Well, Martin, you sort of have me on the spot there. In all modesty, I was at the right place at the right time to have a great many of my writings exert considerable influence and direction at the various meetings and conventions of our government, both before its founding and after. So, in all modesty, I believe one is about as significant as the other. Some people believe that the most important human rights document I ever wrote was my major draft of the Declaration of Independence. Others say that it was something I wrote in 1775 called the Declaration of the Causes and Necessities of Taking Up Arms, or my inaugural speech, when I talked about the rights of minorities parties. Why do you ask, Martin?

King (after a long pause): Well, Tom, I am beginning to reflect on many things written during the era when the Constitution was being put together. I remember that you were a prolific writer and I agree with you that almost everything you wrote had significance regarding the direction the Constitution was to take, not only then, but even to the present day. Since you ask me to tell you which of all your writings was the most significant in regard to human rights, I would not choose any that you have mentioned. Instead, I would choose a document that I came across in a book by A. Leon Higginbotham, one of my wife's classmates. I had never seen or heard of this piece of your writing before, but as soon as I read it, I recognized immediately its importance in the area of human rights. This document was published on September 7, 1769, when you were still a very young man, one who was to mature into a distinguished scholar, statesman, adviser to presidents, and ultimately become president. Let me get the book and read the document to you. It is in the form of an advertisement: "Run away from the subscriber in Albemarle, a mulatto slave called Sandy, about 35 years of age, his stature is rather low, inclining to corpulence." Let me stop there. You know, I am constantly amazed by you, Tom—the eloquence with which you write, even in an advertisement, even for describing a slave. Most of my friends at Morehouse would have simply said, "He's short and fat." But you went beyond that. Your way has a real touch of class: "His stature was rather low, inclining to corpulence." But let me go on:

> Whoever conveys the said slave to me in Albemarle shall have 40 shillings rewards, if taken up within the county, 4 pounds if elsewhere within the colony, and 10 pounds if in any other colony.[7]

That, Tom, from my perspective, is perhaps your most important human rights document. It bears your name, the name that is the second signature on the Declaration of Independence for the Virginia delegation, right below that of your great law teacher, George Wythe; the name that appears on many of our nation's most important archival records: treaties, commissions, statutes. That name, "Thomas Jefferson," is also appended to this advertisement for a human being exercising his self-evident right to seek, among other things, his God-given freedom. I submit to you that that advertisement was probably the most important human rights document you ever penned, at least from Sandy's viewpoint and that of his contemporaries and his heirs.

Jefferson: But Martin, it was customary in those days to advertise for runaway slaves.

King: I am not saying that you were unique, or any worse than any other of your fellow plantation owners. Thumbing through Higginbotham's book, I see another advertisement. I'll read it to you:

> Negroes for sale—A Negro Woman, 24 years of age, and her two children, one eight and the other three years old. Said Ne-

groes will be sold separately or together as desired. The woman is a good seamstress. She will be sold low for cash, or exchanged for groceries. For terms apply to Matthew Bliss and Company.[8]

Here is another one:

One hundred and twenty Negroes for sale—the subscriber has just arrived from Petersburg, Virginia, with one hundred and twenty likely young Negroes of both sexes and every description, which he offers for sale on the most reasonable terms. The lot now on hand consists of plough-boys, several likely and well-qualified house servants of both sexes, several women and children, small girls suitable for nurses, and *several small boys without their mothers.* Planters and traders are earnestly requested to give the subscriber a call previous to making purchases elsewhere, as he is enabled to sell as cheap or cheaper than can be sold by any other person in the trade.

—Hamburg, South Carolina,
Benjamin Davis[9]

Now, tell me frankly, Tom—now that we are in Heaven we don't have to be afraid of the consequences of being candid and truthful—how could the United States Constitution have sanctioned a system where a woman who had committed no crime could have her children snatched away from her and sold, the same way your plantation owners sold corn or cotton, or as is said in the advertisement, groceries? How could it have been that you and other revered leaders such as Washington, Madison, and Monroe, tolerated and legitimized this terrible cruelty? How could your compatriot, Patrick Henry, stand in St. John's Episcopal Church on March 23, 1775, and refer to "chains and slavery" as simply a metaphor for political abuses such as taxation without representation, while there existed throughout most of America, and even on his own plantation, a slavery that was very literal, and chains that were very real?

I am reminded of a statement by Samuel Johnson, which Higginbotham quoted in his book. Johnson was getting a little tired of all the rhetoric coming from this side of the Atlantic about "taxation without representation," and he asked: "How is it that we hear the loudest yelps for liberty from among the drivers of Negroes?" He summed up the colonists' argument (your argument for independence, Tom) as "too foolish for buffoonery and too wild for madness."[10]

But I don't want to deviate too far from a specific and direct question I want to pose especially to you, Tom. How do you justify your condemnation of King George while at the same time you maintained the ownership of 200 slaves? How do you justify Article I, Section 9, of the Constitution, which implicitly sanctioned the international slave trade and the fugitive slave laws? Under these laws, slaves were considered to be nothing more than chattels; they had no more rights than horses, dogs cattle, and any other livestock that could be bought, sold, or slaughtered at the owner's will.

Jefferson: But Martin, aren't you being a little harsh in your judgment? Many of us slaveowners treated our slaves with kindness, even like members of our own families.

King: Well, Tom, I know there were some acts of kindness. When it suited the master's pleasures and purposes, but civilized people don't enslave their family. But most of the time you and your colleagues view the slave solely as a political and economic issue to be exploited for the slave owners' benefit. This is illustrated by the constitutional compromise reached to count the slaves as three-fifths of a person, so that you and other Southerners would have a greater number of representatives in Congress, more power in the Electoral College and thus more power to continue without hindrance the dehumanizing system of slavery. As a matter of fact, it is my understanding that but for the three-fifths clause, you never would have become president.

Jefferson: Martin, I accept your criticism. I admit that there was a lot of hypocrisy. We knew it at the time, but there seemed to be no way we could reconcile our principles of freedom and equality with the economic necessity of continuing the institution of slavery. Because of our failure to do so, maybe none of us slaveholders should ever have been admitted to Heaven.

King: Tom, I have never been in favor of punishing anyone who has been disadvantaged by the culture in which they have been brought up. That is why I worked so hard to get affirmative action and the special point system here. Maybe you don't know what I mean by those terms, so I will explain by telling a story that is going the rounds here in Heaven.

It seems that St. Peter looked over the pool of applicants for entry into Heaven and noticed an extraordinary underrepresentation of certain classes of people. Lawyers in particular were grossly few in number. So he gave lawyers a few extra points, just to put them in the running to be chosen for Heaven. He did the same thing for politicians, rationalizing that over the span of a lifetime, a politician may have done a few good things. So this is how some slaveholders got to Heaven. Even though their overall human rights grade point average was not as good as, say, William Lloyd Garrison's, Frederick Douglass's, Mahatma Gandhi's, Bayard Rustin's, or A. Phillip Randolph's, St. Peter wanted to take into consideration their cultural disadvantages and give them a few extra points to help them qualify for admission to Heaven.

Jefferson: If that was the way I got into heaven, well, I appreciate the little extra pull that got me here. But could it also be that St. Peter recognized that I and others of my generation did not create a system of slavery, we merely inherited it.

King: But, Tom, your forefathers—those who *did* institute the system of slavery in America—did not write that advertisement for the capture of Sandy—you did. And the way you worded that advertisement—it did not sound like you were putting out a report on a lost child. It seemed more like a manhunt for an escaped felon. But I suppose that under the laws that you fashioned in Virginia, Sandy *had* committed a crime, for it was one of the most serious felonies a black could commit in Virginia at that time—stealing himself from his master.

Jefferson: Yes, at that time, that is the way the laws were.

King: I was reading Higginbotham's book, in which your advertisement was quoted. During that time our TV system was running the series by Alex Haley called "Roots." People here were saying how terrible it was that Kunte Kinte's foot was cut off to stop him from running away. But in some ways, Tom, this was an act of mercy, considering the laws of your state of Virginia. After all, under those laws, and under the U.S. Constitution of that time (that is, without the later amendments), Kunte Kinte could have had *both* feet cut off. He could have been castrated. He could even have been killed, without penalty. As a matter of fact, if Kunte had been killed as a runaway slave, his owner would have been reimbursed by the state of Virginia.

Jefferson: I admit, Martin, that those were harsh measures. But the times themselves were harsh. Most of the country was still in a very raw and undeveloped state, and people had to be hard, even cruel, in order to survive.

King: But, Tom, most of the people in America during your lifetime had come of their own volition, or that of their fathers and fore-fathers. It was their personal decision that brought them to what I agree was a harsh and forbidding land. And if they didn't like it, they could always leave for somewhere else, or go back to where they came from. But many others—and I am now refer-ring to my slave ancestors—did *not* leave their homeland by their own choice; and they could *not* leave and return home just by making up their minds to do so. No other group of immi-grants was kidnapped from their homes and families, kept in chains during their boat passage to America, and forcibly de-tained by white masters for the rest of their lives.

No, Tom, your comparison of the hardships suffered by blacks under the slave system to those endured by the early pio-neers in the frontier wilderness simply will not hold. The two en-vironments were as different as night and day. In the one, a per-son was free to reach his or her fullest potential as a human being. In the other, one's very humanity was questioned, deni-grated, or not acknowledged at all, all under the sanction and blessing of the Constitution and legal system of the United States.

For this reason, many blacks were reluctant to celebrate the bi-centennial of the Constitution in its form as ratified in 1787. It is right and proper that those deficiencies be pointed out, for not a few of the troublesome sequels to slavery that persist even today had their foundations in that original Constitution.

Jefferson: Martin, I am glad we are having this discussion. Your viewpoint and insights should have been available to us at our constitu-tional Convention. I do value very highly your thoughts and opinions on this perplexing, long-standing, and almost unsolvable problem involving the conflict between the races, between the helplessness of minorities and the tyranny of the majority.

But it also disturbs me that you put me in an adversarial position. You are drawing selectively from my life and writings to dramatize your point that the Constitution and those who wrote it are not altogether worthy of your wholehearted esteem and respect.

This is a little unfair, Martin, and not like you. Perhaps you are not familiar with some of my less popular writings, such as *Notes on Virginia*. In fact, few scholars, aside from the likes of John Hope Franklin, Benjamin Quarles, Mary Frances Berry, Winthrop Jordan, Daniel Boorstin, and Evelyn Brooks, have given any serious attention and study to my statement on slavery in that book. I can quote the entire section from memory. You may not think my condemnation of slavery was strong enough, but in the context of the times, it took as much courage for me to write it, as it took courage for you to write your Letter from the Birmingham Jail, or your speech for the 1963 March on Washington. Whatever you think of it, at least listen to what I wrote, late one night in my study when I forced myself to come to grips with the question of slavery:

> ... [I]f a slave can have a country in this world, it must be any other in preference to that in which he is born to live and labor for another; in which he must lock up the faculties of his nature, contribute as far as depends on his individual endeavors to the evanishment of the human race, or entail his own miserable condition on the endless generations proceeding from him. With the morals of the people, their industry also is destroyed. For in a warm climate, no man will labor for himself who can make another labor for him. This is so true, that of the proprietors of slaves a very small proportion indeed are ever seen to labor. And can the liberties of a nation be thought secure when we have removed their only firm basis, a conviction in the minds of the people that these liberties are of the gift of God? That they are not to be violated but with his wrath? Indeed I tremble for my country when I reflect that God is just; that his justice cannot sleep forever; that considering numbers, nature and natural means only, a revolution of the wheel of fortune, an exchange of

situation is among possible events; that it may become probable by supernatural interference! The Almighty has no attribute which can take side with us in such a contest.[11]

King: Yes, I am familiar with that passage, and I respect you for having written it. But my point is that you were out of the government, living at Monticello in the year 1782, when you were writing *Notes on Virginia*. Why didn't you present those thoughts and opinions to the Constitutional Convention, where they might have had some influence on the delegates and on the final drafting of the Constitution?

Jefferson: As a matter of fact, I was out of the country in 1787, when the Convention was being held, serving as ambassador to France. But that didn't really matter—others who were there had the same repugnance to slavery. But those views were very unpopular, and given the climate of the times, if anyone tried to force the issue, the Convention would have probably collapsed and we still would not have a Constitution or a Union, even flawed ones.

So, they made compromises, some of which may not be comprehensible to you today. But their hope was to establish a nation that would endure. As tragic as the compromise on slavery was, I believe that it was worth the price, in order to create one nation, the United States of America. For if the colonies had split and there had been a Northern United States and a Southern United States, we would have ended up with a Southern United States where 90 percent of the blacks lived, and I submit that by the present time such a Southern United States would probably not be much different from the current Republic of South Africa. It was the Constitution that made the difference and the binding of the states together in one nation under that Constitution. Without those two elements, slavery in the South would not have been abolished as early as 1865. There would not have been a Civil War because there would have been no Union from which the Southern states could secede. Without the Constitution to begin with, we would not have had the later amendments—the first ten known as the Bill of Rights, and later the Thirteenth, Fourteenth, Fifteenth, and Nineteenth, with the vitality that these measures gave to our society.

King: I agree with you generally, Tom. I speak from experience. Without the protection of the First Amendment, which guaranteed freedom of expression, of the press, and of the right to assemble, my work would have been impossible. My dream for mankind would have died before it had even been born.

You mentioned South Africa—that is a very good example of what happens in a society without a free press. The government there has banned the media from disseminating any information about the cruelties and oppression suffered by blacks and other colored peoples. So the world has no way of knowing precisely what is going on in South Africa. In the absence of international criticism, there seems to be no motivation prodding that government into making positive changes.

But when dogs snarled in Birmingham, and whips cracked in Selma, the news pictures and stories were flashed to Iowa and Nebraska and Utah all across the nation and all over the world. Because of their rights under the First and Fourteenth Amendments the news media were a powerful influence for change, simply by bringing the facts to light.

So I am beginning now to understand the dilemma of your times. The main problem to tackle in the beginning was to bind the individual states into one Union under one flag, one Constitution. Making the Constitution more perfect, smoothing out the rough spots, amending its deficiencies—these would be jobs for the future.

Jefferson: Yes, you understand perfectly. Refining and honing the Constitution was meant to be never-ending. It was written with the view in mind that it would be an evolving document, flexible enough to grow and change as the nation grew and changed. As Justice Benjamin N. Cardozo has written, the Constitution exemplifies "the tendency of a principle to expand itself to the limit of its logic." The genius of the Constitution, and our nation as well, has been the ability to move beyond the original principles and the original vision of those who gathered in 1787, and to cover problems unforeseen at that time concerning freedoms, rights, and privileges of all our citizens. This evolutionary process reflects an inherent and indomitable spirit for justice and liberty that is broader than the limited vision of my generation.

King: I recognized the expansive quality in the Constitution when I
            began my crusade for freedom and justice, Tom.
Jefferson: I am pleased, Martin, that people like you, W. E. B. Du Bois,
            Frederick Douglass, Walter White, Charles Hamilton Houston,
            William Henry Hastie, Thurgood Marshall, and Malcolm X
            pushed America to face up to this unfinished task. It is the bur-
            den of the current generation to use the Constitution to build a
            society where people of all hues are assured dignity and justice,
            and where women, too, can at long last not only be treated seri-
            ously and respectfully, without harassment and impugnment, but
            also develop to the full potential of their talents and abilities.
King: I understand now, Tom, what you meant when you said the
            Founding Fathers had to draft a Constitution that would expand
            to cover problems and issues that could not be foreseen or even
            dreamed of at that time. Who could have dared foretell, in the
            times of Martha Washington and Dolly Madison, harpsichords
            and stately minuets, that there would ever be such a phenome-
            non in our society as lady truck drivers! It would greatly benefit
            the people now on Earth, if they are serious about creating a so-
            ciety that is fairer and more just, if they could also have the ben-
            efit of your wisdom and your hindsight. It is too bad that no one
            on Earth has been able to develop the technology to establish
            electronic and radio contact with Heaven. Tell me, Tom—if you
            were able right now to address the people in the United States,
            what would you tell them?
Jefferson: I would stress that now that the bicentennial celebrations are
            over, Americans should move on. They should not dwell too
            much on the vision of the Founding Fathers or on the world as
            it existed in 1787. Our contributions, important as they were,
            were only a start to what America is now, and a foundation rich
            in its potential for what America someday must be. I would em-
            phasize to the people that they cannot apply our vision mechani-
            cally, for in many ways that vision was flawed and shortsighted.
            It is certainly not a vision to which they should feel bound. In-
            stead, the truly egalitarian spirit of the Thirteenth, Fourteenth,
            Fifteenth, and Nineteenth amendments to the Constitution, and
            the related civil rights acts should be exalted. For without these
            enactments—by which your generation, Martin, repudiated in

part the racism and sexism sanctioned by my generation—many of the rights now held sacred might never have existed.

And Martin, if Earth's outer space technology really was advanced enough to pull in a broadcast from Heaven, I would want to emphasize the importance of studying the lessons of the past in order to recognize where and how mistakes were made. Then I would go on to urge the people not to use those past mistakes as an excuse for hatred or retaliation, or as a basis from which to polarize or further divide the many persons of goodwill who need to work together to build a better society.

I would tell them that in order to do so, they should define the more enduring themes to which the nation must commit itself, not only in the 1990s, but also into the next century and beyond. These themes span from my lifetime, the era of the birth of America, through your lifetime, Martin, and up to the present day. In fact, they are as old as the Talmud, the Koran, and the Sermon on the Mount. These themes draw their value and strength from the depths of a people's hopes and aspirations for a better life. The basic, all-important theme is the need for a society that is totally free from bigotry; where people from all sorts of religious, racial, and ethnic backgrounds can live in dignity and be treated with civility.

When that major priority has been accomplished, other themes could be adopted more easily and naturally. America would become a society where all individuals, including women, could rise to the level of their maximum potential; where children could learn; where governments bow to the dictates of the people, instead of the other way around; where courts dispense justice; where the living and working environments are safe.

King: That's a tall order, Tom—a very ambitious set of priorities on which to ask Americans to set their sights.

Jefferson: But you are no stranger yourself, Martin, to setting ambitious goals and encouraging people to raise their sights a little higher. In one of your last speeches I was impressed with your ringing challenge: "I have the audacity to believe that people everywhere can have three meals a day for their body, education and culture for their minds, and dignity, equality and freedom for their spirits." Those words of yours still have the power to move me, Martin. Your whole life was an inspiration to the American

	people, so much so that your birthday is now celebrated as a national holiday.
King:	If by some means, Tom, we could beam a telecast earthward, one of the first things I would say is that celebrating my birthday is meaningless unless they celebrate also the ideals and attainments of the last two centuries upon which I was able to build my own life and work. I would like for them to celebrate the milestones along the way that mark our progress in the areas of race relations, such as the *Brown* v. *Board of Education* and *Bolling* v. *Sharpe* cases, which determined in 1954 that neither the states nor the federal government could require racial segregation in the public schools of America. I would like to tell them to celebrate the wisdom of those few courageous state judges, such as Chancellor Collins Seitz of Delaware, who ruled, even before the *Brown* case, that Delaware could not provide inferior education to its black students. As a result of his ruling, the public schools in that state were integrated, and black students admitted to the University of Delaware.
Jefferson:	Martin, your deep concern about education reminds me of a very important deficiency in the Constitution. You see, at the time this country was founded, education was not an important priority. The main concerns of the Founding Fathers were things like establishing justice, insuring domestic tranquility, providing for the common defense, and setting up the machinery of government. We could not foresee the supreme importance of mass education in a later age, so we neglected to make any provision for educating children.
	And now, you have probably heard the rumors floating around, reaching even up here to Heaven, that the Supreme Court is preparing to issue a determination that poor children do not have the constitutional right to a quality education. So, if we ever get the chance to communicate directly with the people on Earth, we should warn them that the Supreme Court is a very fragile institution, and they should make sure that only individuals who care deeply about protecting human rights will sit in that great Hall of Justice.
King:	The Supreme Court in the 1950s and 1960s was very helpful in supporting the advancement of blacks, but in other eras it dealt us some severe blows. I am thinking of the unfortunate decisions

in the *Dred Scott* and *Plessy* v. *Ferguson* cases, which represented major setbacks in the cause of freedom and dignity for blacks. The Court can be very ambivalent in the area of human rights, and those rumors, those rumblings on the horizon, seem very ominous to me.

Jefferson: Martin, you may have heard a saying, or watchword, that we in the Revolutionary era used quite often to keep us alert to how fragile our gains really were: "Eternal vigilance is the price of liberty." If the people were firmly committed to that precept, it would make a profound difference in the type of leadership America has, and the kind of society the nation will have in the future.

King: Yes, Tom, I am familiar with that quotation. I have used it often in pep talks to my people when I saw their spirits flag in discouragement and frustration. Sometimes I used Franklin's catchy proverb, too: "We must all hang together or we will surely hang separately." And, Tom, although when I left Earth for Heaven, I left much unfinished business, there was one major feat I did accomplish. In the march on Washington in 1963, without the civil rights leaders, I got together hundreds of thousands of people from all kinds of backgrounds: Jews and Gentiles, Protestants and Catholics, Black and White, rich and poor. I got them to forget their differences for a while and join hands to work together, pray together, and overcome together the barriers to racial justice that seemed so menacing and overpowering.

Jefferson: Those were inspirational times, Martin. It was a thrilling sight to see all those crowds of people marching in demonstrations, hands joined, and singing that moving and inspirational crusade hymn, "We Shall Overcome." What happened to your movement, Martin? I don't hear about demonstrations much any more.

King: In retrospect, Tom, it seems that the major thrust of my endeavors, as they will be remembered in history, was to bring into the glare of publicity all the injustices and indignities suffered by blacks. The marches and demonstrations I organized, the speeches I made, the preaching I did—in fact, almost everything I did, was to sensitize the conscience of the American people, and let them know they had an urgent problem on their hands that they had better do something about. That part of my work for racial justice was fairly well accomplished by the time of my premature entry into Heaven.

My labors have borne fruit, for I understand that many of my old, most intimate comrades during the civil rights struggle have moved on from protesting against the racist policies of yesterday to making the enlightened rainbow policies of tomorrow. I'll tell you about a few of them.

Andrew Young served in the United Nations for a while, and for two terms was mayor of Atlanta. Douglass Wilder was elected lieutenant governor of Virginia and later governor. And then there is, of course, Jesse Jackson. Think of it, Tom—Jesse captured 45 percent of the vote in your Commonwealth of Virginia, and won the Democratic primary. And imagine what Randolph, Madison, and Monroe would think of that event! And along with this flush of success and advancement, think also about this sobering fact: Prior to the 1964 Civil Rights Act, none of these black leaders would have been served a meal in cities of the South like Charlottesville, Virginia, near your estate, Monticello.

So you can see, Tom, that there have been profound changes in the South and in your state of Virginia. The United States is different today from the government you and your colleagues created in 1787. But, as Franklin Roosevelt said in those desperate and dismal depression days of 1932, "Each generation must have its rendezvous with destiny." Your generation had its priorities; my generation had ours; and it is very likely that future generations will have different ones. I believe much will be accomplished by Jesse Jackson and other thoughtful blacks as more Americans become committed to what you proclaimed as a self-evident truth, that all men are created equal. I am reminded of a poem by Langston Hughes, called "Dream of Freedom." It was always such an inspiration for me. Are you familiar with it, Tom?

Dream of Freedom

There's a dream in the land
With its back against the wall
By muddled names and strange
Sometimes the dream is called.

There are those who claim
This dream for theirs alone—
A sin for which, we know
They must atone.

Unless shared in common,
Like sunlight and like air,
The dream will die for lack
Of substance anywhere.

The dream knows no frontier or tongue
The dream, no class or race
The dream cannot be kept secure
In any one locked place.

This dream today embattled,
With its back against the wall
To save the dream for one,
It must be saved for all.[12]

NOTES

1. See James Melvin Washington, ed., *A Testament of Hope: The Essential Writings of Martin Luther King Jr.* (San Francisco: Harper and Row, 1986); David Lewis, *King: A Critical Biography* (Baltimore: Penguin Books, 1970); and Coretta Scott King, *My Life with Martin Luther King Jr.* (New York: Holt, Rinehart and Winston, 1969).

2. Compare Thomas Jefferson, *Notes on the State of Virginia* (Paris: 1784); Julian Boyd, ed., *The Papers of Thomas Jefferson* [to July 4, 1790] (Princeton: 1950–); and Paul L. Ford, ed., *Works of Thomas Jefferson* (New York: 1892–99). See also Daniel T. Boorstin, *The Lost World of Thomas Jefferson* (New York: 1948); and Winthrop D. Jordan, *White over Black* (Chapel Hill: University of North Carolina Press, 1968), chap. 12, "Thomas Jefferson—Self and Society."

3. William Lloyd Garrison, *Selections from the Writings and Speeches of William Lloyd Garrison* (1852; reprint, New York: Negro Universities Press, 1968), 63.

4. See A. Leon Higginbotham, *In the Matter of Color, Race and the Legal Process: The Colonial Period* (New York: Oxford University Press, 1978), 91–97.

5. *Plessy v. Ferguson*, 163 U.S. 537 (1896); Harlan, dissenting.

6. For a more detailed discussion of the impact of Harvard and Yale Law School alumni in *Plessy*, see A. Leon Higginbotham Jr., "The Life of the Law: Values, Commitment, and Craftsmanship," *Harvard Law Review*, 100 (February 1987): 795–816.

7. Leon Higginbotham, *In the Matter of Color*, 478–79, n. 52.

8. Higginbotham, *In the Matter of Color*, 12.

9. Higginbotham, *In the Matter of Color*, 12.

10. Higginbotham, *In the Matter of Color*, 377.

11. See note 2. See also Higginbotham, 383 and, for example, John Hope Franklin, *Racial Equality in America* (Chicago: University of Chicago Press, 1976); and Mary Frances Berry, *Black Resistance/White Law* (Englewood Cliffs, N.J.: Prentice-Hall, 1971).

12. Langston Hughes, "Dream of Freedom" (unpublished poem, ca. April 1964), quoted in *Harvard Law Review* 100 (February 1987): 795.

THURGOOD MARSHALL

RACIAL JUSTICE
AND THE CONSTITUTION

A VIEW FROM THE BENCH

Nineteen Eighty-seven marks the 200th anniversary of the United States Constitution. A commission has been established to coordinate the celebration. The official meetings, essay contests, and festivities have begun.

The planned commemoration will span three years, and I am told 1987 is "dedicated to the memory of the Founders and the document they drafted in Philadelphia."[1] We are to "recall the achievements of our Founders and the knowledge and experience that inspired them, the nature of the government they established, its origins, its character, and its ends, and the rights and privileges of citizenship, as well as its attendant responsibilities."[2]

Like many anniversary celebrations, the plan for 1987 takes particular events and holds them up as the source of all the very best that has followed. Patriotic feelings will surely swell, prompting proud proclamations of the wisdom, foresight, and sense of justice shared by the framers and reflected in a written document now yellowed with age. This is unfortunate—not the patriotism itself, but the tendency for the celebration to oversimplify and overlook the many other events that have been instrumental to our achievements as a nation. The focus of this celebration invites a complacent belief that the vision of those who debated and compromised in Philadelphia yielded the "more prefect Union" it is said we now enjoy.

I cannot accept this invitation, for I do not believe that the meaning of the Constitution was forever "fixed" at the Philadelphia Convention. Nor do I find the wisdom, foresight, and sense of justice exhibited by the framers particularly profound. To the contrary, the government they devised was defective from the start, requiring several amendments, a civil war, and momentous social transformation to attain the system of constitutional government, and its respect for the individual freedoms and human rights, we hold as fundamental today. When contemporary Americans cite "The Constitution," they invoke a concept that is vastly different from what the framers barely began to construct two centuries ago.

For a sense of the evolving nature of the Constitution we need look no further than the first three words of the document's preamble: "We the People." When the Founding Fathers used this phrase in 1787, they did not have in mind the majority of America's citizens. "We the People" included, in the words of the framers, "the whole Number of free Persons."[3] On a matter so basic as the right to vote, for example, Negro slaves were excluded, although they were counted for representational purposes—at three-fifths each. Women did not gain the right to vote for over a hundred and thirty years.[4]

These omissions were intentional. The record of the framers' debates on the slave question is especially clear: The Southern States acceded to the demands of the New England States for giving Congress broad power to regulate commerce, in exchange for the right to continue the slave trade. The economic interests of the regions coalesced: New Englanders engaged in the "carrying trade" would profit from transporting slaves from Africa as well as goods produced in America by slave labor. The perpetuation of slavery ensured the primary source of wealth in the Southern States.

Despite this clear understanding of the role slavery would play in the new republic, use of the words "slaves" and "slavery" was carefully avoided in the original document. Political representation in the lower House of Congress was to be based on the population of "free Persons" in each state, plus three-fifths of all "other Persons."[5] Moral principles against slavery, for those who had them, were compromised, with no explanation of the conflicting principles for which the American Revolutionary War had ostensibly been fought: the self-evident truths "that all men are created equal, that they are endowed by their Creator with certain unalienable Rights, that among these are Life, Liberty and the pursuit of Happiness."[6]

It was not the first such compromise. Even these ringing phrases from the Declaration of Independence are filled with irony, for an early draft of what became that Declaration assailed the King of England for suppressing legislative attempts to end the slave trade and for encouraging slave rebellions.[7] The final draft adopted in 1776 did not contain this criticism. And so again at the Constitutional Convention eloquent objections to the institution of slavery went unheeded, and its opponents eventually consented to a document that laid a foundation for the tragic events that were to follow.

Pennsylvania's Gouverneur Morris provides an example. He opposed slavery and the counting of slaves in determining the basis for representation in Congress. At the Convention he objected that

> the inhabitant of Georgia [or] South Carolina who goes to the coast of Africa, and in defiance of the most sacred laws of humanity tears away his fellow creatures from their dearest connections and damns them to the most cruel bondages, shall have more votes in a Government instituted for protection of the rights of mankind, than the Citizen of Pennsylvania or New Jersey who views with a laudable horror, so nefarious a practice.[8]

And yet Gouverneur Morris eventually accepted the three-fifths accommodation. In fact, he wrote the final draft of the Constitution, the very document the bicentennial will commemorate.

As a result of compromise, the right of the Southern States to continue importing slaves was extended, officially, at least until 1808. We know that it actually lasted a good deal longer, as the framers possessed no monopoly on the ability to trade moral principles for self-interest. But they nevertheless set an unfortunate example. Slaves could be imported, if the commercial interests of the North were protected. To make the compromise even more palatable, customs duties would be imposed at up to ten dollars per slave as a means of raising public revenues.[9]

No doubt it will be said, when the unpleasant truth of the history of slavery in America is mentioned during this bicentennial year, that the Constitution was a product of its times and embodied a compromise that, under other circumstances, would not have been made. But the effects of the framers' compromise have remained for generations. They arose from the contradiction between guaranteeing liberty and justice to all, and denying both to Negroes.

The original intent of the phrase, "We the People," was far too clear for any ameliorating construction. Writing for the Supreme Court in 1857, Chief Justice Roger B. Taney penned the following passage in the *Dred Scott* case, on the issue whether, in the eyes of the framers, slaves were "constituent embers of the sovereignty," and were to be included among "We the People":

We think they are not, and that they are not included, and were not intended to be included. . . . They had for more than a century before been regarded as beings of an inferior order, and altogether unfit to associate with the white race . . . ; and so far inferior, that they had no rights which the white man was bound to respect; and that the negro might justly and lawfully be reduced to slavery for his benefit. . . . [A]ccordingly, a negro of the African race was regarded . . . as an article of property, and held, and bought and sold as such. . . . [N]o one seems to have doubted the correctness of the prevailing opinion of the time.[10]

And so, nearly seven decades after the Constitutional Convention, the Supreme Court reaffirmed the prevailing opinion of the framers regarding the rights of Negroes in America. It took a bloody civil war before the Thirteenth Amendment could be adopted to abolish slavery, though not the consequences slavery would have for future Americans.

While the Union survived the civil war, the Constitution did not. In its place arose a new, more promising basis for justice and equality, the Fourteenth Amendment, ensuring protection of the life, liberty, and property of all persons against deprivations without due process, and guaranteeing equal protection of the laws. And yet almost another century would pass before any significant recognition was obtained of the rights of black Americans to share equally even in such basic opportunities as education, housing, and employment, and to have their votes counted, and counted equally. In the meantime, blacks joined America's military to fight its wars and invested untold hours working in its factories and on its farm, contributing to the development of this country's magnificent wealth and waiting to share in its prosperity.

What is striking is the role legal principles have played throughout America's history in determining the condition of Negroes. They were enslaved by law, emancipated by law, disenfranchised and segregated by law; and, finally, they have begun to win equality by law. Along the way, new constitutional principles have emerged to meet the challenges of a changing society. The progress has been dramatic, and it will continue.

The men who gathered in Philadelphia in 1787 could not have envisioned these changes. They could not have imagined, nor would they have accepted, that the document they were drafting would one day be construed by a Supreme Court to which had been appointed a woman and the descendent of an African slave. "We the People" no longer enslave, but the credit does not belong to the framers. It belongs to those who refused to acquiesce in outdated notions of "liberty," "justice," and "equality," and who strived to better them.

And so we must be careful, when focusing on the events that took place in Philadelphia two centuries ago, that we not overlook the momentous events that followed, and thereby lose our proper sense of perspective. Otherwise, the odds are that for many Americans the bicentennial celebration will be little more than a blind pilgrimage to the shrine of the original document now stored in a vault in the National Archives. If we seek, instead, a sensitive understanding of the Constitution's inherent defects, and its promising evolution through 200 years of history, the celebration of the "Miracle at Philadelphia" will, in my view, be a far more meaningful and humbling experience.[11] We will see that the true miracle was not the birth of the Constitution, but its life, a life nurtured through two turbulent centuries of our own making, and a life embodying much good fortune that was not.

Thus, in this bicentennial year, we may not all participate in the festivities with flag-waving fervor. Some may more quietly commemorate the suffering, struggle, and sacrifice that triumphed over much of what was wrong with the original document, and observe the anniversary with hopes not realized and promises not fulfilled. I plan to celebrate the bicentennial of the Constitution as a living document, including the Bill of Rights and the other amendments protecting individual freedoms and human rights.

NOTES

Remarks at the Annual Seminar of the San Francisco Patent and Trademark Law Association, May 6, 1987, used by permission of Thurgood Marshall, Jr., and the estate of Justice Marshall.

1. Commission on the Bicentennial of the United States Constitution, First Full Year's Report (September 1986), 7.

2. Commission on the Bicentennial of the United States Constitution, First Report (September 17, 1985), 6.

3. U.S. Constitution, Art. 1, § 2 (September 17, 1787).

4. The Nineteenth Amendment (ratified in 1920).

5. U.S. Constitution, Art. 1, § 2 (September 17, 1787)

6. Declaration of Independence (July 4, 1776).

7. See Carl L. Becker, *The Declaration of Independence: A Study in the History of Political Ideas* (New York: Harcourt Brace, 1922), 147.

8. Max Farrand, ed., the Records of the Federal Convention of 1787, vol. 2 (New Haven, Conn., 1911), 222.

9. U.S. Constitution, Art. 1, § 9 (September 17, 1787).

10. *Dred Scott v. Sanford*, 19 How. (60 U.S.) 393, 405, 407–8 (1857).

11. Catherine Drinker Bowen, *Miracle at Philadelphia: The Story of the Constitutional Convention May to September 1787* (Boston: Little, Brown, 1966).

JULIUS L. CHAMBERS

AFTERWORD

RACIAL EQUALITY AND FULL CITIZENSHIP, THE UNFINISHED AGENDA

The modern history of the American Constitution has been, and continues to be, the history of our continuing struggle as a people to ensure equality and protection for citizens and persons within the United States. The effectiveness of the Constitution can be measured by the extent to which that struggle has succeeded in according rights to the historically disadvantaged.

There are still many Americans who are denied equal status and equal protection under the Constitution. Whether the Constitution revives for another bicentennial will depend on whether we can continue a system of fairness and evolution that will extend protection to America's less fortunate—those who for all intent and purpose have been left out of the system.

This, then, is the central theme of these comments. I will focus on four specific points: the legal status of black Americans during colonial times and under the original version of the Constitution; the protection black Americans and other minorities were accorded by the Thirteenth, Fourteenth, and Fifteenth amendments, which changed substantially our legal and constitutional system and history; the continuing protection provided by decisions of courts interpreting those amendments and subsequent congressional legislation; and the way in which civil rights under the Constitution must continue to evolve through decisions, apart from overreliance on "original intent." Finally, I will suggest what these efforts might portend for the future.

THE COLONIAL PERIOD

Any consideration of the Constitution ought to begin with an examination of the sentiments expressed in the Declaration of Independence. These represented the ideals of the American revolutionaries and reflected the principles that would underlie the establishment of a new government. Judge A. Leon Higginbotham, Jr., in his brilliant and seminal work, *In the Matter of Color, Race and the Legal Process: The Colonial Period*, points out that our "first statement as a nation" was that "all men are created equal." That fundamental claim, he wrote, "created a document that put moral demands on all Americans who would ever quote it. . . . By its very language, the Declaration of Independence introduced to a nation, from its inception, the problem of a 'moral overstrain,' a burden from which it has ever since suffered in varying degrees."[1] The discrepancy between our stated ideal of equality for all and the reality of unequal treatment for blacks carried over into the creation of the Constitution and continues to this day.

The framers of the Constitution intended to create a free, fair, and open society in which citizens (as then defined) would participate fully in their own governance and would have a chance to contribute to the nation's growth and well-being. In the words of Judge Higginbotham, the Constitution was designed to "protect the rights of individuals against the will of the government and the whim of the majority." The framers sought to devise a government ruled by law, with constitutional protection and guarantees for the rights and privileges accorded "citizens of the states."[2]

The rights incorporated in the original document, however, extended only to white males, and, for some purposes, only to white males who owned property. The Constitution as written and ratified two hundred years ago stated expressly that black people were to be counted as three-fifths of a person, and only for the purpose of apportioning congressional seats in the new government's congress. Blacks were considered chattel, not persons, and had no legal rights. Women were also excluded from the enumerated rights and privileges.

The Constitution sanctioned slavery and allowed for the unequal treatment of "free" blacks in language that was adopted, not as an afterthought, nor by omission, but as an affirmative act. To be sure, abolition was given lip service by many of the framers, but when it became a choice between abolishing slavery or protecting the economic interests of the majority, property interests won out.

Constitutional support of slavery found further expression in numerous state and federal court rulings. In 1829, a North Carolina court declared in

State v. *Mann* that the "purpose of the legal system was to convince each slave that he had 'no will of his own [and that he must surrender] his will in implicit obedience to that of another. . . . The power of the master must be absolute to render the submission of the slave perfect."[3] The court refused to recognize that slaves had legal recourse, no matter how harsh their treatment: "We cannot allow the right of the master to be brought into discussion in the courts of justice. The slave, to remain a slave, must be made sensible that there is no appeal from his master, that his power is in no instance usurped; but is conferred by the laws of man at least, if not by the law of God."

The view that blacks had no rights under the Constitution was embraced by the Supreme Court in *Dred Scott* v. *Sanford* in 1857.[4] Chief Justice Roger Taney, speaking for the majority, held, first, that no blacks could be citizens of the United States or of the individual states "within the meaning of the constitution"; and, second, that Congress had no power to exclude slavery from federal territories. The decision declared unconstitutional the Missouri Compromise and all other federal legislation embodying the exclusion of slavery.

Although the Supreme Court eventually overturned the *Dred Scott* decision, and the nation fought a war over it, it is impossible to underestimate the long-term effect it has had in denying equal rights to blacks. The spirit of *Dred Scott* lived on in the Jim Crow laws that saw emancipation replaced with legally enforced segregation and discrimination.[5]

THE CIVIL WAR AMENDMENTS

"We cannot escape history," Abraham Lincoln said in his message to Congress on December 1, 1862. "The fiery trial through which we pass will light us down in honor or dishonor to the latest generation." Soon thereafter, in 1863, Lincoln promulgated the Emancipation Proclamation, the first official recognition of the humanity of black people by the government of the United States. It was the Thirteenth Amendment, ratified in 1865, however, that abolished slavery.[6] Three years later, the Fourteenth Amendment, which conferred citizenship upon blacks, was enacted. In 1870, the Fifteenth Amendment prohibited denial of black men's right to vote on the basis of race, color, or previous condition of servitude, eighty-three years after the Constitution was adopted.

The post–Civil War congress passed a series of bills designed to implement the Civil War amendments. By 1866, seven statutes creating special preferences in programs for blacks had been passed, and the Freedmen's Bureau was created to administer the programs.[7] It is important to recall, for later discussions about affirmative action and race-conscious remedies, that the legislative history of the Fourteenth Amendment and of the post–Civil War statutes clearly demonstrates that congress contemplated and expressly authorized such remedies.[8] Congress then, like civil rights advocates today, recognized the need for legislation and other efforts designed and expressly limited to individuals and groups who had been affected by past discriminatory practices.

The post–Civil War legislation was consistent with the objectives of Congress in enacting the Fourteenth Amendment.[9] In addition to establishing national citizenship, the amendment ensured equality of treatment and due process of law for all citizens; it imposed an affirmative obligation on the part of the federal government to ensure that the rights provided by the amendment were extended to all citizens; finally, Congress intentionally used vague terms—"equal protection" and "due process"—in describing the rights established in order to leave to the courts the final determination of what those rights entailed.[10]

In early decisions following passage of the Fourteenth Amendment, the Supreme Court generally gave a broad construct to the equal protection clause.[11] Before *Plessy* v. *Ferguson*, the Court struck down a statute requiring the exclusion of blacks from juries in *Strauder* v. *West Virginia*, decided in 1880.[12] The Court held that the "law in the States shall be the same for the black as for the white." In *The Civil Rights Cases* in 1883, however, the Court limited the reach of the Fourteenth Amendment and the Civil Rights Act of 1875 to governmental practices: "[the Thirteenth and Fourteenth Amendments do] not guard against private wrongs; the redress for such wrongs must be provided by state laws."[13] But later, in 1886, in *Yick Wo* v. *Hopkins*, the Court held that a municipal licensing ordinance, though neutral on its face, was unconstitutional because its enforcement resulted in discrimination against Chinese laundry operators.[14]

The Court was becoming increasingly conservative, however, and later decisions began to limit further the reach of the Fourteenth Amendment, a trend that culminated in the Court's 1896 decision in *Plessy* v. *Ferguson*, which replaced the broad egalitarian sweep of the equal protection clause with the "separate but equal" doctrine. In giving the Court's opinion in *Plessy*, Justice Henry B. Brown wrote:

> The object of the [Fourteenth] amendment was undoubtedly to enforce the absolute equality of the two races before the law, but in the nature of things it

could not have been intended to abolish distinctions based upon color, or to
endorse social, as distinguished from political, equality, or commingling of the
two races upon terms unsatisfactory to either. . . . If one race be inferior to
the other socially, the Constitution of the United States cannot put them on
the same plane.[15]

Plessy kept alive the legal apartheid that had followed emancipation and again
gave constitutional force to laws, customs, and practices that effectively denied blacks all civil rights. There were no serious challenges to *Plessy* until
the 1930s.[16]

THE ROLE OF THE SUPREME COURT

The debate on how to attack *Plessy* under the Constitution began in earnest
in the civil rights community in the 1930s when lawyers for the National
Association Advancement of Colored People (NAACP) made plans to challenge separate schools in the South. A legal strategy was laid out in a report
prepared by Nathan Margold in which he recommended that instead of bringing cases to require equal spending by states and localities for segregated
black and white public schools in every Southern state, segregation itself
should be challenged immediately and directly. This strategy, however, was
rejected after Margold's 1933 notification of his decision to accept an appointment as solicitor of the Department of the Interior and the 1934 recommenda-
tion of Charles Hamilton Houston, a black Harvard-trained law school vice-
dean at Howard University and the first special counsel of the NAACP, that
a different strategy be developed and implemented. Emphasizing a protracted
struggle that would engage black people in their local communities, arouse
their will to struggle, and lay a foundation of precedents for a decision by the
Supreme Court declaring racial segregation unconstitutional, Charles Houston presented a compelling argument to the NAACP. He, therefore, with
black and white lawyers from across the nation litigating local or state cases
and his assistant counsel, Thurgood Marshall, laboring relentlessly on appeals,
systematically prosecuted cases to disestablish constitutional support for "separate but equal."[17] The strategy was ultimately successful when the Court
ruled in the landmark case *Brown* v. *Board of Education* that the "separate-but-
equal" doctrine was unconstitutional.[18]

Brown did not occur in a vacuum. A series of successful challenges that had
been brought against state graduate schools in Maryland, Missouri, Okla-

homa, and Texas in the 1930s and 1940s for failure to provide equal educational opportunities for black students set the stage for *Brown*.[19] The Supreme Court's 1938 *Gaines* ruling held that the University of Missouri, which had offered to pay Lloyd Gaines's tuition to an out-of-state school, had to admit him to its white law school.[20] In 1948 the Court ordered the University of Oklahoma to admit Ada Lois Sipuel to its law school.[21] In two 1950 decisions, the Court overturned an attempt of the University of Texas to create a "Texas Law School for Negroes" in four basement rooms, rather than admit Heman Sweatt to its law school; the same day the Justices ruled illegal the University of Oklahoma's segregation of G. W. McLaurin from white students attending the Graduate School of Education.[22] Within these cases evolved the redefinition of "equal protection" and the broad legal framework that culminated in the historic *Brown* ruling.

The important point here is that within our constitutional framework and judicial review, the Constitution reached out to right an egregious wrong, to recognize a developing America, and to extend meaningful protection to a disadvantaged group of citizens. This effort, though not then complete and not even complete today, permitted our constitutional democracy to work and to continue to operate.

Brown led ultimately to the dismantling of the entire structure of Jim Crow laws that had regulated every aspect of the life of black people in America: movement, marriage, work, education, housing, even death and burial. In turn, *Brown* and subsequent decisions expanding the obligation of government to provide equal educational opportunity for blacks, enabled the courts to advance the rights of other minorities and women. That process has continued to date.

A 1976 Supreme Court ruling affecting Chinese-speaking school children in San Francisco, *Lau* v. *Nichols*, held that the school district was obligated to provide students a *meaningful* education even if it meant conducting lessons in Chinese.[23] Today, bilingual education is an accepted legal principle.

Plyler v. *Doe*, a 1982 Texas case, established that children of illegal aliens had a constitutional right to a public education, since other children in the state were provided a similar education.[24] We have thereby expanded the concept of the right to an education.[25]

In 1979, women benefited from the Court's ruling in *Cannon* v. *University of Chicago*, which opened the door for private individuals to bring suit to enforce Title IX, the congressional statute mandating equal educational opportunity for women.[26]

A ruling in 1985 dealing with the city of Cleburne's use of residential zoning laws to prohibit housing for retarded persons was held to constitute a denial of equal protection; by extension the ruling has implications for educational opportunity for the mentally handicapped.[27]

There has been movement to establish constitutional protection against disparate treatment of the poor based on their economic status. This is an area of emerging constitutional law that will have tremendous impact on civil rights. Just as *Brown* took aim at the "separate-but-equal" doctrine embodied in *Plessy*, the target of the 1980s and 1990s is a 1973 Supreme Court decision, *San Antonio School District* v. *Rodriguez*, which held that it was not a violation of the Constitution for the state of Texas to allow unequal funding among school districts based on the economic status of the districts or the students residing within the districts.[28] In *Papasan* v. *Allain*, the Court significantly liberalized the *Rodriguez* ruling, deciding that a claim against the state of Mississippi challenging the difference in funding of school districts within the state, might establish a violation of equal protection of the law under the Fourteenth Amendment.[29]

Congress has also responded to the momentum created by *Brown*—and the civil rights movement—by passing the Civil Rights Act of 1964, the Voting Rights Act of 1965, 1970, 1972, 1982, and 1991, the fair housing law of 1968, the Civil Rights Restoration Act of 1988, and other legislation that extended protection to disadvantaged groups.[30]

Progress peaked in the 1970s. In the 1990s, civil rights groups and their supporters are committing most of their resources simply to hold the line. Since the Reagan administration in the 1980s, officials of government have undertaken a major effort to halt civil rights progress and reverse past gains. The Justice Department's attack is broadly based: It seeks to undermine established civil rights standards for defining discrimination, consistently challenges the legality of effective remedies, and undertakes legal challenges to civil rights enforcement procedures. This effort not only aims to halt the thrust for equity and equality that gained impetus in 1954 with *Brown* v. *Board of Education* but also to undermine our constitutional system of government. It remains to be seen what the Justice Department under President Bill Clinton will accomplish in the area of civil rights.

THE DANGERS OF THE "ORIGINAL INTENT" DOCTRINE

If the Constitution is to serve us through a second bicentennial, it must continue the evolution that began with its adoption and continued with the ratification of the post–Civil War amendments, the decision in *Brown*, and the passage of the civil rights legislation of the 1960s, 1970s, and 1980s.

This evolutionary process came under an attack led principally by the attorney general of the United States and the Department of Justice under Ronald Reagan and George Bush. The advent of the Reagan administration in 1981 saw a determined assault on civil rights. School desegregation has been attacked as an unwanted invasion of the rights of parents and children. Instead, the Department of Justice would substitute voluntary plans of desegregation, despite the attendant problems of the past and resegregation of schools that would occur by such plans.[31] Affirmative action plans have been attacked as discrimination against nonblacks, as well as a violation of Justice Harlan's declaration in his dissenting opinion in *Plessy*, that the Constitution is color blind. A new form of federalism is advocated with assertions that the federal government should not be involved in the lives of citizens.

These assaults have led to renewed acts of discrimination and racism. Howard Beach, Forsyth County, and racial incidents in the colleges and universities are open expressions of racism that, many insist, are encouraged by practices of Republican administrations. At the same time, we see renewed incidents of blatant discrimination in housing, in employment, and in education. These renewed practices place further demands on the Constitution and the courts for relief.

In addition, the problems of the poor continue to grow with little efforts of relief from the legislative and executive branches of government. As a rationale for attacking the civil rights progress of the past, former attorney general Edwin Meese called for the return to the original intent of the framers. He also challenged judicial review, suggesting an approach that implicates the separation of powers of government. In addition, he advocated less respect for decisions of the courts as distinguished, he suggested, from the constitutional document itself. Although the attorney general and others speaking on his behalf modified the department's positions—after scrutiny by the press, constitutional scholars, historians, and others—it is important that we pause and ask what the adoption of that department of justice's positions would mean to the Constitution, to our governmental system, and to the American people.

Neither the attorney general nor William Bradford Reynolds, former assistant attorney general for civil rights, nor other outspoken proponents of the view of the Department of Justice, has suggested that we abandon judicial review. Indeed, however one settles the debate as to whether the framers contemplated or intended judicial review, we have had judicial review for over 150 years, and I doubt seriously that system will change. What Messrs. Meese and Reynolds advocated instead is that courts, in reviewing constitutional challenges, should discover and apply the original intent of the framers. There are a number of problems with this assertion, three of which are particularly important to examine.

First, Meese and Reynolds would like to forget entirely the Civil War and the constitutional amendments that followed it. Their position instead suggests a return to 1787 when blacks, other minorities, and women were totally excluded from protection under the constitution. Those amendments also changed the relationship of the federal government to the states, thereby limiting state practices, which violated the Bill of Rights or which deprived citizens of due process and equal protection.

The second problem—the impossible search for original intent—was addressed by former Supreme Court Justice William Brennan and, later by U.S. Circuit Court Judge Irving Kaufman. Justice Brennan said:

> There are those who find legitimacy in fidelity to what they call 'the intention of the framers.' In its most doctrinaire incarnation, this view demands that Justices discern exactly what the Framers thought about the question under consideration and simply follow that intention in resolving the case before them. It is a view that feigns self-effacing deference to the specific judgments of those who forged our original social compact. But . . . it is little more than arrogance cloaked as humility. It is arrogant to pretend that from our vantage we can gauge accurately the intent of the Framers on application of principle to specific, contemporary questions.[32]

The third problem with the attorney general's position is that it would completely stifle the ability of the Constitution to extend protection to minorities and other disadvantaged Americans who even today are still seeking to enjoy the same benefits the articles of the Declaration of Independence proclaimed for all Americans.

Nobody suggests that judges should be invested with unbridled discretion in interpreting the Constitution. Indeed, the courts have attempted to determine the framers' intent; but that does not complete the inquiry. Moreover, one cannot expect such an inquiry to produce a definitive answer.

The legacy of the framers, as scholars and jurists have emphasized, is the spirit and the language of the Constitution. There are several legitimate approaches to constitutional interpretation that are in keeping with the language and the spirit of the framers. To be sure, there has always been the risk that some judges may read their personal predilections into the Constitution. But the founders above all were aware that constituting a nation could not be done without risks, and we must be content today with the fact that the framers provided us with general guidance, and not with precision.

As such, the Constitution is more than simply a written document; it incorporates tradition and practices, customs and laws, and everything that has gone into our American democracy. Chief Justice Warren Burger recognized this principle in *U.S. v. Nixon* when overruling President Richard Nixon's claim of executive privilege.[33] Nothing in the specific language of the Constitution, nor decipherable from the framers' intent, provided a clear answer. As others have explained, the Constitution cannot be viewed in isolation.

The efforts of Mr. Meese in the 1980s to carve out a difference between the Constitution and constitutional interpretations raise similar questions about the continuing validity of our Constitution and constitutional democracy. In a speech at Tulane University, Mr. Meese suggested that decisions of the Supreme Court, even those interpreting the Constitution, are not the Constitution and are binding only on parties before the Court and the "executive branch for whatever enforcement is necessary."[34] Although Mr. Reynolds, in a speech at Northwestern Law School, later modified the attorney general's comments, the suggestion that constitutional interpretation by the courts is not of the same order and due the same respect as the Constitution itself ignores the history of the American constitutional system.[35] Even as Mr. Meese argued for separate recognition of the Constitution and judicial decisions, the examples he used—*Plessy v. Ferguson* and *Brown*—support the constitutional approach we have observed rather than Mr. Meese's return to the original intent of the framers.

TOWARD THE TWENTY-FIRST CENTURY

The history of the Constitution, like that of the United States, has been marked by a continuous effort to achieve equal justice and equal opportunity for all Americans. It is a signal history that warrants some commemoration. Today, none who advocate justice is satisfied with the failure to accord equal rights and opportunities to all Americans, but there is appreciation of the efforts that have gone into helping achieve that objective. Some believe that the system and the method by which some advocates of justice have operated historically still offer hope that the millennium we seek is possible.

It is that hope that we must preserve if we are to celebrate future centennials of the U.S. Constitution.

After September 1991, advocates of minority rights were confronted with one of the gravest crises we have faced since the Civil War. The Reagan and Bush administrations largely succeeded in appointing federal judges who tended toward a narrow, restrictive reading of the Constitution and civil rights statutes. As a result, a number of well-established, important civil rights and criminal justice precedents have been overturned, to the detriment of America's disadvantaged and dispossessed. Rather than continuing the process of expanding constitutional guarantees for more and more Americans, the federal courts have begun to threaten and retreat from existing guarantees.

This assault on established civil rights precedents is not based exclusively on the "original intent" doctrine previously discussed, although that pernicious philosophy remains popular in some academic circles. Rather, the ideological basis for the assault is much less complicated: increasingly, federal judges seem to believe that the rights of private industry and of the state should be given much more deference than the rights of minorities and the poor; and that any consideration of race must be seriously questioned even when employed to remedy a history of prior racial discrimination.

For example, in more than a half-dozen decisions in 1989, the Supreme Court made it much more difficult for victims of job discrimination to seek redress in federal courts and posed new threats to race-based remedies for past discrimination. While only one of these adverse rulings applied to the Constitution itself, most of the decisions eviscerated congressional statutes that have been necessary to translate constitutional promises of equality into concrete reality.

In *Patterson* v. *McLean Credit Union,* the Court ruled that the 1866 Civil Rights Act—which bars discrimination in the making and enforcement of contracts—does not protect employees from blatant race discrimination once they have been hired.[36] For more than two decades prior to *Patterson,* the 1866 act had been the most effective legal deterrent against on-the-job racial harassment and other forms of discrimination.

The same Court also made it much easier for discriminatory employers to escape liability under Title VII of the 1964 Civil Rights Act in *Wards Cove Packing Co.* v. *Antonio* and *Price Waterhouse* v. *Hopkins,* overturning legal standards that for two decades had played a major role in opening up the American workplace to minorities and women.[37] In *Martin* v. *Wilks,* the Court allowed white firefighters to challenge an affirmative action settlement that had been in effect for eight years.[38] This practically *invited* challenges under Title VII to long-established affirmative action plans.

In *City of Richmond* v. *Croson,* the Court rejected Richmond's program that set aside 30 percent of contracts for minority contractors.[39] Before this program was established, less than 1 percent of city contracts went to minority businesses. Yet the Court in *Croson* held that Richmond's set-aside violated the rights of *white* contractors to equal protection of the law as spelled out in the Fourteenth Amendment. Under the guise of bringing constitutional protection to white businesses, the Court erected significant barriers to municipalities and states that seek to plan, implement, and defend set-aside programs, which have given black entrepreneurs a "level playing field" with white competitors.

With these and other rulings relating to employment discrimination, the Court in 1989 refused to give the language of civil rights laws and the Constitution the broad, remedial interpretation necessary to ensure that contemporary forms of discrimination and injustice would be addressed. Instead, the Court gave narrow, crabbed readings, demanding explicit language and proof to remedy discrimination in specific situations—even though such specific conduct or remedies could not have been anticipated when the constitutional or statutory language was written.[40]

While most of the 1989 rulings that alarmed civil rights advocates involved employment discrimination, the decisions prompted fears that the Court eventually *would* erect constitutional and statutory barriers to minorities, women, and others who seek equal justice in other areas of the law. Those fears found increased support in the Court's 1993 decision in *Shaw* v. *Reno*.[41] *Shaw* involved North Carolina's effort to redistrict its congressional districts on the basis of the 1990 census and the Voting Rights Act of 1965. Following the U.S. attorney general's rejection of its initial plan based on Section 5 of the Voting Rights Act, North Carolina created a second majority black congressional district. Ruling on a motion to dismiss, Justice Sandra Day O'Connor for the majority (4–5) found the district bizarre, extremely irregular, and facially discriminatory. The Court failed to address who was actually injured by the plan except to suggest that "[racial] classifications of any sort pose the risk of lasting harm to our society"; they may "balkanize us into competing factors" or threaten "to carry us further from the goal of a political system in which race no longer matters."

Justice Byron White, however, appropriately pointed out that the majority's decision ignored precedents, the law, and electoral realities.[42] No cognizable constitutional injury was alleged or could be proved by the plaintiffs, on the basis of their allegations. That did not deter the majority, however, who proceeded to create a new cause of action.

Shaw places in jeopardy established substantive law and remedies governing voting rights. It threatens the recent electoral successes of minorities in Congress and in elected positions across the nation. The two North Carolina Representatives involved in Shaw, are holding positions for the first time since

1901. Other minority representatives are the first since Reconstruction. More ominous, *Shaw* raises serious concerns about our efforts to ensure equal voting rights opportunities for minority citizens.[43]

The Court has equally retrenched its protection for another group of vulnerable citizens, namely death row inmates. A host of recent Court decisions have placed a higher priority on speeding up the process of executing people than on administering rudimentary justice. And that is ominous news for all Americans who would seek shelter under the Constitution's protective cloak.

One alarming example of this trend is the Court's recent approach to "habeas corpus," the time-honored process through which inmates convicted in state courts appeal their convictions and sentences to federal courts. Habeas corpus review has been the single most important means to protect criminal defendants from being incarcerated—or executed—as a result of blatantly unjust and unconstitutional trials. When it comes to death row inmates, however, this Supreme Court seems determined to gut the entire habeas corpus process, denying inmates basic constitutional rights that belong to all Americans citizens.

In *Coleman v. Thompson* (1991), the Court held that the Fourteenth Amendment right to due process did not require a federal court to hear a habeas appeal from a death row inmate, because that inmate's lawyer had inadvertently missed the filing deadline for an appeal in *state* court.[44] In other words, even if inmates are sentenced to death in proceedings that are clearly unconstitutional, federal courts now must let them die because of their lawyers' procedural mistakes.

In *McCleskey v. Zant* (1991), the Court barred death row inmates from filing more than one habeas appeal, except in exceptional circumstances.[45] Because new, potentially life-saving evidence is often discovered after a capital inmate's first round of federal appeals, many inmates prior to *McCleskey* filed second or subsequent habeas corpus appeals. But the Court in *McCleskey* has prevented federal courts from even *considering* on a subsequent habeas corpus appeal meritorious constitutional claims of many death row inmates. While these rights have been taken from the most vulnerable people in this society, this erosion of constitutional protection does not bode well for other Americans.

Justice Thurgood Marshall addressed this subject in his dissent in *Payne v. Tennessee* (1991).[46] In *Payne*, the Court held that the Eighth Amendment's prohibition on cruel and unusual punishment does not bar prosecutors from showing to juries the emotional impact of a capital murder on the victim's relatives. The *Payne* decision overturned two previous rulings, in which the Court had held that such "victim-impact" evidence was unconstitutionally inflammatory and encouraged jurors to make life-or-death decisions based on their emotions, not on a defendant's guilt or culpability. In his *Payne* dissent, Justice Marshall notes: "Today's majority ominously suggests that an even more extensive upheaval of this Court's precedents may be in store. . . . [C]ast aside today are those condemned to face society's ultimate punishment. Tomorrow's victims may be minorities, women or the indigent."[47]

Justice Marshall understood that once the fundamental rights of one group of Americans are taken away in the name of some state interest, it is a short step to denying those rights to *all* Americans. He discussed that possibility in a 1989 speech:

> History teaches that when the Supreme Court has been willing to short-change the equality of rights of minority groups, other basic personal civil liberties like the rights to free speech and to personal security . . . are also threatened. We forget at our peril that less than a generation after the Supreme Court held separate to be equal in *Plessy* v. *Ferguson*, it held in the *Schenck* and *Debs* decisions that the First Amendment allowed the United States to convict under the Espionage Act persons who distributed anti-war pamphlets and delivered anti-war speeches.[48]

Civil rights and all civil liberties, Justice Marshall pointed out, are intertwined. He then provided some prescriptions for their preservation:

> The response to the Court's decisions is not inaction; the Supreme court remains the institution charged with protecting constitutionally guaranteed rights and liberties. Those seeking to vindicate civil rights or equality of rights must continue to press this Court for the enforcement of constitutional and statutory mandates. Moreover, the recent decisions suggest alternate methods to further the goals or equality in contexts other than judicial forums.[49]

Justice Marshall concluded that part of the answer to the current civil rights crisis is to turn to Congress, state legislatures, and "all branches of federal and state governmental units," urging them "to undertake the battles for civil liberties that must be won."[50]

With the retirement of Justices Marshall and Brennan and the appointment of Clarence Thomas, there is a distinct possibility that American law will be shaped by an entrenched majority of activist, conservative justices for decades to come. That prospect makes Justice Marshall's advice about alternative, extrajudicial forums all the more imperative.

The political firestorm over the Civil Rights acts of 1990 and 1991 exemplifies the challenges that civil rights advocates will face when they seek extrajudicial solutions to problems created by the courts. Both bills were designed to restore fair employment law to where it was before the Supreme Court rewrote it in 1989. The 1989 Court apparently found some language in the civil rights laws of the past century to be vague and insufficient to prohibit certain forms of discrimination. Therefore, legislation was drafted to clarify and strengthen that language, so that even a Supreme Court hostile to effective civil rights enforcement would have no leeway for legal interpretations that harmed minorities and women.

Although Congress's initial effort to pass corrective employment discrimination legislature was successfully vetoed by President Bush in 1990, a new Civil Rights Act was enacted in 1991. We must begin the arduous expensive trek of convincing the Court what Congress intended—what proof is required, what discriminatory acts are covered, and what remedies are appropriate when discrimination is established.[51]

Civil rights advocates are also seeking corrective legislation in other areas—voting rights, housing, education—but nothing thus far suggests that these efforts will be easy or even successful. Rather, the vociferous opposition to recent civil rights legislation indicates that the battle to preserve constitutional and statutory rights cannot be won only in courtrooms or in legislative chambers where bills are drafted. The same battle must also be fought and won in the court of public opinion; this will be especially true in the next decade, when, as Justice Marshall noted, constitutional precedents governing civil rights and civil liberties are in danger of being overturned.

In other words, expanded public education is necessary to convince the American people that our Constitution will have little meaning if it is selectively applied to certain Americans, but not to everyone. Americans of all races and economic classes must be persuaded that they have a stake in ensuring that the rights guaranteed in that noble document are extended to all citizens, including the poor, the powerless, people of color, and those with unpopular views. Furthermore, they must be encouraged to let their legislators know that they favor corrective legislation and other governmental action, whenever federal judicial decisions strip away those rights.

In the last analysis, only the expressed demands of the American people can ensure justice and true equality. Unless all of us believe passionately that equal rights must be extended to each and every American, we will seriously threaten the survival of our democratic form of government.

NOTES

1. A. Leon Higginbotham, Jr., *In the Matter of Color, Race and the Legal Process: The Colonial Period* (New York: Oxford University Press, 1978), 371–74, 384.

2. Higginbotham, *In the Matter of Color*, 371–83.

3. *State v. Mann*, 13 N. C. 263 (1829).

4. *Dred Scott v. Sanford*, 60 U.S. 393.

5. See Eric Foner, *Reconstruction: America's Unfinished Revolution, 1863–1877* (New York: Harper and Row, 1988); Vann Woodward, *The Strange Career of Jim Crow* (New York: Oxford University Press, 1957).

6. See Foner, *Reconstruction*, 35–37, 66–67.

7. Foner, *Reconstruction*, 228–80; Robert J. Kaczorowski, *The Politics of Judicial Interpretation: The Federal Courts, Department of Justice and Civil Rights, 1866–1876* (New York: Oceana Publications, 1985); Kaczorowski, "To Begun the Nation Anew: Congress, Citizenship, and Civil Rights after the Civil War," *American History Revised* 92 (1981): 45.

8. Foner, *Reconstruction*, 68–70; Julius Chambers, Book Review, "Protection of Civil Rights: A Constitutional Mandate from the Federal Government," *Michigan Law Review* 87 (1989): 1599.

9. Foner, *Reconstruction*, 256–80.

10. Foner, *Reconstruction*, 256–80.

11. See Robert J. Kaczorowski, "Revolutionary Constitutionalism in the Era of the Civil War and Reconstruction," *New York University Law Review* 61 (1986): 863, 917–40.

12. *Plessy v. Ferguson*, 163 U.S. 537; *Strander v. West Virginia*, 100 U.S. 303.

13. *United States v. Stanley*, 109 U.S. 3.

14. *Yick Wo v. Hopkins*, 118 U.S. 356.

15. *Plessy*, 163 U.S. 537, 543, 552.

16. Jack Greenberg, *Race Relations and American Law* (New York: Columbia University Press, 1969), 32–78

17. Greenberg, *Race Relations*, 32–78.

18. *Brown v. Board of Education*, 47 U.S. 483; Genna Rae McNeil, *Groundwork: Charles Hamilton Houston and Struggle for Civil Rights* (Philadelphia: University of Pennsylvania Press, 1983), 113–17, 132–55, 198–200.

19. Greenberg, *Race Relations*.

20. *Missouri ex rel. Gaines v. Canada*, 305 U.S. 377.

21. *Sipuel v. Oklahoma State Regents*, 332 U.S. 631.

22. *Sweatt v. Painter*, 339 U.S. 629; *McLaurin v. Oklahoma State Regents*, 339 U.S. 637.

23. *Lau v. Nichols*, 414 U.S. 563.

24. *Plyler v. Doe*, 457 U.S. 202 (1982).

25. Compare *San Antonio School Dist. v. Rodriguez*, 411 U.S. 1.

26. *Cannon v. University of Chicago*, 441 U.S. 677.

27. *City of Cleburne, Texas, v. Cleburne Living Center, Inc.*, 473 U.S. 432.

28. *San Antonio School District v. Rodriguez*, 411 U.S. 1.

29. 478 U.S. 265.

30. See Norman C. Amaker, *Civil Rights and the Reagan Administration* (Washington, D.C.: Urban Institute Press, 1988).

31. See Gary Orfield, "The Growth of Segregation in American Schools: Changing Patterns of Segregation and Poverty Since 1968" (Prepared for the National School Board Association, 1993).

32. Speech of Justice William J. Brennan, Jr. to the Text and Teaching Symposium, Georgetown University, October 12, 1985, Washington, D. C., reported in the Federal Society, "The Great Debate: Interpreting Our Written Constitution" (1986), 11, 14.

33. United States v. Nixon, 418 U.S. 683.

34. Edwin Meese, "A Simple Error Lies behind Widespread Misinterpretations" (Bicentennial Lecture at Tulane University, October 21, 1986), Los Angeles Daily Journal, November 4, 1986, p. 4.

35. William Bradford Reynolds, "The 'Burger Years': A Critical Look at the Critics' Intent," Northwestern University Law Review 82 (Spring 1988): 818–36.

36. Patterson v. McLean Credit Union, 491 U.S. 164.

37. Wards Cove Packing Co. v. Antonio, 490 U.S. 1642; Price Waterhouse v. Hopkins, 490 U.S. 228.

38. Martin v. Wilks, 490 U.S. 755.

39. City of Richmond v. J. A. Croson Co., 488 U.S. 469.

40. See United Steelworkers of America v. Weber, 443 U.S. 193, 205 (necessary to apply the spirit of the law rather than literal language in order to achieve the congressional objective. Compare United States v. Nixon).

41. 61 U.S. L. W. 4818 (1993).

42. 61 U.S. L. W. at 4827–31. See also dissenting opinions of Justice Blackmun at 4831; Justice Stevens, 4831, and of Justice Souter, 4832–34.

43. See, for example, LULAC v. Attorney General of Texas, 999 F.2d 831 (5th Cir. 1993) (denying relief to Hispanic and African American plaintiffs who challenged Texas at-large system for electing state court judges), cert. den. 62 U.S. L. W. 3471 (January 14, 1994).

The Supreme Court has similarly limited efforts of civil rights plaintiffs to preserve and promote desegregation of public schools. See, for example, Board of Education of Oklahoma City v. Dowell, 498 U.S. 237. Such decisions and the resulting resegregation led Gary Orfield to conclude that our public schools are about as racially separate today as shortly before Brown. Orfield, "The Growth of Segregation in American Schools."

44. Coleman v. Thompson, 111 S. Ct. 2546.

45. McCleskey v. Zant, 111 S. Ct. 1245 and 111 S. Ct. 1454.

46. Payne v. Tennessee, 111 S. Ct. 2597.

47. Payne, 111 S. Ct. 2597. Dissents are also discussed in American Bar Association Journal 77 (September 1991): 40.

48. Thurgood Marshall, speech delivered to the Second Circuit Judicial Conference, 1989. See Plessy v. Ferguson, 163 U.S. 537 (1896); Schenck v. U.S., 249 U.S. 47 (1919); and Debs v. U.S., 249 U.S. 211 (1919).

49. Marshall, 1989 speech.

50. Marshall, 1989 speech.

51. See The Civil Rights Act of 1991, by the Committee on Federal Legislation, reported in the Record of the Association of the Bar of the City of New York 48 (1993): 75–124.

CONTRIBUTORS

ROBERT McCORMICK ADAMS is secretary emeritus of the Smithsonian Institution. From 1955 to 1984 he was on the faculty of the University of Chicago, where he was director of the Oriental Institute, dean of the Division of the Social Sciences, and provost of the university. His primary academic interests have included agricultural and urban history of the Near and Middle East, geographical and archaeological study of settlement patterns, and comparative economic and social history of premodern societies. He has also devoted attention to institutions and policies for the support of research. He is the author and editor of several books and more than ninety articles. Adams is a member of the National Academy of Sciences, the American Philosophical Society, Middle East Institute, and Council of Foreign Relations, and is a fellow of both the American Academy of Arts and Sciences and the American Anthropological Association.

DERRICK A. BELL, JR., is visiting professor of law at New York University Law School and former professor of law at Harvard University. He served as dean and professor of law at the University of Oregon Law School; executive director of the University of Southern California's Western Center of Law and Poverty; the deputy director, Office of Civil Rights, U.S. Department of Health, Education and Welfare; and the first assistant counsel for the NAACP Legal Defense and Educational Fund, Inc. He is a member of the National

Conference of Black Lawyers, a member of the board of the Howard Thurman Educational Trust, and vice-president of the Society of American Law Teachers. Bell has enjoyed a career of more than thirty years as a litigator, activist, and scholar. Specializing in constitutional law, Professor Bell is the author of numerous scholarly articles and several books, including *Race, Racism and American Law; We Are Not Saved: The Elusive Quest for Racial Justice; Faces at the Bottom of the Well: The Permanence of Racism;* and *Contributing Authority.* He is, as well, the editor of *Shades of Brown: New Perspectives on School Desegregation.*

MARY FRANCES BERRY is the Geraldine R. Segal Professor of American Social Thought and professor of history at the University of Pennsylvania. As a historian and attorney, her chief academic interests have included legal history, African American history, and U.S. social history. She has been a member of the faculties of the University of Michigan, the University of Maryland at College Park, the University of Colorado at Boulder, and Howard University. She also has served as chancellor of the University of Colorado at Boulder and assistant secretary for education in the U.S. Department of Health, Education and Welfare from 1977 to 1980. In addition to more than fifty articles, Berry is the author of several books, including *Black Resistance/White Law: A History of Constitutional Racism in America; Military Necessity and Civil Rights Policy; Stability, Security, and Continuity: Mr. Justice Burton and Decision-Making in the Supreme Court, 1945–1958; Why ERA Failed: Politics, Women's Rights and the Amending Process of the Constitution;* and *The Politics of Parenthood.* With John W. Blassingame, she is the coauthor of *Long Memory: The Black Experience in America.* Named chairperson in 1993, Berry has been a member of the U.S. Civil Rights Commission since 1980. A former vice-president of the American Historical Association and a past president of the Organization of American Historians, Berry has received numerous honorary degrees and awards.

WILEY A. BRANTON was an attorney and partner in the firm of Sidley & Austin until his death in 1988. A civil rights advocate, litigator, and educator, Branton provided major leadership in the struggle for civil rights throughout the years of that movement. He served as chief counsel for the plaintiffs in the Little Rock, Arkansas, school case, *Cooper v. Aaron,* as the director of the Voter Education Project in Atlanta, Georgia, and as a special assistant in the U.S. Justice Department. He was a member of the Arkansas firm of Walker, Kaplan & Mays and partner in the Washington, D. C., firm of Dolphin, Branton, Stafford & Webber for many years. He served thereafter as dean of Howard University's School of Law. He was the recipient of numerous awards and citations for his civil rights work.

ALICE L. BROWN is an assistant counsel at the NAACP Legal Defense and Educational Fund, Inc. with specific responsibility for the environmental justice and low-income housing dockets. Having completed her pre-professional education at Dartmouth College and Northwestern University, she earned her Juris Doctor degree at New York University and is a member of the Pennsylvania Bar. She has served as a law clerk to Judge A. Leon Higginbotham, Jr., and as a program officer at the Ford Foundation, where her portfolio included human rights in South Africa and Namibia. A litigator and advocate, Brown has argued numerous cases to improve the conditions of low-income housing or to protect the environmental quality of African American communities, and she has testified before the U.S. Senate on lead-based paint hazard reduction and distressed housing. Brown has published articles on environmental justice and racism in such periodicals as *Environmental Law* and *Trial*.

JULIUS L. CHAMBERS was installed as the chancellor of North Carolina Central University in 1993. He is an attorney, civil rights leader, and educational administrator. Formerly the director-counsel of the NAACP Legal Defense and Educational Fund, Inc. (LDF), he also served as president of the board of LDF from 1964 to 1984. He has taught and lectured at Columbia University's Law School, Harvard Law School, the University of Michigan School of Law, the University of Virginia's Law School, and the University of Pennsylvania School of Law. Formerly senior partner at Chambers, Ferguson, Watt, Walla & Adkins, Chambers has practiced law before several courts, working principally on civil rights cases in Virginia, North Carolina, Georgia, and Alabama. Before the Supreme Court, he argued *Brenda Patterson* v. *McLean Credit Union* in 1989. His publications include essays on constitutional protection for minority rights and equal educational opportunities in the *National Law Journal, Harvard Civil Rights-Civil Liberties Law Review,* and *Law and Contemporary Problems*. He is the recipient of numerous honorary degrees and awards.

GEORGE WILLIAM CROCKETT, JR., a former member of the U.S. Congress representing the 13th Congressional District of Michigan in Detroit, has had a distinguished career as a public servant, judge, and attorney. He is a member of the bars of West Virginia and Michigan and has been admitted to practice before the U.S. Supreme Court. He was the first African American lawyer to practice at the U.S. Department of Labor and also served as a hearing examiner for the Fair Employment Practices Commission. Crockett founded and directed the Fair Employment Practices Department of the United Auto Workers International Union and for a time served as the union's general counsel. A senior partner in the Detroit law firm of Goodman, Crockett, Eden and Robb, he was elected judge of Detroit's Recorder's Court and served as its presiding judge. He has served, as well, as a visiting judge for the Michigan Court of Appeals and as the acting corporation counsel for the city of Detroit.

JOHN HOPE FRANKLIN is the James B. Duke Professor Emeritus of Duke University and former professor of legal history of Duke University's Law School. Prior to joining the faculty of Duke University, Franklin served as chairperson of the History Department and the John Matthews Manly Distinguished Service Professor Emeritus of the University of Chicago. His career as a scholar spans more than fifty years, during which time he has had faculty appointments at such institutions as Fisk University, North Carolina College (now North Carolina Central University), Howard University, Brooklyn College, and the University of Chicago. Franklin has written extensively in the fields of Southern history and African American history. His work has been recognized by institutions of higher education and governmental agencies, which have bestowed upon him numerous honorary degrees and awards. Among his published works are *The Free Negro in North Carolina, 1790–1860; From Slavery to Freedom: A History of Negro Americans* (now in its seventh edition); *The Militant South, 1800–1860; Reconstruction after the Civil War; George Washington Williams: A Biography; Race and History: Selected Essays, 1938–1988;* and *The Color Line.* His research contributed, as well, to the historical base for the NAACP Legal Defense and Educational Fund's brief in *Brown v. Board of Education* (1954). Franklin has served as president of the American Historical Association, the Organization of American Historians, the Southern Historical Association, and the American Studies Association.

A. LEON HIGGINBOTHAM, JR., serves as a member of the faculty of Harvard Law School after a distinguished career as a federal judge for the Third Circuit of the United States Court of Appeals and for the Eastern District of Pennsylvania. Higginbotham has taught at the University of Michigan, University of Pennsylvania, and University of Hawaii Law Schools. He has, as well, written more than forty scholarly articles and *In the Matter of Color: Race and the American Legal Process—The Colonial Period,* which received the Silver Gavel Award of the American Bar Association. He has served as a federal trade commissioner; a partner in Norris, Green, Harris & Higginbotham; a commissioner for the Human Relations Commission of Pennsylvania; and a citizen regent of the Smithsonian Institution. Higginbotham continues to serve as a member of numerous commissions and national committees.

DARLENE CLARK HINE is John Hannah Professor of American History at Michigan State University and former professor of history as well as vice-provost at Purdue University. She is editor of Carlson's Publishing's sixteen-volume series, *Black Women in United States History: From Colonial Times to the Present.* Her books include *Hine Sight: Black Women and the Re-construction of American History, Black Women in White: Racial Conflict and Cooperation in the Nursing Profession, 1890–1950,* and *Black Victory: The Rise and Fall of the White Primary in Texas.* She has also published more than fifty research articles. Hine is currently the senior editor of *Black Women in America: An Historical Encyclopedia* (the associate editors of which are Elsa Barkley Brown and Rosalyn Terborg Penn). Hine has also edited *The State of Afro-American History, Past, Present, and Future* and coedited (with Clayborne Carson, et al.) *The Eyes on the Prize Civil Rights Reader.*

W. H. KNIGHT is professor of law and former associate dean of academic affairs at the University of Iowa College of Law. He entered the private practice of law in 1979 after having earned his Juris Doctor degree at Columbia University School of Law. From 1979 to 1983, Knight had responsibility for domestic and international banking operations as well as regulatory compliance. Since 1983 he has not only served as a faculty member at the University of Iowa, but also a visiting professor at the law schools of Duke University, Wake Forest University, and Washington University. In his teaching, he has focused on banking, commercial transactions, law and social change, and critical race theory. Publications on regulation, banking, international debt, and human rights have appeared in *Columbia Business Law Review, Journal of Corporation Law, Law and the Status of Women, National Black Law Journal,* and the *St. Louis University Public Law Review.*

CHARLES R. LAWRENCE III is professor of law at the Georgetown University Law Center, having joined its faculty in 1993. During the 1970s he practiced law and began his teaching career in California. He was a member of Public Advocates in San Francisco, a public interest law firm, and Hastie-Lawrence Associates. In 1974 he joined the faculty of the University of San Francisco Law School. From 1986 to 1993 he was professor at the Stanford Law School. He has been a visiting professor at Harvard Law School and the University of Southern California at Berkeley. Professor Lawrence is the author of numerous articles on race and antidiscrimination law and equal protection. Among these are "The Id, the Ego, and Equal Protection" in *Stanford Law Review;* "Promises to Keep: We Are the Constitution's Framers" in *Howard Law Journal;* and "If He Hollers, Let Him Go" in *Duke Law Journal.* Professor Lawrence is a leading voice in the emergent genre of critical race theory. He is coauthor of *The Bakke Case: The Politics of Inequality* and *Words That Wound: Critical Race Theory, Assaultive Speech, and the First Amendment.*

THURGOOD MARSHALL, to whom this volume is dedicated, was the first African American to serve on the highest court of this nation and retired in 1991 after more than two decades as an associate justice of the U.S. Supreme Court. A graduate of Lincoln University in Pennsylvania and Howard University's Law School in Washington, D.C., Justice Marshall began his private practice of law in 1934 and throughout his life—whether as a private practitioner, lawyer for the federal government, or jurist—used his considerable legal skills, intelligence, and talent in the cause of equal justice under the law. Trained by Charles Hamilton Houston to use the law for social change and to engage in "social engineering" for the elimination of racial discrimination under the law, Thurgood Marshall immediately appropriated the Constitution as a weapon, litigating (with Houston and other attorneys) numerous civil rights cases. During the mid-1930s Marshall, with Baltimore's Harold Gosnell and Charles Houston, filed an equal protection claim against the University of Maryland, which had denied admission to Donald Gaines Murray (just as it had earlier to Thurgood Marshall). In 1936 Justice Marshall joined Houston in the legal office of the National Association for the Advancement of Colored People as the assistant special counsel and worked tirelessly for racial justice long after Houston's resignation from the special counselship and his death in 1950. Thurgood Marshall litigated equalization of teachers' salaries and public schools and later desegregation cases, voting rights, protection of the right to protest, and a host of other civil rights causes. He served as the first director-counsel of the separately incorporated NAACP Legal Defense and Educational Fund, Inc., from its inception to 1961. Following legal victories that included *Brown* v. *Board of Education* in 1954, *Cooper* v. *Aaron* (with Wiley Branton) in 1958, and *Garner* v. *Louisiana* in 1961, he was appointed federal judge on the Court of Appeals for the second circuit in September 1961. There followed a distinguished career as the second African American federal judge at the appellate level (after William H. Hastie), solicitor general of the United States from 1965 to the fall of 1967, and thereafter as an associate justice on the U.S. Supreme Court until June 1991. In the latter years of his Supreme Court tenure, the Court became more conservative and Marshall more frequently found it necessary to write dissenting opinions. By the time of his retirement, he had become this century's modern-day "Great Dissenter," having written more than eighteen hundred dissenting opinions. Whether writing majority or dissenting opinions in such cases as *Interstate Circuit* v. *Dallas*, *Furman* v. *Georgia*, *United States* v. *Kras*, *Milliken* v. *Bradley*, *Regents of the University of California* v. *A. Bakke*, *City of Mobile* v. *Bolton*, *Ake* v. *Oklahoma* and *City of Richmond* v. *J. A. Croson*, Justice Marshall placed in the public record his support of First

Amendment protections, desegregated and equal education, the identification of poverty as a suspect classification, the right of privacy and affirmative action, as well as his opposition to capital punishment. On July 4, 1992, Thurgood Marshall was awarded the Liberty Medal in Philadelphia to honor his leadership and vision in the pursuit of freedom. On that occasion he warned: "There's a price to be paid for division and isolation. . . . Justice cannot take root amid rage." Justice Marshall also insisted that "America has no choice but . . . to assure justice for all Americans. . . . Our futures are bound together." Thurgood Marshall died in January 1993. His life of struggle for equal rights and racial justice was celebrated by more than 3,500 persons attending his funeral at the National Cathedral. There they were reminded by Vernon Jordan, African American attorney and former head of the National Urban League, that Thurgood Marshall's mission was "to cleanse our tattered Constitution and our besmirched legal system of the filth of oppressive racism and to restore to all Americans a Constitution and a legal system newly alive to the requirement of justice."

GENNA RAE McNEIL is a professor of history at the University of North Carolina in Chapel Hill. McNeil previously taught in the Department of History of Howard University, which she chaired; at Hunter College; Roosevelt University; and Howard University School of Law. She has also served as a deputy general secretary of the American Baptist Churches in the United States and as an archivist at the New York Public Library. She is the author of *Groundwork: Charles Hamilton Houston and the Struggle for Civil Rights* and other articles on civil rights and African American lawyers. She is coeditor (with Michael Winston) of *Historical Judgments Reconsidered.* She was historian of record on the amicus curiae brief of the National Bar Association, the National Medical Association, and the National Association for Equal Opportunity on Higher Education for *Regents of the University of California* v. *Allan Bakke,* and was consultant historian for the state of Maryland and NAACP Legal Defense Fund, Inc., in *Podberesky* v. *Kirwan.*

MATTHEW HOLDEN, JR., is the Henry L. and Grace M. Doherty Professor of Government and Foreign Affairs at the University of Virginia. Holden has taught political science and public policy or public administration at the University of Pittsburgh, Wayne State University, and the University of Wisconsin. He is, as well, active in professional associations and university governance. He continues to lecture, write, and publish widely in the areas of public administration, public policy, politics, ethnicity, race relations, decision making, and methodology. Among his publications are *Racial Stratification as Accident and Policy* and *The Challenge to Racial Stratification.* He has been a commissioner of the Federal Energy Regulatory Commission and a member of the Public Service Commission. He serves on the editorial board of the *Journal of Politics* and the board of directors of the Committee on the Constitutional System.

CHARLES J. OGLETREE, JR., is professor of law at Harvard Law School and founder-director of Harvard's Criminal Justice Institute. The first years of his practice were devoted to work as a public defender, and he subsequently turned to private practice as a partner in the Washington, D.C., firm of Jessamy, Fort & Ogletree. He began his teaching career at Antioch Law School and American University's Washington College of Law in Washington, D.C., and in 1986 joined the faculty of Harvard Law School. Professor Ogletree has appeared as a guest commentator on "Nightline," "McNeil-Lehrer News Hour," and "Meet the Press"; he has, as well, moderated PBS programs on ethics in America. In 1991 Professor Ogletree served as legal counsel to Professor Anita Hill during the Senate confirmation hearings for Justice Clarence Thomas. His publications appear in numerous journals and include "*Arizona* v. *Fulminante*" and "The Death of Discretion: Reflections on the Federal Sentencing Guidelines" in *Harvard Law Review*; "Reverend Moon and the Black Hebrews: Constitutional Protection of a Defendant's Religion in Criminal Cases" in *Harvard Civil Rights–Civil Liberties Law Review*; and "Does Race Matter in Criminal Prosecutions?" in *The Champion.*

GARY ORFIELD is professor of education and social policy in the Graduate School of Education at Harvard University. He has held faculty appointments at the University of Chicago, the University of Virginia, Princeton University, and the University of Illinois. As a guest scholar at the Brookings Institution, fellow of the Joint Center for Political Studies, and recipient of research grants from such foundations a Carnegie, Ford, MacArthur, and Spencer, Orfield has engaged in scholarly research and writing for more than twenty years. His published works include *The Reconstruction of Southern Education: The Schools and the 1964 Civil Rights Act; Congressional Power; Must We Bus? Segregated Schools and National Policy;* and *Public School Desegregation in the United States, 1968–1980.* Orfield also has been involved in seeking solutions to civic and community problems. He has directed the Chicago Fair Housing Alliance and codirected the Illinois Budget Analysis Project.

FRANK R. PARKER is professor of law at the District of Columbia School of Law and the former director of the Voting Rights Project for the Lawyer's Committee for Civil Rights under Law in Washington, D.C. From 1968 to

1981, he was a staff attorney with the Mississippi Office of the Lawyers' Committee, its assistant chief counsel and chief counsel. Formerly a staff attorney in the Office of the General Counsel for the U.S. Commission on Civil Rights, Parker is a member of the Mississippi and District of Columbia Bars. He is the author of numerous articles, but has focused on litigation concerning congressional redistricting, legislative reapportionment, voting rights, employment discrimination, civil rights protest, and government benefits and services. During 1985–86, Parker was a distinguished scholar at the Joint Center for Political Studies [and Economic] Studies, where he engaged in extensive research on litigation and politics in Mississippi. Parker's 1990 monograph, *Black Votes Count: Political Empowerment in Mississippi after 1965*, has received several prizes, including the American Political Science Association's Ralph Bunche Award.

EDDIE N. WILLIAMS is the president of the Joint Center for Political and Economic Studies in Washington, D.C. He has served as a foreign service reserve officer in the Department of State, vice-president for public affairs and director of the Center for Policy Studies at University of Chicago, and director of the Office of Equal Employment Opportunity. Williams is chairman of the board of directors of the National Coalition on Black Voter Participation and a member of the board of directors of the Children's Defense Fund, the Institute for Educational Leadership, Inc., the National Endowment for Democracy and United Way of America.

ADRIEN K. WING is professor of law at the University of Iowa's College of Law, where she has taught since 1987. Having earned her Juris Doctor degree at Stanford University Law School in 1982, Professor Wing entered private practice in the same year. As a private practitioner, she litigated matters pertaining to contracts, criminal law, corporate transactions, and constitutional law. Wing teaches comparative constitutional law, U.S. constitutional law, and "Race, Racism, and American Law," among other courses. Her professional and civic activities include representation of the National Conference of Black Lawyers at the United Nations, membership in the American Society of International Law, and service on the Board of Directors of the Iowa Peace Institute. Her publications include "Rape, Ethnicity, and Culture: Spirit of Injury from Bosnia to Black America" in *Columbia Human Rights Law Review*, and articles in the areas of international law as well as constitutionalism in *The American Journal of International Law*, *Yale Journal of International Law*, and other scholarly journals.

TABLE OF CASES CITED

INDEX

DATE DUE

		APR 28 '99

Brodart Co. Cat. # 55 137 001 Printed in USA